Answering Challenging Mormon Questions

Answering Challenging Mormon Questions

Replies to *130* Queries by Friends and
Critics of the LDS Church

Michael W. Hickenbotham

Fifth Printing, July, 2004

International Standard Book Number
0-88290-778-6

Horizon Publishers' Catalog and Order Number
H1058

Printed and distributed
in the United States of America by

Address:
925 North Main Street
Springville, Utah 84663

Local Phone: (801) 489-4084
Toll Free: 1 (800) SKYBOOK
FAX: (800)489-1097

E-mail: skybook@cedarfort.com
www.cedarfort.com

Contents

Introduction

1
Latter-day Saints and Christianity

2
Apostasy and Restoration

3
Prophets and Apostles

4
Modern Revelation

5
The Godhead

6
The Plan of Salvation

7
Scripture

8
Specific Modern Scriptural Difficulties

9
The Holy Ghost and Truth

10
Testimony

Introduction

As I started this endeavor, I felt like the Prophet Mormon when he wrote, "I do this for a wise purpose; for thus it whispereth me, according to the workings of the Spirit of the Lord which is in me. And now, I do not know all things; but the Lord knoweth all things which are to come; wherefore, he worketh in me to do according to his will" (Words of Mormon 1:7). Although I was not sure my efforts would ever be published, I hoped that this material might provide members, missionaries, gospel investigators, and members of my own family the benefit of documented insights on specific gospel questions commonly asked by people outside our Church. Questions such as: Why do we believe there can be only one true church? or does the Bible teach that man may become like God?

The Purpose of this Book

Although the answers to many missionary questions are to some extent found in the Church books published today, those answers often are not easily located and, frequently can only be found through time-consuming research. Since extensive time and gospel libraries are not available to many members and missionaries, it is my hope that I can pull together answers to many questions in one resource aid.

While many reference aids help members and missionaries answer general questions on topics such as apostasy, baptism, and the Godhead, they frequently do not answer questions regarding difficult passages of scripture or not-so-general concepts. This text was written to answer some of these more difficult questions. Discussions related to specific questions have been grouped by subject to help the reader locate answers. Additional supporting references are provided in a useful bibliography. Since it is impossible for missionaries to keep an extensive reference library while on a mission, an attempt was made to include as many quotes as possible from authoritative non-scriptural sources. Longer quotations are most often paraphrased. This should aid members who may not have access to a particular work.

It is hoped that this book will help answer many of the common difficult questions about the restored gospel. It is also hoped that the references provided will help the sincere inquirer to further seek prophetic sources and the confirmation of the Spirit.

A Word of Caution—Ravening Wolves

While most questions asked by investigators of the Church will be sincere in their inquiries, there are some people who are as ravening wolves in sheep's clothing (Matt. 7:15). Members and missionaries must use both the gift of discernment (1 Cor. 12:10; D & C 46:23) and the gifts of wisdom and knowledge (1 Cor. 12:8; D & C 46:17-18) while teaching, in order to recognize both when not to respond to their queries (Eccl. 3:7; Matt. 7:6), and to discern how to respond as the Spirit dictates (Luke 12:12; Peter 3:15). Missionaries should realize that they are not obligated to answer all questions, even those asked with honesty and sincerity (see Joseph Fielding McConkie, *Seeking the Spirit,* p. 9). Faith is the first principle of the gospel and leads to perfect knowledge, not vice versa (Ether 3:19).

When a member or missionary tries to document his beliefs using only the scriptures, without relying on testimony and the Spirit, he is relying on intellect. An intellectual testimony will not stand up to the "fiery darts of the adversary" (Eph. 6:16; 1 Nephi 15:24; D & C 3:8; 27:17) and does not lead to salvation (Mosiah 4:7-11); faith does.

The brethren have counselled us to "avoid those who would tear down [our] faith," adding that we should "not contend or debate over points of doctrine" (*1989 Melchizedek Priesthood Manual,* p. 165; Prov. 18:6; Rom. 2:7-8; 1 Cor. 11:16; James 3:16; D & C 10:63; 19:29, 31; 50:32-33). Wise members and missionaries will learn to discern between those inquiring after truth and those seeking to tear down our beliefs for their own selfish and misguided ends. Paul foresaw this dilemma and warned that there would be men in the latter times whose conscience would be "seared with a hot iron," or in other words, permanently scarred by false doctrine (1 Tim. 4:2). He also warned of those having "seducing spirits . . . who are speaking lies in hypocrisy" and trying to induce us to "depart from the faith" (1 Tim. 4:1-3). Therefore, we must be wise so as not to be taken in by their "cunning craftiness, whereby they lie in wait to deceive" (Eph. 4:14). David the Psalmist prophesied: "In that day [when] thou shalt come, O Lord . . . the wicked bend the bow; lo, they make ready their arrow upon the string, that they may privily shoot at the upright in heart, to destroy their foundation" (Joseph Smith Translation, hereafter JST Ps. 11:1-2; see also Ps. 37:12-14).

Joseph Smith set forth the following as the duty of the Saints in relation to their persecutors:

> And also it is an imperative duty that we owe to all the rising generation, and
> to all the pure in heart—For there are many yet on the earth among all sects, par-
> ties, and denominations, who are blinded by the subtle craftiness of men, whereby
> they lie in wait to deceive, and who are only kept from the truth because they know

not where to find it—Therefore, that we should waste and wear out our lives in bringing to light all the hidden things of darkness, wherein we know them; and they are truly manifest from heaven—These should then be attended to with great earnestness" (D & C 123:11-14).

Avoid the Spirit of Contention

Though some may, at times, try to disprove others' religious beliefs, this is not the purpose of this book. Christ taught the Nephites, "he that hath the spirit of contention is not of me, but is of the devil, who is the father of contention, and he stirreth up the hearts of men to contend with anger, one with another" (3 Nephi 11:29). The answers given here are intended to assure not-so-studied Saints and investigators of the strength of the LDS position.

Even though I am fully convinced of the truthfulness of the views expressed in this volume, I by no means expect this work to convince those who declare, "We have received the word of God, and we need no more of the word of God, for we have enough!" (2 Nephi 28:29). The Pharisees and Sadducees constantly demanded proof of Christ's teachings, but rejected it even when it was given to them in abundance. Most often, those who ask for proof do not want it at all. They seek only to establish and prove their own opinions. I believe that the "pure in heart," who are able to view both sides with impartiality, will recognize by the Spirit the truth in the answers given here. If some who are being challenged by proponents of "mainstream Christianity" find cause for reassurance that LDS doctrine embodies the truths preached by Christ and his apostles, then my time preparing this book will have been well spent.

Seek Learning by Study and Faith

Although most of us know that it is the Spirit that converts, many among us have neglected to reinforce the initial spiritual witness we received with consistent scripture study. The Lord tells us in D & C 88:118 and 109:7 that we should "seek learning, even by study and also by faith." When we study prayerfully with faith according to D & C 8:1-3, the spirit of revelation may be manifested to both the mind (rational logic) and the heart (faith, joy, peace and discernment of truthfulness). This is further reinforced in D & C 11:13, where the Lord states that the spirit will "enlighten your mind" and "fill your soul with joy." But this will occur only when we put forth an effort to acquire knowledge (D & C 9:7). God promises to enlighten our minds when we live righteously and seek to obtain his word through study and prayer (D & C 11:20-22).

It is apparent that the average Latter-day Saint's scriptural knowledge is diffused by the necessity of studying the four standard works, statements of our modem prophets and apostles, and the history of the

Church. Our Christian friends, on the other hand, may focus their studies on carefully designed anti-Mormon tactics found in "witnessing" books and tracts. As a result, this more concentrated study makes some anti-Mormon critics anxious to point out what they perceive to be errors in our beliefs. Often they are focused on faultfinding rather than on careful discernment of the saving and exalting truths of the gospel. What a shame it is when truth-seekers mistake a critic's preparation as a sign that he is seeking and speaking the truth. This problem can be overcome, though, if we make the effort to learn the doctrine of the restored Church.

Developing Skills of Scriptural Exegesis

Biblical exegesis (critical scriptural research), as practiced by Joseph Smith and other Church leaders, must be a talent cultivated not just by scholars but by every Latter-day Saint. The purpose of this book is thus two-fold: to inspire the reader to (1) more skillfully "search the scriptures" (John 5:39) and thus obtain his word (D & C 11:21); and (2) thereby develop a deeper understanding of the truth. This will enable us, as Peter exhorted, to "be ready always to give an answer to every man that asketh you a reason of the hope that is in you" (1 Peter 3:15), that under the influence of the Spirit we may show forth "the power of God unto the convincing of men" (D & C 11:21). As our Christian friends say, we have a serious responsibility to "contend earnestly for the faith which was once delivered unto the saints" (Jude 1:3) and, as Paul admonished, to speak "the truth in love" (Eph. 4:15). It is only when one puts forth an effort to "seek learning . . . by study and also by faith" (D & C 88:118; 109:7) by pondering and praying about God's word, that he can insure that he is "rightly dividing the word of truth" (2 Tim. 2:15).

This book is not an official publication of The Church of Jesus Christ of Latter-day Saints and I, the author, am responsible for its contents. It has been written at the request of missionaries and members and is based on years of dialogue and correspondence with those of other faiths. This work represents answers acquired through study and prayer and supported with scriptural and other appropriate or authoritative references. It is hoped that the reader will seek the confirmation of the Spirit that the answers given herein are true. I pray that all who read this work will experience enlightenment, joy, and a stronger testimony of the restored gospel. May the Lord bless you to this end.

1
Latter-day Saints
and Christianity

1. Are Latter-day Saints Christian?

Some critics of The Church of Jesus Christ of Latter-day Saints contend that Latter-day Saints are not really Christians. Their reasons, though accepted by some, are based on erroneous assumptions.

The Random House American College Dictionary defines a Christian as "believing in or belonging to the religion of Jesus Christ, exhibiting a spirit proper to a follower of Jesus Christ (i.e. Christ-like), one who believes in Jesus Christ, an adherent of Christianity, or one who exemplifies in his life the teachings of Christ." Though somewhat broad, all of these definitions include Latter-day Saints; technically, any one of these definitions qualify us as Christians.

In addition, the *Cambridge Bible Dictionary* informs us that the title Christian was "a name first given to believers in Jesus Christ." Interestingly, it also adds that "in the first years of the Church, believers were known among themselves as the brethren, the disciples, the saints, the faithful, and the elect." The title brethren, for example, was used over 500 times in our King James Bible; disciple or disciples was used over 250 times; saint or saints was used over 100 times; faithful was used in reference to his servants over 50 times and elect was used 20 times. By contrast, the word Christian or Christians is used only 3 times throughout the entire Bible. It is probably not a coincidence that the former titles are frequently preferred in modern revelation and among the Latter-day Saints themselves. The official name of the Church, given by revelation, contains both the title "saints" and most importantly, the name "Jesus Christ." Unlike many modern churches, the LDS Church identifies itself first and foremost as being the Church of Jesus Christ. It is not named after any reformer, founder, or Bible principle. The title conforms to Paul's teaching that Christ's church should be associated not with men but with Christ (1 Cor. 1:10-13). Members of The Church of Jesus Christ of Latter-day Saints, though unique in some of their beliefs, are undeniably Christian by standard definitions.

Critics of the LDS Church have taken it upon themselves to redefine the term Christian to mean one who accepts the "orthodox" beliefs to which they adhere. These include extrapolated doctrines such as: belief in the trinity, salvation solely by grace, Bible inerrancy, and other beliefs derived from—but not specifically taught in—the Bible. They also describe unique Mormon beliefs such as man's potential for Godhood, Christ's relationship to us and to Satan, the three degrees of glory, and a need for modem scripture as heretical and cultic, even though these LDS concepts can also be found in or extrapolated from Bible scripture. Their conclusions are, of course, based on the assumption that their doctrines are "orthodox" when judged by Christ's original teachings, and therefore, LDS doctrines are unorthodox. That modem Christian religions arrived at these "orthodox" beliefs as a result of misinterpretations of scripture is unthinkable to these critics, but this will be demonstrated in the remainder of this text.

It is important to note that using some "orthodox beliefs" as criteria for being a "Christian" would disqualify all believers in Christ from the time of his ministry through the next three centuries. Beliefs such as a three-in-one trinity, infant baptism, baptism by sprinkling, asceticism, celibacy, monasticism, abstaining from meats, transubstantiation, denial of continued revelation, the worship of Mary and chosen saints, the intercession of martyrs and saints, the sign of the cross, the immaculate conception, the doctrine of original sin, supererogation (the transfer of surplus good works), indulgences, infallibility, penance, passing the collection plate, pardons, and salvation without works were all introduced much later and were contrary to mainstream Christian thought in the early church. LDS beliefs in these areas are indeed closer to the teachings of the first Fathers and the beliefs of the early Christian church than those of modem "orthodoxy" (see Joseph Fielding Smith, Jr., *Religious Truths Defined,* pp. 155-87; Gilbert W. Scharff, *The Truth About "The God Makers,"* pp. 72 and 123-24).

The Book of Mormon is a profoundly "Christian" book filled with the testimonies of ancient prophets regarding Jesus Christ. The following are two such examples:

> We labor diligently to write, to persuade our children, and also our brethren, to believe in Christ . . . we are made alive in Christ because of our faith; yet we keep the law because of the commandments. And we talk of Christ . . . we prophesy of Christ, and we write according to our prophecies, that our children may know to what source they may look for the remission of their sins . . . the right way is to believe in Christ and deny him not . . . wherefore ye must bow down before him, and worship him with all your might, mind, and strength, and your whole soul (2 Nephi 25:23, 25-26, 29).

Also,

> Wherefore we labored diligently among our people, that we might persuade
> them to come unto Christ, and partake of the goodness of God, that they might
> enter into his rest . . . Wherefore, we would to God that we could persuade all men
> not to rebel against God, to provoke him to anger, but that all men would believe
> in Christ, and view his death, and suffer his cross and bear the shame of the world
> (Jacob 1:7-8).

Joseph Smith, when asked what the fundamental principles of the
Church were, responded: "the fundamental principles of our religion are
the testimony of the Apostles and Prophets, concerning Jesus Christ, that
He died, was buried, and rose again the third day, and ascended into
heaven; and all other things which pertain to our religion are only
appendages to it" (*Teachings of the Prophet Joseph Smith,* hereafter
referred to as *Teachings,* p. 121).

President Ezra Taft Benson taught, "The fundamental principle of
our religion is faith in the Lord Jesus Christ . . . Faith in Him is more
than mere acknowledgement that He lives. It is more than professing
belief. Faith in Jesus Christ consists in complete reliance on Him . . .
His gospel is the perfect prescription for all human problems and social
ills. But His gospel is only effective as it is applied in our lives . . .
Unless we do His teachings, we do not demonstrate faith in Him"
(*Ensign,* June 90, pp. 2-6; see also Ezra Taft Benson, *Come Unto Christ,*
pp. 127, 132).

Daniel Peterson and Stephen Ricks observed that:

> There is, after all, something rather peculiar about the assertion that The Church
> of Jesus Christ of Latter-day Saints is not Christian. It is not a self-evident truth, and
> would even seem to contradict obvious fact. (This is presumably why it is so fre-
> quently announced with an air of breathless discovery.) Mormons declare themselves
> Christian, and are astonished to be told that they are not. They belong to a Church in
> which every prayer is uttered, every sermon is given, and every ordinance is per-
> formed literally in the name of Jesus Christ. Their hymns—the devotional heart of
> their Sunday worship—sing of Christ and his atonement. At Christmas and Easter,
> they join with hundreds of millions of Christians around the world in a celebration
> of his life. In baptism and in the weekly communion they know as "the sacrament,"
> they testify that they are willing to take upon them his name (D & C 20:37, 77). Their
> first Article of Faith announces their belief in "God the Eternal Father, and in His
> Son, Jesus Christ." The Book of Mormon closes with an exhortation to "come unto
> Christ and be perfected in him" (Moroni 10:32). One of the high points of the Doc-
> trine and Covenants is a stirring testimony of Jesus (D & C 76:22-24). Their story
> begins with the claim of a young boy to have seen the Father and the Son. That young
> boy later claimed to be a prophet, defining "the spirit of prophecy" as "the testimo-
> ny of Jesus" His successors, likewise regarded as prophets, are assisted by a presid-
> ing quorum of "Twelve Apostles," or special witnesses of the name of Jesus Christ
> in all the world (D & C 107:23) (*Offenders for a Word,* pp. 176-77).

If members of The Church of Jesus Christ of Latter-day Saints do not
qualify as Christians, then many Catholic and Protestant churches could

be disqualified using the same criteria. For example, if doctrine is used as the criterion, many Catholic and Protestant churches can be eliminated because they teach doctrines foreign to the Bible. Doctrines such as baptism by sprinkling, the infallibility of the Bible, disbelief in the literal resurrection of the body, the elevation and worship of Mary, the immaculate conception, etc. are typical examples (see *Answers to Gospel Questions,* 3:174-84). Since Christians cannot agree among themselves on key points of doctrine such as these, it is absurd to use these or similar doctrines as the criteria for Christianity. If critics wish to ignore the truth, then so be it. Members of the LDS Church are Christian despite unjustified claims to the contrary. Those that so judge should remember that "with what judgement ye judge, ye shall be judged" (Matt. 7:2). Some of those who deny us the title "Christian" may themselves be denied by Christ at the last day (Matt. 7:21-23). See Daniel C. Peterson and Stephen D. Ricks, *Offenders for a Word,* for a scholarly examination of anti-Mormon reasons for denying Latter-day Saints the title of Christian.

2. Do biblical tests exclude the LDS Church from Christianity?

Those who rejected Jesus as the Christ did so while professing a great love for the scriptures and a loyalty to the prophets of ages past. Today, many who criticize our beliefs selectively cite scripture as evidence for their own creeds but ignore some obvious tests given in the Bible. Consider the following tests:

Test 1: Jesus spoke of both true and false prophets in the latter days but cautioned that true prophets could be differentiated from false ones by their fruit (Matt. 7:15-20; 12:33; Luke 6:43-45). Some of the fruit of LDS prophets and the Church are:

a. A strong faith in God and his Son, Jesus Christ, and their divinity (1st Article of Faith; 2 Nephi 25:23, 25, 26, 28; 31:18, 21).

b. Church members who believe in Christ's sacrificial atonement and who are striving to follow in his footsteps by living a Christ-like life (1 Pet. 2:21; 2 Nephi 2:7; 31:16; 3rd and 13th Article of Faith).

c. A membership that is unified in its beliefs and doctrines (1 Cor. 1:10; Mosiah 18:21).

d. Members who are rearing strong, loving families (D & C 68:25-28; Mosiah 4:14-15).

e. Members who believe in the power of God to do miracles today (5th and 7th Article of Faith; D & C 35:8-9).

f. Members who have a love for the scriptures and are striving to live by every word that proceeds forth out of the mouth of God (8th Article of Faith; Deut. 8:3; Matt. 4:4; Moroni 7:25; D & C 1:29-32).

g. Members who are a law-abiding people (12th Article of Faith; D & C 101:76-80).

h. Members who unselfishly give not only tithes and offerings but also of their time and talents to further the Lord's work (D & C 64; Mosiah 18:8-9).

i. A well-educated Church (D & C 88:118; 90:15; 93:36; 109:7).

j. A healthy people who abstain from using alcohol, tobacco, and other substances harmful to their bodies (1 Cor. 6:19; D & C 89).

k. Members who are clean in speech (D & C 63:61-64).

1. A missionary Church (Matt. 28:19; D & C 1; 4; 18).

m. A people who are actively participating in service to the community, state, and nation (D & C 134).

n. A Church that insists that its members obey all of the Ten Commandments including keeping the Sabbath day holy (D & C 59; 68:29).

o. A people who practice charity for those both inside and outside the LDS Church (D & C 121:45; 2 Cor. 9:7).

p. Members who actively participate in Church service and leadership, most often without monetary compensation (D & C 84:103-110).

q. A belief in the importance of temples and in salvation for our ancestors (D & C 124:22-44; 127; 128).

r. A belief that all people are spiritual brothers and sisters and children of our Heavenly Father (D & C 93), and as such have great worth to God and the potential to become like him (Matt. 5:48; 1 John 3:2; D & C 132:19-20).

s. A belief in the Holy Ghost's power to witness and justify (D & C 46).

t. Members who believe in the biblical standards of morality, marriage, and family and oppose abortion and all sexual sins (D & C 42:18-25).

u. A Church which accepts truth from any source, whether secular or religious (D & C 93:23-40; *History of the Church* 5:499, 517).

v. A Church which has a rational claim to the divine authority given by the Savior (D & C 13; JS—H 1:68-75).

w. An organization which is led through revelation from Jesus Christ and thus holds that the Savior is the head and foundation of the Church (Helaman 5:12).

x. A Church which is founded upon apostles and prophets, with Jesus Christ being the chief cornerstone (Eph. 2:20; 6th Article of Faith).

If, as Jesus taught, a corrupt tree cannot bring forth good fruit (Matt. 7:18), how can these good fruits of Mormonism be explained (see Eph. 5:8-10; Titus 2:14; Rev. 14:12-13)? In defending Peter and John, Gamaliel reasoned, "if this counsel or this work be of men, it will come to naught: but if it be of God, ye cannot overthrow it" (Acts 5:38-39). This is also true of LDS beliefs.

Moroni taught the key: "the way to judge is as plain, that ye may know with a perfect knowledge, as the daylight is from the dark night . . . . for every thing which inviteth to do good, and to persuade to believe in Christ, is sent forth by the power and gift of Christ; wherefore ye may know with a perfect knowledge it is of God" (Moroni 7:15-16). Paul taught a similar rule in 1 Thessalonians 5:21.

Test 2. Jesus taught "By this shall all men know that ye are my disciples, if ye have love one to another" (John 13:35). LDS members believe and practice being "benevolent, virtuous, and in doing good to all men" (13th Article of Faith) and in loving our neighbor as ourselves (Gal. 5:13-14; 6:2, 10; Mosiah 23:15; D & C 42:45; 59:6; 88:123; 112:11; Moses 7:33). Latter-day Saints show their love by serving others through inspired activities such as home teaching, visiting teaching, family home evenings, temple work for the salvation of our ancestors, welfare and service projects, fast offerings, as well as through many other personal acts of charity and love.

Test 3. Paul taught that, "no man can say ["know" —*Teachings,* p. 223] that Jesus is the Lord, but by the Holy Ghost" (1 Cor 12:3). LDS leaders and members testify that they know that Jesus Christ is the Lord (Mosiah 3:12, 17; 3 Nephi 19:18; D & C 15:1; 16:1; 17:9; 18:47; 19:1; 20:1; 21:1; 27:1; 35:1-2); therefore, according to scripture, they must have the Holy Ghost.

Test 4. Paul states in Galatians 3:27: "For as many of you as have been baptized into Christ have put on Christ." Jesus taught in Mark 16:16-18: "He that believeth and is baptized shall be saved; but he that believeth not shall be damned." He also taught that believers would have power, in Christ's name, to: (a) cast out demons, (b) speak in tongues, (c) be unharmed by deadly poisons, (d) lay hands on the sick unto recovery. Latter-day Saints believe and practice these principles by (1) being baptized in the name of Christ and thereby putting on Christ and (2) by exercising priesthood power to do miracles and good works as in the New Testament church (see the 4th, 5th and 7th Articles of Faith).

Test 5. Paul also taught that the saints of the household of God are "built upon a foundation of apostles and prophets, Jesus Christ himself being the chief cornerstone" (Eph. 2:19-20). God's people must be led by revelation from Christ through his chosen servants. Without this essential communications link, a church is led by men and not the Lord. Thus the household of God must be founded upon continuing revelation through living oracles. LDS Church beliefs are uniquely founded upon this eternal principle (see the 6th, 7th and 9th Articles of Faith).

Test 6. In Ephesians 4:5, Paul confirmed that there is "One Lord, one faith, one baptism." Latter-day Saints believe there is one Lord, Jesus Christ (1 Cor. 8:6), in whom is salvation (2 Nephi 31:21). Interestingly, Protestants also profess one Lord but hold that the Bible, which speaks of two Lords, is inerrant (Matt. 11:25; 1 Cor. 12:3; 2 Tim. 1:18; Jude 1:4; Rev. 11:15). Latter-day Saints believe there is but one true gospel faith which is taught only in Christ's church. Others today seem to believe that God can have many churches teaching many different versions of the gospel, even though Paul taught otherwise (Cor. 1:10). Last, we believe in one true baptism by immersion at the hands of one having authority. Protestants believe that many kinds of baptism are acceptable, and many even consider baptism optional.

Test 7. The Bible teaches that God's servants must be "called of God, as was Aaron" (Heb. 5:4) through revelation and by ordination of God's chosen servants (Ex. 28:1; Num. 27:18, 23). "We believe that a man must be called of God, by prophecy, and by the laying on of hands by those who are in authority" (5th Article of Faith; Mosiah 18:17). Protestant churches teach a variety of beliefs which contradict the above requirement.

Test 8. John taught "Hereby know ye the Spirit of God: Every spirit that confesseth that Jesus Christ is come in the flesh is of God" (John 4:2). Latter-day Saints confess that Jesus Christ, our Lord and Savior, came in the flesh (1 Nephi 10:11; 15:13; Ether 3:9; D & C 18:11; 20:1, 26; 93:4, 11) and was resurrected with a glorified body of flesh and bone (Luke 24:36-39). The Book of Mormon teaches, "that Christ . . . should take upon him the image of man, and . . . should come down among the children of men, and take upon him flesh and blood, and go forth upon the face of the earth" (Mosiah 7:27). LDS beliefs affirm the importance of obtaining a physical body and of the resurrection of that body. Christ as the first fruits of the resurrection showed the rest of mankind the way. Since we confess and teach that Jesus Christ came in the flesh, we must, as John said, be "of God."

Test 9. John taught in 1 John 5:1: "Whosoever believeth that Jesus is the Christ is born of God" Latter-day Saints believe and teach that Jesus is the Christ (2 Nephi 25:19; 26:12; Moroni 7:44; D & C 29:1; 35:1-2; 38:1-3; 39:1-4), therefore, according to scripture, they are "born of God"

Test 10. John also taught in 1 John 5:5 and 10: "Who is he that over-cometh the world but he that believeth that Jesus is the Son of God? He that believeth on the Son of God hath the witness in himself." Latter-day Saints firmly believe that Jesus is the Son of God (Mosiah 3:8; 4:2; Alma 6:8; 36:17; Helaman 3:28; 5:12; 14:12; 3 Nephi 5:13, 26; 9:15; 20:31; Mormon 5:14; 7:5; Ether 4:7); therefore, they must be among those who will overcome the world and receive his witness (the Holy Ghost) Incidentally, many who call themselves Christians believe that Jesus Christ was conceived of the Holy Ghost, citing Matthew 1:18-20 as proof. The truth is that Jesus Christ always declared that he was the Son of God the Father and not the Holy Ghost. (See p. 95).

Thus the "fruit" of LDS doctrine pass all ten of these Bible tests and fail none. Protestant beliefs, on the other hand, deny a need for true prophets or apostles and also the power and authority whereby the gift of the Holy Ghost is given (2 Tim. 3:5). It should be noted that any religion that fails one or more of the above biblical tests is not teaching the complete gospel of Christ, but instead is teaching a partial gospel made of the precepts of men (Isa. 29:13). Of these the Lord has said, "The kingdom of God shall be taken from you, and given to a nation bringing forth the fruits thereof" (Matt. 21:43).

3. Do Latter-day Saints believe in "another gospel"?

Anti-Mormon detractors sometimes assert that since LDS beliefs regarding salvation, the Godhead, the exaltation of man, and the accuracy of the Bible, differ from Protestant or Catholic beliefs, Mormons must believe "another gospel" than that found in the Bible (Gal. 1:6). Though others do have a portion of the gospel as found in the Bible, they lack the fullness of the everlasting gospel spoken of in Revelation 14:6; 3 Nephi 27:13-21; D & C 14:10; and 20:9. The fullness of the gospel is defined in Bruce R. McConkie's *Mormon Doctrine* (p. 333) as "those laws, doctrines, ordinances, powers, and authorities needed to enable men to gain the fullness of salvation" (i.e. exaltation in the celestial kingdom). Since the power and authority to administer the saving ordinances resides solely in Christ's church, only that church has the fullness of his gospel. The fullness of the gospel as taught by the LDS Church is in agreement with Bible teachings. Latter-day Saints generally list five principles and ordinances as essential to salvation. These are:

1. Faith in the Lord Jesus Christ as Savior and Redeemer (Mark 16:15-18; John 3:16-18; 8:24; Acts 16:31; Rom. 1:16-17; 10:8; Heb. 3:17-19; 10:38-39; 1 Peter 1:9; 1 John 5:5).

2. Repentance of personal sin (Isa. 55:6-7: Ezek. 33:14-15; Matt. 21:28-32; Luke 13:3; Acts 2:38; 3:19; 11:18; Heb. 6:1-2; 1 John 1:8-9).

3. Baptism by immersion by those having authority (Matt. 28:19; Mark 16:15-16; Luke 7:28-30; John 3:5; Acts 2:37-38; 10:47-48; Gal. 3:27; Titus 3:5; 1 Peter 3:21).

4. Receipt of the Holy Ghost (Matt. 3:11; Luke 3:16; John 3:5; Acts 2:37-38; 11:16; 1 Cor. 2:11-14; 12:3; 2 Thes. 2:13).

5. Enduring to the end through obedience to gospel teachings (Eccl. 12:13; Matt. 10:22; 24:13; Mark 13:13; Heb. 6:15; James 1:12, 22, 27; 3 John 11; Rev. 2:26; 3:21; 21:7).

These principles are taught clearly in the Book of Mormon: "And it shall come to pass, that whoso repenteth and is baptized in my name shall be filled; and if he endureth to the end, behold, him will I hold guiltless before my Father at that day when I shall stand to judge the world. And no unclean thing can enter into his kingdom; therefore nothing entereth into his rest save it be those who have washed their garments in my blood, because of their faith, and the repentance of all their sins, and their faithfulness to the end. Now this is the commandment: Repent, all ye ends of the earth, and come unto me and be baptized in my name, that ye may be sanctified by the reception of the Holy Ghost, that ye may stand spotless before me at the last day" (3 Nephi 27:16, 19-20).

In contrast, fundamentalist Christians believe that in order to be saved one must (1) accept Jesus Christ as his Savior and (2) accept certain "orthodox Christian beliefs" which they define as:

1. Accepting the deity of Christ.

2. Accepting the bodily resurrection of Jesus.

3. Believing in salvation solely by the grace of God, through faith alone, since Christ's atonement pays for all sin.

4. Believing in the trinity.

5. Believing in the virgin birth of Christ.

The first question that must be asked is: are these tenets propounded by fundamentalist Christians in agreement with Bible scripture? Members of the LDS Church would agree that the first two stated "basic Christian beliefs" are true and are in accordance with the Bible. They are also basic Mormon beliefs; but only the first, as it pertains to faith in the Lord Jesus Christ, is defined in the scriptures as essential to salvation. Evangelicals also perceive the deity of Christ as meaning that the one "triune" God the Father came to earth and manifested himself as the Son, a distinctly different understanding of Christ's divine nature than that held by Latter-day Saints.

Although a belief in the bodily resurrection of Jesus Christ is an important part of understanding his mission on earth and having faith in him, it is not listed in the Bible as a requirement for salvation.

The third tenet is accurate if one understands the conditional nature of Christ's atonement for personal sin. He died for all mankind on condition that we accept his sacrifice and follow him (Heb. 5:9; 1 Peter 2:21 and other references found in chapter 6 of this text). Eternal life is gained through knowing God (John 17:3) and keeping his commandments (1 John 2:3-5). It thus becomes part of enduring.

The fourth tenet would be true (per John 17:3) if the doctrine of the trinity were true. The word trinity is not found in the Bible and the concept of biblical oneness implies only unity of purpose and action. An unbiased reading of John 17:11, 21-22; Romans 12:5, 16; 15:6; 1 Corinthians 1:10; 6:17; 8:6; 10:17; 12:13; Galatians 3:28; Ephesians 1:10; and Hebrews 2:11 demonstrates this conclusively (See chapter 5 of this text for further details).

Last, belief in the virgin birth, as taught by fundamentalist Christians, is in no way a biblical requirement for salvation. Although the LDS Church acknowledges that the Savior was born of a virgin, many other Christians assert that both Christ's conception and birth were miraculous and that Mary remained a virgin for the remainder of her life. This teaching, like those of the trinity, transubstantiation, indulgences, limbo, and others, was introduced during the apostasy following the death of the apostles and has no basis in scripture.

In summary, the gospel as taught in the LDS church, especially in the critical area of salvation, is in harmony with the Bible, while "fundamentalist" doctrines generally ignore references to principles other than faith. Any additional requirements for salvation which are found in the scriptures, such as baptism or obedience to commandments, are often rationalized or dismissed as optional. To this the Lord has said: "Woe to the rebellious . . . that take counsel, but not of me; and that cover with a covering, but not of my spirit, that they may add sin to sin" (Isa. 30:1).

Latter-day Saints do not ignore Bible passages which refer to repentance, baptism, or the gift of the Holy Ghost, nor do they think that through their works they can somehow be saved without Jesus Christ. Latter-day Saints cannot be accused of professing to know God but in works deny him (Titus 1:16), but instead are by patient continuance in well doing, seeking for glory, honor, immortality, and eternal life (Rom. 2:7). The reader is referred to chapter 6 of this text and following for further information in this regard.

4. Do Latter-day Saints believe in another Jesus?

Although some believe that Mormons teach "another Jesus" than the Jesus described in the Bible (2 Cor. 11:4), our concept of Jesus Christ is entitled *A New Witness for the Articles of Faith* (pp. 639-40) usually satisfies the honest inquirer:

> [Members of the LDS Church believe in Jesus Christ who was Jehovah of the Old Testament; the only begotten Son of God born to Mary as] foretold by the prophets; [the baby] cradled in a manger [and] welcomed by angelic hosts; [the child] circumcised when eight days old [and later] worshipped by the wise men from the east; exiled to Egypt; disciplined in Nazareth; trained in carpentry in Galilee; matured and grown in grace in the Holy Land; baptized at Bethabara; tested in the wilderness; a Holy Man who ministered in Judea, Galilee, Samaria, and beyond the borders of Israel; preached and wrought miracles throughout the land; cast out devils; healed lepers; cured the lame; opened blind eyes; walked on the Sea of Galilee; fed thousands with a few loaves and fishes; raised the dead in Capernaum, Nain, and Bethany; proclaimed his own divine Sonship; the Son who was transfigured on the mount; atoned in Gethsemane; tried before Annas, Caiaphas, Herod, and Pilate; crucified on Calvary; resurrected in the Garden; and ascended from Olivet. . . . [This Son of Man] who "made himself of no reputation, and took upon him the form of a servant, and was made in the likeness of men" (Phil. 2:7), shall come again as the Immortal King [of Kings and Lord of Lords (Rev. 19:16)], to rule and reign over [his people] and all the earth for a thousand years!

This is the Jesus Christ in whom Latter-day Saints believe. He is our Lord, our Savior, and our Redeemer (1 Nephi 22:12) and we pray that all men may come to know him and his Father and return to their presence someday. Additional details regarding the divinity of Jesus Christ may be found in chapter 5 of this text.

5. Does the LDS Church have secret social and political objectives?

That some of our critics suspect the Church of sinister motives and secret conspiratorial intentions is, to most members of our Church, unbelievable. Unfortunately, these accusations have been made since the beginning of the Church and are still being made today.

President Wilford Woodruff, as early as December 1889, answered similar charges being made by critics of the Church. These included accusations that the LDS Church: (1) claimed to be the kingdom of God on earth and thus had authority to administer capital punishment, including the killing of apostates and (2) sought the overthrow of the U.S. Government, since the temple endowment ceremony was hostile to the Government and contained an oath to avenge the blood of the prophet.

The following is quoted from an Official Declaration by the First Presidency and Quorum of the Twelve Apostles, dated December 12th, 1889:

To whom it May Concern:

In consequence of gross misrepresentations of the doctrines, aims and practices of The Church of Jesus Christ of Latter-day Saints, commonly called the "Mormon" Church, which have recently been revived for political purposes and to prevent all aliens, otherwise qualified, who are members of the "Mormon" Church from acquiring citizenship, we deem it proper on behalf of said Church to publicly deny these calumnies and enter our protest against them.

We solemnly make the following declarations, viz:

That this Church views the shedding of human blood with the utmost abhorrence. That we regard the killing of a human being, except in conformity with the civil law, as a capital crime which should be punished by shedding the blood of the criminal, after a public trial before a legally constituted court of the land.

Notwithstanding all the stories told about the killing of apostates, no case of this kind has ever occurred, and of course has never been established against the Church we represent . . .

The revelations of God to this Church make death the penalty for capital crime, and require that offenders against life and property shall be delivered up to be tried by the laws of the land.

We declare that no Bishop's court or other court in this Church claims or exercises the right to supersede, annul or modify a judgement of any civil court. Such courts, while established to regulate Christian conduct, are purely ecclesiastical, and their punitive powers go no further than the suspension or excommunication of members from Church fellowship . . .

We declare that there is nothing in the ceremony of the Endowment, or in any doctrine, tenet, obligation or injunction of this Church, either private or public, which is hostile or intended to be hostile to the Government of the United States. On the contrary, its members are under divine commandment to revere the Constitution as a heaven-inspired instrument.

Utterances of prominent men in the Church at a time of great excitement have been selected and grouped, to convey the impression that present members are seditious. Those expressions were made more than thirty years ago, when through the falsehoods of recent officials, afterward demonstrated to be baseless, troops were sent to this Territory and were viewed . . . as an armed mob coming to renew the bloody persecutions of years before. At that time, excitement prevailed and strong language was used; but no words of disloyalty against the Government or its institutions were uttered; public speakers confined their remarks to denouncing traitorous officials who were prostituting the powers of their position to accomplish nefarious ends . . .

We also declare that this Church does not claim to be an independent, temporal kingdom of God, or to be an imperium in imperio aiming to overthrow the United States or any other civil government. It has been organized by divine revelation preparatory to the second advent of the Redeemer. It proclaims that "the kingdom of heaven is at hand." Its members are commanded of God to be subject unto the powers that be until Christ comes, whose right it is to reign . . .

We desire to be in harmony with the Government and people of the United States as an integral part of the nation (*Messages of the First Presidency,* vol. 3, pp. 184-87; see also D & C 134:1, 8-10).

Our 10th Article of Faith states: We believe . . . that Christ will reign personally upon the earth and, that the earth will be renewed and receive its paradisiacal glory." It is in this sense as confirmed by Bible scripture

(Isa. 9:6-7; 24:23; 32:1; Zech. 14:9; Luke 1:31-33; 21:10-27; Rev. 5:10; 19:6, 15; 20:4-6) and modern revelation (1 Nephi 22:24; D & C 1:36; 29:11; 45:59; 103:5-7; 133:25) that the nations of the earth will be overthrown by Christ and not men.

Elder L. Tom Perry (*Ensign,* Nov. 89, p. 71) has confirmed more recently that the Church has no hidden agenda but is seeking to build up Christ's kingdom and not man's.

As John the Revelator said: We await the day when "The kingdoms of this world are become the kingdoms of our Lord, and of his Christ; and he shall reign for ever and ever" (Rev. 11:15), and "we shall reign" with him "on the earth" (Rev. 5:10).

It is ironic, when the Book of Mormon warns against secret combinations (Ether 8:14-26), that Latter-day Saints are being wrongly accused of this very thing. While it is true that the devil often works in secret, it is also true that gospel truths may be kept secret. Bible scriptures illustrate this point, referring frequently to secret teachings and knowledge among the saints of old (Deut. 29:29; Jud. 13:18; Job 29:4; Ps. 25:14; Prov. 3:32; Dan. 2:28; Amos 3:7; Matt. 13:11, 35; 17:9; Mark 4:11; Luke 8:10; John 16:12; Rom. 11:25; 16:25; 1 Cor. 2:7; 4:1; 13:2; 14:2; 15:51; Eph. 1:9; 3:3-5; 5:32; 6:19; Col. 1:26; 2:2; 1 Tim. 3:16; Rev. 2:17). See also JST Matthew 7:9-11.

John 18:19-23 or Luke 8:17 are often cited as proof that Christ kept no secrets. A careful study of the passages cited in the previous paragraph and Christ's parables leads one to conclude that Christ revealed truths only to those prepared to receive them (Matt. 13:11). His comments in John 18:19-23 were not as much a statement about openness in teaching the gospel as it was a challenge to produce his accusers as required by law. He recognized the attempt by his captors to force him into self-incrimination rather than rely on the testimony of witnesses as the law specified. Likewise, his statement in Luke was not about secret ideas but rather about works (Luke 8:15).

In his book entitled *Signs of the True Church of Christ,* Michael T. Griffith stated:

> When the pagan critic Celsius accused the early Christians of secrecy, Origen freely admitted that the Early Church had secret doctrines, and he defended their existence: ". . . that there should be certain doctrines, not made known to the multitude, which are revealed after the exoteric [public] ones have been taught, is not a peculiarity of Christianity alone, but also of philosophic systems, in which certain truths are exoteric and others esoteric [confidential, limited to a select few]. Some of the hearers of Pythagora were content with his ipse dixit; while others were taught in secret those doctrines which were not deemed fit to be communicated to profane and insufficiently prepared ears. Moreover, all the mysteries that are celebrated throughout Greece and barbarous countries, although held in secret,

have no discredit thrown upon them. So that it is in vain that he [Celsius] endeavors to calumniate [slander] the secret doctrines of Christianity, seeing he does not correctly understand its nature" (*The Ante-Nicene Fathers,* vol. 4, p. 399).

Clement of Alexandria (150-215 A.D.) was an elder and a prominent scholar in the early church. Under Clement, the Christian school at Alexandria became one of the most outstanding schools of the eastern branch of the ancient Christian church. Historian Frank N. MaGill has given us the following interesting analysis of Clement's teachings on the early Christian gospel:

Clement concedes that the Scriptures open salvation to the many, who experience the 'first saving change,' when they pass from heathenism to faith, or from law to Gospel. But these are saved only in the first degree. Besides his public teachings, Christ also taught his Apostles the gnosis [sacred knowledge] which leads to perfection. This knowledge, Clement claims, has descended by transmission to a few, having been imparted unwritten by the apostles. Great preparation and previous training are necessary to receive it. But those who can obey it achieve here and now a foretaste of eternal bliss, and, in the world to come, will take their places with the Apostles in the highest sphere (*Masterpieces of Christian Literature,* p. 47).

Ian Barber has made some relevant observations on the subject under discussion:

. . . important pieces of Jewish/Christian literature, such as the Ethiopian text, "The Combat of Adam and Eve against Satan," introduce elements that have relevance not only to the theological instruction of the [Mormon temple] endowment ceremony, but to material found in such LDS sources as the Book of Moses (e.g. in "The Combat . . .") Satan continually tries to intimidate and confront Adam while he and Eve offer sacrifice in similitude of the true sacrifice of Christ. God sends heavenly messengers to comfort them, including three messengers who bring "the signs of the priesthood and Kingship," which are signs of the atonement to come . . .

It [the fact that there were secret teachings in the Early Church] goes back to the earliest Patristic writers, and is stated clearly by Eusebius [an early Christian historian, 260-339 A.D.], Irenaeus [an ancient bishop and apologist, 115-200 A.D.], and Ignatius [another Early Church bishop, 35-107 A.D.]. Indeed, gnosis is an authentic New Testament Greek word meaning sacred knowledge, and as Nibley points out . . . [there was a] gnosis centered like the Mormon endowment around the living Christ. It was this that Eusebius asserted the Lord gave secretly to Peter, James, and John in a post-resurrectional setting. . . . In [an article] in the prestigious religious journal "Vigiliae Christinae" (reprinted in *When the Lights Went Out*), Nibley notes that . . . a consistently organic body of material argues for the authenticity of a true post-resurrectional gnosis, as Eusebius suggested, involving sacred ordinances ("What Mormonism Isn't: A Response to the Research of Jerald and Sandra Tanner," pp. H/1H/2). (Griffith, *Signs of the True Church of Christ,* pp. 122-24).

Truths revealed in the early days of the LDS Church were not evil but uplifting. The same is true of LDS temple ceremonies. They involve righteous covenants which Latter-day Saints hold as sacred. In accordance with Christ's teaching in Matthew 7:6, we do not speak of the details of our temple worship to the world but we encourage all to become temple worthy and then to enter the temple and learn the sacred truths taught there. They involve no sinister social or political objective such as avenging wrongs done by our enemies, but rather promote righteousness among God's people. See also Hugh Nibley, *Since Cumorah,* chapter 4 and Darrick Evenson, *The Gainsayers,* pp. 75-83 for additional information on this subject.

6. Why do Latter-day Saints believe there can be only one true church?

D & C 1:30 tells us, "those to whom these commandments were given . . . have power to lay the foundation of this church, and to bring it forth out of obscurity and out of darkness, the *only* true and living church upon the face of the whole earth"

Paul taught that we should be "of the same mind and the same judgement" and that there should be "no divisions" among us (1 Cor. 1:10). He also spoke of "one body," "one faith" and "one baptism" and of the importance of "edifying the body of Christ: Till we all come in the unity of the faith, and of the knowledge of the Son of God" (Eph. 4:4, 5, 12, 13). Peter, in like manner, exhorted the Lord's people to be of "one mind" (1 Peter 3:8). It follows that there can be only one true fold and one true shepherd, as the Savior's teachings imply in John 10:16, and he that is not with Christ is against him (Matt. 12:30; Mark 9:40; 2 Nephi 10:16). If we are not one, we are not his (D & C 38:27). God's true Church cannot be divided in faith, teachings, or doctrines. If it is, it is not his Church (Matt. 12:25, 1 Cor. 12:25; 14:33).

Last, Paul instructed us to "mark them which cause divisions and offenses contrary to the doctrine which [we] have learned; and avoid them. For they that are such serve not our Lord Jesus Christ" (Rom. 16:17-18). Thus the scriptures affirm that Christ's kingdom is one of unity and order and there can only be one unified body of believers. Divisions, confusion, and conflict have no part in Christ's church. Those who would have you believe that we should reject any church which claims to be the only true church are teaching that "wide is the gate and broad is the way [which] leadeth unto life," but Christ taught differently (Matt. 7:13-14). Truth cannot be self-contradictory, so any group of churches which disagrees on points of doctrine cannot logically claim to have unflawed doctrine. Pure truth can only be found in Christ's church (see also page 12 of this text; Ps. 133:1; John 17:11; Acts 1:14; 4:32; Rom. 12:5; 2 Cor. 13:11; Gal. 3:28; Eph. 4:3; Phil. 1:27; 2:2; Titus 3:10; and Heb. 2:11).

2
Apostasy and Restoration

7. Why does the LDS Church claim to have power and authority which Catholics and Protestants do not?

Christ's gospel and church were established with power—the power of the priesthood (Matt. 10:1; Mark 3:14-15; 6:7; 9:1; Luke 24:49; D & C 84:19-21; 107:18; 113:8; 121:41).

The literal nature of the power of the priesthood is clearly demonstrated in the miracles where Jesus remarked that "virtue had gone out of him" (Mark 5:30; Luke 6:19; 8:46). The misleading use of the word "virtue" might cause some to think that Jesus could have been less virtuous after this encounter. In reality, the Greek word "dunamis," which was translated in the above-mentioned scriptures as "virtue," was most often rendered as "power" in other Bible passages. This miraculous priesthood power is a healing strength which can be transferred by touch when faith is present, and apparently, occasionally even when the bearer is unaware. The same Greek word was used in Luke 9:1 immediately following the healing of the woman with an issue of blood. At that time, Jesus "called his twelve disciples together, and gave them power [dunamis] and authority over all devils, and to cure diseases." After receiving this power and authority, "he sent them to preach the kingdom of God, and to heal the sick" (Luke 9:2), the healing being done by the laying on of hands (Mark 16:15-18) by those so empowered.

Many scriptures also emphasize the importance of the priesthood power. The Apostle Peter taught that the disciples were "built up a spiritual house, an holy priesthood, to offer up spiritual sacrifices, acceptable to God by Jesus Christ." He called them "a chosen generation, a royal priesthood, an holy nation, [and] a peculiar people" (I Peter 2:5, 9). Paul said his "preaching was not with enticing words of man's wisdom, but in demonstration of the Spirit and of power. That [the disciples'] faith should not stand in the wisdom of men but in the power of God" (1 Cor. 2:4-5). He also taught the Thessalonian saints that the "gospel came not unto you in word only, but also in power, and in the Holy Ghost" (1 Thes. 1:5). To Timothy Paul said, "Neglect not the gift that is in thee, which was given thee by prophecy, with the laying on of hands of the presbytery (elders)" (1 Tim. 4:14; 2 Tim. 1:6). Paul speaks in these passages of the power of the priesthood to give the gift of the Holy Ghost.

The priesthood and gift of the Holy Ghost are conferred "by the laying on of hands of the elders, so that all things may be done in order" (D & C 20:41, 68; JS-H 1:68).

We might then ask, "How and from whom did modern Protestant preachers and ministers receive their power and authority?" If from other ministers, from what source did those ministers ultimately receive it?

As reported in Acts 8:17, 20, Peter and John laid their hands on those of Samaria who had been baptized that they might receive the gift of the Holy Ghost. When the difference between the Holy Ghost and the gift of the Holy Ghost is understood, it is apparent that the standard method of giving this gift in the New Testament church was by the laying on of hands (see chapter 9 for additional details). Catholic and Protestant churches, to the author's knowledge, observe no such procedure today. Even if Protestant churches did confer this gift by the laying on of hands, they have no legitimate claim to the priesthood power. They were long ago cut off by the Catholic Church, the only possible line of authority through which they could have received this power.

Paul, in his epistle to the Hebrews, spoke of men ordained to the priesthood that they might "offer both gifts and sacrifices for sins" but cautioned that "no man taketh this honour [the priesthood] unto himself, but he that is called of God, as was Aaron" (Heb. 5:1, 4). Aaron was called by the prophet Moses (Ex. 28:1). Neither Catholics nor Protestants have a priesthood called and ordained by revelation from God as Aaron. In most cases, they deny the possibility of modern revelation and therefore cannot have the power and authority of God. The Protestant world does not recognize the fact that "the kingdom of God is not in word, but in power" (1 Cor. 4:20). Even today they claim the Bible (the word) as the source of their authority. They thus have "a form of godliness but [deny] the power thereof" (2 Tim. 3:5).

It is important to note that the Bible contains no instances of a prophet who is self-called or self-ordained. Paul stated in 2 Corinthians 10:8 and 18 that authority is given by the Lord—not by scripture. Ordination to the priesthood was accomplished, as shown previously, by the laying on of hands (Acts 13:1-3; 1 Tim. 4:14).

A man must receive this ordination by the laying on of hands before he may baptize or confer the gift of the Holy Ghost. Kirk Holland Vestal and Arthur Wallace in *The Firm Foundation of Mormonism* discuss authority in the early church, citing the following:

The early Church father, Cyprian, discussed this vital doctrine in his 69th Letter, written about 255 A.D., when he was questioned about authority to baptize and to preside in a congregation without having been ordained to the priesthood through the proper channels. Cyprian summarized that "one who was not ordained in the Church cannot conceivably have or maintain any authority over the Church" (Cyprian, 69th Letter, iii).

Latter-day Saints are unique among Christians of the world in claiming a restoration of the priesthood power and authority. This was accomplished in the spring of 1829 by the return of John the Baptist and later the Apostles Peter, James, and John (D & C 13; JS-H 1:68-72). These ministers of God conferred both the Aaronic and Melchizedek priesthoods upon Joseph Smith and Oliver Cowdery. These priesthoods are conferred upon others in the Church when a recipient has been called through inspiration (revelation) by those having authority (Titus 1:5; see also 1 Tim. 5:22; Heb. 5:4).

Since the LDS Church received its authority directly from Christ's apostles and not through a questionable line of apostolic succession spanning many hundreds of years of apostasy, LDS priesthood bearers are uniquely qualified to claim the priesthood of God. As there is only one power of God, it follows that there can be only one true priesthood here upon the earth. The priesthood restored in this dispensation is that priesthood. It is the power and authority of God delegated to man on earth to act in all things for the salvation of men. It is the power by which the ordinances of salvation are performed so that they will be binding on earth and in heaven (Matt. 16:19; *Mormon Doctrine,* p. 594). In conclusion, the "power of God unto salvation" (Rom. 1:16) is available only in the Church Jesus Christ established himself, The Church of Jesus Christ of Latter-day Saints. See also Joseph Fielding Smith Jr., *Religious Truths Defined,* pp. 170-87; Richard Lloyd Anderson, *Understanding Paul,* pp. 209-15.

8. Why do Latter-day Saints teach that an apostasy and restoration occurred when the Bible says that the gospel was "once delivered unto the saints" (Jude 1:3)?

The word "once," as used in Jude 1:3 should be translated as "before" or "previously" to be more accurate. As proof of this, note that the same Greek word was used in verse 5 and was also translated in the King James Version (KJV) as "once." The context used in verse five makes it clear that to interpret the use in verse two as "one time" is not correct. The KJV translates the Greek as "ye once knew this" (i.e. He knew it in the past but may have forgotten it). The New International

Version confirms this by translating this same Greek word (once-verse 5) as "already," meaning formerly.

Other scriptures confirm that many general apostasies have taken place (Deut. 9:7, 25; 29:25; 30:15-19; Jud. 3:7; 1 Kings 11:2; 14:22; 2 Kings 17:7; 21:2; Ps. 106:36; Isa. 2:8; 3:9; 24:5; 29:13-14; 59:2; Jer. 2:17; 7:11; 35:15; Ezek. 2:3; 11:12; 22:26; Hos. 4:6, 17; Amos 8:11; Micah 3:11; Matt. 13:15; 15:9) and that the gospel had been formerly delivered to ancient Israel following these apostasies. Paul taught the Galatians that "God . . . preached before the gospel unto Abraham" (Gal. 3:8) and in Hebrews 4:2 he declared that, "unto us was the gospel preached, as well as unto them [Israel in the days of Moses—1 Cor. 10:4; Heb. 3:16-17]: but the word preached did not profit them, not being mixed with faith in them that heard it" (Heb. 4:2). If the gospel was preached to Abraham in 2000 BC, to the people of Israel during the exodus in 1350 BC, and then to Israel of Christ's day, it was delivered more than one time. See also Isaiah 40:9; 52:7; 61:1; Moses 5:58-59; 6:51-68; *Teachings,* pp. 59-61; Seaich, *Mormonism the Dead Sea Scrolls and the Nag Hammadi Texts,* pp. 54-55.

It is clear that an apostasy was predicted by Jesus Christ and his apostles. Jesus taught that, "many shall come in my name, saying, I am Christ; and shall deceive many" (Matt. 24:5). Paul declared: "be not soon shaken in mind, or troubled, neither by spirit, nor by word, nor by letter as from us, as that the day of Christ is at hand. Let no man deceive you by any means: for that day shall not come, except there come a falling away first" (2 Thes. 2:2-3). We should note that the Greek word "apostasia" was translated as "falling away" in the King James version. Thus, Paul is saying that the early Christians should not be fooled by false Christs since there would be an unmistakable apostasy before Christ's return. Consider also the following: Matthew 24:4, 9-13, 24; John 16:2-3; Acts 20:29-30; 1 Corinthians 1:10-13; Galatians 1:6-8; 2 Thessalonians 2:1-12; 1 Timothy 4:1-3; 2 Timothy 3:1-9, 12-13; 4:3-4; Titus 1:10-16; 2 Peter 2:1-3; 3:3; 1 John 2:18-19; Jude 3-4; Revelation 13:4-8.

During the sixteenth century, the Church of England said, "Laity and clergy, learned and unlearned, all ages, sects, and degrees, have been drowned in abominable idolatry most detested by God and damnable to man for eight hundred years and more" (Church of England "Homily on Perils of Idolatry," p. 3).

John Wesley, the founder of the Methodist Church, observed: "It does not appear that these extraordinary gifts of the Holy Ghost were common in the Church for more than two or three centuries. We seldom hear of them after that fatal period when the Emperor Constantine called himself a Christian. . . . From this time they almost totally ceased. . . . The Christians had no more the Spirit of Christ than the other heathens . . . This was the real cause why the extraordinary gifts of the Holy Ghost were no longer to be found in the Christian Church; because the Christians were turned heathen again, and had only a dead form left" (The More Excellent Way, *John Wesley's Works,* Vol. 7, Sermon 89, pp. 26-27).

Roger Williams, the founder of the Baptist Church of America, declared, "There is no regularly constituted church on earth, nor any person qualified to administer any church ordinances; nor can there be until new apostles are sent by the Great Head of the Church for whose coming I am seeking" (*Picturesque America,* edited by William Cullen Bryant, vol. 1, pp. 500-02).

On another occasion Williams proclaimed: "The apostasy . . . hath so far corrupted all, that there can be no recovery out of that apostasy until Christ shall send forth new apostles to plant churches anew (Underhill, Edward, *Struggles and Triumphs of Religious Liberty,* cited in William F. Anderson, *Apostasy or Succession, Which?,* pp. 238-39).

Other Bible verses such as Matthew 17:11; Acts 1:6-7; 3:19-21; Ephesians 1:10; and Revelation 14:6 confirm the LDS belief that a restoration of the gospel was prophesied to occur in these latter days. Some may be tempted to cite the Protestant reformation as the fulfillment of these prophecies, but it is clear that the promised restoration was to be accomplished not through man's effort but in spite of it (Dan. 2:44-45; Matt. 5:13; 1 Tim. 4:1-2; 2 Tim. 3:1-7; 4:3-4; Heb. 6:4-8). Such a renewal came at the time of the Savior's mortal ministry. Jesus Christ made no attempt to reform the doctrines and institutions of his day, he simply restored the true gospel to the earth. It was taught not as reformed Judaism but rather as a new alternative to it. As Jesus taught, new wine cannot be put in old bottles or both the wine and the bottles will be lost (Matt. 9:16-17). The multitude of Protestant churches existing today are proof of the fact that a reformation cannot succeed in restoring absolute truth. God has always accomplished this end through new revelation to his chosen prophets and not through self-appointed reformers. See also Hugh Nibley, *The World and the Prophets,* chapter 14.

9. Didn't the Savior say he would build his church upon the "rock" of Peter (Matthew 16:18)?

The Roman Catholic Church claims that Peter was the "rock" mentioned in Matthew 16:18, while Protestants generally claim that Peter's

confession of faith was the "rock." We believe as was taught by Joseph
Fielding Smith that "The expression the rock is used in the scriptures
with different meanings that must be interpreted according to the context. There are times when it refers to Christ, and times when it refers to
the gospel and other times when the reference is to revelation and again
to the Church" (*Answers to Gospel Questions,* 1:95). It is thus essential
to examine the scriptural context in which the word is used to determine
its meaning. First let us examine the Catholic and Protestant claims.

The Catholic Church claims that Peter was the rock and consequently the first Pope of the church which Christ established. But Peter could
not have been the "rock" since, in context, it was promised that the gates
of hell would not prevail against this "rock." In Matthew 16:23, just five
verses later, Christ strongly rebukes Peter's suggestion that he avoid persecution, calling Peter "Satan" The implications of this are largely
ignored by those who hold that Peter was the "rock." Other similar passages of scripture will be considered shortly.

We should also note that although Matthew, Mark, and Luke all mention the discussion of Christ's identity and Peter's testimony (Matt.
16:13-20; Mark 8:27-30; Luke 9:18-22), it was only Matthew who mentioned the "rock" upon which Christ's church would be built. Significantly, John mentions nothing of this announcement. If this event
actually carried the importance that Catholics have attached to it, why
would it have been ignored or incompletely reported by three of the four
gospel writers? (see C. Johann Perrie, *What Every Christian Should
Know,* Chapter 16)

Historians such as John Foxe record the fate of the Apostle Peter,
telling us he was crucified upside-down in Rome before AD 68. A.
Melvin McDonald, in his booklet entitled *The Day of Defense,* makes a
very good point. He asks, "if Clement were Pope in AD 96, like Catholic
tradition informs us, why didn't he, instead of John, receive the revelation on the Isle of Patmos? Why wasn't he or the Church of Rome recognized by John? Why are the scriptures completely void of any transfer
of authority when the apostles were to guide us in all truth and unity?
Why haven't the signs nor the power followed" as scripture prescribe
(Matt. 10:8; Mark 16:17-18)? He further asks why the Pope is not called
a prophet or apostle (A. Melvin McDonald, *The Day of Defense,* p. 63).
We could also ask why the Catholic Church completely changed the
original church organization and added new offices and titles such as
popes, cardinals, archbishops, monsignors, monks, nuns, and so forth.
(See also Joseph Fielding Smith, Jr., *Religious Truths Defined,* pages
170-174 for a more detailed discussion of papal succession.)

The original grammar, context, and Greek words for Peter and rock are very important to an adequate understanding of this scripture. The grammar of the verses makes reference to the rock as the way Peter received this truth (i.e. as revealed from the Father by revelation). Also, the first word translated as "Peter" comes from the Greek word "petros," meaning a piece of rock or fragmented stone (see John 1:42). The Greek word translated as "rock" in the KJV was "petra," meaning a mass of rock such as bedrock or a sure rock or foundation. No builder would build upon a "petros" or fragmented stone foundation, so the comparison Christ made was obvious to those present at the time. It was also obvious to Peter. In 1 Peter 2:3-8, Peter uses a third Greek word (lithos), meaning a smaller stone, to describe the position of Christ and his disciples relative to the church. Peter explains that Jesus Christ himself was both a living stone in the overall church and a (petra) rock of offense. His disciples were likened only to the smaller (lithos) stones used to "built up a spiritual house" with Christ himself being the "chief corner stone" (See also Eph. 2:20). Thus Peter and the other disciples were smaller stones in the edifice, but Christ was the principal stone and the sure foundation (petra) of the church.

The Protestant world claims that Peter's confession of Christ as Son of God was the "rock." 1 Peter 2:6 and 2 Timothy 2:19 do seem to support this assertion. Although it is clear that faith in Christ is a fundamental principle of the gospel, several problems arise when the Protestant assertion is examined.

Despite Peter's confession of faith in this instance, he later denied Christ three times (Matt. 26:69-75). In addition, Christ's words in Luke 22:32-34, "When thou art converted," show that Peter still had not become fully converted at the time of Christ's betrayal. These scriptures cast doubt on the Protestant premise and lead to a conclusion that the gates of hell did prevail against Peter's faith, even if only for a time.

The LDS view that the "rock" referred to in this case was revelation, is probably based on a comment made by Joseph Smith about this passage. He is reported to have said that Jesus in his teaching stated, "Upon this rock I will build my Church, and the gates of hell shall not prevail against it. What rock? Revelation" (*Teachings*, p. 274). There is substantial internal evidence in these verses of Matthew to support this conclusion. Note that Jesus stated, "flesh and blood hath not revealed it unto thee, but my Father which is in heaven" (Matt. 16:17). The antecedent of the word "rock" was the "revealed" phrase in the preceding verse (See *Answers to Gospel Questions*, 1:95-99).

Any truth that is revealed by the Father or any member of the Godhead is revelation. This is especially true of the testimony of Christ. John stated, "the testimony of Jesus is the spirit of prophecy," (Rev. 19:10) or in other words, revelation. We all must obtain a testimony in the same manner as Peter. Paul, for example, claimed that his gospel knowledge was received not "of man . . . but the by revelation of Jesus Christ" (Gal. 1:12). Peter also spoke of revelation or prophecy saying "We have also a more sure word of prophecy; whereunto ye do well that ye take heed" (2 Peter 1:19).

Isaiah, in speaking of the word of the Lord to men, said it would be given "precept upon precept . . . line upon line . . . here a little, and there a little: For with stammering lips and another tongue will he speak to this people. . . . Therefore thus saith the Lord God, behold, I lay in Zion for a foundation a stone, a tried stone, a sure foundation: he that believeth shall not make haste" (Isa. 28:10-11, 16; see also Romans 9:33).

It is significant that early Christian writers prior to 300 AD interpreted the rock to be revelation by the Spirit. In about 200 AD Hippolytus said, 'By the Spirit Peter spoke the blessed word 'Thou art the Christ, the Son of the living God.' By this Spirit the rock of the church was established. This is the Spirit, the comforter, that is sent because of thee to be the child of God" (Hippolytus, *Discourse on the Holy Theophany* as quoted in the 1952 Melchizedek Priesthood Manual entitled *The Divine Church* by James L. Barker, pp. 155-57; see this reference for additional quotes). Thus, the revealed testimony of Jesus Christ is a sure word of prophecy (revelation) and a sure foundation stone, but as will now be shown, not the only one spoken of in scripture.

Jesus himself is a Rock, as testified in numerous scriptures. Paul taught the Corinthian saints: "Moreover, brethren, I would not that ye should be ignorant, how that all our fathers were under the cloud and all passed through the sea; and were all baptized unto Moses in the cloud and in the sea . . . and all did drink the same spiritual drink: for they drank of that spiritual Rock that followed them: and that Rock [petra or bedrock] was Christ" (1 Cor. 10:1-4; see also Jacob 4:15-17). Paul also likened Christ to a solid foundation (1 Cor. 3:11) and Peter testified that Christ was the "living stone," the "chief corner stone," "a stone of stumbling" and "a rock of offense" (1 Peter 2:4-8; see also 1 Samuel 2:2).

Though Christ was the chief corner stone of God's kingdom, Paul and John make it clear that Christ's apostles and prophets shared the designation of "foundation" (Eph. 2:20; Rev. 21:14). Modem scriptures also confirm that Christ was the rock and sure foundation (1 Nephi 13:36; Jacob 4:15-17; Helaman 5:12; D & C 50:44; see also "Peter" in the *LDS Bible Dictionary*, p. 749).

The gospel is also clearly spoken of as a foundation or rock. Paul speaks of "the foundation of repentance from dead works, and of faith toward God, of the doctrine of baptisms, and of the laying on of hands, and of resurrection of the dead, and of eternal judgement" (Heb. 6:1-2). These "principles of the doctrine of Christ" are, in the final analysis, the gospel. 3 Nephi 11:39-40; D & C 11:24-25; 18:4-5; 33:12-13; and other modem scriptures confirm that Christ's gospel is also a rock upon which we must build along with revelation (D & C 11:24-25) and faith in Christ (D & C 33:12-13).

Although the rock spoken of in Matthew 16:18 is clearly the revelation of Christ's divinity, we should not categorically assume that the "rock" always refers to revelation and nothing else. Ancient and modern scriptures confirm that Jesus Christ and his gospel were also referred to as rocks and all are solid foundations upon which we should build our faith.

10. Why do Latter-day Saints believe in an apostasy when Christ taught that the gates of hell would not prevail against his Church (Matt. 16:18)?

The interpretation that apostasy could not occur in the church because of Christ's statement to Peter (i.e. that "the gates of hell shall not prevail against it") is neither in harmony with history nor the remainder of scripture.

Jesus Christ taught the Nephites: "Verily, verily, I say unto you, that this is my doctrine, and whoso buildeth upon this buildeth upon my rock, and the gates of hell will not prevail against them. And whoso shall declare more or less than this, and establish it for my doctrine . . . buildeth upon a sandy foundation, and the gates of hell stand open to receive such" (3 Nephi 11:39-40).

The Greek word translated as "church" in Matthew 16:18 is "ecclesia," which literally means a "calling out" Thus, the word translated as "church" in our King James New Testament referred not to an institution but a select group of righteous believers (See *Ensign,* Aug. 1993, p. 52). This is further substantiated in D & C 10:67, 69 where we are told that those who endure to the end will be established upon Christ's rock and "the gates of hell shall not prevail against them." Indeed, Jesus prophesied correctly, for the gates of hell did not prevail against those built upon Christ and his revelation to the prophets. Rather, the church fell into general apostasy when members began to rely on the philosophies of men, setting aside prophecy and Christ himself. The many firm believers in Christ, those who were "called out," died firm and untainted by the apostasy.

A. Melvin McDonald, in his book *The Day of Defense* (pp. 61-62), summarized the fate of the Lord's chosen apostles and other church leaders as recorded by early historians (such as Eusebius) and the traditions of the early church as related by Foxe in his *Book of Martyrs*. Most scholars today consider much of this information as only legends with little historical evidence, although the deaths of Peter and Paul are well documented by several early writers. A similar summary (with some corrections and additions) is included here for reference:

Fate of the Early Christian Apostles and Leaders

Apostles*	Person	Method of Death	+Year AD	Location
1.*	Judas Iscariot	Suicide—hanging (Matt 27:5; Acts 1:18)	34	Jerusalem
2.	Steven	Stoned (Acts 7:58-60)	36	Jerusalem
3.*	James the Great, brother of John, Son of Zebedee	beheaded with the sword (Acts 12:1-2)	44	Jerusalem
4.*	Thomas (doubting or Didymus)	run through with a lance	52	Calamina, East India
5.*	Philip	scourged, stoned imprisoned, crucified	52	Hierapolis Phrygia (Turkey)
6.*	Bartholomew	dragged, flailed alive, crucified, beheaded	52	Albinopolis, Armenia
7.	Matthew, Called Levi, Son of Alphaeus	slain with a lance or battle-ax	60	Nadabah
8.*	James the Less, Son of Alphaeus	thrown from the pinnacle, beaten stoned, brains dashed out with a fuller's club	60-62	?
9.*	Simon Peter	crucified upside down	64-68	Rome

10.*	Paul	beheaded by Nero	64-68	Rome
11.*	Matthias	stoned, beheaded	70	Ethiopia
12.*	Thaddaeus, brother of James (could be Jude)	shot with arrows or crucified	72-76	Edessa, Greece
13	Timothy	beaten with clubs	73	?
14.	Luke	hanged on olive tree	73	Boeotia, Greece
15.*	Barnabas	stoned to death	73	Salancan or Cyprus
16.	Mark	dragged to pieces, burned to death	74	Alexandria, Egypt
17.*	Simon (Zelotes)	crucified	74	Presia, Britain
18.*	Andrew, brother of Peter	burned to death or crucified	74	Patras, Greece
19.*	John the Beloved, brother of James the Great	banished to the Isle of Patmos until AD 97 and to Ephesus until AD 100 (Rev 1:9)	no record	no record

* Indicates disciples referred to in the Bible as apostles
+ *Dates are approximate (See also The Life and Teachings of Jesus and His Apostles,* New Testament Institute Manual, pp. 214-15, for a New Testament chronological history).

John Foxe's *Book of Martyrs* was first published in 1563. In his book he contended that the gates of hell had not prevailed against the church since it had "endured" from the days of Christ to his time despite "the uttermost strength and powers of all hell." This having been stated, he later describes the state of religion in AD 1371 at the time of the persecutions of John Wickliff (also known as Wycliff):

> This is out of all doubt, that at what time all the world was in most desperate and vile estate, and the lamentable ignorance and darkness of God's truth had overshadowed the whole earth . . .
> In these days the whole state of religion was depraved and corrupted: the name only of Christ remained amongst Christians, but his true and lively doctrine was as far unknown to the most part as his name was common to all men. As touching faith, consolation, the end and use of the law, the office of Christ, our impotency and weakness, the Holy Ghost, the greatness and strength of sin, true works, grace

and free justification by faith, the liberty of a Christian man, there was almost no mention.

The world, forsaking the lively power of God's spiritual Word, was altogether led and blinded with outward ceremonies and human traditions; in these was all hope of obtaining salvation fully fixed; insomuch that scarcely any other thing was seen in the temples or churches, taught or spoken of in sermons, or finally intended or gone about in their whole life, but only heaping up of certain shadowy ceremonies upon ceremonies; neither was there any end of this their heaping.

The Church did fall into all kinds of extreme tyranny; whereas the poverty and simplicity of Christ were changed into cruelty and abomination of life . . . The simple and unlearned people, being far from all knowledge of the holy scripture, thought it quite enough for them to know only those things which were delivered them by their pastors; and they, on their other part, taught in a manner nothing else but such things as came forth of the court of Rome; whereof the most part tended to profit of their order, more than to the glory of Christ.

What time there seemed to be no spark of pure doctrine remaining . . . This Wickliff, perceiving the true doctrine of Christ's gospel to be adulterated and defiled with so many filthy inventions and dark errors of bishops and monks . . . could no longer abide the same. . . .

Foxe goes on to describe the Church in the days of John Huss:

During all this time of Pope John [XXIII] there were three Popes reigning together, neither was yet the schism ceased, which had continued the space, already of thirty-six years; by reason whereof a General Council was holden at Constance in AD 1414, being called by Sigismund the Emperor, and Pope John XXIII. These three Popes were John, whom the Italians set up; Gregory, whom the Frenchmen set up; Benedict, whom the Spaniards placed. In this schismatical ambitious conflict everyone defended his Pope . . .

Pope John was deposed by the decree of the council, more than three and forty most grievous and heinous crimes being proved against him: as that he had hired Marcilius Parmensis, physician, to poison Alexander, his predecessor; further that he was a heretic, a simoniac, a liar, a hypocrite, a murderer, an enchanter, and a dice-player . . .

The correct interpretation of Matthew 16:18 becomes clear when one understands that, to early Christians, "the gates of hell" were the entrance to spirit prison or the place of departed spirits (see *Mormon Doctrine,* p. 342, Hades). As such, these gates figuratively symbolized physical and spiritual death. Since the gospel was soon to be preached to those in spirit prison (1 Peter 3:18-19; 4:6) and since the resurrection would overcome the effects of physical death, death and hell would not triumph over the church. However, this does not mean that an apostasy would not occur. Christ's atonement would still vanquish physical and spiritual death even if the church itself were lost for a time (see also *Ensign,* August 1993, pp. 52-53).

It is obvious from the foregoing history and the many prophecies found throughout the remainder of the New Testament that apostasy would prevail after the deaths of the apostles and prophets (see John

16:1-4; Acts 20:29; Gal. 1:6; 2 Thes. 2:3; 2 Tim. 1:15; 2 Tim. 3:1-5; 4:34; 2 Peter 2:1-2, 18-21; Rev. 13:7).

It is clear that Old Testament prophets also foresaw a complete apostasy in the "latter days" when men would "reject knowledge" and God would reject them (Hosea 3:4-5; 4:1-6). Isaiah, speaking of this time, said: "The earth also is defiled under the inhabitants thereof; because they have transgressed the laws, changed the ordinances, [and] broken the everlasting covenant" (Isa. 24:5). The law of Moses did not contain an everlasting covenant; it was only by the blood of Christ's sacrifice that God established his everlasting covenant (Ezek. 37:26-27; Heb. 13:20). Isaiah further states, "For, behold, the darkness shall cover the earth, and gross darkness the people" (Isa. 60:2). Amos spoke in like manner of a day when God would send "a famine of. . .hearing the words of the Lord," that would extend "from sea to sea, and from north even to the east, they shall run to and fro to seek the word of the Lord, and shall not find it" (Amos 8:11-12).

Even during Israel's days of transgression they retained their scriptures and prophets. It was only during the so-called dark ages of the earth's history that the scriptures were unavailable to the majority of mankind and the prophets were absent for nearly two millennia. If a universal apostasy did not occur, then John's prophecy that he "saw another angel fly in the midst of heaven, having the everlasting gospel to preach unto them that dwell on the earth" (Rev. 14:6) would make no sense.

The time for a "restitution of all" of God's words (Acts 3:21) has come, and a restoration of his heavenly kingdom is imminent. Latter-day Saints declare with sincerity that God has raised up a prophet in our day to restore his true church and the fullness of the gospel of Christ. Only that church (The Church of Jesus Christ of Latter-day Saints) is teaching the fullness of Christ's gospel and has God's authority to perform the saving ordinances. All others have "a form of godliness but [deny] the power thereof" (2 Tim 3:5: see *History of the Church* vol. 1, Introduction B. H. Roberts, for further information on the apostasy).

3
Prophets and Apostles

11. Why do Latter-day Saints teach that the foundation of apostles and prophets had to be laid again a second time?

Some Protestants believe that the foundation of the church spoken of in Ephesians 2:20 was meant to be laid only once and was not intended to last any longer than the original apostles. One critic asked, "How many foundations can a house have?" The answer to this is clear to those who truly understand the extent to which the apostasy destroyed the original church.

Just as building foundations are not removed when construction of a building is completed, Christ's apostles and prophets were not meant to be removed when the church was established, but were meant to remain, as were the other offices mentioned in Ephesians 4:11. There are at least 15 and possibly as many as 22 apostles named in the New Testament, and no fewer than three prophets are named in the book of Acts. Consider the following references:

Apostles

1-12	Original 12 apostles—Matt. 10:2-4 (also Mark 3:16-19; Luke 6:14-16)
13	Matthias—Acts 1:26
14	Paul—Acts 13:2; 14:14; Rom. 1:1
15	Barnabas—Acts 13:2; 14:14
16	Andronicus—Rom. 16:7
17	Junia—Rom. 16:7
18	Apollos—1 Cor. 4:6-9
19	James (the brother of Jesus)—Gal. 1:19
20	Silvanus—1 Thes. 1:1; 2:4-6
21	Timotheus—Thes. 1:1; 2:4-6
22	Jesus—Heb. 3:1

Prophets

1	Agabus—Acts 11:27-28; 21:10
2	Judas—Acts 15:22, 32
3	Silas—Acts 15:22, 32
—	Others—Acts 11:27; 13:1; 21:9; Rev. 11:3-10

We should ask why Matthias was chosen to replace Judas if that foundation were not meant to remain? Why also were Paul and Barnabas first mentioned as apostles following the death of James the brother of John and the imprisonment of Peter (Acts 12:2-3; 13:1-3; 14:14)? Why did the early church accept and refer to so many post-resurrection prophets by name?

If prophets existed throughout the Bible, why do we not need them now? Amos 3:7 indicates that God will do nothing save he reveal his will to his prophets. Also, 1 Corinthians 12:27-29, 14:29-33 and 37-39 indicate that prophets and the gift of prophecy were part of the original church. Their principle duty was to prevent error and confusion among the saints. Where does the Bible indicate that they were not meant to continue? A careful reading of Ephesians 4:11-14 indicates not only that prophets and apostles were meant to remain to maintain a "unity of the faith" and a "knowledge of the Son of God," but also that without them, men would be "tossed to and fro, and carried about with every wind of doctrine" (verse 14). This is exactly the condition of "mainstream Christianity" today!

In Ephesians 3:3-5, Paul makes it clear that in that day, knowledge was "revealed unto his holy apostles and prophets by the Spirit" (see also Acts 1:2; 2:18). It should also be noted that a careful reading of Luke chapter 11 reveals that Christ taught that slaying the apostles and prophets would cause the "key of knowledge" to be "taken away" (verses 49-52). Based on these verses, it seems safe to assume that any church not claiming to have these officers also cannot claim any unique understanding of God's truth or be his Church.

Hegesippus, a historian of the period immediately following apostolic times, is quoted by Eusebius in his *Ecclesiastical History* as saying:

> The church continued until then as a pure and uncorrupt virgin; whilst if there were any at all that attempted to pervert the sound doctrine of the saving gospel, they were yet skulking in dark retreats; but when the sacred choir of apostles became extinct, and the generation of those that had been privileged to hear their inspired wisdom had passed away, then also the combination of impious errors arose by fraud and delusions of false teachers. These also, as there were none of the apostles left, henceforth attempted, without shame to preach their false doctrine against the gospel of truth. Such is the statement of Hegesippus (Eusebius, *Ecclesiastical History,* Book III, chapter 32).

Psalms 11:3 asks: "If the foundation be destroyed, what can the righteous do?" The answer to this question is found in Acts 3:19-21: "Repent ye therefore, and be converted, that your sins may be blotted out, when the times of refreshing shall come from the presence of the Lord; And he shall send Jesus Christ, which before was preached unto you: Whom the heaven must receive until the times of restitution of all things, which

God hath spoken by the mouth of all his holy prophets since the world began" (see also Acts 1:6-7).

The time of refreshing has come and the restitution of all things has begun in preparation for the Second Coming of Jesus Christ. That restoration included the priesthood power and authority held by ancient apostles and prophets and making possible the calling of modem apostles and prophets in these latter days (D & C 1:30).

12. How can Latter-day Saints accept Joseph Smith as a prophet when he received the Book of Mormon from an unknown and possibly false spirit?

2 Corinthians 11:13-15 states: "For such are false apostles, deceitful workers, transforming themselves into the apostles of Christ. And no marvel; for Satan himself is transformed into an angel of light. Therefore it is no great thing if his ministers also be transformed as the ministers of righteousness; whose end shall be according to their works." Some have asked if Satan can appear as an angel of light, couldn't he have deceived Joseph Smith by claiming to be Moroni or any of the other messengers who appeared to him?

This is certainly a possibility that should be considered seriously, since the Book of Mormon describes two instances where this occurred (2 Nephi 9:9; Alma 30:53). Joseph Smith also briefly described several incidents of this nature associated with the restoration (D & C 128:20; Teachings p. 214). Nevertheless, it appears that Joseph was well aware of this tactic and taught the saints how to recognize this ruse (*Teachings,* pp. 202, 204, 214, 227; see also Bruce R McConkie's *Doctrinal New Testament Commentary,* vol. 2, pp. 440-41).

The Bible also contains a test to enable us to judge, or as John says, to "try spirits whether they are of God" (1 John 4:1-3). If Moroni or any of the other messengers who appeared to Joseph Smith failed this test we would know he was a minister of Satan.

John states: "Hereby know ye the Spirit of God: Every spirit that confesseth that Jesus Christ is come in the flesh is of God: And every spirit that confesseth not that Jesus Christ is come in the flesh is not of God. Joseph Smith likewise taught, "If I profess to be a witness or teacher, and have not the spirit of prophecy, which is the *testimony of Jesus,* I must be a false witness . . . any man who says he is a teacher or preacher of righteousness and denies the spirit of prophecy, is a liar, and the truth is not in him; and by this key false teachers and impostors may be detected" (Teachings, p. 269).

Moroni not only confirmed that Jesus Christ was "come in the flesh," but quoted Old and New Testament scriptures which were fulfilled with his coming (JS—H 1:40). Moroni also stated that his purpose was to reveal a book "giving an account of the former inhabitants of this continent" and containing the "everlasting Gospel . . . as delivered by the Savior" (JS—H 1:34) following his mortal ministry. The stated purpose of the Book of Mormon is in fact to convince both "Jew and Gentile that Jesus is the Christ." As such, it is subtitled "Another Testament of Jesus Christ." We believe it to be a second witness, after the Bible, of Jesus Christ's divine mission. If Moroni were Satan or one of Satan's ministers acting as an instrument of evil, he surely would not have done so much to convince mankind to believe in Christ—it goes counter to Satan's purpose (Matt. 12:25).

The Book of Mormon was written to bring us to Christ as was stated in 2 Nephi 33:10-11: "And now, my beloved brethren, and also Jew, and all ye ends of the earth, hearken unto these words and believe in Christ; and if ye believe not in these words believe in Christ. And if ye shall believe in Christ ye will believe in these words, for they are the words of Christ, and he hath given them unto me; and they teach all men that they should do good. And if they are not the words of Christ, judge ye— for Christ will show unto you with power and great glory, that they are his words, at the last day; and you and I shall stand face to face before his bar; and ye shall know that I have been commanded of him to write these things, notwithstanding my weakness"

The Book of Mormon contains an account of Christ's visit to those upon this continent wherein he allows them to "feel the prints of the nails" in his flesh (3 Nephi 11:14) that they might understand that he died for them also. Thus Moroni and the book which he brought both testify that Jesus Christ is the Messiah and was come in the flesh "manifesting himself unto all nations" (Book of Mormon title page; 1 Nephi 10:4-11; 11:18-21, 27-33; 15:13; Mosiah 7:27; 15:1-2; Ether 3:6, 9, 16-17; Moroni 9:25).

None of the messengers which appeared to Joseph Smith ever denied that Jesus Christ was the Messiah come in the flesh (D & C 13:1; 18:11-12; 19:16-19; 20:1; 110:4); to the contrary, they all testified of him and his divinity. Verse 15 of 2 Corinthians 11 contains a final key to detection of false messengers. It states that their "end shall be according to their works" If their works be evil or unrighteous we will know they are not from God. "By their fruits ye shall know them" (Matt 7:20; see also p. 8).

13. How can Latter-Day Saints accept Joseph Smith as a prophet when he made mistakes and admitted he was a sinner?

Much of the anti-Mormon literature available today attempts to discredit Joseph Smith. The majority use stories which attack his integrity. Hugh Nibley has systematically examined the claims of some of Joseph's accusers and demonstrated that their charges cannot stand the test of investigation. Cleverly trumped up accusations have poisoned the minds of many and continue to be presented to the world as truth. But an unbiased examination of Joseph Smith's life will convince the impartial investigator that he was an honest man called of God (See Hugh Nibley, *Myth Makers*).

As anti-Mormon critics well know, "there is none righteous" (Rom. 3:10) even among the prophets; "all have sinned and come short of the glory of God" (Rom. 3:23); "if we say we have no sin, we deceive ourselves" (1 John 1:8-10). All men, including prophets, have failings and are subject to sin. Joseph Smith was no exception. Joseph freely admitted in recounting his history that he "frequently fell into many foolish errors, and displayed the weakness of youth, and the foibles of human nature; which . . . led [him] into divers temptations, offensive in the sight of God. . . . [Not] of any great or malignant sins . . . [but he] was guilty of levity, and sometimes associated with jovial company, etc., not consistent with that character which ought to be maintained by one who was called of God as [he] had been" (JS-H 1:28; see also D & C 3:9-11; 5:21; 93:47).

He also stated: "Although I do wrong, I do not the wrongs that I am charged with doing; the wrong that I do is through the frailty of human nature, like other men. No man lives without fault. Do you think that even Jesus, if He were here, would be without fault in your eyes? His enemies said all manner of evil against Him-they all watched for iniquity in Him" (*Teachings,* p. 258).

Indeed they said of Jesus: "The Son of Man came eating and drinking . . . Behold a man gluttonous, and a winebibber, a friend of publicans and sinners" (Matt. 11:19). Jesus was also accused of being one of Satan's servants (Matt. 9:34; 12:24; Mark 3:22), a blasphemer (Matt. 26:65-66; John 19:7), a rebel and malefactor (Luke 23:2, 5; John 18:30), and a false Christ and king (Luke 23:2; John 18:33, 37). While rejecting him as the Christ, they claimed a great love for the scriptures and a loyalty to the prophets of the past-prophets who their ancestors had persecuted when they were sent to them (Matt. 23:37; *LDS Topical Guide*—Rejection of Prophets, p. 398).

These same prophets sometimes erred despite their callings as men of God. Consider, for example: Noah's drunkenness (Gen. 9:21); Abraham's lie (Gen. 12:12-18); Aaron's golden calf (Ex. 32:1-4); Moses' pride (Num. 20:12); Eli's misjudgment of Hannah (1 Sam. 1:12-16) and failure to correct his sons' behavior (1 Sam. 3:13); Jonah's reluctance to obey the Lord (Jonah 1:2-3); and contentions between Paul and Barnabas (Acts 15:2, 39) and Peter and Paul (Gal. 2:11-14; 2 Peter 3:16). Elijah was described by James as "a man subject to like passions as we are" (James 5:17) and Jeremiah said the Lord had "deceived" him (Jer. 20:7). Balaam was lured by the promise of riches and was destroyed with the wicked (Num. 22:9-20; 31:8, 16; 2 Peter 2:15; Jude 11; Rev. 2:14) and David, though a murderer and an adulterer (2 Sam. 12:9) was yet called a prophet by Peter (Acts 2:29-30; see also Scrapbook of Mormon Polemics, Num. 1, p. 9 and James K. and Rosel Seastrand, *Journey to Eternal Life and Distractions along the Way,* pp. 166, 178).

In the words of Elder B. H. Roberts, "Joseph Smith . . . claimed for himself no special sanctity, no faultless life, no perfection of character, no inerrancy for every word spoken by him . . . Yet to Joseph Smith was given access to the mind of Deity, through the revelations of God to him" (*A Comprehensive History of the Church of Jesus Christ of Latter-day Saints,* 2:360-61). Joseph Smith, like many of the prophets, was rejected by men (Luke 4:24; John 4:44) and sealed his mission and his works with his own blood (D & C 135:3). It is true that his "name should be had for good and evil among all nations, kindreds, and tongues . . . [and] should be both good and evil spoken of among all people." Moroni foretold this and Joseph recorded it in his history (JS—H 1:33). As Christ said: "Blessed are they which are persecuted for righteousness' sake: for theirs is the kingdom of heaven" (Matt. 5:10). Joseph may now rejoice as his reward in heaven is assured, for in like manner did the world persecute the prophets of old (Luke 6:23).

14. How can Latter-day Saints accept Joseph Smith as a prophet when he destroyed the *Nauvoo Expositor* press after it criticized him?

Some critics of the Church refer to this incident as a "treason to destroy the press." It is interesting that these same critics ignore the destruction of a Mormon printing press by an anti-Mormon mob eleven years earlier.

In regard to the *Nauvoo Expositor* press, the following should be considered: the Nauvoo city council declared the *Nauvoo Expositor* libelous and a public nuisance endangering civil order. The council directed the city marshal to destroy that issue of the paper and the press itself, and not the printing office, as is often alleged. The city council, which included at least one non-Mormon, concurred that the paper was "exciting the Spirit of mobocracy . . . and bringing death and destruction" upon

Mormons (Leonard Arrington and Davis Bitton, *The Mormon Experience,* p. 78).

At that time, there were many vigilante groups dedicated to the destruction of Mormonism and looking for excuses to carry out their violent intentions, a fact that should weigh heavily in any judgment about this act of the council. Under the circumstances, it appears that this action would more accurately be characterized as self-defense than "treason." Most certainly, the crime of treason is in no way related to the putting down of a public nuisance.

The murder of the Prophet and his brother less than three weeks later by an armed mob further substantiates the fact that the council's fears concerning the highly inflammatory material printed by the *Nauvoo Expositor* were well founded and the action taken was clearly justified. Even today, courts are making judgements against libelous statements made in the press. Can this also be called treason?

Joseph went to Carthage to deliver himself up to the pretended requirements of the law, two or three days previous to his assassination. He said: "I am going like a lamb to the slaughter; but I am calm as a summer's morning; I have a conscience void of offense towards God, and towards all men. I SHALL DIE INNOCENT AND IT SHALL YET BE SAID OF ME—HE WAS MURDERED IN COLD BLOOD" (D&C 135:4). It was an improbable prophecy for a false prophet, but not for a true prophet of the Lord.

15. How can Latter-day Saints accept Joseph Smith as a prophet when he was a money-digger and dabbled in magic?

This allegation was commonly made in Joseph Smith's day. His response is found in his own history:

> As my father's worldly circumstances were very limited, we were under the necessity of laboring with our hands, hiring out by day's work and otherwise, as we could get opportunity. Sometimes we were at home, and sometimes abroad, and by continuous labor were enabled to get a comfortable maintenance.
>
> In the year 1823 my father's family met with a great affliction by the death of my eldest brother, Alvin. In the month of October 1825, I hired with an old gentleman by the name of Josiah Stoal, who lived in Chenango county, State of New York. He had heard something of a silver mine having been opened by the Spaniards in Harmony, Susquehanna county, State of Pennsylvania; and had, previous to my hiring to him, been digging, in order, if possible, to discover the mine. After I went to live with him, he took me, with the rest of his hands, to dig for the silver mine, at which I continued to work for nearly a month, without success in our undertaking, and finally I prevailed with the old gentleman to cease digging after it. Hence arose the very prevalent story of my having been a money-digger (JS—H 1:55-56).

Other records indicate that Joseph initially rejected the request of Josiah Stowell (also spelled Stoal), but the financial situation of the Smith family caused him to accept the offer of $14 per month, room and board, and the hiring of his father. This was done just two months before the family would lose their Manchester farm because they could not make the annual $100 payment (*History of the Church,* 1:17; *History of Joseph Smith by his Mother Lucy Mack Smith,* pp. 91-99; Elder's Journal, July 1838, p. 43).

It should be remembered that digging all day long was hard, hard work. To accept employment to perform such arduous labor is not a sign of a lack of character but of good character. Society today does not regard gold miners, or silver miners, or coal miners as ne'er-do-wells, but as honest, hard-working individuals. Why is Joseph Smith judged by a different standard?

The following additional information is taken from *The Truth About "The God Makers,"* by Gilbert W. Scharffs, p. 145:

> Joseph Smith was undoubtedly involved in "money-digging," as he has always admitted and perhaps some form of "magic" which at the time he and his associates did not sense as in any way inappropriate. Such conduct was not unusual for the times as the 1930 quote from the Comprehensive History of the Church . . . pointed out (B. H. Roberts, *Comprehensive History of the Church,* 1:26-27].
>
> The Lord took Joseph Smith, a man innocently caught up in the superstition of his day, and turned him in the right direction. Joseph Smith himself was reported as saying, "I am a rough stone. The sound of the hammer and chisel was never heard on me until the Lord took me in hand. I desire the learning and wisdom of heaven alone" (*History of the Church,* 5:423; see also *The Truth About "The God Makers,"* p. 138).

Similar allegations were made about Jesus Christ and his family, as anti-Christ critics attempted to discredit him. Hugh Nibley summarized accusations found in early literature as follows:

> All sources, early and late, Christian and anti-Christian, agree that Jesus' family was often in trouble and moved about a good deal. The early anti-Christian writers made much of this: a family of improvident ne'er-do-wells, tramping about the country looking for odd jobs; Mary, a woman of the lowest classes and the loosest morals, working as a ladies hairdresser, kicked out by her husband when she had an affair with a Roman soldier (they furnished the name, rank, and serial number), giving birth in disgrace to Jesus, the ambitious boy who picked up a bag of tricks in Egypt along with exalted ideas about His own divinity, and who gathered about Him a band of vagabonds and desperadoes with whom He ranged the countryside picking up a living by questionable means (Hugh Nibley, "Early Accounts of Jesus' Childhood," Instructor 1965, p. 35; see also John 8:41; Hugh Nibley, *The World and the Prophets,* PP. 17-18).

16. How can Latter-day Saints accept Joseph Smith as a prophet when he prophesied falsely?

Critics of Joseph Smith sometimes cite Deuteronomy 18:20-22 and state that God's test for a prophet requires 100 percent accuracy in fulfillment of his prophecies or the prophet is a false prophet. D&C 84:2-5 is occasionally used as an example of a what they consider to be false prophecy. It is asserted that this prophecy predicted that the New Jerusalem would be built in Joseph Smith's day. Several factors should be considered in judging this prophecy:

It should be noted that the time of accomplishment uses the identical words "this generation" which Jesus used in referring to his Second Coming and "the gathering of his elect" (Matt. 24:27-34). It appears that the word "generation," as used in scripture, may have no set time limit (D&C 5:8,10; 6:9; and others). Jesus stated, for example: "an evil and adulterous generation seeketh after a sign; and there shall be no sign given it" (Matt. 12:39).

Similar problems are found with words like "eternal," "forever," "ever-lasting," "hereafter," "quickly," and others. John Taylor explained: "The word forever used in the Old Testament does not necessarily mean to the end of time but to the end of a period" (John Taylor, *Mediation and Atonement*). Thus, it seems quite possible that D&C 84:2-5 and other similar scriptures are simply being misinterpreted because the Lord's perspective of time is not the same as man's (See also Matt. 10:23; 12:39-42; 24:34; 26:64 [hereafter]; Rev. 22:6-7, 12, 20 [quickly]).

Furthermore, it is clear to Latter-day Saints that promised blessings may be revoked when man does not obey God (Jer. 18:8-10; D&C 58:31-33; 130:21). That the blessing in D&C 84:2-5 was revoked "for a little season" is made clear by the Lord in D & C 105:1-9 and 124:49. This particular promise was made contingent on obedience to the commandment "that they shall not boast themselves of these things . . . before the world" (D&C 84:73). In this case, the Saints did boast, and the blessing was withdrawn for a time. Some may scoff at this explanation, but God nevertheless frequently grants and revokes blessings based on obedience. The reader might note that the children of Israel were similarly denied blessings as a result of disobedience at Mount Sinai (Ex. 32) and in the borders of Canaan (Num. 14). Other promises, as will be noted shortly, were revoked for thousands of years. Many prophetic teachings and prophecies as contained in our present King James Bible are difficult to understand or appear to be conditional:

1. Passover feast to be an eternal ordinance (Ex. 12:14) and circumcision an eternal covenant (Gen. 17:13; Acts 15:1-11).
2. Jacob prophesied that Judah would not be without a ruler until Shiloh (the Messiah) had come (Gen. 49:10; see also Talmage, *Jesus the Christ*, pp. 54-55).
3. Children of Israel given "a place of their own, and move no more; neither shall the children of wickedness afflict them any more" (2 Sam. 7:10).
4. Isaiah's prophecy of Hezekiah's death (Isa. 38:1-5).
5. Jeremiah's prophecy concerning Zedekiah (Jer. 34:4-5; 52:10-11).
6. Jonah's prophecy concerning Nineveh (Jonah 3:4, 10).
7. Jesus prophesied that "the end would come" after the gospel was "preached in all the world for a witness unto all nations" (Matt. 24:14). Paul later stated that, in that day, the "gospel . . . was preached to every creature which is under heaven" (Col. 1:23; see also Mark 16:15 and Matt. 28:19). Many other prophecies of Christ seemed to confirm the nearness of fulfillment to that day but have not yet been fulfilled. (Matt. 10:23; 16:28; 24:34; 26:64; Mark 13:30; Luke 21:24-27, 32; see also Heb. 9:26; 1 John 2:18; JS—M 1:34-35).

Were Abraham, Jacob, Moses, Nathan, Isaiah, Jeremiah, Jonah, and Jesus false prophets? If we use Deuteronomy 18:20-22 as an absolute rule and believe the Bible to be inerrant, we might be led to this conclusion. It is clear that the information presented above must be considered in judging prophecies. As Paul said, "We know in part, and we prophesy in part. But when that which is perfect is come, then that which is in part shall be done away" (Cor. 13:9-10). The time element and the conditions specified must be clearly understood and we must be patient and exercise faith in the Lord's servants (D&C 21:4-5). Most importantly, we must rely on the Spirit, not man's understanding, to guide us in all truth (John 16:13).

Duane S. Crowther and other authors have made exhaustive lists of hundreds of modern prophecies which have been fulfilled. Brother Crowther lists 141 prophecies made or recorded by Joseph Smith alone which have been fulfilled (*The Prophecies of Joseph Smith;* see also Kirk Holland Vestal and Arthur Wallace, *The Firm Foundation of Mormonism,* chapter 21; Gilbert W. Scharffs, *The Truth About "The God Makers,* "Appendix C, pp. 387-98. For additional information on prophets and prophecy see *Sustaining and Defending the Faith,* pp. 69-71; *Teachings,* pp. 255 and 278; and *Answers to Gospel Questions,* 4:111-15. Additional details concerning the qualifications of a prophet as described in Deuteronomy 18:21-22 may be found on p. 49 of this text).

17. How can Latter-day Saints accept Joseph Smith as a prophet when he attacked all Christians and their churches?

Some opponents of the LDS faith distort and misrepresent Latter-day Saint acceptance of other religions by claiming that we dogmatically assert that all other beliefs are wrong. They frequently justify their own criticism of our beliefs by stating that Joseph Smith first attacked all other Christian churches, declaring them to be "wrong" (JS—H 1:19). They reason that because he attacked them, they are justified in "defending" themselves. Consider the fact that the Christian denominations in Joseph Smith's day all claimed to be right and yet taught conflicting doctrines (JS—H 1:8-11). All of them could not have been right while believing different doctrines, but all could have been "wrong," as a whole, if only a portion of the beliefs of each was wrong (i.e. all could have been "wrong" and yet still have had some truth).

The source of the criticism mentioned earlier is what the LDS Church refers to as the "first vision" found in Joseph Smith's History, chapter 1. Verse 19 of that chapter is the Lord's response to Joseph Smith's inquiry as to which church he should join. Joseph Smith was not the author of this declaration; he was only the messenger. The message itself was from Jesus Christ and was made up principally of scriptural quotes from Isaiah 29:13 and 2 Timothy 3:5 concerning the last days (note: Isa. 29:13 was also quoted by Christ in Matt. 15:8-9 concerning the orthodox Jews of that day).

An examination of the context of these quotes is revealing. Paul said in 2 Timothy 3:1-5, "This know also, that in the last days perilous times shall come. For men shall be lovers of their own selves . . . false accusers, incontinent, fierce, despisers of those that are good . . . Having a form of godliness, but denying the power thereof: from such turn away" The religions of Joseph Smith's day did have a "form of godliness" but denied the power of God to call new prophets and reveal new scripture, and lacked priesthood authority.

The context of Isaiah's quote speaks of the coming forth of a sealed book, associated with a marvelous work and a wonder (Isa. 29:10-14), that would show the error of the learned because they preferred the precepts of men to the revelations of God. He says that "in that day shall the deaf hear the words of the book, and the eyes of the blind shall see out of obscurity . . . They also that erred in spirit shall come to understanding and . . . learn doctrine" (verses 18 and 24).

It appears that our critics are condemning the words of their own Bible. If Paul and Isaiah were not speaking of our day, of what were they speaking? Is it just coincidence that the work that Joseph Smith was called to do involved the restoration of God's priesthood power and a new scriptural witness translated from a sealed book?

As to the Latter-day Saint view of other Christian churches, the following statements by Joseph Smith should also be considered:

> Have the Presbyterians any truth? Yes. Have the Baptists, Methodists, etc., any truth? Yes. They all have a little truth mixed with error. We should gather all the good and true principles in the world and treasure them up or we shall not come out true "Mormons" [or true Christians either] (*History of the Church,* 5:517).

Also:

> The inquiry is frequently made of me, "Wherein do you differ from others in your religious views?" In reality and essence we do not differ so far in our religious views, but that we could all drink into one principle of love. One of the grand fundamental principles of "Mormonism" is to receive truth, let it come from whence it may (*History of the Church,* 5:499).

Note that Joseph Smith acknowledges truth in other churches, even truths not then found in Mormonism, and declares that true Mormons must look for truths throughout the world and treasure them up (Additional information may be found in *A Sure Foundation,* pp. 210-14 and *Scrapbook of Mormon Polemics,* Mormon Miscellaneous Scrapbook number 2, pp. 21-22).

18. How can Latter-day Saints accept Joseph Smith as a prophet when he failed to document his first vision until years later?

Although the official account of Joseph Smith's first vision was not published until 1842, earlier accounts were written in 1832, 1835, and 1838. Historical evidence indicates that Joseph Smith was reluctant to speak or write of the first vision because of the ridicule he received about it when he first shared it with others and because of its sacred nature. Joseph's young age (about 14) and available documentation lend support to this claim (see Milton V. Bachman, Jr., *Joseph Smith's First Vision*).

The recording of major biblical events was also delayed for substantial periods. Most Bible scholars believe that the earliest Gospel was probably written by Mark in Rome at about 68 AD (*Encyclopedia Americana,* 1972, 18:298). Some scholars hold that the Gospel of

Matthew might have preceded that of Mark, but concede that it could not have been composed before the late fifties. By these calculations, the first Gospel would have been written between 25 to 35 years after Christ's death. An LDS historian recommends that those who are critical of Joseph Smith's delay in recording the first vision should consider the fact that Paul's "first known mention of the Damascus appearance [of Christ] is in 1 Corinthians 9:1, written about two dozen years after it happened" (Richard Lloyd Anderson, *Parallel Prophets: Paul and Joseph Smith,* BYU Devotional Address, 9 Aug. 83, pp. 4-5).

It is interesting to compare later, more complete accounts of Paul's vision as found in Acts 9:3-8; 22:6-11; and 26:13-18. Not only do they differ in details but they conflict in some of these details. Similar problems may be found in the Gospel narratives of the crucifixion and resurrection. See chapter 7 of this text for further details.

In light of the above circumstances, it is not unreasonable that Joseph did not immediately record the details of his first vision.

19. How can Latter-day Saints explain Joseph Smith's and Brigham Young's comments about the moon and the sun being inhabited?

Gilbert W. Scharffs has done an excellent job of answering this question in his book *The Truth About "The God Makers"* :

> No original sources verifying [that Joseph Smith declared that the moon was inhabited] have been found of which I am aware. The book [*The God Makers*] quotes from an 1881 journal entry, published in 1892 by Oliver B. Huntington, who claimed Joseph Smith said there were moonmen. Huntington would have been about eleven years of age at the time, if he heard this from Joseph Smith personally, or even if the idea came from someone else. In fact, indications are that he heard it second-hand at best.

Van Hale answered the criticism against this assertion in his pamphlet, "How Could a Prophet Believe in Moonmen?" One excerpt:

> Did Joseph Smith believe in an inhabited moon? From the historical evidence now available the answer must be: Not proven. But, all things considered, the possibility, or probability, that he did cannot reasonably be denied. For all others of that era the question seems quite insignificant, especially given contemporary beliefs. But in the case of Joseph Smith, he claimed to be a prophet. Some extremists contend that his claim demands that his knowledge in every area be superior to that of others in his era. If he believed any false notion of his day, so these critics say, his credibility must be doubted. Others, not so demanding of infallible insight in a prophet, would be more comfortable with a description of God's revelation which allowed for the human and the divine. As Rev. J. R. Dummelow so aptly described the authors of the Bible, so might one say of Joseph Smith:

Though purified and ennobled by the influence of His Holy Spirit, these men each had his own peculiarities of manner and disposition—each with his own education or want of education—each with his own way of looking at things—each influenced differently from one another by the different experiences and disciplines of his life. Their inspiration did not involve a suspension of their natural faculties; it did not even make them free from earthly passion; it did not make them into machines—it left them men.

Therefore we find their knowledge sometimes no higher than that of their contemporaries. . . . (J. R. Dummelow, *One Volume Bible Commentary,* p. cxxxv). Dummelow's description of the author of Genesis is equally applicable:

His scientific knowledge may be bounded by the horizon of the age in which he lived, but the religious truths he teaches are irrefutable and eternal (*Ibid.* p. xxx).

Dummelow, who is not LDS, is considered to be one of the foremost commentators on the Bible.

Biblical prophets sometimes apparently erred, but that does not detract from their being men of God. . . . Latter-day Saints do not believe their prophets are infallible, not every word they utter always true. . . . (pp. 119-20)

Of Brigham Young's comment about the sun being inhabited, Gilbert Scharffs asks:

Are the authors equally critical of the Apostle John, in his vision of heaven, who claimed, "I saw an angel standing in the sun"? (Rev. 19:17).

The question comes from the *Journal of Discourses* which has never been sanctioned by the LDS Church as being authoritative. Many LDS and non-LDS historians admit to the limitations of this source. Actually Brigham Young is reported as saying, speaking of the sun, "Do you think it is inhabited? I rather think it is."

The early members of the LDS Church believed in creations of other spheres. If the recorded account of what Brigham Young said is accurate (and it might not be), Brigham Young's opinion may have been in error. It is wrong to claim Latter-day Saints believe every idea expressed by their prophet is infallible. Taking a quote from a public meeting, written by a clerk in shorthand, before the availability of a tape recorder and where Brigham Young added "I think," is using questionable evidence to attack the LDS Church. Since biblical prophets were not infallible, why do the authors demand more from LDS prophets? (Gilbert W. Scharffs, *The Truth About "The God Makers,"* pp. 120-21)

It is interesting to note that a contemporary astronomer of Brigham Young's day also believed that there was life on the sun. Sir William Herschel (1738-1822), who is famous for the discovery of Uranus, pioneered virtually every branch of modern physical astronomy. He charted and classified over 2,500 star clusters and nebulae and over 800 double stars. He also first suggested that the sun itself moves, determined its direction, measured the heat generated by solar radiation, and inferred the existence of infrared radiation. It is no exaggeration to say that he was probably the preeminent astronomer and expert on the sun in that day, and yet he believed it possible that the sun was inhabited by some form of life. If one of the foremost astronomers of that day believed the sun was inhabited, it should come as no surprise that Brigham Young might have also held a similar belief based on his own human knowledge.

Ancient prophets also expressed some of the erroneous opinions of their generation. *The New American Bible* published by the Catholic Book Publishing Company states: "The ancient Hebrews saw the earth as a large plate with a huge vault over it. Above the vault was God's palace" (New American Bible, p. 23). They include a diagram which indicates the relative positions of the heavenly seat of divinity, the waters above the firmament, the firmament of the sky with its floodgates and celestial bodies and all being held up by the pillars of heaven, the earth, and beneath the earth, Sheol (the home of the dead), the pillars of the earth, and a watery abyss (inferior waters which surrounded the pillars holding up the earth). Through the floodgates in the vault of the firmament water could fall to the earth in the form of rain or snow. If this picture sounds strange, consider the following Bible verses which seem to confirm this concept:

1. Heavenly Seat—Deut. 26:15; Ps. 33:14
2. Firmament—Gen. 1:6-8, 14-17; Ps. 19:1
3. Windows of Heaven (Floodgates)—Gen. 7:11; 8:2; 2 Kings 7:19; Isa. 24:18; Mal. 3:10
4. Pillars of Heaven—Job 26:11
5. Sheol (hell or hades)—Isa. 14:9; Ezek. 31:16-17; Luke 10:15
6. Pillars of Earth—1 Sam. 2:8; Job 9:6; Ps. 75:3
7. Abyss (Fountains of the deep)—Gen. 7:11; 8:2; Prov. 8:28
8. Earth founded upon seas—Ps. 24:1-2

Although Moses and some of the prophets understood the nature of the earth better than the men of their time, some apparently also believed the misconceptions of their day.

That prophets can err in scientific thought should only convince us that as Joseph Smith taught, a "prophet was a prophet only when acting as such" (*History of the Church,* 5:265). Prophets, even Bible prophets, when they speak as men, are susceptible to error (see also p. 170 of this text; a discussion of Moses' proper understanding of the firmament is found in Joseph Fielding Smith's *Answers to Gospel Questions,* 4:116-21 and Teachings, p. 118 note, and p. 278).

20. Does Joseph Smith meet the biblical qualifications of a prophet?

Numbers 12:6 teaches: "If there be a prophet among you, I the Lord will make myself known unto him in a vision, and will speak unto him in a dream." Verse 7 and 8 go on to say that under certain conditions (i.e.

Moses), the Lord will appear to his prophet and "speak mouth to mouth" with him clearly. Such was also the case with Joseph Smith. The Lord appeared to Joseph Smith and spoke to him clearly face to face (JS—H 1:17-20, 25) as with Moses (Ex. 33:11). Though this event in Joseph Smith's life is referred to as "the first vision," it was much more than a vision or dream. The Lord at other times did indeed speak to the prophet in dreams and visions (See *Teachings,* pp. 368-69, 393; D&C 76, 110, 137; JS—H 1:42).

Deuteronomy 18:21-22 asks, "How shall we know the word which the Lord hath not spoken? When a prophet speaketh in the name of the Lord, if that thing follow not, nor come to pass, that is the thing which the Lord hath not spoken, but the prophet hath spoken it presumptuously: thou shalt not be afraid of him."

Section 87 of the Doctrine and Covenants contains just such a prophecy pronounced in the name of the Lord in 1832. It proclaims: "Verily, thus saith the Lord concerning the wars that will shortly come to pass, beginning at the rebellion of South Carolina, which will eventually terminate in the death and misery of many souls; And the time will come that war will be poured out upon all nations, beginning at this place. For behold, the Southern States shall be divided against the Northern States, and the Southern States will call on other nations, even the nation of Great Britain, as it is called, and they shall also call upon other nations, in order to defend themselves against other nations; and then war shall be poured out upon all nations. And it shall come to pass, after many days, slaves shall rise up against their masters, who shall be marshaled and disciplined for war" (D&C 87:1-4).

The Civil War fulfilled this prophecy on every point. The first shot was fired at Fort Sumter at Charleston, South Carolina, on April 12, 1861 and resulted in much death and misery. From that time, wars *have* spread to all nations (i.e. World Wars). It was a conflict between the Northern and Southern states where the South did call on the nation of Great Britain and other nations for assistance. The primary issue was that of slavery (see also D&C 130:12-13). This prophecy was clearly made in the name of the Lord and has "come to pass." The prophecy was recorded nearly thirty years prior to its fulfillment and was fulfilled in every detail.

This prophecy is only one example of many prophecies pronounced by the Prophet Joseph Smith. Those that "will not hearken unto" these words would do well to note that, the Lord has declared, "I will require it of him" (Deut. 18:19). Those who reject the word of the Lord will answer for it at the judgment day (2 Nephi 33: 10-11). (See also p. 41 this text.)

21. Can LDS apostles meet the qualifications in Acts 1:21-22?

Some contend that LDS apostles cannot be true apostles because they are not witnesses of Christ's resurrection. Modern apostles can not only witness" of Christ's resurrection but according to John 14:18-19, they can see Christ and be eyewitnesses of him as well.

Oliver Cowdery set forth this charge to the first latter-day Council of the Twelve: "The ancients . . . had this testimony—that they had seen the Savior after he arose from the dead. You must bear the same testimony. . . . Never cease striving until you have seen God face to face. . . . Your ordination is not complete till God has laid his hand upon you. We require as much to qualify us, as did those who have gone before us; God is the same. . . . Therefore call upon him in faith in mighty prayer till you prevail, for it is your duty and your privilege to bear such a testimony for yourselves" (*History of the Church,* 2:192-98).

Doctrine and Covenants 67:10 contains the Lord's promise to his servants "that inasmuch as you strip yourselves from jealousies and fears, and humble yourselves before me . . . the veil shall be rent and you shall see me and know that I am."

Critics may be surprised at the number of people the Bible confirms have seen the Lord in glory: Adam and Eve (Genesis 3); Abraham (Genesis 17: 1; Acts 7:2); Abimelech (Genesis 20:3); Jacob (Gen. 32:30); Moses (Ex. 33:11; Deuteronomy 34:10); Moses, Aaron, Nadab, Abihu and 70 elders of Israel (Exodus 24:9-11); Joshua (Joshua 5:12-15); Manoah and his wife (Judges 13:22); Solomon (I Kings 3:5-14; 9:2-9); Job (Job 42:5); Isaiah (Isaiah 6:1-5); Ezekiel (Ezekiel 1:1; 8:1-4; 10:4); Daniel (Daniel 10:5-6); Mary Magdalene (John 20:11-18); Peter (Luke 24:34; I Corinthians 15:5); the 10 (Mark 16:14); 2 disciples (Luke 24:13-15, 30-34); the 11 and others (Luke 24:33; John 20:24-29); disciples at the Sea of Tiberias (John 21:1-14); disciples in Galilee (Matthew 28:16-20; Mark 16:15-18); above 500 brethren (I Corinthians 15:6); James (I Corinthians 15:7); Paul (Acts 22:17-18; I Corinthians. 15:8); Steven (Acts 7:51-60); John (Revelation 1:13-18).

According to John 6:40, "seeing the Son" seems to be a requirement for everlasting life. The Savior likewise taught "Blessed are the pure in heart: for they shall see God" (Matt. 5:8). Joseph Smith also spoke of this requirement in connection with the "second comforter" and "calling and election. (See *Teachings,* pp. 150-51; 298; 305). Some in this dispensation have received this great blessing but because of its sacred nature, do not speak of it openly. Two scriptural accounts of the Lord's appearance in our day are found in Doctrine and Covenants 76 and 110 (see also Heb.50 12:21-24; 2 Peter 1:10-11, 19; 2 Nephi 31:14-21; 3 Nephi 11:14-15; D&C 88:3-4; 93:1; 130:3; 131:5).

4
Modern Revelation

22. Is revelation still necessary?

Many believe that revelation from God ceased after the death of the first apostles. They often cite Revelation 22:18-19 as what they regard as proof that the Bible forbids man from "adding unto" or "taking away from" revealed scripture. Some believe that LDS leaders, with their additional scriptures, have added to revealed scripture and thus are defying God's word. Multiple problems with this line of reasoning have been stated for years, but this question continues to be asked of LDS missionaries. The following facts should be considered in responding:

1. If prohibiting further revelation was the intent of these verses, then the Saints of John's day and for more than a thousand years afterwards misunderstood this scripture. The book entitled "The Revelation of John" was a separate document for hundreds of years before it was assembled with other writings into the scriptural library we call the Bible. The word "Bible" comes from the Greek "ta biblia" meaning "the books" (see *LDS Bible Dictionary*—Bible). Thus, John was referring only to "the words of the prophecy of this book," or in other words, only to the book called "The Revelation of John" (Rev. 22:18-19). It seems apparent that John was concerned that men would change his prophecies and thereby alter and destroy the truths they contained (1 Nephi 13:26-34).

2. This injunction specifies only that "man" shall not add to or take away from these revealed words (Rev. 22:18; D&C 20:35). God may add and does add to his word as he desires. Modern LDS scripture was written "by way of commandment" from the Lord and was given "by the gift and power of God" (Book of Mormon Title Page; D&C 1:1, 6; 45:60-61).

3. Essentially the same prohibition is found in Deuteronomy 4:2 and 12:32. Does this invalidate all scripture given after the Pentateuch (the first five books of the Old Testament)? All would agree that it certainly does not. Why then should a similar statement found in a New Testament book invalidate all modern scripture?

4. Evidence indicates that John himself wrote additional scripture after his own "Revelation" Bible scholars generally agree that John recorded his book of "Revelation" at about 95 or 96 AD on the Isle of Patmos.

The Gospel of John is dated to 96 to 104 AD and was thought to have been written at Ephesus. John's three epistles were thought to have been written at about the same time as the Gospel of John (96 to 104 AD; see Daniel-Rops, *L'Eglise des Apotres et des Martyrs,* pp. 304-06; 1952 Melchizedek Priesthood Manual; James L. Barker, *The Divine Church,* pp. 11, 17). Thus, the book of "Revelation" was not intended to be the end of revealed scripture but only a warning of future events.

5. The Bible itself speaks of the coming forth of additional scripture (Isa. 29; Ezek. 37) and future revelations (Matt. 17:11; Luke 10:22; John 16:12-15; Acts 2:17-18; James 1:5). Even the book of Revelation itself alludes to future prophets and revelations from heaven (Rev. 11:3; 14:6).

Though the Bible indicates that revelation is part and parcel of the true church (Amos 3:7; 1 Cor. 14:29-33, 37-39), many denominations today teach that revelation has ceased. Some go one step further and condemn those who believe in modern revelation. Hugh Nibley has observed that anti-Mormon literature generally shows a "singular lack of variety and imagination in accusations, all of which can be readily reduced to one standard indictment, monotonously repeated and mechanically transmitted from one writer to the next: the crime of believing in continuous revelation. Claims to the possession of prophetic powers, to exclusive knowledge of the true gospel and the priesthood that goes with it and to all the other charismatic gifts, are simply corollaries of the basic proposition that God still speaks to men" (Hugh Nibley, *The World and the Prophets,* p. 284).

Brother Nibley also noted that one non-Mormon scholar has concluded that: "If one dares to claim revelation, it follows . . . that one must claim to have the only true church, since revelation is necessarily the truth" (*Ibid.,* p. 270, as taken from R. Bultmann, in *ztschr f neutest Wiss.* 27:118)

Edouard Meyer singled out the LDS Church as one of the great original religions of the world. He found that "Most other churches and sects are really only episodes in the history of a going concern, variations on an accepted theme, reforms or innovations undertaken by men who thought that they may have felt aware of a special calling or a special talent for the job, were simply doing what other men did. But three religions—primitive Christianity, Islam, and Mormonism—actually claim to have been founded not by men but by direct revelation from heaven" (Ibid., p. 18, as taken from Edouard Meyer, *Ursprung and Geschichte der Mormonen,* pp. 68-69, n. 2).

Without direct and continuing revelation, a church is no longer directed by God and cannot claim Christ as its head. Only when constant corrections are made by the Master will the ship remain on course.

Churches which claim the Bible as their standard are like ships with fixed rudders. Their course may appear to be straight in the short run, but with time will diverge from the true heading originally intended. Paul alluded to this same symbolism in Ephesians 4:11-15, teaching that unless Christ is directing his church through his chosen apostles, prophets and other inspired leaders (by revelation), the disciples will be as "children, tossed to and fro, and carried about with every wind of doctrine."

Of the three revealed religions singled out by Edouard Meyer, only Mormonism lays claim to continuing modem revelation. What remains of the other two religions now relies totally on the writings of ancient prophets (the Bible and Koran) for direction today. Without modem revelation it is impossible to arrive at a proper understanding of those ancient writings since even inspired words may be misunderstood. Witness the diversity among various Protestant and Catholic church beliefs concerning baptism, miracles, spiritual gifts, and even salvation. Though most claim the same scriptures and origin, they vary widely in their teachings and practices in these and many other important doctrines.

Joseph Fielding McConkie notes that "no one would argue that a library containing the memoirs of great generals fills the need for generals in today's armies. Great books may instruct and inspire those who would be leaders, but they will never replace those leaders. Just as strategy and courage of dead warriors will not win today's battles, the faith and repentance of meridian Saints will not remit our sins. . . . If God who is the same yesterday, today, and forever, gave them priesthood and power, he must in justice give us priesthood and power; if he gave them prophets and revelation, he must in justice give us the same. Our battle is not less than theirs. Satan as well as God is the same yesterday, today, and forever. He still commissions prophets to represent him in leading his knights of darkness. Can the God of heaven do less?" (Joseph Fielding McConkie, *Prophets and Prophecy,* p. 15)

The real power of God cannot be dissociated from revelation. Authority and priesthood power are inseparably linked to revelation (see Ex. 28:1; Num. 27:18; Rom. 10:14-15; Heb. 5:4) as was shown at the beginning of chapter 2 of this text. Salvation comes from receiving revelation, not from reading about the revelations experienced by others (Bruce R. McConkie, *Doctrines of the Restoration,* p. 218). Brother Nibley observes that ". . . when Justin [Martyr] wishes to prove to a Jewish friend that the truth has now passed from the Jewish to the Christian community, his argument is that the gift of prophecy, once enjoyed by the Jews, has now been transferred to his own people the proof of which, he says, is 'that prophetic gifts are to be found among us to the present day such as were anciently among you'" (Hugh Nibley, *The World and the Prophets,* p. 4, as taken from Dialogue with Trypho, VI, 669).

Apostolic succession is often touted as proof of authority in the Catholic church. But apostolic succession, even if it could be proved, does not establish authority. Authorization to act in God's name may be withdrawn. No modem church can prove that, in the course of centuries, the power and authority originally given to the apostles was not withdrawn due to sin and apostasy (*Ibid.,* pp. 264-69).

As proof that Christians also eventually lost this gift of prophecy, Brother Nibley cites John Chrysostom as saying that members of the church (ca. 400 AD) were always and everywhere asking him, "What has happened to the spiritual gifts? Why do we no longer have the gift of tongues? Where are the prophets? Why are men not chosen for office as they were anciently by direct revelation from above?" (Ibid., p. 221, as taken from John Chrysostom, in Patrologia Graec., 50:453, 455, 459, 488; 51:81, 85; 55:402; 58:479; 61:269, 279; 62:526; 63:623; etc.; see also Micah 3:6-7).

Brother Joseph Fielding McConkie declared: "The Bible and all other scripture are but a sealed book to any who seek to understand them independent of the spirit in which they were written. The eternal verity is that those professing a sealed canon—those announcing that all necessary scripture has been given, and that God will give no more—shall have taken from them even that understanding which they have (See 2 Nephi 28:29-30). The professing Christian who refuses to admit the necessity of the spirit of revelation in understanding the New Testament will see no more of the true meaning of that book than the professing Jew can see the true meaning and intent of the Old Testament writers. Jews who could quote and expound scripture endlessly failed to recognize the Christ when he came, because they rejected the spirit of prophecy [Rev. 19:10] and the responsibility to live worthy of it. Similarly, there is no shortage of Bible believers in our day who also quote and expound that book endlessly but will fail to recognize either Christ or his gospel because they too have rejected the spirit of prophecy and the necessity of living worthy of it" (*Prophets and Prophecy,* pp. 114-15).

The scriptures exhort us to "Despise not prophesyings" (1 Thes. 5:20), to seek "that ye may prophesy" (1 Cor. 14:1), to look to God that he "may give you the spirit of wisdom and revelation" (Eph. 1:17). Modem revelation also warns, "Yea, wo unto him that shall deny the revelations of the Lord, and that shall say the Lord no longer worketh by revelation, or by prophecy" (3 Nephi 29:6). The Lord has also warned us to "Deny not the spirit of revelation, nor the spirit of prophecy, for wo unto him that denieth these things" (D&C 11:25). Those who ignore these warnings do so to their own condemnation (see 2 Nephi 28:21, 26-31).

23. Has the LDS Church changed its beliefs and teachings about the gathering of the Saints?

Members of the Church believe in a literal gathering of the ten tribes, as stated in their 10th Article of Faith, but this gathering can take many forms. Just as the Jews were confused by the dual nature of Christ's advent as described in the Old Testament, many today seem to be confused by the gathering of the elect. Even as death, baptism, the creation, the resurrection, and man himself have both a physical and spiritual aspect, so also does the gathering of God's children (John 11:52).

At the direction of the Prophet Joseph Smith, the Apostle Orson Hyde was sent on a mission to Palestine to dedicate the Holy Land for the return of the Jews. On October 24, 1841, he stood on the Mount of Olives and offered a dedicatory prayer. ("Orson Hyde's 1841 mission to the Holy Land," *Ensign,* Oct. 91, pp. 16-19). At this time Israel was designated as the literal or physical gathering place for Judah.

Although we tend to think that the physical gathering of the Jews started after 1948 with the establishment of the State of Israel, the return of the Jews and the rise of Zionism actually dates from the last half of the 1800s. Immigration between 1882 and 1919 actually exceeded 30 thousand, and over 600 thousand Jews had returned prior to 1946. With respect to the rise of Zionism, we should note that the expression of a modern desire for a Jewish homeland in Palestine dates back to a book written by Moses Hess in 1862, and the first Zionist Congress was held at Basel Switzerland in 1897 (*Encyclopedia Americana,* Jewish History and Society—Zionism, 16:108-09, 1972 Edition).

The gathering of the Jews has only just begun, however, since the scriptures indicate that it will continue not just until the Second Coming, but beyond. Some of the Bible scriptures which describe this event are: Deuteronomy 30:1-5; Isaiah 11:11-12; Jeremiah 3:17; 30:3; 32:37-38; Ezekiel. 11:16-17; 20:34-36, 42; 34:13.

The scriptures mention a second physical gathering for the people of Israel, as distinguished from those of Judah (Isa. 14:1-2; Jer. 3:12-14; Ezek. 28:25; Amos 9:14-15; Micah 4:1-2). A significant aspect of the gathering of Israel is the physical return of the ten lost tribes. This event is plainly referred to in Bible scripture (Jer. 3:18; 16:14-16; 23:7-8; 31:7-8), but will not be accomplished until after the Second Coming of Christ (3 Nephi 21:25-28).

A spiritual gathering was prophesied for both Israel and Judah. The importance of this event is not the place (although it may be mentioned) but that they who are gathered will be converted to the way of the Lord. This is not true of the present gathering of Judah. Judah will, for the most part, still be an unbelieving people at Christ's Second Coming (Zech. 12:9-11; 13:6). The spiritual gathering of Israel will be accomplished by missionaries who are sent out to "teach all nations" the gospel of Jesus Christ (Matt. 28:19; Mark 16:15) and gather the elect into his fold (John 10:16). Many Bible scriptures describe this spiritual gathering: Leviticus 26:44-45; Nehemiah 1:8-9; Psalms 14:7; 107:1-7; Isaiah 2:2-3; 4:2-4; 5:25-26; 43:5-7; 54:7-8; Jeremiah 3:17-18; 12:14-15; 23:2-6; 31:10-12; 33:7-11; 50:4-5; Ezekiel 37:21-27; Zephaniah 3:20; Matthew 24:31; Mark 13:26-27; Revelation 18:4. We believe the gathering is in progress today primarily among the non-Jewish descendants of Israel.

Deuteronomy 33:17 is especially interesting in this regard. This passage predicts that the descendants of Joseph will "push" Israel together "to the ends of the earth" and that the gathering will include "the ten thousands of Ephraim and . . . the thousands of Manasseh." This ratio of tribes is nearly identical to that found in the LDS Church today (Vestal and Wallace, *The Firm Foundation of Mormonism,* p. 206).

In connection with the above, the scriptures mention another event as occurring at the time of the Second Coming—the establishment of the New Jerusalem. The Bible mentions it only rarely (Heb. 12:22; Rev. 3:12; 21:1-2, 9-11). This New Jerusalem is linked to the physical gathering of Israel to Zion by modem LDS revelation (3 Nephi 21:23-25, Ether 13:3-11) and will be built upon the American continent. Although it appears that the early members of the church believed, as Paul and others of his day, that redemption and the Second Coming of Christ was near at hand (1 Thes. 4:15-17), it is apparent that the final redemption of Zion is yet to be accomplished in conjunction with Christ's' return. Of this important event even the prophets are not privileged to know the precise time (Matt. 24:36; Mark 13:32).

Although early converts to the LDS Church did gather to America to strengthen the then small body of believers, the final gathering is still in the future (D&C 45:64-75). As was discussed in chapter 3 of this text (p. 41, the final physical gathering has been delayed at the Lord's direction (D&C 105:1-9), but the spiritual gathering of the elect continues in the form of missionary work being carried on throughout the world.

Bruce R. McConkie explained that the Church has asked modem converts in other countries to stay in their own lands to aid in strengthening the stakes of the "tent of Zion" (Isa. 54:2; D&C 82:14) and in taking the gospel "into all the world" (Mark 16:15). He told the Saints of Mexico and Central America in August of 1972: "The place of gathering for the Mexican Saints is Mexico; the place of gathering for the Guatemalan Saints is in Guatemala; . . . and so it goes throughout the length and breadth of the whole earth. . . . Every nation is the gathering place for its own people" (Cited by Harold B. Lee in *Conference Report* for April 1973, pp. 6-7 and in *Sustaining and Defending the Faith* by McConkie and Millet, p. 75). Spencer W. Kimball taught the same doctrine (*Teachings of Spencer W. Kimball*, p. 439, 1982; see also *Rediscovering the Book of Mormon*, p. 196). Although this may be cited as evidence of change, it in no way goes counter to the Lord's purposes. The gathering will continue according to the Lord's plan until his purposes are fulfilled (D&C 76:3; see also *Book of Mormon Student Manual*, p. 74).

24. Has the LDS Church changed its beliefs and teachings about Adam-God?

Some who ask this question are like the Pharisees of Christ's day who sought by their questions to trap Jesus. Others may be sincerely seeking an answer but are being challenged by anti-Mormon literature or detractors. It is essential that missionaries rely on the Spirit and exercise discernment in giving a response. The following information may be useful in responding to this question:

1. Bruce R. McConkie has stated:

> Cultists and other enemies of the restored truth, for their own peculiar purposes, sometimes try to make it appear that Latter-day Saints worship Adam as their Father in heaven. In support of their false assumptions, they quote such statements as that of Brigham Young to the effect that Adam is our father and our god and the only god with whom we have to do. This statement, and others of a similar nature, is perfectly consistent and rational, when viewed in full gospel perspective and understood in the light of the revelations relative to the patriarchal chain binding exalted beings together. . . .
>
> Faithful members of the Church worship the Father, in the name of the Son, by the power of the Holy Spirit, and view Adam in his proper high place as the pre-existent Michael, the first man and presiding high priest (under Christ) over all the earth for all time, and as one who will again lead the armies of heaven in the final great war with Lucifer. There is a sense, of course, in which Adam is god. But so also, in the same sense, are Abraham, Isaac, and Jacob; Moses and all ancient prophets [Matt. 8:11; Luke 13:28]; Peter, James, and John [Luke 22:30]; and all the righteous saints of all ages, including those of both high and low degree. All exalted beings become joint-heirs with Christ [Rom. 8:17] and inherit the fulness of the Father's kingdom [see also Matt. 25:34; Eph. 5:5; Rev. 21:7] (*Mormon Doctrine*, p. 18).

Michael's preeminence among the angels is affirmed by both scripture (Dan 10:13; Jude 1:9) and Jewish tradition. An ancient Hebrew text called The Ascension of Isaiah speaks of Michael as "chief of the holy angels" and as one of the angels who opened the sepulchre of Christ (L. Lamar Adams, *The Living Message of Isaiah,* Salt Lake City, Utah, Deseret Book, 1981, p. 110).

2. Joseph Fielding Smith said that the statements of Brigham Young so often quoted by critics "in all probability [were] erroneously tran-scribed" (Doctrines of Salvation, 1:96-106).

3. The Adam-God theory is inconsistent with numerous ancient and modem scriptures (Gen. 2:7; 3:9; Luke 3:38; D&C 29:34, 36, 42; 78:15-16; 107:54; Moses 2:27; 5:6-9; 6:1, 8-9, 50-53; Abr. 5:7, 13-15).

4. Adam-God statements are primarily found in Church journals which are not considered to be Church doctrine unless they conform to the standard works. The often quoted *Journal of Discourses* is a 26-vol-ume record of speeches by early LDS leaders from 1854 to 1886. Although it is a valuable and basically accurate source of LDS thought, it cannot be considered a source of official doctrine for several reasons: (1) it was not an official publication of the Church, (2) limitations of hand-recording by scribes of that day may have introduced errors into the sermons, and most importantly, (3) its contents, outside those por-tions found in modern scripture, were not ratified as official canon by the Priesthood or the general Church membership.

5. Statements of Brigham Young as contained in the *Journal of Dis-courses* are at times contradictory. In the same sermon where statements referring to Adam-God are found, Brigham Young also taught that there were three that created the earth: "Eloheim, Yahovah, and Michael" or Adam (Journal of Discourses, 1:50-51; see also D&C 27:11; 107:54). Note that Brigham Young taught in this same sermon that (1) Adam was Michael, (2) Adam was a "God," (3) the first earthly tabernacles (those of Adam and Eve) were "originated by the Father," and (4) "earth was organized by Eloheim, Yahovah, and Michael, these three forming a quorum" Later, Brigham Young also taught that "Adam was as conver-sant with his Father who placed him upon this earth as we are conver-sant with our earthly parents. The Father frequently came to visit his son Adam, and talked and walked with him . . ." (*Journal of Discourses,* 9:148).

6. The theory was not considered Church doctrine by other General Authorities and has been denounced by prophets of the Church since its inception (Eugene Seaich, *Ancient Texts and Mormonism,* pp. 101-03; Van Hale, "What About the Adam-God Theory?" (Brochure), Mormon Misc. Response #3, pp. 2-4).

7. There is no doctrine of infallibility in the LDS Church (See Con-ference Report, Spencer W. Kimball, April 1970, p. 120). Prophets, like all men, gain understanding "line upon line, precept upon precept" (Isa.

28:10; 2 Nephi 28:30; D&C 98:12; 128:21) and until they do so on a particular subject, may lack knowledge and may err in their understanding. He may still be a prophet and yet hold opinions which are incorrect (see also p. 41 and p. 170 of this text).

8. As was pointed out in the previous chapter, a prophet is only a prophet when acting as such (*History of the Church*, 5:265; Teachings, p. 278). Brigham Young himself provided a superb example of this principle while speaking in Church conference. After giving a fiery speech in the morning session of conference, he returned that afternoon and announced: "This morning you heard what Brigham Young thinks about this subject, and now I would like to tell you what the Lord thinks about it." Although the Prophet completely reversed himself on the subject, we should not conclude that this demeans or belittles him in any sense. It exalts and ennobles him in the eternal perspective in that he, getting the spirit of inspiration and learning what should have been presented, was willing to humble himself and announce the Lord's will (Bruce R. McConkie, "Are the General Authorities Human?," University of Utah address to the Institute of Religion on 28 October 1966, script copy p. 6, as quoted in *Sustaining and Defending the Faith*, p. 54).

9. The Adam-God theory is contrary to the teachings of the temple endowment which was given by revelation. Historical facts indicate that Brigham Young was intimately familiar with the temple endowment as it was taught to him by Joseph Smith in May of 1842 (*History of the Church*, 5:2-3, *Comprehensive History of the Church of Jesus Christ of Latter-day Saints*, 2:134-135). It also seems clear that Brigham Young thoroughly understood the meaning and purpose of the endowment since he actively directed this work and administered the ordinances to many others in the Nauvoo temple (*History of the Church*, 7:542-5, 547, 556-7, etc.). If Church leaders later taught uninspired concepts which were contrary to those contained in the endowment, this in no way makes them true. We must rely upon the sure witness of the Holy Ghost to teach us "all truth" (John 16:13).

10. No revelation was ever presented by Brigham Young on the Adam-God theory. In a private letter outlined by President Wilford Woodruff and written by Apostle Joseph F. Smith, it was stated that, "The doctrine was never submitted to the councils of the Priesthood nor to the Church for approval or ratification, and was never formally or otherwise accepted by the Church. It is therefore in no sense binding on the Church" (Van Hale, "What about the Adam-God Theory?" brochure, pp. 3-5). Also the theory, though mentioned, was never advocated in any official Church statements issued by the First Presidency or Quorum of

the Twelve (*Ibid.*, p.2; Eugene Seaich, *Ancient Texts and Mormonism*, pp. 101-03; see p. 61 of this text).

The words of Joseph Fielding Smith can help us in discerning gospel truths. He has said:

> It makes no difference what is written or what anyone has said, if what has been said is in conflict with what the Lord has revealed, we can set it aside. My words, and the teachings of any other member of the Church, high or low, if they do not square with the revelations, we need not accept them. Let us have this matter clear. We have accepted the four standard works as the measuring yardsticks, or balances, by which we measure every man's doctrine.
>
> You cannot accept the books written by the authorities of the Church as standards of doctrine, only in so far as they accord with the revealed word in the standard works.
>
> Every man who writes is responsible, not the Church, for what he writes. If Joseph Fielding Smith writes something which is out of harmony with the revelations, then every member of the Church is duty bound to reject it. If he writes that which is in perfect harmony with the revealed word of the Lord, then it should be accepted (Joseph Fielding Smith, *Doctrines of Salvation*, 3:203-04).

25. Has the LDS Church changed its beliefs and teachings about plural marriage?

The Church no longer practices plural marriage (often referred to as polygamy) because the Lord no longer requires it. In Official Declaration #1 (Excerpts), President Wilford Woodruff makes it clear that he would "have let all the temples go out of our hands . . . gone to prison . . . and let every other man go there, had not the God of heaven commanded" him to stop the practice of plural marriage. He further adds that he was shown "by vision and revelation exactly what would take place if we did not stop."

The Protestant world generally ignores the fact that the Lord condoned polygamy in the Old Testament (Gen. 16:3-4, 7-11; 17:15-17; 25:1-2, 6; 29:23-35; 30:1-26; 32:22; Ex. 2:21-22; 21:10-11; Num. 12:1-10; Deut. 21:15-17; 25:5; Jud. 8:30; 1 Sam. 1:1-2, 19-20; 2 Sam. 2:2; 5:13; 12:7-12; 1 Kings 11:1-11; 15:5; 2 Chron. 13:21-22; 20:7; 24:2-3; Hos. 1:2-3; 3:1, 3). According to scripture, the practice was part of the law of Moses (Ex. 21:10-11 and Deut. 21:15-17; 25:5) and Nathan, God's prophet, stated that God gave David his wives (2 Sam. 12:7-8; D&C 132:39). The Lord later affirmed that polygamists would be "in the kingdom of heaven" (Matt. 8:11; Luke 13:28; D&C 132:37).

In New Testament times the Lord abolished many portions of the Law of Moses and replaced them with higher laws (Matt. 5:21-48), but plural marriage was not specifically addressed. It is true that Paul recommended that bishops be "the husband of one wife" (1 Tim. 3:2; Titus

1:6), but he also alluded to worthy elders taking care of widows if they "be counted worthy of double honour" (1 Tim. 5:16-17).

The Lord has made it clear in the Book of Mormon under what circumstances plural marriage would be required. He stated, "if I will, saith the Lord of Hosts, raise up seed unto me, I will command my people [to have more than one wife]; otherwise they shall hearken to these things" (Jacob 2:30).

The Lord reveals different principles to his people based on their needs and their abilities to live those principles. Higher laws may be revealed to those who are worthy but "unto whom much is given much is required; and he who sins against the greater light shall receive the greater condemnation" (D&C 82:3; see also D&C 58:21-22; 124:49). Plural marriage is not a product of man's sinful nature. It is a higher law of marriage which was practiced by prophets and other worthy men when directed by the Lord (see also *Answers to Gospel Questions,* 3:158-162; 4:143-146, 212-215; and Daniel Peterson & Stephen Ricks, *Offenders for a Word,* pp. 153-56).

26. Has the LDS Church changed its beliefs and teachings about blacks and the priesthood?

The teachings of the Church concerning blacks and the priesthood provide one of the most impressive proofs that the LDS Church is led, as was the ancient church, by revelation. When one recognizes that the priesthood was anciently restricted to a select group among the House of Israel (Ezra 2:62-63; Neh. 7:63-65) and later made available to others, it should not be surprising that the restored priesthood was also restricted in the beginning. We do not totally understand the reason for this, but believe it was related to the curse given by the Lord to Cain and his descendants. Bruce R. McConkie stated the following on this subject:

> The ancient curse is no more. The seed of Cain and Ham and Canaan and Egyptus and Pharaoh (Abr. 1:20-27; Moses 5:16-41; 7:8, 22)—all these now have power to rise up and bless Abraham as their father. All these, Gentile in lineage, may now come and inherit by adoption all the blessings of Abraham, Isaac, and Jacob (Rom. 8:14-24; 9:4; Gal. 4:5; Eph. 1:5; *Teachings,* pp. 149-50)—all these may now be numbered with those in the one fold of the one shepherd who is Lord of all (*Doctrines of the Restoration,* p. 161; see also *Mormon Doctrine,* Negroes).

The curse pronounced on Cain and his descendants by the Lord is alluded to in the Bible (Gen. 4:9-16; 9:19-27; 24:3), but was more fully described in modern revelation (Moses 7:7-8, 22). It is this modern scripture which describes the means by which the mark of Cain was continued after the flood (Abr. 1:21-27). A vague allegorical reference in Genesis is all that remains in the Bible to give a hint of this truth to other

Christians (Gen. 9:20-27). Although it is not generally known among many LDS or non-LDS Christians today, another hint is provided by the name "Cush" which was given to the son of Ham. The name "Cush" means both "black" and "Ethiopian" in Hebrew (see *LDS Bible Dict.*— Cush; Strong's *Exhaustive Bible Concordance*—Cush; see also Jer. 13:23). Thus the mark of Cain was preserved after the flood through Cush, the son of Ham. This is in complete agreement with modern scripture (Abr. 1:21-27).

The revelation given to President Spencer W. Kimball on the 1st of June 1978 is perhaps one of the best examples we have of how modern revelation is received in the Church. Bruce R. McConkie, one of the apostles at the time the revelation was received, described this historic spiritual event:

> . . . the First Presidency and the Twelve, after full discussion of the proposition and all the premises and principles that are involved, importuned the Lord for a revelation.
>
> President Kimball was mouth, and he prayed with great faith and great fervor; this was one of those occasions when an inspired prayer was offered . . .
>
> On this occasion, because of the importuning and the faith, and because the hour and time had arrived, the Lord in his providence poured out the Holy Ghost upon the First Presidency and the Twelve in a miraculous and marvelous manner, beyond anything that any then present had ever experienced. The revelation came to the President of the Church; it also came to each individual present. There were ten members of the Council of the Twelve and three of the First Presidency there assembled. The result was that President Kimball knew and each one of us knew, independent of any other person, by direct and personal revelation to us, that the time had now come to extend the gospel and all its blessings . . . to those of every nation, culture, and race, including the black race. There was no question whatsoever as to what happened or as to the word and message that came.
>
> The revelation came to the President of the Church, and in harmony with Church government, was announced by him; the announcement was made eight days later over the signature of the first presidency (*Doctrines of the Restoration,* pp. 166-67; see also *Priesthood,* pp. 126-37).

It is interesting to note the similarities between the revelation described above and those described in Acts chapters 11 and 15. Acts chapter 11 concerns the preaching of the gospel to the Gentiles, while chapter 15 deals with the continuation of circumcision among Gentile converts. Each involved a significant change in a practice and not a doctrine of the church. These practices were instituted by God many years previous (over 3000 years in the biblical examples). In all three instances the process by which the revelation came was essentially the same: on each occasion a discussion of the proposition was held (Acts 11:2-3; 15:2-6); the man who was called to lead the church (also called the prophet) presented what the Lord had revealed to him (Acts 11:4-17; 15:7-11); then the apostles and other leaders present received a personal witness of the revelation, confirming what had been revealed to the prophet (Acts 11:18; 15:13-19); and following this, it was officially made known to the church by those chosen and authorized to do so (Acts 13:46-48; 15:20-32); and last, it was recorded as scripture (Acts 13:49; 15:23, 30-31; Official Declaration #2).

True revelations, including Official Declaration #2, are revealed strictly in accordance with procedures established by the Lord. Rejection of such duly-received revelation constitutes rejection of God's word (see Deut. 8:3; 18:15, 19; Matt. 4:4; Joseph Fielding Smith, The Way to Perfection, pp. 97-111; Bruce R. McConkie, *Mormon Doctrine,* pp. 526-28; Richard Lloyd Anderson, *Understanding Paul,* p. 53).

27. Do Bible teachings contradict modern revelation regarding a need for the priesthood and temples?

Orthodox Protestants incorrectly assume that every Christian is automatically a member of the priesthood. They cite 1 Peter 2:9, Revelation 1:4-6, and Hebrews 7:21 as proof-texts, asserting that all Christians are now priests and that Christ is the one and only high priest forever. Some claim there is no official priesthood in the New Testament. They ask why we would need official priests now since Christ came and shed his own blood as a sacrifice for us. They also claim that there was no further need for a temple since blood sacrifices were done away with after Calvary.

We should first note that the above cited scriptures were not written simply to the general membership of the church, but to the elect (1 Peter 1:2, 22-23), and especially to those called as priesthood bearers (Heb. 3:1; 1 Peter 2:5; Rev. 1:4; JST Rev. 2:1).

Christ was "Called of God an high priest" (Heb. 5:10; 6:20) but he was not the only one (Heb. 5:1). Despite Protestant claims to the contrary, there are absolutely no scriptures stating that Christ was the last high priest. Christ was one among other high priests but not the only high priest or the last high priest. He was also a priest (Heb. 7:15-17), a bishop (1 Peter 2:25), an apostle (Heb. 3:1), and a prophet (Matt. 21:11; John 4:19; 6:14; 7:40)—positions also held by other men. Paul wrote to the Hebrew saints after the ascension of Christ into heaven: "the law maketh men high priests which have infirmity" (Heb. 7:28). "For every high priest is ordained to offer gifts and sacrifices [not blood sacrifices]" (Heb. 8:3). John the Apostle also testified that Jesus Christ "hath made us kings and priests unto God and his Father" (Rev. 1:6).

While there are few New Testament references to priests other than Jesus Christ and converted Levite priests (Acts 6:7), we should not assume that this office was abolished. The early church had priests along with bishops and deacons. Origen (ca. 240 AD) spoke of the church hierarchy in the 2nd century, describing the priest's office as being between that of the deacon and bishop (Jean Danielou, *Origen,* p. 44-45, 49-50; Cel. 5, 3, 1; De Princ. 3, 2, 4; Hom. Luc., 35; Hom. Ez. 1, 7). Eusebius (ca. 300 AD) clearly distinguished between those holding the priesthood (i.e. bishops, presbyters or elders, priests, deacons, etc.) and the lay members, both men and women (Eusebius, *History of the Church,* 6:19, 23, 43; 7:30; 10:3, 4).

Eugene Seaich observes that "documents from the early Church show that the Aaronic Priesthood did not immediately disappear from Christianity. 1 Clement (ca. 96 AD) divides the priesthood into High Priests, Priests and Levites. The latter were also called "Deacons" and, according to Justin's First Apology (ca. 150 AD), were responsible for passing the bread and wine to those attending service" (*Ancient Texts and Mormonism,* p. 59). Though the title "priest" was rarely used in the New Testament, so also were similar priesthood titles such as pastor (Eph. 4:11), evangelist (Acts 21:8; Eph. 4:11; 2 Tim. 4:5), presbytery (1 Tim. 4:14), and seventy (Luke 10:1, 17).

Perhaps this question is raised because those Protestants who admit there was an official priesthood have a problem. They have no claim to authority by succession, since the Catholic Church long ago cut them off. On the other hand, if Protestants can claim that priesthood is legitimately inherent in Christianity, then this justifies their claim to authority. However, if the Protestant line of reasoning is correct, then anyone can start a new church and claim the same authority. Unfortunately, this is exactly what has happened today as confusion reigns among the hundreds of Christian churches. This cannot be God's way, for his is a house of order, not of confusion (D&C 132:8).

There was definitely an official, unchangeable (Heb. 7:24) and everlasting (Ex. 40:15; Num. 25:13) priesthood in the early church which was given to those called and ordained (John 15:16; Acts 1:22; 14:23; 15:22-23, 32; Eph. 2:20; 4:11-12; 1 Tim. 2:7; 2 Tim. 1:9; Titus 1:5) by the laying on of hands (Acts 6:1-6; 13:1-3). These priesthood holders, referred to as elders (Acts 15:2, 4, 6, 22, 23; 16:4; 20:17, etc.), bishops (1 Tim. 3:1, 2; Titus 1:7; 1 Peter 2:25), deacons (Phil. 1:11; Tim. 3:8, 10, 12, 13), the presbytery (1 Tim. 4:14), and other titles, accomplished healings (James 5:14-15) and other miracles (Mark 16:17-18) and led the church (Acts 15:2-6).

By the same reasoning some today also see no more need for temples. Those that hold to this belief ignore the fact that Jesus frequently went to the temple and even called it his "Father's house" (John 2:16). It is also evident that the disciples, even after the resurrection, often went to worship at the temple (Luke 24:53; Acts 2:46; 5:42; 22:17). Much more could be said about the importance of the temple to early Christians, but this goes beyond the scope of this discussion and the understanding of most Christians outside the Church. Questions in this area are often referred to as mysteries and are not basic gospel principles (the milk) essential to conversion (Isa. 28:9-10; 1 Peter 2:2). The meat is best left for those who have a firm foundation in the gospel (1 Cor. 3:2; Heb. 5:12-13).

28. Do Bible teachings contradict modern revelation regarding family history work?

Critics of the Church often quote 1 Timothy 1:4 and Titus 3:9 as proof-texts, asserting that genealogy records are "unprofitable" and thus unnecessary. It is important to understand that these two scriptures are not reproving the practice of searching out one's own ancestry but were instead referring to common deceptions in Paul's day. Joseph Fielding Smith, quoting from Clark's Commentary, volume 6, page 555, says these references refer to "doubtful and untruthful genealogies which had been tampered with for improper purposes" (*Answers to Gospel Questions,* 1:212-215; 5:131-132).

The Cambridge Bible Society confirms the above interpretation of these two scriptures, saying they refer to "exaggerated stories . . . popular among the Jews" of that day (*Cambridge Bible Dictionary,* see Genealogy). These tall tales of the heroes and patriarchs of early Hebrew history called attention away from the essential doctrines of the Christian faith and promoted the belief that one could be saved by virtue of one's lineage. In this regard, John the Baptist rebuked those who put too much emphasis on ancestry and attempted to use lineage as a substitute for righteousness (see Matt. 3:9; Luke 3:8).

Leland Gentry, a Salt Lake Institute of Religion instructor, further elaborated on the above explanations, stating that the endless genealogies were specifically referring to an "endless chain of gods, or aeons as they were called, each one inferior to the one above." This false doctrine was espoused to explain how God, a spiritual entity beyond the corrupting contamination of the physical world, could be creator of the material universe" (*The New Testament and the Latter-day Saints,* p. 79).

In addition to the above, it should be noted that both Matthew chapter 1 and Luke chapter 3 include genealogies of Christ. These are true genealogies bearing no resemblance to the "fables and endless genealogies" mentioned by Paul. Also, the Prophet Malachi emphasized in the last chapter and last verse of the Old Testament the critical importance that ancestral relationships would take on in the last days (Mal. 4:5-6). Malachi knew that it was "necessary in the ushering in of the dispensation of the fulness of times . . . that a whole and complete and perfect union, and welding together of dispensations, and keys, and powers, and glories should take place, and be revealed from the days of Adam even to the present time." The curse mentioned had reference to salvation. "For we without them cannot be made perfect; neither can they without us be made perfect" (D&C 128:18). Only through genealogical research and the associated temple work can our ancestors receive the required ordinances of salvation, performed in their behalf (see also D&C 2:1-3; 110:13-16).

29. Do inspired teachings and practices change?

An anti-Mormon newspaper article once asked the question "When did the apostles ever change what they taught in the New Testament?" In order to convince us that they did not, Matthew 24:35 was cited as proof that gospel teachings and practices would not change (i.e. God's word would not pass away). It should be apparent that this scripture provides a very weak proof of this assertion, since the survival of God's word has little to do with continuing revelation and change. The assumption is that because God is an unchanging being, his requirements and commandments never change. Yet, many examples of change may be found throughout the Bible and especially in the New Testament. Consider the following:

1. Killing
   a. Forbidden—Ex. 20:13; Deut. 5:17
   b. Condoned—Ex. 32:26-28; Deut. 7:2; Jos. 6:17, 21;
      1 Sam. 15:2-3, 33; 1 Kings 18:40; Eccl. 3:3
2. Animal Sacrifices
   a. A statute forever—Lev. 7:34; 16:33-34
   b. Done away—Heb. 7:27; 9:12, 26, 28
3. The Sabbath
   a. A perpetual covenant—Ex. 31:13, 16
   b. To cease—Lam. 2:6; Hos. 2:11
   c. Strictly practiced—Ex. 20:10; Num. 15:32-36; Jer. 17:21-22; Ez. 20:20-21
   d. Liberally practiced—Matt. 12:1-13; Luke 13:11-17; John 5:10-18; Col. 2:16
4. The Priesthood
   a. An everlasting responsibility—Ex. 40:15; Lev. 7:35-36
   b. Changed—Heb. 7:12

5. The Passover
   a. A memorial ordinance forever—Ex. 12:14, 24-27; Lev. 16:34
   b. Changed—1 Cor. 5:7-8
6. Circumcision
   a. An everlasting covenant—Gen. 17:9-14
   b. Discontinued—Acts 15:1-9; Rom. 2:25-26; Gal. 6:15
7. Proselyting
   a. Not to the Gentiles—Matt. 10:5-6; 15:24
   b. To all nations including Gentiles —Matt. 28:19; Mark 16:15; Acts 13:46
   c. Take neither money nor scrip (baggage) nor staff nor shoes—Matt. 10:9-10; Luke 10:4; 22:35
   d. Take staff and sandals—Mark 6:8-9
   e. Take purse and scrip—Luke 22:36
   f. Go without a sword—Matt. 26:52; Rev. 13:10
   g. Take a sword—Luke 22:36
   h. Go not house to house—Luke 10:7
   i. Go house to house—Acts 2:46; 20:20
8. Paid Ministry
   a. Prohibited—Micah 3:11; Acts 20:33-34; 1 Cor. 9:18; 2 Cor. 11:7; 1 Peter 5:2
   b. Allowed—Luke 10:7; 1 Tim. 5:18
9. Marriage
   a. Not necessary—1 Cor. 7:7-9
   b. Necessary—1 Cor. 11:11
10. Divorce
   a. Prohibited—Luke 16:18
   b. Allowed at times—Matt. 19:7-9
11. Women
   a. To be silent and not teach—1 Cor. 14:34-35; 1 Tim. 2:9-12
   b. Women prophetesses—Luke 2:36; Acts 2:16-18; 21:8-9; 1 Cor. 11:5
   c. Women missionaries with Paul—Rom. 16:1-4; Phil. 4:2-3
12. Drinking Wine
   a. To be avoided—Lev. 10:8-9; Prov. 20:1; 23:29-35; Jer. 35:13-14; Hos. 3:1; 4:11; Rom. 14:21; Eph. 5:18; 1 Tim. 3:3; Titus 1:7
   b. Allowed—Gen. 14:18; 27:28; Deut. 14:26; Ps. 104:15; Prov. 9:5; 31:6; Isa. 25:6; Luke 5:39; John 2:1-11; 1 Tim. 3:8; 5:23
13. Christ's Gospel
   a. Brings peace—John 14:27
   b. Brings the sword—Matt. 10:34

c. Yoke is easy—Matt. 11:28-30

d. Converts to be hated and persecuted—Matt. 10:22-23; 24:9

Although a few of the above contradictions may be the result of translational errors, it seems clear that the Lord can also reveal different principles at different times because circumstances and the needs of his people change. He may change the organization, procedures and at times even the commandments and laws we live by, inasmuch as we progress toward Christ and perfection (Moroni 10:32; D&C 82:3), but the central doctrines remain fixed. Changes in organization or procedures are a testimony that revelation is ongoing (Boyd K. Packer, October 1989 General Conference Talk, *Ensign,* Nov. 89, pp. 14-16).

God has told us that his ways are higher than our ways and his thoughts are higher than our thoughts (Isa. 55:8-9). Our object should be to be obedient to his will as revealed through his chosen servants either past or present (Eccl. 12:13; 1 John 2:17; Rev. 2:26; D&C 1:38).

Latter-day Saints accept God's right to expand upon his previously revealed word, choosing to live "by every word that proceedeth out of the mouth of God" (Deut. 8:3; Matt. 4:4; Moroni 7:25). On the other hand, those who deny modem revelation have chosen to live by bread alone and have fallen into the same trap as the Jews of Christ's day. They refuse to admit that God's word is never complete and that God has declared that he will reveal line upon line, precept upon precept (Isa. 28:10-13). They also ignore the fact that the Prophet Amos has said: "Surely the Lord God will do nothing, but he revealeth his secret unto his servants the prophets" (Amos 3:7). Since God has not stopped speaking to man, those outside his church must have stopped living by God's word spoken through his prophets today. As has been mentioned previously, those who do so will suffer the consequences and put their salvation at risk (Deut. 18:19).

30. Which is the correct Sabbath day—Saturday or Sunday?

Some denominations today believe that much of Christianity is observing the wrong day of the week as the Sabbath. They contend that Saturday is the seventh day and should, according to Bible scripture, be observed as the true Sabbath (Ex. 16:29-30; 20:8-11; Lev. 23:1-3; Deut. 5:12-15). There are several flaws with this assertion:

1. The research of Samuel Walter Gamble, a Methodist minister, suggests that the original Hebrew calendar was not like our modem calendar. His findings published in a study called "Sunday, the True Sabbath of God" (reprinted in Kenneth E. Coombs, *The True Sabbath—Saturday or Sunday*), indicate that differences in the Hebrew calendar caused a

one day shift in the Sabbath each year when compared to our modern calendars. He points out that the Hebrew calendar was composed of a system of fixed-date Sabbaths each seventh day until the day of Pentecost (a high holy day). At that point, a 48-hour Sabbath was celebrated. This double Sabbath effectively shifted the Sabbath one day each year when compared to our own calendar (see also *Mormon Doctrine,* p. 658, *Doctrinal New Testament Commentary,* 1:841; 3:440-441).

2. It appears that the Sabbath day was changed by early Christians to the first day of the week to commemorate the resurrection of the Lord (Matt. 28:1; Mark 16:2, 9; Luke 24:1; John 20:1, 19; Acts 20:7; 1 Cor. 16:2). Note that the resurrection day is referred to in all Greek Testaments as "Sabbath" [sabbaton] and was translated in the King James Version as "the first day of the week" to avoid confusing the two Sabbaths. John thereafter referred to it as the Lord's day to differentiate it from the Jewish Sabbath (Rev. 1:10). Both Old and New Testament scripture foretold this change (Hos. 2:11; Heb. 4:7-9; 10:9) and early Christians affirmed it.

Ignatius, in about AD 110, said that Christians were "no longer keeping the Sabbath but . . . the Lord's day on which our life also arose through him" (*Letters of Ignatius,* 2:9). Barnabas (ca. 75 to 130 AD) declared, "This is why we spend the eight day in celebration, the day which Jesus both arose from the dead and . . . ascended into heaven" (*Epistle of Barnabas,* 15:8). Justin Martyr (ca. 140 AD) also recorded that Christian services were held on Sunday "because Jesus Christ—our Redeeming Savior—rose from the dead on the same day" (*First Apology,* pp. 65-67; quoted more fully on p. 132 of this text).

If this is not sufficient proof that the Sabbath day was changed, we can add the testimonies of Bardaisan (b. 154 AD); Irenaeus (ca. 178 AD); Clement of Alexandria (ca. 194 AD); Cyprian (200-258 AD); Origen (201 AD); Eusebius (ca. 315 AD); Peter, Bishop of Alexandria (ca. 300 AD); and the author of the Didache (80-120 AD). Each of these men affirmed that early Christians observed the "Lord's day" on the first day of the week rather than the Jewish Sabbath (see also *LDS Bible Dictionary,* pp. 725, 765; LeGrand Richards, *A Marvelous Work and a Wonder,* pp. 342-50).

3. The Latter-day Saints keep the Sunday Sabbath because the Lord so commanded them by direct revelation (D&C 59:9-13-Note: this revelation was given on Sunday; see also James E. Talmage, *Articles of Faith,* pp. 451-52; Joseph Fielding Smith, *Answers to Gospel Questions,* 2:58-63).

4. Paul taught that we should let no man judge us with respect to observance of Sabbath days (Col. 2:16).

The above demonstrates two things relative to revelation: first, not all revelations given to the early Church were recorded in the Bible; and second, without modern revelation, men can err in interpreting scripture and God's will today.

5
The Godhead

31. Is the God of Mormonism a changeable God?

Some have criticized the LDS concept of deity, saying the God of Mormonism often changes his mind. Issues such as plural marriage, blacks and the priesthood, and other questions treated in chapter 4 are often cited as examples of changes made by the "Mormon God" This, they assert, conflicts with Bible scriptures which describe God as unchanging (Ps. 90:2; Mal. 3:6; Heb. 13:8; James 1:17). The obvious conclusion they draw is that our God is not the same as the God of the Bible.

LDS scripture, including the Bible, affirm that our God and his Son are the same yesterday, today, and forever (1 Nephi 10:18-19; Alma 41:8; 3 Nephi 24:6; Mormon 9:9, 19; Moroni 8:18; D&C 20:17), but at the same time they clarify the meaning of "unchanging" Alma, for example, teaches us that God's justice with respect to sin is "unalterable" (Alma 41:3-10). Third Nephi 24 taught, as did Malachi, that we could trust in the consistency of God's blessings and judgements. The words of Moroni also confirm God's unchangeable nature but then he warns that those who "deny the revelations of God, and say that they are done away" (Mormon 9:7-9) have themselves "imagined" a changeable god (Mormon 9:10, 19). Moroni effectively turns the tables by asking our critics why they no longer believe in the biblical God of prophecy, miracles, and continuing revelation. God's love for his children, if truly constant, should be manifest in revelation to prophets yesterday, today, and forever. The lack of prophets and modern revelation in today's Protestant and Catholic churches is in essence a denial that God is the same today.

Those who believe an unchanging God must be unwavering in his approach do not understand God's role as our *Father.* If one could imagine a perfect earthly parent, one that is all-knowing and unchanging, one would hardly expect him to treat each child the same at all times, regardless of age, behavior, or circumstance. Likewise, God has never changed his position on eternal principles. However, He has often varied his approach according to our righteousness, our readiness, and our willingness to receive his correction (Ps. 103:13). Promises have been made then revoked because of unrighteousness, and a few organizational matters have been modified as our understanding and circumstances have changed. Indeed, God has not changed, but the needs of his kingdom have changed. Critics could just as easily reprove a righteous father for holding his two-year-old and eighteen-year-old to different standards as they could attack the "Mormon God" for revealing "line upon line" to an increasingly prepared flock.

This brings us to the matter of consistency. Anti-Mormon critics contend that modern revelation is inconsistent both internally and externally with regard to Bible scripture, and therefore reflects a changeable God. We should first make it clear that God is always unchanging in his purpose, which is to help us gain faith in Christ and "bring to pass the immortality and eternal life of man" (Moses 1:39). God may reveal different principles at different times because mankind has different needs in each age, but his ultimate goal remains fixed (Eph. 3:11-12; Alma 37:7; 42:26; Mormon 5:14; 8:22; D&C 76:3-4). God's love and mercy are also unchanging (Moroni 8:17-19; John 3:15-16), but just as a mortal father adjusts the guidance given to his children as they mature, so our Heavenly Father will adjust the laws and commandments he gives us based on our obedience and spiritual maturity. He is teaching us line upon line and precept upon precept (Isa. 28:10) in order to lead us step by step to salvation and exaltation (Rom. 2:7; Moses 1:39). His guidance may vary with circumstances and our ability to obey, but an unchanging God will consistently give guidance to the faithful (see *Lectures on Faith,* Lecture 3).

Those who try to imply more than is justified by the "unchangeable" quality of God's nature should first consider the fact that scripture describes several areas in which deity can change. For example, Hebrews 13:8 states that "Jesus Christ [is] the same yesterday, and to day, and for ever," but this certainly does not apply to his physical nature. Jesus Christ was anciently known as Jehovah the God of the Old Testament (John 1:1, 10, 14; 1 Cor. 10:4) and as such had a body of spirit (Ether 3:16). As the mortal Messiah, he took upon himself a physical body of flesh and blood and became a man (John 1:14; 19:34; Phil. 2:8; 1 Tim. 2:5; 1 John 1:7; Mosiah 7:27) in order to bring to pass the atonement. After giving his life on the cross, he broke the bonds of death through the resurrection and became an exalted and glorified being with a body of "flesh and bones" (Luke 24:39). He thus changed first from a being of spirit to a mortal being of flesh and blood and lastly to an immortal being of flesh and bone. Thus, the unchangeable nature of deity does not apply to his physical nature. It also does not apply to his attitude toward man as reflected by specific directives, blessings, and punishments.

Divine direction to man will vary significantly based on needs, circumstances, and man's righteousness. In addition to the contrasting decrees previously discussed in chapter 4 (pp. 66-68), it is clear that God does, under certain circumstances, repent (i.e. change his mind and modify or delay decreed actions because of changed circumstances), despite scriptural statements to the contrary. Consider the following Old Testament passages:

1. God does not repent—Num. 23:19; 1 Sam. 15:29; Ps. 110:4; Jer. 4:28; Ezek. 24:14; Zech. 8:14

2. God repents—Gen. 6:6-7; Ex. 32:14; Deut. 32:36; Jud. 2:18; 1 Sam. 15:11, 35; 2 Sam. 24:16; 1 Chron. 21:15; Ps. 90:13; 106:45; 135:14; Jer. 18:8; 26:3, 13, 19; 42:10; Joel 2:13; Amos 7:3, 6; Jonah 3:10

Although the above references to God repenting are apparently mistranslations of the Hebrew word "nacham" (see JST for those scriptures noted in paragraph 2 above), the meaning still conveys a change in attitude and the associated blessings or consequences. This is illustrated by God's declaration to Jeremiah (Jer. 18:8-10): "If that nation, against whom I have pronounced, turn from their evil, I will repent (nacham) of the evil that I thought to do unto them. And at what instant I shall speak concerning a nation, and concerning a kingdom, to build and to plant [i.e. bless] it; If it do evil in my sight, that it obey not my voice, then I will repent (nacham) of the good, wherein I said I would benefit them" Simply put, the Lord is bound by his promises when we do what he says, but when we do not obey him we have no promise (D&C 82:10).

The New Testament likewise describes Jesus Christ as God (John 1:1, 14) and as such omnipotent, omniscient, and eternal but, as pointed out by Van Hale ("What about the Adam-God Theory," brochure, *Mormon Misc. Response #3,* p. 8), the mortal Jesus:

1. "grew, and waxed strong"—Luke 2:40

2. "increased in wisdom and stature, and in favor with God and man"—Luke 2:52

3. "learned . . . obedience by the things which he suffered"—Heb. 5:8

4. "was in all points tempted like as we are"—Heb. 4:15

5. experienced birth, pain, joy, sorrow, anger, and death (see also Matt. 21:12-13; Mark 8:2; John 11:35; Mosiah 3:7; D&C 93:13, 17).

Latter-day Saints "know there is a God in heaven, who is infinite and eternal, from everlasting to everlasting the same unchangeable God, the framer of heaven and earth, and all things which are in them" (D&C 20:17).

Jehovah in the Old Testament was at times a God of anger and wrath (Ex. 22:24; Deut. 9:7; Ps. 110:5; Jer. 10:10; Hos. 5:10; Zeph. 1:15), and at times a God of love and mercy (Ex. 20:6; 34:6; Deut. 4:31; 2 Chron. 30:9; Neh. 9:17; Ps. 52:8; Mic. 7:18) and yet he was described as unchanging by himself (Mal. 3:6) and by his prophets (Ps. 15:4; 102:27). In the New Testament, God was described as a God of wrath to the unrighteous (John 3:36; Rom. 1:18) and a God of mercy to the repentant (Eph. 2:4; Titus 3:4-5; James 5:10-11).

Although the principles by which the Lord operates are somewhat obscure in Bible scripture, there should be no doubt that his wisdom is vastly superior to ours (Isa. 55:8-9). Though God's ultimate purpose is unchanging, it is clear that his promises have always been contingent upon righteousness. God is compassionate to those who obey him and unforgiving to those who unrepentantly rebel against him (Ex. 20:5-6). In the eternal scheme, justice demands that we be warned of the punishment for sin (Rom. 4:15), but God's mercy will be extended when we heed that warning. Likewise, promised blessings will be bestowed upon the righteous but withdrawn from the disobedient (D&C 58:31-33). In this regard, God may appear to change when he is, in reality, fulfilling his eternal purpose within the limits of the unchanging laws of justice and mercy. Though God's plan may at times be difficult for us to understand, we can take comfort in the promise that the "eternal purposes of the Lord shall roll on, until all his promises [of immortality and eternal life] shall be fulfilled" (Mormon 8:22; see also 1 John 2:25; Joseph F. Smith, Gospel Doctrine, p. 33).

32. Do Latter-day Saints believe in the trinity?

The answer to this question depends entirely on the inquirer's definition of trinity. Webster's New Collegiate Dictionary defines the word trinity as "the unity of Father, Son, and Holy Spirit as three persons in one Godhead." The Random House College Dictionary adds a second alternative to this definition which allows also "the threefold personality of one Divine Being." Although Webster's definition would be considered a valid LDS description of the Godhead, the second Random House alternative would be considered by Latter-day Saints to be an apostate view.

Today, some people assert that a belief in a mysterious unknowable trinitarian god is essential to a claim of Christianity, even though this requirement is not biblical. At times they use Colossians 2:9 as a proof-text to support their trinitarian concept: "in him [Christ] dwelleth all the fulness of the Godhead bodily." Though this scripture could appear to vindicate belief in a trinity, the Greek text does not justify this interpretation. The Greek word translated as Godhead in this verse is "theotes" This word actually means "deity" and is translated as such in many modern Bible translations. Accurately translated, this verse should read "in

Christ the fulness of deity dwells in bodily form" (see New Internation-al Version). Thus, the qualities of Godhood are manifest to us in Christ, but Christ is not God the Father (see also p. 81 of this text).

It is important to note that the word "trinity" does not appear any-where in the King James Version nor any other reputable translation of the Bible. The present trinitarian concept cannot be derived from an impartial reading of the Bible. Justification of this doctrine using cita-tions of biblical verses is weak and inconclusive at best. The term God-head, on the other hand, is an accepted biblical term (Acts 17:29; Rom. 1: 20; Col. 2:9) and the preferred title in the LDS Church (*History of the Church*, 6:473; *Lectures on Faith*, Lecture 5; *A New Witness for the Arti-cles of Faith*, pp. 58-59). References to the Godhead as the trinity are found in Church literature (*Articles of Faith*, pp. 39-41; *Journal of Dis-courses*, 6:95; *History of the Church*, vol. 1, Intro., pp. 80-81), but such usage clearly denotes a three-person Godhead and not a one-being con-cept (See also Van Hale, "Defining the Mormon Doctrine of Deity," brochure, *Mormon Misc. Reprint #6*, p. 9).

The latter concept of the trinity, now held by much of "mainstream Christianity," seems to have originated under the influence of Greek and other oriental philosophies during the period of apostasy following the death of the apostles (*History of the Church*, vol. 1, Intro., pp. 82-87). A study of Christianity prior to AD 325 reveals that the LDS interpretation of the Godhead was then the prevailing belief. Church fathers such as Ignatius, Justin Martyr, Origen, Athanasius and others argued that the Godhead consisted of separate Beings (see J. D. N. Kelly, *Early Christ-ian Doctrines*, pp. 93, 96, 129, 233). The first person to use the term trin-ity appears to have been Tertullian in about AD 200. He used the term to refer to ideas which mentioned three and one.

Over a century later, in AD 325, the Roman Emperor Constantine convened a delegation composed of about one-sixth of the bishops from throughout the Roman Empire. The stated purpose of this Council of Nicea, as it was called, was to achieve unity among the factions then existent. The three major groups with differing views regarding God's nature at length became two factions. The eastern (Arian) Christian view favored a three-God concept while the western (Roman) view favored one supreme God to whom all others were subordinated. Under extreme intimidation by the emperor, the Arian group was compelled to yield to the Roman view. Arius and the bishops and priests who opposed the Nicean Creed and the "one substance" terminology adopted by the council were exiled. Constantine, in order to ensure future unity, also commanded that the writings of these men be burned (James K. and

Rose Seastrand, *Journey to Eternal Life and Distractions Along the Way,* p. 132; *History of the Church,* vol. 1, Intro., pp. 79-90).

The Nicean Creed stated that there was "one God and one Lord Jesus Christ the Son of God" who was "one substance with the Father." The Athanasian creed, which was an outgrowth of the Nicean Creed, typifies the modern "orthodox" concept of the trinity. It speaks of an "incomprehensible" God which is completely foreign to Christ's teachings. Jesus taught that "this is life eternal, that [we] might *know* . . . the only true God, and Jesus Christ whom [God had] sent" (John 17:3; see also Jeremiah 31:34; John 8:19, 14:7-9, Hebrews 8:10-11, 1 John 2:3-4, and 1 John 3:1-2, 6; 5:20).

Thus, the accepted trinitarian concept of deity is the result of a compromise achieved without the benefit of apostles, prophets, or revelation and arrived at only when extreme pressure was exerted by a then-pagan emperor. The true concept of God is not that of an "unknown" or unknowable God (Acts 17:23) but one whose offspring we are (Acts 17:28-29) and in whose image we were created (Gen. 1:26-27). Our Heavenly Father loves us and wants us to know him and become like him (Matt. 5:48; 1 John 3:1-2; for further information on the Godhead see the additional questions which follow; see also *Answers to Gospel Questions,* 3:165-69).

33. Do Latter-day Saints believe in one God or three?

LDS prophets since Joseph Smith have taught clearly that there are three separate members of the Godhead, each of which is a God. As Joseph Smith stated: "these personages . . . are called God the first, the Creator; God the second, the Redeemer; and God the third, the Witness or Testator" (*Teachings,* p. 190). He further taught: "I have always declared God to be a distinct personage, Jesus Christ a separate and distinct personage from God the Father, and that the Holy Ghost was a distinct personage and a Spirit: and these three constitute three distinct personages and three Gods" (*Teachings,* p. 370, see also *History of the Church,* 6:474).

Bruce R. McConkie states concerning the Godhead that "Three glorified, exalted, and perfected personages comprise the Godhead or supreme presidency of the universe. . . . Though each God in the Godhead is a personage, separate and distinct from each of the others, yet they are one God (Testimony of the Three Witnesses in the Book of Mormon), meaning that they are unified as one in their purposes and objectives, and also in the attributes of perfection. For instance, each has the fulness of truth, knowledge, charity, power, justice, judgement, mercy and faith. Accordingly they all think, act, speak, and are alike in all things; and yet they are three separate and distinct entities" (*Mormon Doctrine,* p. 319). In a latter work, Brother McConkie confirmed that "the Father, the Son, and the Holy Ghost are one. . . . They are one in plan, one in possession of the attributes of godliness, and one in every good thing. The whole system of salvation is so ordained that we may become one with Deity. If we do not, we are not like him" (Bruce R. McConkie, *Doctrines of the Restoration,* p. 380). Thus the oneness of the Godhead is a perfect example of the unity that should exist among the Saints of God (3 Nephi 28:10-11; D&C 35:2, *Teachings,* pp. 311-12; *Lectures on Faith,* Lecture 5).

The Bible contains numerous examples of the separate nature of the Father and the Son (see pp. 81-82). There also are important instances where all three members of the Godhead are clearly portrayed as separate and distinct. The best example is the baptism of Jesus Christ (Matt. 3:13-17; Mark 1:9-11: Luke 3:21-22; John 1:29-32). In all but John's account, all three members of the Godhead are identified: the Father bearing witness "from heaven" (Matt. 3:17; Mark 1:11; Luke 3:22), the Son "coming up out of the water" (Mark 1:10), and the Holy Ghost descending "in a bodily shape like a dove" (Luke 3:22). All three members of the Godhead are clearly separate entities who, in this instance, are physically separated also.

John provides another scriptural witness that "there are three that bear record in heaven, the Father, the Word [Jesus Christ], and the Holy Ghost" (1 John 5:7). John adds that "these three are [actually] one," apparently meaning one witness because they, like the witnesses of the spirit, the water, and the blood "agree in one" (1 John 5:8). Bible scholars have noted that 1 John 5:7 and 8 are not found in the early Greek manuscripts and may therefore be of questionable authority. Whether or not these verses are authentic, it is clear from other Bible passages that the Father and the Son are in fact separate witnesses. John himself records in John 8:17-18 and 28-29 that Jesus taught: "It is also written in your law, that the testimony of two men is true. I am one that bear witness of myself, and the Father that sent me beareth witness of me . . . I do nothing of myself; but as my Father hath taught me, I speak these things. And he that sent me is with me: the Father hath not left me alone; for I do always those things that please him." It is clear that Jesus considered his Father a separate being and witness.

Many who espouse the triune concept point to Old Testament scriptures as proof that there is only one God (Gen. 1:1; Isa. 43:10-12; 44:6, 8; 46:9). But these verses, as originally written, made no such claim. Although our King James Version (KJV) states in Genesis 1:1 that, "In the beginning God created the heaven and the earth," the Hebrew identified Eloheim as the creator. Eloheim is the plural form of eloah (as used in Isa. 44:8) which means God or Deity. Thus, "eloheim" literally means Gods or Deities, so Genesis 1:1 could be translated: "In the beginning Gods created the heaven and the earth" (see Abraham 4:1). Use of "us" and "our" in Genesis 1:26 further justifies this conclusion.

Examination of the Hebrew text also helps us understand Isaiah's references (chapters 43 and 44) to one God. Isaiah 43:10-12 in the KJV reads: "Ye are my witnesses saith the Lord [Jehovah in Hebrew] . . . understand that I am he: before me there was no God [Eloheim in Hebrew] formed neither shall there be after me. I, even I, am the Lord [Jehovah]; and beside me there is no saviour. . . . ye are my witnesses, saith the Lord [Jehovah], that I am God [El]." Knowing that Jehovah was Jesus Christ (see 1 Cor. 10:4 and other references, pp. 99 and following), we are confronted with a contradiction. Paul the apostle later taught that "there is but one God, the Father . . . and one Lord Jesus Christ, by whom are all things" (1 Cor. 8:6, see also 1 Tim. 2:5). If Jesus as Jehovah was saying that he was the only God, then how could the Father also be the only God and still be separate from Jesus Christ? Isaiah 44:10 helps explain this apparent contradiction by clarifying the meaning of the word "formed" in the last portion of Isaiah 43:10. The Hebrew reads: "who has formed a god, or poured out an image [i.e. idol], to no profit?" (Hendrickson Interlinear Bible). Thus, the Lord is not claiming to be the only God in existence but is warning Israel not to worship false idol gods (see also Isa. 17:7-8; 42:8, 17; 43:12; 44:6-18). When these chapters are read in context in the KJV, it is clear that Isaiah's reference to forming god is speaking of graven images of metal and wood. Isaiah 44:8-18 makes it unmistakably clear that the prophet is condemning idolatry and not a belief in more than one God.

Isaiah 43:10 also teaches us more about God's names. In Hebrew it reads: "Ye are my witnesses saith Jehovah, I (or I AM), El (short form of Eloheim) and no other eloheim [gods; in this case false gods] no none are like me." This verse actually uses three names for deity together. The contraction of Jehovah-Eloheim (translated LORD God in the KJV) is a similar, commonly found, grouping of names found in the Hebrew Old Testament. It appears that these compound name-titles were an attempt by ancient writers or scribes to refer to more than one member of the Godhead by a compound name (*Articles of Faith,* p. 49). Thus the Hebrew of the above verse might more accurately be translated "Ye are our witnesses saith Jehovah and Eloheim and no other gods are like us."

Although the New Testament also speaks of the "oneness" of the Godhead (John 10:30; 17:11, 21, 22; 1 Cor. 8:4-6; 1 John 5:7), the context of the verses generally provides the key to a correct interpretation. John, for example, quotes the Savior's reference to his own oneness with the Father but also indicates that the disciples need to be one (using the same Greek word) with himself, God, and other believers (John 6:56; 14:20; 17:11, 21-22; 1 John 3:24; 4:13, 15). The context of many of Paul's references to oneness make it clear that he is speaking of a oneness of mind and spirit. Paul speaks, in 1 Corinthians 2:16, of having "the mind of Christ" He likewise tells the Philippians "stand fast in one spirit with one mind striving together for the faith of the gospel" (Phil. 1: 27; see also Gal. 5:22-25 and 1 Cor. 1:10). Paul also made frequent reference to a oneness of the saints (again using the same Greek word) with God and Christ as well as with other members (Rom. 8: 1; 12: 16; 15:6; 1 Cor. 3: 16; 6:17; 10:17; 12:13; 2 Cor. 5:17; 6:16; Gal. 2:20; 3:28; Eph. 1:10; 3:17; Phil. 1:27; Col. 1:27; 2:10; Heb. 2:11).

It is especially significant that Paul used the same verbal construction as Christ used in saying, "I and my Father are one" (John 10:30) to describe his relationship to Apollos. He wrote, "I have planted, Apollos watered; but God gave the increase. Now he that planteth and he that watereth are one" (1 Cor. 3:6, 8). From the above-cited references it should be clear that both John's and Paul's concept of "oneness" was not a merging of substance but was instead an expression of unity of purpose, mind, and heart. Modem scripture also confirms this interpretation (D&C 35:2; 50:43; 130:22).

The early church fathers Hippolytus, Origen, and Tertullian, also affirmed that God the Father and Jesus Christ were separate and distinct personages with unity of purpose and power. Hippolytus taught that Christ and the Father "are one . . . but it refers to two persons and one power . . . and disposition of unity of mind . . . God the Father Almighty, and Christ Jesus the Son of God, who being God, became man . . . and the Holy Spirit . . . are three" (*Against the Heresy of Noetus,* 7, 11 as quoted in James L. Barker, *Apostasy from the Divine Church*, p. 44). Origen wrote that the Father and Son "are two separate persons, but one in unity and concord of mind and in identity of will" (Henry Bettenson, *The Early Christian Fathers,* p. 336). Tertullian declared that "the Father is one, and the Son one, and the Spirit one, and that they are distinct from Each other" (*The Ante-Nicene Fathers,* 3:603; see also Darrick Evenson, *The Gainsayers,* pp. 66-68; James L. Barker, *Apostasy from the Divine Church,* pp. 42-44 for further quotes on this subject).

34. Are Latter-day Saints polytheists?

Some outside our Church contend that the LDS belief that there are three Gods in the Godhead make us polytheists. Though dictionaries (basing definitions on term definitions devised many years ago in theological seminaries) generally define polytheism as a belief in the existence of more than one god, Latter-day Saints refuse to accept this term as descriptive of our religious worship. The reason for this is that the commonly accepted meaning that most people give this term differs radically from its technical definition. The commonly accepted meaning of polytheism is typically associated with a multiplicity of deities as worshiped by primitive pagan religions. This system of gods is totally foreign to LDS beliefs and is considered by Church members to be an apostate perversion of the original truths revealed to Old Testament prophets beginning with Adam.

To worship is to give profound reverence, respect and love to a Divine Being; to give praise and honor; to recognize the omnipotence and the divine qualities of deity; to be cognizant of divine grace, love and concern; and to be desirous of maintaining a closeness, a personal relationship and an ongoing communication. Latter-day Saints worship God the Father; Jesus Christ, the only-begotten Son of God the Father, and the Holy Ghost. They regard each of the three as possessing the divine attributes of Godhood. They believe each of the three plays a significant role in directing the affairs of mankind here on earth, and that their influence upon mankind will be eternal in nature, continuing in the exalted realms of heaven.

The major responsibility for the central role in creation of the earth was delegated by the Father to Jesus Christ (Heb. 1:2; Col. 1:16). Jesus also governed the affairs of mankind as the Old Testament Jehovah, then came to earth in the meridian of time in the role of Savior and Redeemer. He will return in a glorious Second Coming and rule as King of Kings and Lord of Lords (Rev. 19:12). He will judge all mankind (John 5:22-29). When he has completed and perfected his work, he will present it to the Father, then be crowned with glory and given power to reign forever (D&C 76:106-108) as the Father's appointed "heir of all things" (Heb. 1:2).

Yet Christ has directed us to acknowledge God the Father's overall authority over man, since he is the literal Father of our spirits (Heb. 12:9; Matt. 5:48; Acts 17:29). Though we recognize Jesus' role as assigned administrator of this earth's affairs, our Savior himself instructed us to address our prayers to the Father (Matt. 6:9) and to always pray to the Father in the name of Jesus Christ (3 Nephi 18:19-24). Thus, our worship of the Father, Son and Holy Ghost is primarily channeled to the Father.

Bible scripture speaks of a "God of gods and Lord of lords" (Deut. 10:17; see also Ex. 15:11; 18:11; Ps. 97:9; 135:5; 136:2; 138:1; Dan. 11:36) and Paul taught that while there were many gods, mortals of this earth should worship only God the Father (1 Cor. 8:5-6; Col. 3:17). Members of the LDS Church do in fact worship God the Father in the name of Christ as is taught in both ancient and modem scripture (Matt. 6:9; John 15:16; 2 Nephi 32:9; Jacob 4:5; 3 Nephi 18:19; Moroni 10:4; D&C 18:40; 20:19, 29; Moses 1:17).

Latter-day Saints also literally accept the many scriptural passages which tell us that man, as spirit offspring of God the Father, may eventually be granted the powers of Godhood (Rom 8:16-17; Gal. 4:6-7; Titus 3:7; Heb. 1:14; 11:7; James. 2:5; Matt. 5:48; D&C 76:50-60; 132:19-20). However, while recognizing that man has the God-given potential to attain personal exaltation and godhood, we worship only God since we recognize that their attaining of this exalted station by men and women is a future event.

Latter-day Saints recognize that there is a oneness of unity and purpose of the Father, Son and Holy Ghost (John 17:20-23). Evangelicals, with their concept of the trinity, believe that the Father, Son and Holy Ghost are three separate beings but still (in some manner which they are unable to "comprehend" or satisfactorily define) one God, and hence they call themselves "monotheistic." Yet they sometimes attempt to play word games, asserting that Latter-day Saints are "polytheistic" in their worship of those same three beings. It is hypocritical to call Protestants monotheists, and Latter-day Saints, polytheists since we worship the "Godhead" in the same manner they worship the trinity.

35. Are God and Christ separate beings?

Joseph Fielding Smith leaves no doubt that God the Father and Jesus Christ are separate and distinct beings. He has declared: "How plain it is that the Father and Son are separate Personages, yet one in power, wisdom and unity. Hence they are, with the Holy Spirit which carries out their will—one God or Presiding Council!" (*Answers to Gospel Questions,* 1:4; see also p. 76 of this text).

Jesus Christ likewise taught: "And now . . . I come to thee. Holy Father, keep through thine own name those whom thou hast given me, that they may be one [in purpose and unity], as we are" (John 17:11).

The scriptures are replete with examples of the separate nature and substance of the Father and the Son. Consider the following:

1. God spoke from heaven while Christ was on the earth—Matt. 3:17; 17:5; Mark 1:11; Luke 3:22; John 12:28-30
2. God is a separate witness of Christ—John 5:36-37; 8:17-18

3. Christ was "with" God in the beginning—John 1:1-3,10,14; 6:38; 16:28; 17:3, 5, 24; 20:21; Eph. 3:9; 1 John 4:14

4. Christ is God's Son—Mark 9:7; John 3:16; 9:35-37; 17:1; 20:17, 21, 31; Eph. 3:14; Heb. 1:6; 5:5

5. Christ prayed to his Father—Matt. 6:6-9; 26:39; 27:46; Luke 23:34; John 12:27-28; 16:26; 17:5-11

6. Christ is at the right hand of God—Mark 16:19; Luke 22:69; Acts 2:33; 7:55-57; Rom. 8:34; Eph. 1:20; Col. 3:1; Heb. 1:3; 10:12; 1 Peter 3:22; Rev. 3:21

7. The Father committed all judgment unto the Son—John 5:17-20, 22-23, 27; Rom. 2:16; 2 Tim. 4:1

8. God anointed Jesus Christ—Acts 10:38; Heb. 1:9

9. God honored, blessed and glorified Christ—Matt. 12:18; John 5:26; 12:23; 17:1, 5, 24; Acts 3:13; 5:30-31; Philip. 2:9; 2 Peter 1:17-18

10. Jesus was raised up by God—Acts 5:30-31; 1 Peter 1:21

11. God and Jesus are plural (we, our, us)—Gen. 1:26; Isa. 6:8; John 14:23; 17: 11, 21-22

12. God "sent" Christ to atone for us—Mark 9:37; John 3:16; 5:24; 6:38; 7:28-29; 8:42; 12:44-45; 17:3-4, 6-10, 18, 25; 20:21; 1 John 4: 14

13. Christ commanded us to pray to God in his name—Matt. 6:6, 9; Luke 11:2; Col. 3:17; Heb. 7:25-26

14. Christ spoke of his Father in heaven—Matt. 6:9; 10:33; 16:17; Luke 11:2; John 14:12; 20:17

15. Only God knew the exact time of the end; Christ did not then know—Matt. 24:36; Mark 13:32

16. God the Father is Christ's God—Mark 15:34; John 20:17; Eph. 1:17; 1 Peter 1:3

17. Christ's will and doctrine were separate from God's—Matt. 26:3942; Luke 22:41-42; John 5:30; 7:16-17; 14:10

18. Christ did his Father's work, not his own—Luke 2:49-50; John 17:3-4

19. Christ came in his Father's name—John 5:43

20. Christ came from and returned to God—John 14: 12; 16:27-28, 30; 1 Peter 3:21-22

21. The Father was "greater than" the Son—John 10:29; 14:28; 1 Cor. 15:28

22. We come to the Father only by the Son—John 14:6

23. Christ will deliver up the kingdom to God the Father—1 Cor. 15:24

24. Christ is mediator between God and men—1 Tim. 2:5; Heb. 8:6; 12:24

Since proponents of the "one substance" doctrine have never been able to explain how God can be his own son, stand beside himself, or why he would pray to himself, they must describe it as a mystery. A mysterious God is not the God Christ taught us we should come to "know" (John 17:3; see also James E. Talmage, *Articles of Faith,* chapter 2).

36. Do God and Christ resemble each other?

The Savior's teaching in John 14:7-9, that "he that hath seen me hath seen the Father," is often misinterpreted to mean that Jesus is the Father. The teachings of modern apostles as well as those of the primitive church teach that Jesus Christ was similar in appearance to God the Father. James E. Talmage stated that the Lord, when importuned by Philip to show him the Father, was teaching the apostles that "even in bodily appearance the Father and the Son are alike" (*Articles of Faith,* p. 41). "The scriptures . . . reveal the personality, powers, and perfections of the Son of God who is in the express image and likeness of the Father. The mere fact of knowing the Son and those things which unto him do appertain is of itself sufficient to reveal and identify the Father, because they are like each other in personality and appearance and in character, perfections, and attributes. Hence, the saying of Jesus, 'He that hath seen me hath seen the Father' (John 14:9)" (*Promised Messiah,* p. 475).

That the Father and Son resemble each other is confirmed in four separate epistles of Paul. In two of these (2 Cor. 4:4 and Col. 1:15), he taught that Christ was the "image of God" He used the Greek word "eikon" which means likeness, statue, profile, or representation. It is from this word that our modem English word "icon" comes. In Philippians 2:6, Paul described Christ as "being in the form of God." In this case Paul used the Greek word "morphe" meaning shape, nature, or form. Last of all, Paul described Christ as "the express image of his [God's] person" (Heb. 1:3). This reference used the Greek word "charakter" which means exact copy or reproduction. The New International Version of the Bible translates the Greek word "charakter" as "exact representation of his being." In each case, the word carries not only the connotation of an image or copy but of a duplicate or twin. This could in fact be the case since Christ was the "only begotten Son" of the Father (John 1:14, 18; 3:16, 18; Heb. 5:5; 1 John 4:9; 5:1, 18; Moses 2:26-27) in the flesh (John 1:14; 1 Tim. 3:16; 1 Peter 3:18; 4:1; 1 John 4:2; 2 John 7).

Some may argue our interpretation of these verses, but the words of the apostles are clear—Christ and his Father are alike in character, personality and bodily appearance. To know one is to know the other and to see one is to see the other. (See also Michael T. Griffith, *Signs of the True Church of Christ,* pp. 17-18; Bruce R. McConkie, *The Mortal Messiah,* 4:71).

37. Are God and Christ identical in knowledge?

There are some who hold that because Jesus was God prior to coming to the earth, he had to have had all knowledge, even in mortality. If this were true, he could not have "increased in wisdom" as Luke 2:52 states, nor could he have "learned obedience" as Paul taught in Hebrews 5:8. If he had all knowledge from birth, he also could not have been "tempted . . . as we are" (Heb. 4: 15). It seems clear that in order for the mortal Messiah to be truly tried and tempted, he had to live, as we do, by faith. As Moroni taught, those who have a sure knowledge have "faith no longer, for [they know], nothing doubting" (Ether 3:19).

Christ came to this earth, as all men, with no remembrance of the preexistence. He "increased . . . in favor with God" (Luke 2:52) by developing faith, and "increased in wisdom" through communion with his Father (Matt. 11: 27). It is reasonable to assume that he learned line upon line and precept upon precept as we do and therefore "increased" in knowledge throughout his life (see also Luke 13:32; 18:19).

That all knowledge was not revealed to him, even in the last days of his life, is indicated by Christ's words on the Mount of Olives. Both Matthew and Mark record that Jesus taught that only the Father knew the exact time of the Second Coming (Matt. 24:36; Mark 13:32). Additionally, Mark adds the phrase "neither the Son," indicating that Jesus himself did not have this knowledge, though this phrase was deleted in Joseph Smith's translation of Mark 13:32 (See James E. Talmage, *Jesus the Christ,* p. 575, note j, p. 589 note 3). Christ's prayer, in which he confessed "not as I will, but as thou wilt" (Matt. 26:39; Mark 14:36; Luke 22:42; see also John 5:30) also indicates that Christ's desires at that time were not necessarily those of his Father, but that he desired to set aside his will to do the will of the Father.

Though Jesus was apparently lacking in knowledge in certain areas while yet in mortality, it should be clear that this constraint was of a temporary nature. He now knows all things, including the exact time of his return (Rev. 22:7, 12, 20; D&C 33:18; 49:28; 51:20; 87:8). That his knowledge was less than that of his Father's during his mortal sojourn on earth is added proof that God and Christ are separate and distinct personages.

38. Is God a spirit?

It is widely believed by other Christians that God is a spirit essence without shape or form that fills the immensity of space and is everywhere present. This doctrine, which has very little scriptural support, was devised by councils in the early days of apostasy following the death of the apostles and prophets. Most Protestant scholars today refuse to base any doctrine on only one scripture, but this is apparently what most of Christianity has done. One passage of the Gospel of John in the King James Bible is cited in support of this doctrine. It states "God is a Spirit: and they that worship him must worship him in spirit and in truth" (John 4:24). The fact is that this verse has been mistranslated. This passage should read: "The hour cometh, and now is, when the true worshipper shall worship the Father in spirit and in truth; for the Father seeketh such to worship him. For unto such hath God promised his Spirit. And they who worship him, must worship in spirit and in truth" (JST John 4:24-26).

Eugene Seaich has pointed out that:

> The original Greek says only that "God is spirit" (pneume ho theos), i.e. spiritual in nature, the noun being anarthrous (without the definite article). As Raymond E. Brown—undoubtedly the world's leading scholarly authority on John's Gospel—explains, "This is not an essential definition of God, but a description of God's dealings with men, it means that God is spirit toward men because he gives the spirit (xiv. 16) which begets them anew" (*Anchor Bible,* John, p. 172). There are in fact two other such descriptions in John's writing, "God is light" (1 John 1:5), and "God is love" (1 John 4:8), though no one has argued that God is a light, or a species of love! In short, one must worship the Father through the Spirit which he has given to the Church (John 14:16), there being no hint of suggestion that he is himself "a spirit" (Eugene Seaich, *Ancient Texts and Mormonism,* p. 26).

The Greek word "pneuma" which is translated as spirit in John 4:24 also means "life" or "breath." The King James Version of Revelation 13:15, for example, renders the word "pneuma" as life. Thus "God is life" or "God is the breath of life" are alternative translations of this verse. John 6:63 also uses the Greek word "pneuma": "the words that I speak unto you, they are [pneuma]" Although most versions render this as "spirit," the following phrase "and they are life" clarifies the meaning as does the context (see John 4:10, 14; 6:35, 40, 47-48, 51). Words are not "spirit" in the sense we normally think of spirit, but are a spiritual source of eternal life when believed. In the same way, God is not "a spirit" but a spiritual source of eternal life to those who worship him in spirit and truth. To believe otherwise is to believe the absurd notion that we must in some way leave our bodies to worship him since "they that worship him must worship him in spirit" (John 4:24).

Some have also cited Alma 22:9-10 as proof that God is a spirit, but as with John 4:24 the context does not justify this meaning. These verses speak of God as the "Great Spirit," which was apparently a title for

God among the Lamanites. Aaron, who knew that a lesson on the nature of God could come later, was merely using a term for deity that the king of the Lamanites was familiar with. Joseph Smith also used the title "Great Spirit" as a title for God when teaching the American Indians (*History of the Church,* 5:480). Both Joseph Smith and Aaron used the same teaching technique used by Paul on Mars Hill (Acts 17:22-28) to teach the gospel to men unfamiliar with the true God. Note that Aaron also teaches, as Paul, that we were created in God's image (Alma 22:12; Acts 17:28-29) and that Christ was God's Son (Alma 21:7; Acts 17:31).

Although there is a sense in which God may be said to be a Spirit (Bruce R. McConkie, *Mormon Doctrine,* p. 319, and *Doctrines of the Restoration,* p. 31), man must also be considered a spirit in the same sense (Job 32:8; Eccl. 12:7; 1 Cor. 6:17; Philemon 25; D&C 93:33). Spirits are not an immaterial vaporous essence that fills the immensity of space, but personages with form like our tangible bodies (see 1 Nephi 11:11; Ether 3:16; D&C 77:2; *LDS Bible Dictionary,* p. 776).

Latter-day Saints believe that the real essence of man is his spirit, and although it might be proper to say that man is a spirit, it would be more correct to say man is a soul since the spirit and body together are the "soul of man" (D&C 88:15). Although we often think of the mortal body as the tangible substance and the spirit as the intangible being within the body, the spirit is substance also. Our spirit bodies are made of a more refined substance that cannot be handled or felt in the physical realm (D&C 129:1-7; 131:7-8).

Jesus taught the apostles after the resurrection that they could verify that he was both spirit and body "for a spirit hath not flesh and bones" as he had. By touching the wounds in his hands and feet, they confirmed that he was not only the spirit of the crucified Lord but a bodily resur-rected being with "flesh and bones" (Luke 24:36-39; John 20:27). We believe as Paul taught that a resurrected being rises a "spiritual body" (1 Cor. 15:44; D&C 88:27) having both a spirit and body "restored to their proper and perfect frame" (Alma 40:23). When we realize that Jesus did only that which he had seen his Father do (John 5:19; *Teachings,* p. 312), it is reasonable to conclude that the Father also has a glorified body of flesh and bones.

Modern revelation provides a final clear witness that God has a glo-rified and immortal body in which is housed his spirit. Joseph Smith instructed us that, "The Father has a body of flesh and bones as tangible as man's; the Son also; but the Holy Ghost has not a body of flesh and bones, but is a personage of Spirit. Were it not so, the Holy Ghost could not dwell in us" (D&C 130:22). This knowledge is called the greatest truth of eternity by Bruce R. McConkie (*Doctrines of the Restoration,* p.

48), for it confirms that we are truly created in the image of God and are his spirit offspring (Acts 17:28-29). As such we have the potential to become like him (1 John 3:2) in the eternities and thereby gain eternal life (John 17:3; 1 John 5:20; see also *Doctrines of the Restoration,* pp.31, 34).

39. Can God or Christ dwell in our hearts?

Some believe that God and Christ are omnipresent and can therefore dwell in all believers everywhere simultaneously. They cite 2 Corinthians 13:5; Galatians 2:20; Ephesians 3:16-17; and Colossians 1:27 as biblical proof-texts. Joseph Smith taught that "the idea that the Father and the Son dwell in man's heart is an old sectarian notion, and is false" (D&C 130:3). The Bible verses cited above do speak of Christ dwelling "in" us, but as discussed earlier (p. 79), many Bible verses also speak of believers being "in Christ" and God the Father. Thus we can be "in them" as they can be "in us", but this does not enable us to dwell in God the Father's or Christ's heart. According to John 17:21, Jesus prayed, "That they all may be one; as thou, Father, art in me, and I in thee, that they also may be one in us."

The Bible verses 1 John 3:24 and 4:13, 15 help us understand these expressions of indwelling. John explains that "he that keepeth his commandments dwelleth in him, and he [Jesus Christ] . . . abideth in us, by the Spirit which he hath given us" (1 John 3:24). "Hereby know we that we dwell in him, and he in us, because he hath given us of his Spirit" (1 John 4: 13; see Rom. 5 :5). John further clarifies the meaning in 1 John 1 :3 when he refers to the "fellowship" of believers with "the Father, and with his Son Jesus Christ." As stated earlier, this fellowship occurs by the Spirit, also called the Holy Ghost.

Paul also taught that it is "by his Spirit in the inner man; that Christ may dwell in your hearts by faith" (Eph. 3:16-17).

Joseph Smith confirmed this concept in D&C 130:22. It states that "the Holy Ghost . . . is a personage of Spirit. Were it not so, the Holy Ghost could not dwell in us."

40. Is God omniscient, omnipotent, and omnipresent?

These terms are seldom used by members of the LDS Church, and only the word omnipotent appears in scripture (see Rev. 19:6; Mosiah 3:5, 17-18, 21; 5:2, 15); however, all three are commonly used in Catholic and Protestant creeds and theology.

Although the *Lectures on Faith* speaks of God the Eternal Father as "omnipotent, omnipresent and omniscient" (*Lectures on Faith,* p. 9), it is evident from D&C 130:22 that God's omnipresence is achieved through the Holy Ghost.

The Prophet Brigham Young taught the following:

> He is our Heavenly Father; he is also our God, and the Maker and upholder of all things in heaven and on earth. He sends forth his counsels and extends his providences to all living. He is the Supreme Controller of the universe. . . . he is everywhere present by the power of his Spirit—his minister, the Holy Ghost. He is the Father of all, is above all, through all, and in you all; he knoweth all things pertaining to this earth, and he knows all things pertaining to millions of earths like this (*Journal of Discourses*, 11:41; also quoted in John A. Widtsoe, *Discourses of Brigham Young*, p. 19; see also pp. 23-24).

James E. Talmage affirmed God's omnipresence stating, "There is no part of creation, however remote, into which God cannot penetrate; through the medium of the Spirit the Godhead is in direct communication with all things at all times" (*Articles of Faith*, pp. 42-43). Brother Talmage also affirms God's omniscience and omnipotence along with other godly attributes (*Ibid.*, pp. 43-44).

The Bible implies that God the Father is not an omnipresent spirit when it teaches us that he dwells in heaven (a specific location). If God were everywhere present, there would be no need to go to heaven to be with him. Peter, for example, taught that "Jesus Christ . . . is gone into heaven, and is on the right hand of God" (1 Peter 3:21-22; see also John 7:33; 14:12, 28; 16:10, 16-17, 27-28, 30; Rev. 3:12; 20:9). In like manner, we are told that "the spirit [of man] shall return unto God who gave it (Eccl. 12:7). It is also significant that the New Testament always speaks of men being "filled" with the Holy Ghost (Luke 1:15, 41, 67; 4:1; Acts 2:1-4; 4:8; 6:3-5; 7:55; 11:24; 13:9, 52) and never "filled" with the Father or the Son.

As was mentioned in the response to the previous question, the Bible also affirms that God dwelleth in us "by the Spirit" (John 14:16; Rom. 8:9-11; 1 John 3:24; 4:13). It is thus, through the Spirit of truth, that we are guided "into all truth" (John 14:26; 16:13) and knowledge (Ex. 31:1-3; 1 Cor. 2:9-16; Eph. 1:17). The Holy Ghost is a witness (John 15:26; Rom. 8:16; 1 Cor. 12:3; Heb. 10:15), a comforter (John 14:16, 26; 15:26; 16:7), a revelator (Luke 12:12; John 14:26; 2 Peter 1:21), and a sanctifier (John 3:5; Rom. 15:16; 2 Thes. 2:13; Titus 3:5; Alma 13:12; 3 Nephi 27:20; Moses 6:65). It is also by the Holy Ghost that the "love of God is spread abroad in our hearts" (Rom. 5:5; Gal. 5:22) and we are enabled to dwell in God (1 John 3:24; 4:12-13). Therefore it is principally by the Holy Ghost that the Godhead communicates and blesses man, and it is through the omnipresence of that Spirit that they dwell in us (Ps. 51:11;

139:7-13; Rom. 8:9; 1 John 3:24; 4:1213; see chapter 9 of this text for additional information on the Holy Ghost).

41. Doesn't a belief that God has a physical body like man's make him a finite God?

Most modern scholars admit that the biblical conception of God presupposes his human form—or more correctly stated, man's divine form. Eugene Seaich has observed that:

> In the Old Testament, the Israelites likewise "conceived even Jahweh himself as having human form" (Gerhard von Rad, *Theology of the Old Testament*, I:145). For this reason, "a doctrine of God as spirit in the philosophical sense will be sought in vain in the pages of the Old Testament." In fact, "an unprejudiced evaluation of the Old Testament's humanizing of deity leads us to see . . . that in fact it is not the spiritual nature of God which is the foundation of the Old Testament faith. It is his personhood—a personhood which is fully alive, and a life which is fully personal (Walter Eichrodt, *Theology of the Old Testament*, Philadelphia, 1961, 1:212).
>
> But even in the Old Testament it would be incorrect to say that God has a human form, "for according to the ideas of Jahwism, it cannot be said that Israel regarded God anthropomorphically, but the reverse, that she considered man as theomorphic" (*Ibid.*, I:144). In other words, man was created in God's image (Gen. 1:26), not the other way around.
>
> The reason for this is obvious. "God took the pattern for this, his last work of creation, from the heavenly world above. In no other work of creation is everything referred so very immediately to God himself" (*Ibid.*). Man, in short, possesses the same divine image that Christ possessed, for which reason the author of Hebrews could say, "Both he that sanctifieth and they that are sanctified are of one origin" (ex henos, masc., 2:11; see Kasemann, op. cit., p. 90") (*Ancient Texts and Mormonism*, pp. 26-27).

Those who believe God is an "immaterial being" have a difficult time explaining in what way we, as men, are made in the "similitude of God" the Father (James 3:9) if it is not in a physical sense. Man's basic nature, as scripture says, is sinful (1 John 1:8; Mosiah 3:19) and nothing like God's (Heb. 4:15). Our thoughts are not his thoughts and our ways are not his ways (Isa. 55:8-9). Notwithstanding, Genesis teaches clearly that man was created in both the image and likeness of God (Gen. 1:26-27). A few chapters later, we are told that Adam's son, Seth, resembled Adam in like manner, using the identical Hebrew words translated in the King James Version as: "in his own likeness" and "after his own image" (Gen. 5:3). Thus it is clear that we must resemble God and his Son just as mortal sons physically resemble their fathers. Paul applied the same literal meaning to these words by explaining that as man "is the image and glory of God," so "the woman is the glory of the man" (1 Cor. 11:7).

The Old Testament describes Jacob's encounters with God, stating that he did see "God face to face" (Gen. 32:30) and that God spoke to Moses "face to face, as a man speaketh unto his friend" (Ex. 33:11). We are also told that "Enoch walked with God" (Gen. 5:22-24). How could this possibly be, unless God had a bodily shape like that of man?

The New Testament also confirms that Christ is in the "image of God" (2 Cor. 4:4; Col. 1:15; Heb. 1:3) and the "form of God" (Phil. 2:6). It further tells us that in the resurrection our vile bodies will be made like Christ's "glorious body" (Phil 3:21) so that when he returns, "we shall be like him" (1 John 3:2) and "see his face" (Rev. 22:4). If we were created in the similitude of both God and Christ, and Christ is in image and form like his Father, then God the Father and his Son must have corporeal bodies like ourselves.

The Church of England teaches that "there is but one living and true God, everlasting, without body, parts, or passions; of infinite power, wisdom, and goodness" (*Book of Common Prayer,* Articles of Religion, Article 1-Of Faith in the Holy Trinity, p. 685). This immaterial God is at variance with scripture since the original God of the Bible is described as having body, parts, and passions:

1. Body—Ex. 24:10-11; 33:23; Num. 12:5; Jud. 13:22; 1 Kings 11:9; Isa. 6:5; Matt. 5:8; John 5:37; Acts 7:55-56; and other scriptures cited above and on p. 82, paragraph 6 this text.

2. Parts—Gen. 8:21; Ex. 24:10-11; 31:18; 33:23; Num. 12:8; Deut. 9:10; 34:10; Job 19:25; Ps. 94:7-11; Matt. 4:4; Rev. 19:12; 22:4

3. Passions—Ex. 20:5-6; 34:6-7, 14; Deut. 4:24, 31; 6:15; 7:8-9; 10:15, 18; Josh. 24:19; Jud. 2:14; 3:8; 1 Kings 22:53; 2 Kings 13:3; Neh. 9:17; Ps. 69:16; 116:5; Isa. 30:27; Jer. 4:8; 7:19-20; 44:4-6; Hosea 11:1; Zech. 8:17; John 16:27; Rom. 1:18; James 5:11; 1 John 3:1; Rev. 15:1

Furthermore, it is inaccurate to claim that members of the LDS Church believe in a God with a physical body like man's. James E. Talmage has affirmed that God, unlike man, is "of infinite power; His mind of unlimited capacity; his powers of transferring Himself from place to place are infinite; plainly, however, His person cannot be in more than one place at any one time. Admitting the personality of God, we are compelled to accept the fact of his materiality; indeed, an immaterial being under which meaningless name some have sought to designate the condition of God, cannot exist, for the very expression is a contradiction in terms" (James E. Talmage, *Articles of Faith,* p. 43).

Bruce R. McConkie, after reviewing several personal appearances of the resurrected Christ (Luke 24:18-25, 37-43; John 20:15-17, 25-27; 21:5-7; Acts 1:11 and others), pointed out:

From this brief review we learn several important things: we know that resurrected beings, containing their glory within themselves, can walk as mortals do on earth; that they can converse and reason and teach as they once did in mortality; that they can both withhold and manifest their true identities; that they can pass with corporeal bodies through solid walls; that they have bodies of flesh and bones which can be felt and handled; that if need be (and at special times) they can retain the scars and wounds of the flesh; that they can eat and digest food; that they can vanish from mortal eyes and transport themselves by means unknown to us (*Doctrines of the Restoration,* pp. 123-24).

Christ was God even before the creation of the world (John 1:1-3, 14; 1 Cor. 10:1-4; Heb. 1:1-3; Isa. 9:6) and he followed in the footsteps of the Father (John 5:19-20; Phil. 2:5-6) to become exalted (Phil. 2:9-11; Rev. 3:21). If we further realize that Jesus Christ, being God, now has a body of flesh and bones in appearance as man's (Luke 24:15-16, 30-31, 36-39, John 20:27) and yet can pass through walls (John 20:19) and influence mankind through his power (Phil. 1:19; Moroni 7:16), it should not be difficult to realize that God the Father likewise is an exalted Man of Holiness (Moses 6:57; see also John 3:13). Christ has become like him (Rom. 8:29; 2 Cor. 4:4; Phil. 2:6; Col. 1:15; Heb. 1:3) in both appearance and physical attributes (John 14:9; D&C 130:22). As such, Christ chose in mortality to call himself the "Son of man which is in heaven" (John 3:13) or simply "Son of man" (see *LDS Topical Guide,* p. 256).

Two scriptures are generally cited by critics to show that God is not a man. Numbers 23:19 informs us that "God is not a man, that he should lie; neither the son of man, that he should repent." Nevertheless Jesus called himself Son of man (Matt. 8:20) and yet was himself God (John 1:1-3; Heb. 1:8-9). First Samuel 15:29 informs us: "And also the Strength of Israel will not lie nor repent: for he is not a man, that he should repent" (note that 1 Sam 15:11 contradicts this verse in part). God and Jesus Christ are perfect and, as such, are not *as man* that they will lie or need to repent. The Bible clearly teaches that Jesus Christ was the God of the Old Testament (John 1:1-3, 14, etc.) and that Jesus Christ was a man, even after his resurrection (1 Tim. 2:5; 1 Cor. 15:21-22, 47; Phil. 2:8). Thus, the above-mentioned scriptures are saying that God is not weak like "corruptible man" (Rom. 1:23) and therefore not susceptible to sin (Matt. 5:48; 1 Peter 2:22).

Though much of Christendom is as Thomas and will not believe that God has a glorified and exalted body of flesh and bone (D&C 130:22) unless they are shown, we may be sure of this fact. Blessed are they that have not seen, and yet have believed, for they truly know God and his Son (John 17:3; Eph. 4:13; see also *Teachings,* p. 181).

42. How do you explain the fact that
Isaiah 9:6 calls Christ the Father?

Some believers in the three-in-one concept of trinitarian theology have pointed to Isaiah 9:6 as a proof-text for their belief that Jesus is the "everlasting Father." A doctrinal exposition issued by the First Presidency and the Quorum of the Twelve explains several ways in which Jesus is the "Father."

The first way Christ is the "Father" is that he is the Creator. This is shown in the Book of Mormon where the meaning of the title "Father" is clarified. Mosiah 3:8 states, for example, that "he shall be called Jesus Christ, the Son of God, *the Father of heaven and earth, the Creator of all things from the beginning;* and his mother shall be called Mary" (see also Mosiah 15:4; 16:15; Alma 11:38-39; Ether 4:7).

In a second meaning of the term, Christ is also referred to as the Father of all those who are born again (Eph. 1:3-5; Mosiah 5:7; 27:24-29; Ether 3:14; see also John 8:41; 17:6-12, 20-21; 1 Cor. 4:15; Rev. 21:7; D&C 25:1; 34:3; 76:24, 59; 121:7).

Third, Christ represents the Father by divine investiture of authority (John 5:43; 10:25). The authority to speak and act in behalf of His Heavenly Father has been conveyed to Jesus. As Bruce R. McConkie states in *Mormon Doctrine:* "Since he is one with the Father in all of the attributes of perfection, and since he exercises the power and authority of the Father . . . the Father puts his own name on the Son and authorizes him to speak in the first person as though he were the Father" (Bruce R. McConkie, *Mormon Doctrine,* pp. 130-131). The scriptures include numerous examples of divine investiture, where others speak in behalf of others. The clearest biblical examples involve angels speaking in behalf of God or Christ (Gen. 22:11-12; Ex. 3:2, 6; 23:20-21; Acts 7:30-33, 38; Rev. 1:1; 19:9-13; 22:8-16), though Christ also spoke "as though he were the Father" on many occasions throughout the Old Testament (Gen. 17:1; 35:11; Ex. 6:3). Christ was also referred to as the Almighty (Rev. 1:8, 18; 4:8; 11:17, pp. 101-02 of this text). It is for this reason that many today mistakenly identify Jehovah and Eloheim as the same person. (For a detailed explanation see p. 104 of this text). The concept of Christ as the Father is clearly set forth in a statement entitled, "The Father and the Son: A Doctrinal Exposition by the First Presidency and the Twelve" dated June 30, 1916. This exposition is cited in full in James E. Talmage's *Articles of Faith,* pages 465-73, and in Joseph Fielding Smith's *Man: His Origin and Destiny,* pages 117-29. See also Joseph Fielding Smith, *Answers to Gospel Questions,* 4:176-80; *Messages of the First Presidency,* 5:26-34).

43. Why do Latter-day Saints teach that God is the Father of our spirits?

Christ consistently referred to God the Eternal Father as not only his own Father but also as our Father (Matt. 5:45, 48; 6:1, 4, 6, 8, etc.). He taught all men to approach God in prayer by saying "Our Father which art in heaven" (Matt. 6:9). After the resurrection he told Mary Magdalene: "I ascend unto my Father, and your Father; and to my God, and your God" (John 20:17). These verses and modern revelation (Moses 3:5-7; Abr. 3:22; D&C 76:24; *Journal of Discourses,* 1:50; 4:27, 216, 218; *Discourses of Brigham Young,* pp. 24; 50-51) affirm that the title Father is to be understood literally. The scriptures teach that there is a Being who is the Father of the spirits of all men (Num. 16:22; 27:16; Deut. 14:1; Ps. 82:6; Eccl. 12:7; Hosea 1:10). He is more commonly called our Heavenly Father (Matt. 6:6, 9, 14, 26, 32; 7:11; 15:13; 18:35; Luke 11:13). The apostle Paul taught that all men, Christian and non-Christian alike, are the "offspring of God" (Acts 17:22-24, 28-29). He further informs us that God is the "Father of all" and the "Father of spirits" (Eph. 4:6; Heb. 12:9).

It is important to differentiate between the "Father of Spirits" (God the Father) and the God whose sons and daughters we may become (Jesus Christ). Those who accept the Gospel and are spiritually born again on earth become sons and daughters of God the Son (Jesus Christ) (John 1:12; 2 Cor. 5:17; Eph. 2: 8-10; 1 John 2:25-29; 3:2, 9-10; *LDS Topical Guide,* p. 306). In the first instance, God the Father is the father of the spirits of all mankind. All of us were born as his spirit offspring in the premortal life. In the second instance, God the Son (Jesus Christ) is the regenerative Father of those that truly believe in him and in his gospel (John 1:12-13). A spiritual rebirth occurs when the Holy Spirit transforms us and our hearts are changed so that we have "no more disposition to do evil" (Mosiah 5:2, 7; see also Rom. 12:2; Alma 5:14; 19:33). God commands us to become like him (Matt. 5:48; Luke 13:24; Rom. 2:10) so that we may be spiritually born again unto eternal life (Rom. 2:6-7, 6:4, 23) and thus become his sons and daughters eternally (Rom. 8:14-17; Gal. 3:26). They are those whom God the Father has given to his Son Jesus (John 3:35; 6:37; 10:27-29; 17:2, 24-25). When we are born again of the spirit of the Holy Ghost, we are born into the kingdom of heaven (John 3:5; Moses 6:59, 65; see also *Articles of Faith,* p. 466).

44. Is Jesus our spirit brother?

God our Father is called by Moses the "God of the spirits of all flesh" (Num. 16:22; 27:16) and by Paul "the Father of spirits" (Heb. 12:9). As such, he is the Father of the spirits of all men including Jesus Christ. Though Christ is our spiritual brother, he holds a preeminent position as the "first begotten" (Heb. 1:6) among all pre-existent spirits. For this reason he is also called the "firstborn among many brethren" (Rom. 8:29) and the "firstborn of every creature" (Col. 1:15; see also D&C 93:21-23). Though it may be argued that Christ was the "firstfruits" of the resurrection (1 Cor. 15:20-23; Col. 1:18) and therefore was "firstborn" in that sense, other scriptures relate this preeminence to the pre-existence of Christ and man (Ps. 89:27; Rom. 8:29; Heb. 1:2-6). Significantly, Revelation 3:14 affirms that Jesus Christ was "Amen, the faithful and true witness, the beginning of the creation of God" He was the first of all the spirit progeny of our Father in heaven and thus our elder brother. When men follow him and become one with him "he is not ashamed to call them brethren" (Heb. 2:11).

President Joseph Fielding Smith has stated that "We accept Jesus Christ as God—the Only Begotten Son of the Father in the flesh, and the first begotten in the Spirit. Therefore he is our eldest brother, for we also are the offspring of God" (*Answers to Gospel Questions,* 2:127-28).

Our critics often ask how Lucifer can be the spirit brother of Jesus when their characters are diametrically opposite. We must first understand that Lucifer (meaning "lightbringer") was in the beginning a "son of the morning" (Isa. 14:12-14) and was perfect in all his ways from the day of his creation till iniquity was found in him (Ezek. 28:15). Thereafter, he aspired to exalt himself and become "like the most High" (Isa. 14:13-14). Lucifer's lust for power led to his downfall. Because of his rebellion against God he was cast out and "became Satan" (Moses 4:3-4; Luke 10:18; Rev. 12:79).

This concept was understood even centuries after the apostasy had started, although in a degraded form. Origen (ca. 240 AD) taught that "Before the aeons existed, all spirits were pure; demons, souls and angels alike, all served God and did what he commanded them. The devil was one of them. He had free-will and wanted to set himself up against God, but God cast him down. The biggest sinners became demons, lesser ones angels, the least archangels" (De Princ. 1, 8, 1 as quoted in Jean Danielou, *Origen,* p. 214).

We should note that Lucifer was not created as an evil being but became Satan by his own choice. It may seem ironic that Satan could be evil when Christ his brother was righteous, but we should remember that he was one among many who were spirit brothers. That some had a spirit of rebellion should come as no surprise (Isaiah 14:12-15 and Revelation 12:7-9). We also find similar opposites among men of the scriptures (Cain and Abel, Gen. 4; Jacob and Esau, Gen. 25:29-34; 27:41-42; Joseph and his brothers, Gen. 37:17-28). We should also note that even among the apostles chosen by Christ was found Judas Iscariot; a man who must have been, at least initially, worthy of that calling. (See also Peterson and Ricks, *Offenders for a Word,* pp. 149-51; Michael T. Griffith, *Signs of the True Church of Christ,* pp. 37-41 and *A Sure Foundation,* p. 223).

45. Was Jesus begotten of the Father or of the Holy Ghost, and by what means?

Members of the LDS Church may be surprised to learn that many Christians teach that Christ was begotten of the Holy Ghost. The Apostle's Creed, a doctrinal statement which is nearly universally accepted among Catholics and Protestants, states that "Jesus Christ . . . was conceived by the Holy Ghost" (Book of *Common Prayer,* p. 52; see also *Mormon Doctrine,* pp. 47-48, 535-37). The creed, sung in conjunction with the Holy Communion of the Church of England, says: "Jesus Christ . . . Begotten not made, was incarnate by the Holy Ghost of the Virgin Mary" (*Ibid.* pp. 291-92).

Although Matthew states that Mary was "found with child of the Holy Ghost" (1:18) and "that which is conceived in her is of the Holy Ghost" (1:20), Luke provides us a more detailed and clear account. While Matthew describes the visit of an unnamed angel to Joseph in only two verses, Luke takes ten verses to describe the visit of the angel Gabriel to Mary. The additional insight provided by Luke's account helps clarify Matthew's statement in this instance. He tells us initially that Jesus "shall be called the Son of the Highest" (1:32) and thereafter affirms Christ's divine sonship by informing us that the angel told Mary: "The Holy Ghost shall come upon thee, and the power of the Highest shall overshadow thee: therefore also that holy thing which shall be born of thee shall be called the Son of God" (1:35)—not of the Holy Ghost. Luke and other inspired writers clearly used the titles "highest" and "Majesty on high" to refer to God the Father (Luke 1:76; 6:35-36; Heb. 1:1-3; see also 1 John 3:1, 10; 5:2, 5, 10-12). They also unmistakably believed that Jesus Christ was the Son of God the Father (2 John 3; see also Ps. 2:7, John 20:17; Acts 13:33; Rom. 15:6; 2 Cor. 11:31; Eph. 1:3, 17; Col. 1:3,12-14; Heb. 1:5; 5:5; 1 Peter 1:3).

Three of the four Gospel accounts of the baptism of Jesus Christ also testify that Jesus Christ is Son of God the Father. Luke, for example, tells us that "the Holy Ghost descended in bodily shape like a dove upon him [Christ], and a voice came from heaven, which said, Thou art my beloved Son; in thee I am well pleased" (Luke 3:22). It is clear that the Holy Ghost was present at the baptism while God the Father spoke from heaven, declaring Jesus Christ to be his Son (see also Matt. 3:16-17; 28:19; Mark 1:10-11; John 12:26-30). It was not the Holy Ghost who spoke to Jesus from the heavens.

Irenaeus (ca. 190 AD) in his exposition "Against Heresies" confirmed "that the Holy Ghost came upon Mary, and the power of the Most High overshadowed her, and so what was born (of her) is holy and the Son of God Most High, the Father of all" (v. 3 as quoted in Cyril Richardson, *Early Christian Fathers,* p. 388).

The Book of Mormon also clearly identifies God the Father as Christ's Father. First Nephi 11:18-21 reads:

> Behold the virgin whom thou seest is the mother of the Son of God, after the manner of the flesh. And it came to pass that I beheld that she was carried away in the Spirit; and after she had been carried away in the Spirit for the space of a time the angel spake unto me saying: Look! And I looked and beheld the virgin again, bearing a child in her arms. And the angel said unto me: Behold the Lamb of God, yea, even the Son of the Eternal Father!

Alma testified that he knew "that Jesus Christ shall come, yea, the Son, the Only Begotten of the Father" (Alma 5:48). This statement is not unique to the Book of Mormon; New Testament authors, as well, used the phrase "only begotten of the Father" (John 1:14, 18; 3:16; 1 John 4:9). It is interesting to note that Isaac was similarly referred to as Abraham's "only begotten son" (Heb. 11:17; see also Gen. 22:2, 16; Jacob 4:5). The scriptural witness is clear: Jesus Christ is the literal Son of God the Father and Mary and of none else (Matt. 3:17; 16:16, 27; 17:5; 26:63-64; John 3:13-17; 5:18-20; 8:19; 20:17, 31; Heb. 1:1-3; 1 Peter 1:3; 1 John 1:3; 5:11; 2 John 3; Rev. 1:6; 1 Nephi 13:40; 2 Nephi 25:12; Alma 13:9; 3 Nephi 11:7; D&C 20:21; 93:11; Moses 1:6, 33; 2:1, 26-27; 5:7).

The second part of this question asks by what means Christ was conceived. Although this would seem a delicate subject to most of us, the writers of the gospels apparently felt it was very important. The previously cited verses from Matthew, for example, are quite explicit concerning Mary's conception. Matthew and Luke clearly believed that this information was proof of the fulfillment of prophecy (Isa. 7:14; Matt. 1:22-23) and crucial to the establishment of Christ's divinity (Isa. 9:6-7; Luke 1:35). Unfortunately, despite these scriptural accounts, Christians are highly divided on the facts concerning this event. In discussing this issue, some Christians often introduce misleading terms such as virgin birth and Immaculate Conception, which can cause further confusion and misunderstanding.

Although most of Christianity agrees that Jesus Christ was born of the Virgin Mary, there is ample disagreement as to what this actually means. Catholics, for example, believe that Mary remained a virgin after the birth of Christ and for the rest of her life, while Protestant scholars are largely divided on whether only the conception was miraculous or whether virginity was retained after both conception and birth.

LDS apostles and prophets affirm that Jesus was conceived of a virgin, but also make it clear that the actual birth of the Savior was "as natural as the births of our children" (Brigham Young, *Journal of Discourses,* 8:211; see also Joseph Fielding Smith Jr., *Religious Truths Defined,* p. 44; Bruce R. McConkie *Mormon Doctrine,* pp. 741-42, 822). Latter-day Saints, therefore, do not believe in a miraculous birth (i.e. delivery) nor that Mary remained a virgin throughout her life. Luke confirms this view, stating that Mary had to accomplish the required purification, following Mosaic law, after the opening of her womb at birth (Luke 2:22-23; see also Lev. 12:2-6). The fact that Mary later had other children is also made abundantly clear in Bible scripture (Matt. 1:25; 12:46; 13:55-56; Mark 6:3; Gal. 1:19).

The term "immaculate conception," mentioned earlier, is defined as the view that Mary was conceived in her own mother's womb without the stain of original sin. This false belief has no basis in scripture and is not accepted by the LDS Church (Bruce R. McConkie, *Mormon Doctrine,* p. 375). The "original sin" of Adam brought death into the world (1 Cor. 21-22) but it is our own sins that spiritually separate us from God. Jesus Christ atoned unconditionally for Adam's transgression (Rom. 5:11-18; Moses 6:54) and conditionally atoned for our personal sins (Heb. 5:9).

Enemies of the Church have, through the years, made attempts to portray LDS doctrine on this subject as radically anti-Christian. Some, for example, have tried to use the above cited words of our apostles and prophets and others to show that Mormons believe that God had "sexual intercourse with the virgin Mary." Quotes from Bruce R. McConkie's Mormon Doctrine on the topic "Son of God" (pp. 741-42) and others by Brigham Young (*Journal of Discourses;* 1:51) and Joseph Fielding Smith (*Doctrines of Salvation,* 1:18) are misconstrued to convey this false concept. These quotes, when read in context, simply emphasize the fact that Christ was both the spiritual and physical Son of God and that Christ's *birth* (not conception) was as normal as any other child's.

None of the above sources state that God had "sexual relations with Mary" as some critics contend, seeking to extract "shock value" from their statements. Indeed, even LDS scripture affirms our belief in a virgin conception (1 Nephi 11:13-21). While we do believe that Christ is the "only begotten Son" of God in the flesh (Ezra Taft Benson, *Come Unto Christ,* pp. 2-4, 128), the author is unaware of any speculation by LDS leaders as to how this was accomplished. In this day of test-tube babies and artificial insemination, various possibilities as to how the Virgin Mary conceived can be considered. The scriptures give a specific explanation on this matter, and LDS doctrine does not go beyond the scriptures. On the other hand, Christ is clearly identified as the "Son" of God, and the importance of Christ's divine Sonship as the "only begotten" is found throughout our scriptures and other LDS writings (John 1:14, 18; 3:16, 18; Heb. 5:5; 1 John 4:9; 1 Nephi 11:18-21; Jacob 4:5, 11; Alma 12:33-34; 13:5; D&C 20:21; 29:42; 49:5; 76: 13, 23-25; Moses 1: 6, 33; 2: 1, 26-27; 3:18; 4:1; 5:9; *Jesus the Christ,* p. 81; *Mormon Doctrine,* p. 546-547; *Mortal Messiah,* 1: 313- 15).

The only satisfactory interpretation of Christ's Sonship is a physical one, since all men may be spiritually "begotten of God" by being born again (1 John 5:18; Mosiah 5:7). Christ alone is the only begotten Son of God in the flesh (John 1: 14). An understanding of this concept is critical, since those who are not unified in the faith and of the Son of God (Eph. 4:13) and who deny his divine Sonship will not be among those who overcome (1 John 5:5).

46. Do Latter-day Saints believe Christ was God prior to his birth into mortality?

The wording of this question is "loaded"—it has an entirely different meaning to Latter-day Saints than it has to many evangelicals. Those with a trinitarian viewpoint hear the question as meaning "was Christ God the Father prior to his birth into mortality?" Latter-day Saints understand it to mean "Did Jesus, the Son of God the Father, attain the status of Godhood in his premortal state—and thus become a god at that time?"

Though members of the Church have been accused of believing that Jesus Christ was not God prior to his birth, nothing could be further from the truth. We believe not only that Christ was God prior to his birth but that he was the God of the Old Testament (John 1:1-3; 1 Cor. 10:1-4; Joseph Fielding Smith, *Doctrines of Salvation,* 1: 27, 32). The author is amazed that those who criticize us in this area have so utterly failed to understand this important LDS doctrine. The clarity with which modern scripture sets forth this doctrine is unequalled in Bible scripture. Consider the following passages:

And it came to pass that the Lord spake unto them saying: Arise and come forth unto me, that ye may thrust your hands into my side, and also that ye may feel the prints of the nails in my hands and in my feet, that ye may know that I am the God of Israel, and the God of the whole earth, and have been slain for the sins of the world (3 Nephi 11:13-14).

Behold, I say unto you that the law is fulfilled that was given unto Moses. Behold, I'am he that gave the law, and I am he who covenanted with my people Israel; therefore, the law in me is fulfilled, for I have come to fulfill the law; therefore it hath an end (3 Nephi 15:4-5).

The veil was taken from our minds, and the eyes of our understanding were opened. We saw the Lord standing upon the breastwork of the pulpit, before us; and under his feet was a paved work of pure gold, in color like amber. His eyes were as a flame of fire; the hair of his head was white like the pure snow; his countenance shone above the brightness of the sun; and his voice was as the sound of the rushing of great waters, even the voice of Jehovah, saying: I am the first and the last; I am he who liveth, I am he who was slain; I am your advocate with the Father (D&C 110:1-4).

This same doctrine is found throughout LDS scripture and the writings of the prophets (1 Nephi 19:7, 10, 13-14; 2 Nephi 25:29; Mosiah 3:5, 8; 4:2; 7:27; Helaman 8:22-23; 3 Nephi 9:15, 19; Ether 3:14-18; D&C 29:1; 39:1; see also *Jesus the Christ,* pp. 32, 37-38; *Mormon Doctrine,* p. 392). Since this teaching is clearly found in the Book of Mormon, there can be no doubt that it is LDS doctrine; those who say we believe Christ was not God prior to his birth have been misled. It is interesting to note that although LDS scriptures revealed this doctrine over 160 years ago, some Protestant denominations seem to have just discovered this truth, while others still seem to be divided over the true identity of Jehovah.

47. Do Bible scriptures support the belief that Jesus Christ was Jehovah of the Old Testament?

That Jesus Christ was the Lord and Savior of the New Testament is understood by all Christianity. The fact that he was also Jehovah of the Old Testament is understood by a relative few. Indeed, Jehovah's Witnesses have completely misunderstood this truth. David H. Yarn, Jr., in his book entitled *The Gospel: God, Man, and Truth,* explained:

"Jehovah" is the anglicized form of the Hebrew name Yahweh or Jahveh. It means the Self-existent One or The Eternal. This name is essentially the same as that revealed to Moses when he was instructed to tell the children of Israel, "I Am hath sent me unto you." Identifying himself for Moses, the Lord declared his name to be "I Am That I AM" (Ex. 3:13-14). In effect the Lord was saying to Moses that he is without beginning of days or end of years, that he is identical with existence, that he did not come to be nor will he cease to be. The connotation is essentially the same as another of his names used in the scriptures, Alpha and Omega, the first and the last, or the beginning and the end. Similarly, his names mean I am he who really is, or I am he who eternally exists.

The name by which he is most frequently called in the Christian world is Jesus Christ, "Jesus" meaning Savior (Matt. 1:21), and "Christ" meaning Messiah (John 1:41). The words "Savior" and "Messiah" are sometimes used along with other sacred titles such as the Only Begotten Son, Son of God, Son of Man, Emmanuel, the Anointed One, Redeemer, the Holy One of Israel, Lamb of God, Lamb without spot and without blemish, and firstborn (*The Gospel: God, Man, and Truth,* p. 13; see also James E. Talmage, *Jesus the Christ,* pp. 35-41).

Although modern scripture makes it clear that Jehovah, the God of the Old Testament, was truly Jesus Christ (see previous question), biblical scripture also provides numerous witnesses to this doctrine when studied by the Spirit. If we compare the scriptural titles and characteristics attributed to both the Jehovah of the Old Testament and Jesus Christ of the New Testament it becomes plain that they are the same individual:

1. *Jehovah—Creator* (Gen. 1:1; 2 Kings 19:15; Neh. 9:6; Ps. 33:6; 90:2; Isa. 40:28; 41:20; 42:5; 43:15; 44:24; 45:12, 18; Jer. 51:15) *Jesus—Creator* (John 1:1-3, 10-14; 1 Cor. 8:6; Eph. 3:9; Col. 1:1516; Heb. 1:1-3, 10; Rev. 4:11; see also Mosiah 3:8; 3 Nephi 9:15)

2. *Jehovah—Savior or Salvation* (Deut. 32:15; Ps. 27:1; 62:2; 2 Samuel 22:3, 47; Isaiah 12:2; 43:3, 11; 45:15, 17, 21; 49:26; 60:16; 63:8; Hosea 13:4) *Jesus—Savior or Salvation* (Matt. 1:21; Luke 2: 11; John 4:42; Acts 4:10-12; 5:30-32; 13:23; Phil. 3:20; Titus 1:4; 2:13; 3:6; 1 John 4:14)

3. *Jehovah—Redeemer* (Job 19:25-26; Ps. 19:14; 78:35; Isa. 41:14; 43:14; 44:24; 47:4; 48:17; 49:7, 26; 54:5, 8; 59:20; 63:16; Jer. 50:34) *Jesus—Redeemer* (John 1:29; Rom. 3:24; Gal. 3:13; Eph. 1:5-7; Col. 1:14; Titus 2:14; Heb. 9:12; Rev. 5:9)

4. *Jehovah—Rock* (Deut. 32:4, 15,   18, 30-31; 1 Sam. 2:2; 2 Sam. 22:2-3, 32, 47; 23:3; Ps. 18:2, 31, 46; 28:1; 31:3; 42:9; 61:2, 7; 62:2; 71:3; 78:35; 89:26; 92:15; 94:22; 95:1; Isa. 8:13-14; 17:10) *Jesus—Rock* (1 Cor. 10:4; Rom. 9:32-33; I Peter 2:5-8; see also 1 Nephi 13:36; Helaman 5:12)

5. *Jehovah—Stone or Cornerstone* (Gen. 49:24; Ps. 118:22; Isa. 8: 13-14; 28: 16) *Jesus—Stone or Cornerstone* (Matt. 21:42; Mark 12:10; Luke 20:17; Acts 4:10-12; Rom. 9:32-33; Eph. 2:19-21; 1 Peter 2:4, 6-8; see also Jacob 4:15-17; D&C 50:44)

6. *Every knee to bow to Jehovah* (Isa. 45:23) *Every knee to bow to Christ* (Rom. 14:10-11; Phil. 2:9-11)

7. *Jehovah—Judge* (Gen. 15:14; 18:25; Deut. 32:36; 1 Chron. 16:33; Ps. 9:7-8; 50:6; 96:13; 98:9; 105:7; Isa. 3:13; 33:22) *Jesus—Judge* (John 5:22, 27; Acts 10:42; 1 Cor. 4:4; 2 Tim. 4:1, 8)

8. *Jehovah—I Am* (Ex. 3:14; 6:6-8; Deut. 32:39; Isa. 41:4; 43:10-13, 15, 25; 46:4; 48:12)
   Jesus—I Am (John 8:56-58 (see also Matt. 14:27; Mark 14:62; Luke 22:70; John 4:26; 6:20; 8:24; 13:19; 18:5-6; D&C 38:1; Mormon Doctrine, p. 340)

9. *Jehovah—First and Last, Beginning and End* (Isa. 41: 4; 44:6; 48: 12; see also D&C 110:1-4)
   Jesus—First and Last, Beginning and End (Col. 1:18-19; Rev. 1:8, 11, 17, 18; 2:8; 21:6; 22:12-13, 16; see also 3 Nephi 9:15-18; D&C 63:60)

10. *Jehovah—Holy One* (Ps. 16:10; 89:18; Isa. 29:23; 41:14, 20; 43:3, 14-15; 45:11; 49:7; 54:5; Ezek. 39:7; Hab. 1:12; see also *LDS Bible Dictionary,* p. 704)
    Jesus—Holy One (Mark 1:24; Luke 4:34; Acts 2:27; 3:13-15; 13:35-37; 1 John 2:20; Rev. 3:7; see also 1 Nephi 19:13-15; 2 Nephi 25:28-29; 30:2; Omni 1:26; *Mormon Doctrine,* p. 360)

11. *Jehovah—Our Father* (Ps. 89:26; Isa. 22:21; 63:16; 64:8; Mal. 2:10; see also Isa. 43:1-7)
    Jesus—Our Father (Isa. 9:6; Eph. 1:3-5; Rev. 21:6-7; see Ether 3:14)

12. *Jehovah—God* (Ps. 90:2; Isa. 40:3, 28; 43:10-12; 44:6-8; 45:21)
    Jesus—God (Isa. 9:6; John 1:1; 20:28; Titus 2:13; Heb. 1:8; Rev. 1:6; see also 1 Nephi 19:7-13, Helaman 8:22-23; 3 Nephi 11:14)

13. *Jehovah—Shepherd* (Gen. 49:24; Ps. 23:1; 80:1; 95:7; 100:3; Isa. 40:11; Ezek. 34:11-15; 37:24)
    Jesus—Shepherd (Matt. 25:31-33; John 10:11, 14, 16, 27; 21:15-17; Heb. 13:20; 1 Peter 2:25; 5:4; see also Alma 5:38; Mormon 5:17)

14. *Jehovah—Servant* (Isa. 42:1; 52:13; Zech. 3:8)
    Jesus—Servant (Matt. 12:18: Luke 22:27; John 5:19; Phil. 2:7)

15. *Jehovah—King* (Ps. 24:7-10; 48:1-2; 74:12; 95:3; 149:2; Isa. 6:5; 41:21; 43:15; 44:6; Jer. 10:10; Dan. 4:37; Zech. 9:9; 14:9, 16-17)
    Jesus—King (Matt. 2:1-2; 21:1-5; 27:11, 29, 37; John 1:49; 12:13; 1 Tim. 6:15; Rev. 1:5; 15:3; 17:14; 19:16; see also 2 Nephi 10:14; Alma 5:50; D&C 45:51-53)

16. *Jehovah—Lamb* (Isa. 53:7; Jer. 11:19)
    Jesus—Lamb (John 1:29, 36; 1 Peter 1:19; Rev. 5:6, 9-13; 7:14; 12:11; 13:8; 21:23; see also 1 Nephi 11:34-36; 12:6, 11; 13:40; D&C 76:85)

17. *Jehovah—Lord of Hosts* (Isa. 2:12; 5:7, 16; 48:2; 51:15; Jer. 31:35; Mal. 1:8, 11, 14; 4:1)
    Jesus—Lord of Hosts (Mal. 3:1; see also D&C 29:1, 9)

18. *Jehovah—A Well or Fountain of Living Water* (Isa. 58:11; Jer. 2:13; Zech. 14:8)

Jesus—A Well or Fountain of Living Water (John 4:10, 13-14; 7:38; 1 Cor. 10:4; Rev. 21:6)

19. *Jehovah—The Pierced One* (Zech. 12:8-10; 13:6)
    Jesus—The Pierced One (John 19:34-37; Rev. 1:7)

20. *Jehovah—The Almighty* (Gen. 17:1; 28:3; 49:25; Ex. 6:3; Num. 24:4; Job 11:7)
    Jesus—The Almighty (Rev. 1:8; 4:8; 11:17 (see also Helaman 10:11; D&C 84:118-119)

21. *Jehovah—The Purchaser* (Ex. 15:16; Ps. 74:2) *Jesus—The Purchaser* (Acts 20:28; Eph. 1:12-14)

22. *Jehovah—His Way Prepared* (Isa. 40:3 LORD from Yehovah in Hebrew)
    Jesus—His Way Prepared (Matt. 3:1, 3; Mark 1:3; Luke 1:17, 76; 3:4; John 1:21-23; 3:28)

23. *Jehovah—Come unto him* (Isa. 55:3) *Jesus—Come unto him* (Matt. 11:28; Mark 1:17; see also D&C 10:67)

24. *Jehovah—Look to him* (Isa. 45:22 (see also Num 21:7-9) *Jesus—Look to him* (Heb. 9:28; 12:2; see also Alma 33:19; Helaman 8:14-15; D&C 6:36)

25. *Jehovah—Victory over death and the grave* (Isa. 25:6-8; Ezek. 37:1213; Hosea 13:14)
    Jesus—Victory over death and the grave (1 Cor. 15:21-22, 26; 54-57; see also Mosiah 15:8-9; 16:7-8; Alma 22:14; Mormon 7:5)

26. *Jehovah—Love him and keep his commandments* (Ex. 20:6; Deut. 6:56; 7:9)
    Jesus—Love him and keep his commandments (John 14:15; 1 John 5:2-3; see also D&C 20:19)

27. *Jehovah—Not to be tempted* (Deut. 6:16; Ex. 17:2, 7) *Jesus Not to be tempted* (Matt. 4:1, 5-7; 1 Cor. 10:9)

28. *Jehovah—Light and Life* (Ps. 27:1; 36:9; (see also Job 33:4; Ps. 4:6; 43:3; 89:15; Isa. 2:5; 60:19)
    Jesus—Light and Life (John 1:4, 9; 8: 12; see also D&C 10:70; 93:9)

29. *Jehovah—Sun* (Ps. 84:11; Isa. 60:19; Mal. 4:2)
    Jesus—Sun (Luke 1:78-79; 2 Peter 1:19; Rev. 2:28; 7:16-17; 22:16; see also D&C 88:7)

30. *Jehovah—To come with fire* (Ps. 50:3; Isa. 29:6; 64: 1-2; 66: 15-16; Joel 1:15-19; Micah 1:3-4; Mal. 3:2-3)
    Jesus—To come with fire (Luke 12:49; 2 Thes. 1:7-8; 1 Peter 1:7; 2 Peter 3:12; see also D&C 97:26; 133:41)

31. *Jehovah—To come on his day with all the Saints* (Isa. 13:3-6; Joel 1:15; 2: 1, 11, 31; 3:11, 14; Amos 5:18-20; Zeph. 1:7, 14; Zech.

14:5) *Jesus—To come on his day with all his Saints* (Acts 2:20; 1 Cor.1:8; 2 Cor. 1:14; Phil. 1:6, 10; 1 Thes. 3:13; 5:2; 2 Thes. 2:2; 2 Peter 3:10-12)

32. *Jehovah—Stills the sea* (Ps. 89:8-9)
    Jesus—Stills the sea (Matt. 8:23-27; Mark 4:37-41)

33. *Jehovah—Husband of the church* (Isa. 54:5; Jer. 3:14; 31:32; Hosea 2: 19-20)
    Jesus—Husband of the church (Eph. 5:23-25; Rev. 19:7-9)

34. *Jehovah—Bridegroom* (Isa. 62:5; Jer. 2:2; Ezek. 16:8; Hos. 2:19)
    Jesus—Bridegroom (Matt. 9:14-15; 22:2-24; 25:1-13; Mark 2:19-20; Luke 5:34-35; John 3:29; 2 Cor. 11: 2; Rev. 19:7-9)

35. *Jehovah—King of Kings and Lord of Lords* (Deut. 10:17; Isa. 49:7; Jer. 10:7; Dan. 2:47; Zech. 14:9)
    Jesus—King of Kings and Lord of Lords (1 Tim. 6:14-15; Rev. 17:14; 19:13-16)

36. *Jehovah—Tread the winepress* (Isa. 63:1-9; Lam. 1:15)
    Jesus—Tread the winepress (Rev. 14:19; 19:15)

37. *Jehovah—Forgives sin* (Isa. 1:16, 18; 43:25; 44:22)
    Jesus—Forgives sin (Mark 2:7, 10; Acts 5:30-31)

38. *Jehovah—Sat at the Lord's right hand* (Ps. 110:1)
    Jesus—Sat at the Lord's right hand (Mark 12:35-37; Acts 7:55-56; Heb. 1:3)

39. *Jehovah—A visible God* (Gen. 32:30; Ex. 24:10-11; 33:11; Isa. 6:1,5; Ezek. 1:26-28)
    Jesus—A visible God (John 1:1, 18; Col. 1:15; Heb. 1:3; 11:24-27)

40. *Jehovah—Rewards according to works* (Deut. 15:10; Ps. 62:12; Jer. 50:29)
    Jesus—Rewards according to works (Matt. 16:27; 2 Cor. 5:10; Rev. 2:23, 26; 20:12)

41. *Jehovah—Faithful* (Deut. 7:9; Isa. 49:7; I Peter 4:19)
    Jesus—Faithful (2 Thes. 3:3; 1 John 1:9; Rev. 1:5; 3:14; 19:11-13)

42. *Jehovah—Righteous* (Ex. 9:27; 2 Chron. 12:6; Ezra 9:15; Ps. 11:7; 119:137; 129:4; 145:17; Jer. 12:1; Lam. 1:18; Dan. 9:14)
    Jesus—Righteous (2 Tim. 4:8; 1 John 2:1, 29; Rev. 16:5; 19:2)

For additional information see Bruce R. McConkie, *Promised Messiah,* chapter 10 and 20; A. Melvin McDonald, *Day of Defense,* pp. 10-11; *Signs of the True Church of Christ,* pp. 27-30; Thomas E. Uharriet, "Who is Jehovah?" (brochure).

In addition to Bible scripture, the earliest Christian writers affirmed that Jesus was Jehovah. Justin Martyr, Theophilus of Antioch, Irenaeus, Tertullian, Clement of Alexandria, Eusebius, and Origen all insisted "that it was the word (Jesus) who was revealed to man in the divine appearances of the Old Testament" (Mourett, *Histoire Generale de l'Eglise,* 1:316 as quoted in James L. Barker, *Apostasy from the Divine Church,* pp. 48, 83; see also Eusebius, *History of the Church,* 1:4:12-13; Justin, *Dialogue with Trypho,* 63, 4; Irenaeus, *Against Heresies,* 4, 7, 2 and 4).

48. Doesn't the Old Testament identify Jehovah and Eloheim as the same person?

It has been asserted by some that Eloheim, Jehovah, Adonai and other similar Old Testament Hebrew names for deity are simply different titles which emphasize different attributes of the "one true God." They often cite Old Testament scriptures such as Deuteronomy 6:4: "The LORD [Jehovah in Hebrew] our God [Eloheim] is one LORD [Jehovah]"; Deuteronomy 4:24: "the LORD [Jehovah] thy God [Eloheim]"; or Deuteronomy 4:35: "LORD [Jehovah] he is God [Eloheim]"as proof that these are different titles for the same God.

The confusion that can occur with divine names is further illustrated in the following scriptures: Exodus 34:23 combines the Hebrew words Adonai (Lord), Jehovah (LORD) and Eloheim (God) of Israel into one title which is translated "Lord God, the God of Israel" or "Lord Jehovah, God of Israel." The Hebrew version of Psalms 82:1 declares: "God [Eloheim] stands in the assembly of God [El]; he judges in the midst of the gods [Eloheim]". Psalms 110:1 reads: "The LORD [Jehovah] said unto my Lord [Adonai], Sit thou at my right hand, until I make thine enemies thy footstool" (Hebrews 1:1-3 indicates that God the Father said this to Jesus Christ; see also Matt. 22:44; Mark 12:36; Luke 20:42 and Jack N. Sparks, *The Apostolic Fathers,* pp. 38, 290).

In one instance, the word Eloheim is even translated as "angels" (Ps. 8:5). The Hebrew text states that Jehovah made the son of man "a little less than Eloheim" [KJV—angels]. Though most literal translations render Eloheim as "God" in this verse, there is justification for translating it as angels. Hebrews 2:7, quotes this verse, using the Greek word "aggelos" or angels in place of Eloheim. We also find that Eloheim is translated in four instances as "judges" (KJV Ex. 21:6; 22:8-9) though "God's representative" is probably the intended meaning. This nevertheless shows that divine names were used by inspired writers with different meanings.

Although "Eloheim" is understood and used in the restored Church of Jesus Christ as the name/title of God the Eternal Father and the name "Jehovah" is reserved for "His Only Begotten Son," Jesus Christ (James E. Talmage, *Jesus the Christ,* p. 38), we also recognize that the Hebrew word eloheim was used anciently as a generic word for god (*Teachings,* p. 371; Eugene Seaich, *Ancient Texts and Mormonism,* p. 20).

The title *Eloheim* emphasizes the strong, covenant-keeping qualities of God; the name *Jehovah,* the self-existent and eternal attributes; and *Adonai,* the characteristics of a sovereign lord. However, they have not always been applied to just one God. The following tables illustrate this point:

Hebrew Titles for Deity in the King James Old Testament

Hebrew words translated as God	Occurrences	Percentage
1. Eloheim (plural of Eloah)	2310	85
2. Jehovah (Yehovah or Yehovih)	160	6
3. El (pronounced ale)	115	4
4. Elah (Chaldean)	77	3
5. Eloah (singular poetic form)	45	1.7
6. Tsoor (also meaning rock)	2	<0.1
	2709	

Hebrew words for deity other than God (i.e. false gods)	Occurrences
1. Eloheim (Ex. 7:1; 22:20; Deut. 32:39; etc.)	242
2. El (Ex. 34:14; Deut. 32:12; Jud. 9:46; etc.)	15
3. Elah (Dan. 2:11; 3:28; 4:8; etc.)	15
4. Eloah (2 Chron. 32:15; Dan. 11:37-39)	4
	276

Hebrew words translated as LORD (Deity)	Occurrences	Percentage of Total Occurrences
1. Jehovah (translated as LORD)	6402	92.7
2. Adonai or Adonay	418	6.1
3. Yahh or Jah (short form of 1)	46	0.7
4. Adon (Short form of 2)	36	0.5
5. Mare (Chaldean—master)	2	—
	6904	

Hebrew words translated as lord (other than deity)	Occurrences
1. Adon (Gen. 18:12; 1 Sam. 1:26; Dan. 1:10; etc.)	170
2. Jehovah (Jud. 4:18; Ruth 2:13; 1 Samuel 26:15; etc.)	7
3. Adonai (1 Sam. 25:31; Ezra 10:3; Isa. 21:8; etc.)	5
4. Mare (Dan. 4:19, 24)	2

5. Yahh (Ps. 105:21)   1
6. Others   <u>38</u>
                                      223

(Source—*Strong's Exhaustive Concordance of the Bible*)

The use of the same name-titles in the preceding examples, for both true and false gods as well as for human leaders, demonstrates that these words were often used in a generic sense. Such usage could cause confusion, especially if the text were later modified. Eugene Seaich has thoroughly researched the confusion of titles for deity in *Ancient Texts and Mormonism* and has indicated that scholars have found that early Canaanite and Israelite theology recognized two separate and distinct sets of divine traits: one for a "Father of gods" and "Father of men" and the other for a son of the former who was a "dying-and-resurrecting god, who gave life to all creatures" and "managed the cosmos for his Father."

Brother Seaich explains that the High God was called "El and his son was called Ba'al at least through the time of the Israelite monarchy." The Israelites who returned from the desert with the Mosaic religion, referred to El's son as Yahweh. Some evidence of this distinction still survives in our Old Testament scriptures (see Deut. 32:8-9; Ps. 82; Prov. 30:4).

He also notes that Genesis Chapter one speaks of Eloheim (the longer form of El) as the creator while Chapter two speaks of Yahweh—Eloheim. Brother Seaich states that "the Mosaic reform, which only began as an attempt to root out the licentious excesses to which the old polytheism had sunk (Ex. 32), took at least a half-dozen centuries to establish itself as Israel's 'true' religion, eliminating in the process many former truths, before emerging as the 'ethical monotheism' of late Judaism. . . . In the new monotheism . . . the earlier Eloheim and Yahweh became the single Yahweh—Eloheim' of Deut. 6:4. . . . The complete assimilation of two gods into one probably took as long as the 'Monotheistic Reform' itself, i.e. from ca. 1500 to 500 BC. . . . Finally, the OT itself was thoroughly subjected to a corresponding revision (known as the 'Deuteronomic Revision')" (Eugene Seaich, *Ancient Texts and Mormonism,* pp. 15-21, see actual text for complete listing of references).

In addition to the above, we should recall that Jesus as Jehovah spoke by divine investiture. As explained earlier in this chapter (p. 92), the Lord often spoke as though he were God the Father (D&C 29:1, 41-46). We also find that angels frequently presented their messages as though they were Jesus Christ or God the Father (Rev. 1:1; 19:9-10; 22:8-14).

Additional support for the Latter-day Saint differentiation in the use of divine titles is found in both New and Old Testament scriptures.

Matthew and Mark reported that Jesus, while on the cross, cried out to his Father using the name Eli (Matt. 27:46) or Eloi (Mark 15:34). Both of these names are regarded by scholars to be the Chaldean equivalent of El or Eloheim (see *Strong's Greek Dictionary of the New Testament,* p. 35, Elah and Eloah).

Although references to Christ's Sonship are somewhat rare in the Old Testament, they nevertheless exist. Daniel 3:25 describes a fourth individual in Nebuchadnezzar's furnace whose form was like a "Son of God [Elah]." Proverbs 30:4 speaks of the "son" of the creator, and Daniel 7:13 refers to the glorious coming of the "Son of man" (compare John 3:13 and Moses 6:57). Hosea 11:1 was quoted by Matthew (2:15) as a prophecy that God's "son" would be called out of Egypt. We also should not forget that Isaiah's famous messianic prophecy foretold the birth of a son who would also be known by the titles "everlasting Father" and "mighty God" (Isa. 7:14; 9:6). All of these scriptures provide proof that as Nephi stated, many do now "stumble exceedingly" because of the "plain and precious things which have been taken away" from the scriptures (1 Nephi 13:26-30, 34, 40).

Eloheim was anciently the Almighty God and Father of us all and Jehovah was and is Jesus the Christ, his Son. This knowledge has been restored by revelation in modern scripture (D&C 110:1-4 and other references on pp. 98-104 of this text) and is confirmed in the teachings of apostles and prophets today. President Joseph F. Smith taught: "Among the spirit children of Eloheim the firstborn was and is Jehovah or Jesus Christ to whom all others are juniors" (*Improvement Era,* Dec. 1916, pp. 940-41; also quoted in 1990 *Melchizedek Priesthood Personal Study Guide,* p. 39; see also Talmage, *Jesus the Christ,* pp. 36-38; Joseph Fielding McConkie and Donald W. Parry, *A Guide to Scriptural Symbols,* parts 2 & 3).

49. Did Jesus Christ attain godhood at some point in time?

Joseph Fielding Smith has told us that, "Our Savior was God before he was born into this world, and he brought with him that same status when he came here. He was as much a God when he was born into the world as he was before" (*Doctrines of Salvation,* 1:32). Thus, Christ did not attain godhood on this earth as some have falsely supposed, but achieved this status while yet a spirit (John 1:1-3). We make no claim to know when Christ became God but we do know it was prior to the "foundation of the earth" (Heb. 1:8-10; see also Col. 1:15-16; 1 Peter 1:19-20; Rev. 13:8). We likewise know that he did not, as some say, attain godhood in another world prior to this one. We do teach that Jesus Christ created other worlds (Moses 1:33) and that he died only once to atone for our sins (Heb. 9:28) forever (Heb. 10:10-12). Christ's atonement was infinite (2 Nephi 9:7) and eternal (Alma 34:10) and "brought about the great and eternal plan of redemption" for "all those who shall believe on his name" (Alma 34:15-16; see also p. 98 of this text).

50. Was God once a man?

We believe, as was taught by Joseph Smith, that "God himself was once as we are now, and is an exalted man, and sits enthroned in yonder heavens! That is the great secret. If the veil were rent today, and the great God who holds this world in its orbit, and who upholds all worlds and all things by his power, was to make himself visible, I say, if you were to see him today, you would see him like a man in form—like yourselves in all the person, image, and very form as a man; for Adam was created in the very fashion, image, and likeness of God, and received instructions from and conversed with him, as one man talks and communes with another" (*Teachings of the Prophet Joseph Smith,* p. 345).

D&C 130:1 states: "When the Savior shall appear we shall see him as he is. We shall see that he is a man like ourselves."

It is for this reason that Jesus Christ is called both "Son of God" (Mark 1:1; 3:11) and "Son of man" (Mark 2:10, 28). John makes it clear that both titles are synonymous when he calls Jesus Christ "Son of man which is in heaven" (John 3:13). "Man of Holiness" was an ancient title given to God the Father; thus Christ was literally the "Son of Man of Holiness" (Moses 6:57; see also Joseph Fielding Smith, *Answers to Gospel Questions,* 1:10-11; *Jesus the Christ,* pp. 142-44).

In John 5:19-20 Jesus declares: "The Son can do nothing of himself, but what he seeth the Father do: for what things soever [the Father] doeth, these also doeth the Son likewise. For the Father loveth the Son, and sheweth him all things that himself doeth" What did Jesus do? He was born of a woman, lived a sinless life, and after atoning for our sins, was glorified with a resurrected body of "flesh and bones" (Luke 24:36-39). If Christ followed the example of his Father, then it is clear that God the Father was once a man just as Christ, and both of them are now glorified and exalted beings (see also Bruce R. McConkie, *Mortal Messiah,* 1:315).

As the Prophet Joseph Smith taught:

> It is the first principle of the Gospel to know for a certainty the Character of God, and to know that we may converse with him as one man converses with another, and that he was once a man like us; yea that God himself, the Father of us all, dwelt on an earth, the same as Jesus Christ himself did (*Teachings,* pp. 345-46).

6
The Plan of Salvation

51. Does the Bible teach that man may become like God?

The objections of Christian "Orthodoxy" to what they call the heretical doctrine of deification are generally supported by the following false premises:

1. God is not a man (Num. 23:19; 1 Sam. 15:29; Hos. 11:9) and therefore man can never be a God—see pp. 89-91 and 108 for a detailed response.

2. Scriptural references to men as "gods" are figurative since the Bible affirms that there is only one God (Deut. 4:35-39; Isa. 43:10; 44:6-8; 1 Cor. 8:4-6; 1 Tim. 2:5; James 2:19)—see responses pp. 76-79 and p. 104 and following.

3. A belief in the existence of more than one God constitutes polytheism (a non-biblical pagan worship)—see p. 80 for a response to this assertion.

4. A belief that man was created in God's physical image is demeaning to God—See reply p. 89.

Since all four of the above premises were discussed in the previous chapter, the reader should refer to the referenced pages for a more detailed response in these areas. Additional comments in this section will pertain to those scriptures and writings which support man's potential to become like God. Before beginning our discussion though, we should first clarify the LDS doctrine of deification since some often misrepresent what Latter-day Saints actually believe. We do not believe, for example, that man can become God's equal in the domains where he rules, nor be independent of him despite the claims of our critics (D&C 76:58-62). We do believe that man may be exalted and yet remain subordinate to God if we overcome the world through the atonement of Jesus Christ (1 John 5:4-5; Rev. 5:9; 7:14; D&C 76:69-70). It is only in this way that we can become heirs of God and joint-heirs with Christ (Rom. 8:17; Gal. 4:6-7; James 2:5; D&C 84:37-38) and inherit all things as Christ has inherited all things (1 Cor. 3:21-23; Heb. 1:2; Rev. 21:7).

Many Bible passages support the belief that man has the potential to become like God and Christ. The Bible teaches first and foremost that we are children of a loving God (Deut. 14:1; Ps. 82:6; Hos. 1:10; Mal.

2:10; Luke 3:38; Acts 17:28-29; Rom. 8:16; Gal. 3:26; Eph. 4:6) created in his image and likeness (Gen. 1:26; 5:1; 9:6; 1 Cor. 11:7; James
3:9). It also teaches that man occupies a position of preeminence in
God's creation. Psalms 8:4-6 affirms that man was "made a little lower
than the angels" (this should actually be translated "gods" since the
Hebrew word "Eloheim" was used; see also Ps. 82:1, 6; 97:9).

God commands men to be holy and perfect like himself (Lev. 19:2;
Matt. 5:48; Heb. 12:10; 1 Peter 1:15; 2 Peter 1:3), that thereby they
"might be partakers of the divine nature" (2 Peter 1:4) and be spiritually reborn as his sons and daughters (John 1:12; 3:5-7; 2 Cor. 6:18; 1 John
3:9-10). The scriptures further affirm that the righteous, at his coming,
will not only inherit all things (Rev. 21:7), but will be like the Lord (1
John 3:2-3; 1 Cor. 15:49; 2 Cor. 3:18; Phil. 3:21) and receive of his glory
(2 Thes. 2:14; see also Ps. 8:4-6; 1 Cor. 2:7; Col. 3:4; 2 Peter 1:3)
becoming one with both God and Christ (John 17:21-23; 1 John 1:3). We
are also informed that the righteous will reign forever with them upon
their throne (Rev. 3:21; 5:10; 22:5) as "kings and priests unto God and
his Father" (Rev. 1:6; 5:10). Indeed, the Bible affirms that, "Eye hath not
seen, nor ear heard, neither have entered into the heart of man, the things
which God hath prepared for them that love him" (1 Cor. 2:9; see also
Isa. 64:4). As God's children we all are capable of growth beyond our
wildest expectations if we but pattern our lives after the Son's as he pat-
terned his life after the Father's (John 5:19; 1 Peter 2:21).

Despite the clarity of the above Bible scriptures, some attempt to
rationalize these teachings. Typical of this is the "Ye are gods" passage
found in Psalms 82:6 and cited by Jesus Christ in John 10:34-35. The
usual rationalized explanation is that Psalms 82 refers to Israelite judges
who by virtue of their position represent God and are therefore referred
to as gods in a figurative sense. Christ's reference to this scripture, by
their line of reasoning, should be understood to mean that if God called
wicked judges "gods," how much more appropriate for Jesus to be
called God or Son of God. An alternate interpretation explains the use of
the term "gods" as an ironic (some even say sarcastic) figure of speech.
They point to the statement "but ye shall die like men" in support of this
view.

Although the above explanations seem superficially plausible, they
seem to ignore the context of the full Psalm. Psalms 82:1 states, for
example, "God standeth in the congregation of the mighty; he judgeth
among the gods" (note the similarity to Abr. 3:22-23 where God stood
among pre-existent spirits). The interpretation that this passage is speaking of earthly men is contradicted by several facts. First, in comparison
to God, it is difficult to see how wicked judges could be considered

mighty. It is also hard to understand at what point God has stood among them to judge. Verse 6 also contradicts the belief that wicked judges are the subject of this discussion. It states, "all of you are children of the most high." Protestant scholars agree this would not be in keeping with the Old Testament use of the term "children of God," which they understood to refer to the righteous (Deut. 14:1-2). Last, irony seems to be totally absent in both of these verses and in Christ's latter use of this passage. Indeed, why would Christ use an ironic remark to establish that he was the Son of God when he was being accused of blasphemy? This would only have given those ready to kill him (John 10:39) additional reason to condemn him.

As further proof that the doctrine of deification was originally an accepted biblical teaching, consider the following statements by orthodox Christian saints as quoted by Stephen E. Robinson:

> In the second century Saint Irenaeus, the most important Christian theologian of his time, said
>> If the word became a man it was so men may become gods [Against Heresies, book 5, preface]
>
> Indeed, Saint Irenaeus had more than this to say on the subject of deification:
> Do we cast blame on him [God] because we were not made gods from the beginning, but were at first created merely as men, and then later as gods? Although God has adopted this course out of his pure benevolence, that no one may charge him with discrimination or stinginess, he declares, "I have said, Ye are gods; and all of you are sons of the Most High" . . . For it was necessary at first that nature be exhibited, then all that was mortal would be conquered and swallowed up in immortality . . ."But man receives progression and increase towards God. For as God is always the same, so also man, when found in God, shall always progress towards God"
>
> Also in the Second Century, Saint Clement of Alexandria wrote, "Yea, I say, the Word of God became a man so that you might learn from a man how to become a god" (*Exhortation to the Greeks,* (1) . . . Clement also said that "if one knows himself, he will know God, and knowing God will become like God. . . . His is beauty, true beauty, for it is God, and that man becomes a god, since God wills it. So Heraclitus was right when he said, 'Men are gods, and gods are men.'" (*The Instructor,* 3:1; see also Clement, *Stromateis,* p. 23).
>
> Still in the Second Century, Saint Justin Martyr insisted that in the beginning men "were made like God, free from suffering and death," and that they are thus "deemed worthy of becoming gods and of having power to become sons of the highest" (*Dialogue with Trypho,* p. 124).
>
> In the early Fourth Century Saint Athanasius—that tireless foe of heresy after whom the orthodox Athanasian Creed is named—also stated his belief in deification: "The word was made flesh in order that we might be enabled to be made gods. . . . Just as the Lord, putting on the body, became a man, so also we men are both deified through his flesh, and henceforth inherit everlasting life." (*Against the Arians,* 1:39, 3:34) On another occasion Athanasius stated, "He became man that we might be made divine" (*De Inc.,* p. 54; see also Athenasius, *On the Incarnation of the Word,* p. 65).

Finally, Saint Augustine himself, the greatest of the Christian Fathers, said: "But he himself that justifies also deifies, for by justifying he makes sons of God [John 1:12]. If then we have been made sons of God, we also have been made gods" (*On the Psalms*, 50:2) (Stephen E. Robinson, *Are Mormons Christian*, pp. 60-61).

Brother Robinson goes on to quote *The Westminster Dictionary of Christian Theology* on the subject of deification:

Deification (Greek theosis) is for Orthodoxy the goal of every Christian. Man, according to the Bible, is "made in the image and likeness of God". . . . It is possible for man to become like God, to become deified, to become god by grace. This doctrine is based on many passages of both OT and NT (see Ps. 82:6; 2 Peter 1:4), and it is essentially the teaching both of St. Paul, though he tends to use the language of filial adoption (see Rom. 8.9-17; Gal. 4.5-7), and the Fourth Gospel (see John 17:21-23).

The language of 2 Peter is taken up by St. Irenaeus, in his famous phrase, "if the word has been made man, it is so that man may be made gods" (*Adv. Haer*, V, Pref.), and becomes the standard in Greek theology. In the fourth century St. Athanasius repeats Irenaeus almost word for word, and in the fifth century St. Cyril of Alexandria says that we shall become sons "by participation" (Greek methexis). Deification is the central idea in the spirituality of St. Maximus the Confessor, for whom the doctrine is the corollary of the Incarnation: "Deification, briefly, is the encompassing and fulfillment of all times and ages," . . . and St. Symeon the New Theologian at the end of the tenth century writes, "He who is God by nature converses with those whom he has made gods by grace, as a friend converses with his friends, face to face"

. . . Finally, it should be noted that deification does not mean absorption into God, since the deified creature remains itself and distinct. It is the whole human being, body and soul, who is transfigured in the Spirit into the likeness of the divine nature, and deification is the goal of every Christian (Symeon Lash, *The Westminster Dictionary of Christian Theology*, ed. Alan Richardson and John Bowden, Philadelphia: Westminster Press, 1983, pp. 147-48; as quoted in *Are Mormons Christian*, p. 62).

Eugene Seaich made the following comment about the passage in 2 Peter 1:4:

That "partaking of the divine nature" actually meant deification is still clearly recorded by Hippolytus, Bishop of Portus, at the start of the third century. "And thou shalt be a companion of the Deity, and a co-heir with Christ, no longer enslaved with lusts or passions, and never again wasted by disease, for thou hast become God . . . Whatever it is consistent with God to impart, these God has promised to bestow upon thee, because thou hast been deified, and begotten unto immortality" (*Refutation of Heresies*, X.30).

Modern "orthodoxy," of course, has since invented an "unbridgeable gulf" separating Man from God, supposing that it somehow "magnifies" the one to belittle the other. Unfortunately, "orthodoxy" only belittles God's ability to do whatever he pleases . . . the early Church preferred to believe that "provided thou obeyest His solemn injunctions, and becomest a faithful follower of Him who is good, then shalt thou resemble Him, inasmuch as thou shalt have honor conferred upon thee by Him. For the Deity by condescension does not diminish aught of the dignity of

His divine perfection, having made thee even God to His glory (*Ibid.,* X:30)" (Eugene Seaich, *Ancient Texts and Mormonism,* pp. 45-46).

In the third century, Origen likewise held that "we should flee with all power from being men and make haste to become gods" (*On the Gospel of John,* 11, 13, 19). Origen's teacher, Clement of Alexandria, said, "The soul [which is kept pure], receiving the Lord's power, studies to become a god" (excerpted from Philip Barlow, "Unorthodox Orthodoxy: The Idea of Deification in Christian History," *Sunstone,* vol 8, no. 5, pp. 13-16).

In the fifth century, Jerome commented on Psalms 82:6 saying that God "made man for that purpose, that from men they may become gods" (*The Homilies of St. Jerome,* pp. 106-07). He also wrote, "Give thanks to the God of Gods . . . They who cease to be mere men, abandon the ways of vice and are become perfect, are gods and sons of the Most High" (*Ibid,* p. 353).

To these we add two other fourth century Fathers, Basil of Caesaria and Gregory of Nazianzus. Basil of Caesaria taught, "The Holy Spirit aids man in being made like God and the highest of all, being made God" (*On the Holy Spirit,* ix:23). Gregory of Nazianzus likewise taught, "I may become God to the same extent as He became man" (*Orations,* 29:19; 43:82; 7:23). In the thirteenth century, Thomas Aquinas said, "God became man, that man might become God" C. S. Lewis, considered by many as the twentieth century's foremost proponent of "orthodox" Christianity, stated, "There are no ordinary people. We live in a society of possible gods and goddesses" (*Weight of Glory,* pp. 14-15, as excerpted from Gilbert W. Scharffs, *The Truth About "The God Makers,"* p. 78).

Although this summary of comments by the first Fathers and other respected Christians is admittedly incomplete, it nevertheless shows that the doctrine of deification was accepted and taught since the very beginning of the church. The fact that theologians and saints, from Justin Martyr in the second century to C. S. Lewis in the twentieth century considered it an "orthodox" doctrine, makes it somewhat ironic that those who now call themselves "orthodox" Christians have labeled this doctrine as heretical. For further quotes see Darrick Evenson, *The Gainsayers,* pp. 49-57.

52. Why do Latter-day Saints accept Satan's lie to Eve that man may become as Gods?

Although Satan is the father of all lies (John 8:44; 2 Nephi 2:18; Moses 4:4), he is also cunning (D&C 10:23) and often mixes truth with error in order to deceive. The scriptures contain many examples where

Satan or his servants have told partial or whole truths to further their own purposes (Job 1:9-10; Matt. 4:6; 8:29; Mark 5:7; Luke 4:10-11; 8:28; Acts 16:17). We find, for example, devils declaring Jesus to be the "Holy One of God" (Mark 1:23-24; Luke 4:33-34) and also "Christ the Son of God" (Luke 4:41; see also Matt. 8:28-29, Mark 3:11; 5:7-8; Luke 8:28; Jesus the Christ, pp. 181-82).

On the occasion in question, Genesis 3:4-5 informs us that Satan told Eve that eating of the fruit of the tree of knowledge of good and evil would (1) surely not cause death (a lie—Gen. 2:17; 5:5) but (2) would cause their eyes to be opened so that they might know good from evil and therefore "be as gods" (true—Gen. 3:7, 22). Thus, in this instance, Satan told a half truth. It is important to note that the Lord himself affirmed, in Genesis 3:22, that the second half of Satan's statement was true by declaring, "Behold, the man is become as one of us, to know good and evil." Could there be any clearer witness than this one from God? We should understand by this that Satan was not promising godhood to Eve. He was mixing the truth that she would become like the gods (having the ability to discern between good and evil) with the lie that she could not die. The fact is, we do become as God when we gain knowledge of truth (good and evil) and learn obedience to God's commandments (Rom. 2:6-8; 1 Tim. 2:3-4; Titus 1:16; 2 Peter 2:20-21; 1 John 2:3-5; 20-21; 3:9-10).

53. Is the LDS belief in the pre-existence of man biblical?

Although serious Bible scholars acknowledge that a belief in the pre-existence of man was a genuine Jewish and early Christian doctrine (see *Interpreter's Dictionary of the Bible,* III:869-70; Hastings *Dictionary of the Bible,* IV:64; Hamerton-Kelly, *Pre-Existence, Wisdom and the Son of Man in the New Testament,* p. 15), only traces of this teaching are found in our modern Bible. It seems probable that because this doctrine was so widely accepted as genuine until the council of Constantinople in AD 553, both Old and New Testament writers and early church theologians presupposed its veracity and acceptance by later readers (Hastings *Encyclopedia of Religion and Ethics,* p. 239; Hamerton-Kelly, *Wisdom and the Son of Man in the New Testament,* p. 15).

Early examples of scriptural presupposition of man's pre-existence are found in Job, Proverbs, Jeremiah, and Ecclesiastes. Job 15:7 refers to the pre-existence of Adam, who was "made before the hills," and an allusion to the pre-existent spirits of men is found in Job 38:4-7 when the "sons of God shouted for joy" at the creation of the earth. Solomon declares that he "was set up from everlasting" and was "brought forth" even before the Lord "made the earth" (Prov. 8:23-26). He also proclaims that when the Lord "prepared the heavens, I was there . . . by him, as one brought up with him: and I was daily his delight, rejoicing always before him" (Prov. 8:27-30). Jeremiah 1:5 similarly speaks of the pre-existence of the prophet Jeremiah, whom God "knew" before he was formed in his mother's womb. Not only was Jeremiah known, but he was "sanctified" and "ordained . . . a prophet unto the nations" as Christ was similarly ordained the Savior in the pre-existence (1 Cor. 2:7; 1 Peter 1:20). The "preacher" of Ecclesiastes likewise affirms that at death "the spirit shall return unto God who gave it" (Eccl. 12:7). More will be said about this shortly.

Although modern "orthodoxy" theorizes that biblical allusions to the pre-existence of man are only examples of God's "foreknowledge," this theory fails to explain the five scriptures cited above. New Testament scriptures likewise allude indirectly to man's pre-existence. This premise was, for example, the basis of the disciples question about the blind man: "Master, who did sin, this man or his parents, that he was born blind?" (John 9:2). This man could only have sinned prior to his birth if he had pre-existed. That sin prior to birth was considered possible is confirmed by Peter's reference to the "angels that sinned" (2 Peter 2:4) and Jude's mention of the same event (Jude 1: 6).

The many scriptural references to the divine origin of our spirits discussed in the last chapter (p. 93) further attest to the fact that our spirits can, in reality, "return unto God" (Eccl. 12:7) the Father of all spirits (Eph. 4:6; Heb. 12:9). When we examine Paul's references to God's foreknowledge of those "called according to his purpose" (Rom. 8:28-29), we find the same Greek word "proginosko," which is translated as "foreordained" in 1 Peter 1:20. Therefore, just as Christ was foreordained to his calling "before the foundation of the world," so the saints were also foreordained "to be conformed to the image of his Son . . . the firstborn among many [spirit] brethren" (Rom. 8:29; see also Alma 13:3-5). Paul, in his other epistles, confirms the fact that we were "chosen . . . in him before the foundation of the world" (Eph. 1:4; 2 Tim. 1:9) and were there (in heaven) given "hope" of redemption "in the word of truth of the gospel" (Col. 1:5; Titus 1:2).

Though a statement in Zechariah 12:1, that God "formeth the spirit of man within him," appears to contradict the fact that our spirits were created long before our bodies, the rest of the scriptures and Jewish and Christian writings affirms this fact (see Josephus, *Wars of the Jews* book 2, chapter 8 and quotes which follow). A possible explanation for the above centers around the translation of the Hebrew word "yatsar." Although most translators render it "formeth" or "forms," it might also be translated as "frames," meaning "places within." Support for this is found in other Old Testament scriptures [see Gen. 2:7 (note that breath and spirit are the same word in Hebrew); Job 32:8; Isa. 42:5; Ez. 37:5-10]. When a careful study is made, it is clear that God places spirits into our earthly bodies of flesh.

Clement, the Bishop of Rome (ca. 90 AD), affirmed this view by teaching, "For this reason the world has existed through the ages, so that the spirits destined to come here might fulfill their number, and here make their choice between the upper and the lower worlds.." (*Clementine Recognitions,* III:26, *Patrologia Graec.,* 1:1249 f).

This principle was also taught by Origen in 220 AD in his essay *On First Principles.* He there described an initial spiritual creation of heaven and earth and the spirits of all the later inhabitants of the physical creation. From this spiritual pre-existence, some were born into one of three different glories which Origen called "supercelestial, terrestrial, and subterrestrial" (*On First Principles,* 1I:9, iii as excerpted from Vestal and Wallace, *The Firm Foundation of Mormonism,* p. 229; see also Origen's *Against Celsus,* 5:29 which refers to "the doctrine of souls entry into bodies"). Origen also informs us that the "primeval spirits" of Abraham, Isaac, and Jacob were created "before any other works of God" (Joseph's Prayer, *Commentary on John,* II:25; for additional information on Jewish and Christian writings about man's pre-existence see Eugene Seaich, *Mormonism, the Dead Sea Scrolls, and the Nag Hammadi Texts,* pp. 7 through 12).

Modern revelation provides the clearest affirmation of the pre-existence of man. To Joseph Smith it was revealed in D&C 93:29, 33 that "Man was also in the beginning with God. Intelligence, or the light of truth, was not created or made, neither indeed can be. For man is spirit. The elements are eternal, and spirit and element, inseparably connected, receive a fulness of joy" (see also D&C 138:53; Moses 3:5; Abr. 3:22; 5:7; *Teachings,* pp. 352-54).

54. Aren't angels a different species of creation from man?

Through ancient and modern revelation we know that angels are our spiritual brothers and sisters. All have either been born or will be born on this earth, and all are ministering spirits or resurrected beings sent from the presence of the Father and the Son. The scriptures often use the terms "angels" and "ministering spirits" interchangeably. Psalms 104:4 rhetorically asks, "Who maketh his angels spirits; his ministers a flaming fire"? (see also Heb. 1:7). Hebrews 1:13-14 reads, "But to which of the angels said he at any time, Sit on my right hand, until I make thine enemies thy footstool? Are they not all ministering spirits, sent forth to minister for them who shall be the heirs of salvation?" As has already been shown, we all existed as spirits before birth (see Matt. 18:10; note "angels" in this verse should be "spirits;" see also pp. 93, 114-116 of this text). Men, like angels, often act as messengers of God (Hag. 1:13; Mal. 2:7; 3:1; Matt. 11:10; Mark 1:2; Luke 7:27). Angels appear as men and were actually called men by inspired writers, as attested in scripture (Gen. 18:1-2; 19:1, 15; Ezek. 40:1-4; Matt. 28:2-6; Mark 16:5; Luke 24:3-4; John 20:1-12; Acts 1:10; 10:3, 30; Heb. 13:2; Rev. 21:17).

We are instructed that we are not to worship angels (Col. 2:18; Rev. 19:10; 22:8-9; see also Jud. 13:15-16). It is only when we read the account of an angel's appearance to John the Revelator that this injunction is explained. John records, "And when . . . I fell down to worship before the feet of the angel . . . Then saith he unto me, See thou do it not: for I am thy fellowservant, and of thy brethren the prophets" (Rev. 22:8-9). The angel thus identifies himself as a righteous man who had returned as an angelic messenger even as Moses, Elias, and others have done (Matt. 17:2-3; Mark 9:4; Luke 9:30). He was not just man's equal but a spirit brother (Rev. 19:10) and a son of God as man is (Num. 16:22; 27:16; Acts 17:22-29; Eph. 4:6; Heb. 12:9).

Joseph Smith has also affirmed that angelic messengers can be either resurrected men or spirits who are not yet resurrected (D&C 129:1-3; *History of the Church*, 4:425). Bruce R. McConkie further subdivides these two general groups into five categories (*Mormon Doctrine*, pp. 35-37) while at the same time making it clear that all "angels of the Almighty are chosen from among his offspring and are themselves pressing forward along the course of progression and salvation . . . because angels are of the same race as man and God" (see also D&C 130:5).

Some Christians mistakenly conclude that angels are "sexless" because they view Matthew 22:30 as supporting this belief. This scripture implies nothing about the ability of angels to procreate but only states that they are unmarried (single). Since marriage and procreation are only part of mortal life and exaltation, it seems clear that unexalted angels, whether pre-existent spirits or resurrected beings, will necessarily be single (see D&C 132:15-17). A more detailed discussion of Matthew 22:30 as it relates to eternal marriage may be found on p. 152 of this text.

55. Why does Paul seem to be teaching predestination in Romans 8 and Ephesians 1?

Eldon R. Taylor's answer to this question in the December 1990 *Ensign* is as good as any the author has found. As his response is fairly long, his answer will be excerpted. He indicates that:

> The problem is one of definition and interpretation. Many Christian church-
> es regard the words predestine and foreordain as synonymous. [Even Webster's

Dictionary defines foreordain as "to dispose or appoint in advance: PREDES-TINE" (*Webster's Ninth New Collegiate Dictionary*, Springfield, Mass.: Merriam Webster, Inc., p. 483, s.v., "foreordain")] However, our modern-day Church leaders have distinguished between them. Predestination is not a part of Latter-day Saint doctrine; foreordination is.

The Prophet Joseph Smith clearly taught that individuals were foreordained in premortality to certain missions in mortality. "Every man who has a calling to minister to the inhabitants of the world was foreordained to that very purpose in the Grand Council in Heaven before this world was," [*Teachings,* sel. Joseph Fielding Smith, Salt Lake City: Deseret Book Co., 1977, p. 365].

. . . To discover what Paul meant in Romans 8:29-30, we must study his other writings. In his letter to Timothy, Paul wrote that God "will have all men to be saved, and to come unto the knowledge of the truth" (1 Tim. 2:4; see also 2 Nephi 26:33).

. . . On the question of agency and accountability, Paul taught that God "will render to every man according to his deeds. . . . For there is no respect of persons with God" (Rom. 2:6-11; see also 2 Nephi 2:27).

In the same letter, Paul told the Romans that their conduct would determine their eternal reward: "Know ye not . . . his servants ye are to whom ye obey; whether of sin unto death, or of obedience unto righteousness?" (Rom. 6:16).

Paul's letters also make it clear that "the elect" can fall from grace and thus lose their reward (See Rom. 11:17-21). In fact, Paul claimed no guarantee of his own salvation; one of his favorite themes was the necessity of holding "stedfast unto the end" (Heb. 3:14; see also 1 Cor. 9:27). Such constant exhortations to righteousness would hardly seem necessary if he had believed that human beings did not help determine their own eternal destinies by their conduct during mortality.

From these scriptures, it seems clear that Paul did not believe in predestination—at least as a Calvinist defines the term. But then we might ask, did Paul believe in and teach the doctrine of foreordination—as we define the term?

Again to find out, we need to study Paul's writings. He himself said that he had been set apart "before [he] was born" (Gal. 1:15, Revised Standard Version). He wrote to Timothy of their "holy calling" given "before the world began" (2 Tim. 1:9). To the Ephesians, he said that the Lord "hath chosen us in him before the foundation of the world" to receive the gospel and its blessings (Eph. 1:3-5; see also verse 11). He told the Thessalonian members that "God hath from the beginning chosen you to salvation through sanctification of the Spirit and belief of the truth" (2 Thes. 2:13). Indeed, all people are foreordained to salvation and exaltation, but to fulfill that fore-ordination they must accept the ordinances of the gospel, keep the commandments, and endure to the end.

But if Paul did not believe in predestination, why does the passage in Hebrews refer to it? Could those who translated the King James Version have erred in using the English word predestinate to convey the meaning of foreordain?

Possibly. The problem arises because the Greek word proorizo, which is made up of the prefix pro (meaning "before or in front of; beforehand, or earlier"; Liddell and Scott, *Greek-English Lexicon,* Oxford: Clarendon Press, 1959) and the verb orizo (meaning "to determine, mark out, designate, destine, ordain or appoint," or "to divide or separate from . . . to preappoint or pre-ordain"; Arndt and Gingrich, *A Greek-English Lexicon of the New Testament and other Early Christian Literature,* Chicago: Univ. of Chicago Press, 1957; Moulton and Milligan, *The Vocabulary of the Greek Testament,* Grand Rapids, Mich.: Wm. B. Eerdmans, 1952) can be translated a number of different ways. In fact, various combinations of words have been used to translate the term over a period covering hundreds of years [See Acts 4:27-28; 1 Cor. 2:7]. The [following] examples . . . come from various translations of Romans 8:29-30. Note how the same idea is translated in a number of different ways.

Translation	Year	Romans 8:29	Romans 8:30
Wycliff	1380	bifor ordeyned	bifor ordeyned
Tyndale	1534	ordeyned before	appoynted before
Cranmer	1539	ordeyned before	appoynted before
Geneva	1657	ordeyned before	appoynted before
Rheims	1582	predestinated	predestinated
Standard Rev.	1881	foreordained	foreordained
James Moffatt	1913	decreed of old	has thus decreed
J.B. Phillips	1958	chose them	chose them long ago
Wm. F. Beck	1963	appointed long ago	appointed long ago
New Test. in Today's English	1966	had also set apart	had already set apart

In addition to these translations, the Greek word proorizo can be translated several other ways—for example, with such English words as allotted, planned, and fore-approved. Obviously, the most correct way to translate the word cannot be determined by simply referring to a dictionary. And the word chosen may not fully or accurately convey the original author's intent. The accuracy of any translation depends on the translator's ability to determine what the original author had in mind and then to convey that idea to the reader in another language.

. . . From the tenor of Paul's letter, we may determine that the English word predestinate does not accurately convey what Paul meant in Romans 8:29-30. What then did he mean? To understand that, we need to look at the verses in context. In verses 4 through 6, Paul tells members to "walk not after the flesh, but after the Spirit. . . . For to be carnally minded is death; but to be spiritually minded is life and peace" [see also Mosiah 3:16]. In verses 14 through 17, he explains, "For as many as are led by the Spirit of God, they are the sons of God. . . . We are the children of God: And if children, then heirs; heirs of God, and joint-heirs with Christ." In verse 24, Paul explains the need for hope in order to attain promised blessings [see also 2 Nephi 31:20; Ether 12:4, 8, 28,32; and Moroni 7], and in verse 28 he says that "all things work together for good to them that love God" and who are foreordained to accept the gospel and become like Christ.

Further, those who are thus foreordained are "justified," "sanctified," and "glorified" (see v. 30) through receiving the saving ordinances of the gospel and obeying the commandments—which is Paul's theme throughout his epistles.

Overall, Paul's teachings cannot be reconciled with the concept of Calvinistic predestination, and to translate proorizo as predestination does not accurately convey the apostle's intended meaning.

. . . In summary, Paul did not believe in predestination as Calvinists have defined the word. It has been his interpreters who have confused the doctrine. Paul himself taught that God loves all his children and has offered salvation to all who come unto Christ and are justified and sanctified through obedience to the covenants they make with him (Eldon R. Taylor, *Ensign*, Dec. 90, pp. 29-31).

Although the words predestinate or predestinated were used only four times in the King James version of the New Testament (Rom. 8:29, 30; Eph. 1:5, 11), from these short references has come one of the most destructive false doctrines ever conceived. Paul spoke of this saying, "they will not endure sound doctrine; but . . . shall turn away their ears from the truth, and shall be turned unto fables" (2 Tim. 4:3-4). Because many modern churches have turned away from the truth of the pre-existence of man, they have turned to the fable of predestination.

The reluctance of scholars to use "before ordained" or "foreordained" may have resulted from the abundance of Greek words meaning "ordained" which were used throughout the New Testament. There are at least twelve different Greek words which were translated as ordained by King James translators, though the word ordained or ordain is found only twenty-three times in all the New Testament (James Strong, Strong's *Exhaustive Concordance of the Bible*). In an effort to avoid the more frequent use of the word ordained, it is possible that the word predestined may have been substituted as what was thought to be an equivalent word in the four instances in Romans 8 and Ephesians 1.

Even today, expert translators fail to distinguish between foreordained or predestined when translating the Greek word *proorizo*. The Nestle Greek Text Literal English Translation by Reverend Alfred Marshall (*The Zondervan Parallel New Testament in Greek and English,* Zondervan Bible Publishers, Grand Rapids, Mich., 1975) translates proorizo as foreordained in Romans 8 but uses predestined in Ephesians 1.

Despite modern uncertainty regarding this doctrine, it is important to note that Romans 8:30 links foreordination to being "called" The rest of that verse seems to say that once a man is called, he will also be justified and glorified, but this is not always the case. Matthew 22:14 teaches, "many are called, but few are chosen" (see also Matt. 20:16; Luke 13:23; D&C 95:5; 121:34). Thus being called (foreordained) does not automatically imply salvation (being chosen). We are called to follow in Christ's footsteps (1 Peter 2:21) but yet may be rejected if we are not obedient to that call (Heb. 10:26; Rev. 2:5). To return to live with God and Christ we must be called, chosen, and faithful (Rev. 17:14; see also Jer. 1:5; 2 Thes. 2:13; 1 Peter 1:2; Alma 13:3-6; Abraham 3:22-23; *Mormon Doctrine,* p. 588; *Answers to Gospel Questions,* 4:147-54).

56. Was Adam's fall part of God's plan?

As was mentioned in the previous question, Calvinist doctrine taught that all mankind is "predestined" to salvation or damnation through the foreknowledge of God. Calvinist Protestants today still affirm a belief in predestination, yet at the same time hold that Adam's fall was an unexpected "hitch" in God's plan (see also Eugene Seaich, *Ancient Texts and Mormonism*, p. 41). The contradiction that God's knowledge extends to our day but not to Adam's is difficult to justify, but some still try.

Latter-day Saints understand that when God created the earth and man, he chose to create them in an eternal and perfect form. He thereafter pronounced them as "very good" (Gen. 1:31). When God created the Garden of Eden he placed the tree of knowledge of good and evil in it. If he never intended for Adam or Eve to partake of it, why was it there? Surely an all wise God could have eliminated the tree or placed a barrier around it like he did with the tree of life (Gen. 3:24) if the fall were not part of his plan. It seems clear that the fall was part of God's plan because God purposefully planted this tree in the garden. By doing so, he gave Adam and Eve the freedom to choose (2 Nephi 2:26-27; Moses 4:3) either to remain as he had created them or to begin an imperfect world where both physical and spiritual death were possible.

Knowing that man would fall, God also prepared ahead of time "a way for our escape" from both kinds of death (2 Nephi 9:8-10) through the resurrection and the atonement of Jesus Christ (2 Nephi 9:19-25). That his mission and sacrifice were prepared even "before the foundation of the world" is attested to throughout the scriptures (Eph. 1:3-4; 1 Peter 1:19-20; Rev. 13:8; Mosiah 4:6-8; Alma 22:13-14; Moses 4:1-2). When we understand that the Savior's mission was "foreordained" from the beginning, reason should satisfy us that Adam's *fall* was also "foreordained" (1 Nephi 9:6; 2 Nephi 9:6, 10; Mosiah 4:6-7; Mormon 9:12-13; Bruce R. McConkie, *The Promised Messiah*, p. 217) to bring about God's eternal purposes (Eph. 3:11; 2 Nephi 2:24-25; Moses 1:39). As Nephi testified, "Adam fell that men might be; and men are, that they might have joy" and eternal life (2 Nephi 2:25, 27).

57. What is salvation?

One would think that the subject of salvation would be particularly well defined in scripture and thoroughly understood by all Christians. Instead, it is a highly debated topic about which the Bible gives only occasional details, and which few Christians really understand. We should also add that virtually no one, LDS or otherwise, claims a complete understanding of the miraculous means by which the atonement was accomplished for all mankind (2 Nephi 9:21). Just as an understanding of the infinite universe exceeds man's grasp, so also Christ's infinite atonement (2 Nephi 9:7) exceeds man's finite comprehension (see James E. Talmage, *Jesus the Christ*, p. 613). This having been said, let us examine what the scriptures reveal about salvation and the atonement.

The words "salvation" and "saved," as they are used in the scriptures, may refer to deliverance from:

1. Captivity—Ex. 14:13, 30; Jude 5
2. Enemies—Num. 10:9; 2 Chron. 20:17; Luke 1:71
3. Sin—Ps. 51:1-12; Eph. 2:5
4. Physical death—Gen. 47:25; 2 Peter 2:5
5. Spiritual death—Ps. 35:9; John 3:16; 1 Peter 1:9
6. God's wrath—Rom. 5:9

Unfortunately, many Christians today have a tendency to interpret scriptural references to salvation as meaning unlimited forgiveness and the assured promise of eternal life in God's kingdom. This assumption has, in turn, led much of Christendom to believe in a simple, one-step path to eternal life. Some of the fallacies of this belief will be examined later in this chapter (see p. 134 and following). At this point we will only define these terms in light of scripture and modern revelation.

Although no succinct definition of salvation is contained in the scriptures, we can deduce the following:

1. Salvation is deliverance from sin and death or from other forms of repression (see references cited previously).

2. The gospel is referred to as the power of God unto salvation to those who believe (Rom. 1:16; 10:13-17; 1 Cor. 1:18; D&C 68:4).

3. The source of salvation is God's grace (Eph. 2:5, 8; Titus 2:11; 2 Nephi 10:24; 25:23) or in other words God's mercy and love (Rom. 5:8-9; Titus 3:5; *LDS Bible Dictionary*—grace, p. 697).

4. God's grace and love were manifest in Christ's vicarious sacrifice (John 3:16; 2 Tim. 1:9; 3 Nephi 27:14; Moroni 10:32-33) and is effective solely through that "means" (also referred to as "the way," John 1:12; 14:6; Acts 4:12; Rom. 5:2, 19-21; 6:23; Heb. 10:10; 2 Nephi 31:20-21; Mosiah 4:78; 5:7-8; D&C 18:23; Moses 6:52).

5. Full salvation (i.e. exaltation and eternal life) is contingent upon obedience to the gospel and enduring in personal righteousness (see Matthew 7:21, further information below, and p. 123).

6. Salvation is a free gift from God (Rom. 3:24; 5:15-16, 18; Eph. 3:7; 2 Nephi 2:4; 26:27; D&C 6:13; 14:7; Bruce R. McConkie, *The Promised Messiah,* pp. 346-47; see also pp. 138 and following of this text).

Modern revelation provides additional insight relative to salvation and the atonement. James E. Talmage in *Jesus the Christ,* page 23, explains:

> The effect of the atonement may be conveniently considered as two-fold:
> 1—The universal redemption of the human race from [physical] death invoked by the fall of our first parents; and
> 2—Salvation, whereby means of relief from the results of individual sin are provided.

The dual meaning of salvation is illustrated by Paul's statement in 1 Timothy 4:10: "For therefore we both labour and suffer reproach, because we trust in the living God, who is the Saviour of all men, specially of those that believe." Christ is the Savior of all men because of his victory over physical death (John 5:28; 1 Cor. 15:21-22), but only the believer is saved from individual sin through his atoning sacrifice (Rom. 1:16; Alma 34:15). The believer is thus "specially" saved from both death and the consequences of sin. The two-fold purpose of Christ's mission is further attested to through the symbols of the sacrament or Lord's Supper. The bread symbolizes the resurrection of the body while the wine symbolizes Christ's blood, shed to atone for our sins (see also Moses 1:39). Bruce R. McConkie explained that there are three categories of salvation:

1. Unconditional or general salvation, that comes by grace alone without obedience to gospel law, consists in the mere fact of being resurrected. In this sense salvation is synonymous with immortality . . . This kind of salvation eventually will come to all mankind [John 5:28-29; 1 Cor. 15:22] . . . But this is not the salvation of righteousness, the salvation which the saints seek. . . .

2. Conditional or individual salvation, that which comes by grace coupled with gospel obedience, consists in receiving an inheritance in the celestial kingdom of God. This kind of salvation follows faith, repentance, baptism, receipt of the Holy Ghost, and continued righteousness to the end of one's mortal probation . . . Even those in the celestial kingdom, however, who do not go on to exaltation, will have immortality only and not eternal life . . .

3. Salvation in its true and full meaning is synonymous with exaltation and eternal life and consists in gaining an inheritance in the highest of the three kingdoms within the celestial kingdom. With few exceptions this is the salvation of which the scriptures speak. It is this salvation which the saints seek (*Mormon Doctrine,* pp. 669-70; see also *Doctrines of Salvation,* vol. 2, pp. 9-13).

Additional information on the necessity of works and the conditional nature of salvation will be presented later in this chapter.

58. What must we do to be saved?

The scriptures indicate that no man will be saved in the kingdom of God (i.e. receive exaltation and eternal life) in unrighteousness (see Gal. 5:16-25; Eph. 5:1-9; 3 Nephi 27:19-20; D&C 59:23). The scriptures also indicate that obedience to the following gospel requirements is necessary:

a. *Faith in the Lord Jesus Christ*—John 3:17-18; Acts 16:30-31; Rom. 10:9-10; 2 Tim. 3:15; Mosiah 3:9, 12; 3 Nephi 27:19; D&C 33:12

b. *Repentance of all our sins*—Mark 1:15; Luke 13:3; Acts 2:38-40; 3:19; 11:18; 2 Cor. 7:10; 2 Nephi 9:23; 3 Nephi 27:19; D&C 18:12

c. *Baptism by immersion for the remission of sins*—Mark 16:16; John 3:5; Acts 2:37-38; Titus 3:5; 1 Peter 3:21; 2 Nephi 9:23; 3 Nephi 11:33; D&C 68:9

d. *Reception of the Holy Ghost and sanctification by the Spirit*—John 3:5; Acts 2:38; 2 Thes 2:13; Mosiah 5:2, 7-9; 3 Nephi 27:20

e. *Enduring to the end through obedience to the gospel*—Matt. 10:22; 24:13; Mark 13:13; Rom. 2:68; Heb. 5:9; 6:15; James 2:24; Rev. 2:26; 2 Nephi 31:15-16, 20; Mosiah 4:30; 3 Nephi 15:9; 27:6, 16; D&C 18:22; 76:50-53

f. *Prayer*—Acts 2:21; Rom. 10:13; Mosiah 4:11, 20; Moroni 10:4-5 (Note: Although prayer is not considered one of the first principles and ordinances of the gospel, its importance, as stressed in the above scriptures, seems to justify its inclusion in this list:)

Note how these requirements tie in with Romans 1:15-18 and the essentials of the gospel outlined on p. 12 and following of this text. Hearing the gospel (verse 15) is the first step toward salvation; believing (verse 16-i.e. hope leading to prayer and faith—Rom. 1:17; Alma 32:21-22, 27) is the second step; obeying the gospel (steps a through f above) could be considered the final life-long step (see Rom. 1:17-18; see also *Doctrines of the Restoration,* pages 78-79, 107).

59. Is baptism essential to salvation?

Although some Christians today believe that baptism by water is optional, the scriptures teach otherwise. Baptism is not just a sign of conversion but is a necessary step in receiving a remission of sins. In so doing, we follow Christ in fulfilling all righteousness and in turn receive of his Spirit (Matt. 3:13-15; Gal. 3:27; 2 Nephi 31:5-13).

Before we can adequately answer the question posed above, we must first establish what baptism is and is not. Baptism, as used in the New Testament, is the English translation of the Greek word baptisma (plural—baptismos) which was also translated as washing or washings (Mark 7:8; Heb. 9:10). Baptisma was derived from the word baptizo which means to baptize or make fully wet. This word was only used in the New Testament to refer to ceremonial ablutions or cleansings and especially to the Christian ordinance itself (James Strong, *Greek Dictionary of the New Testament,* p. 18). Baptizo was also translated as "wash" (Mark 7:4) or "washed" (Luke 11:38), meaning to cleanse with water. Common usage of these terms by both Latin and Greek writers make it clear that complete immersion was the understood meaning (see *LDS Missionary Bible Ready References,* pp. 40-42). Bible narratives also confirm this interpretation (Matt. 3:16; Mark 1:5, 9-10; John 3:23; Acts 8:38-39; Rom. 6:4; Col. 2:12).

Immersion was the proper method of baptizing according to second, third, and fourth century Christian writers such as Cyrill, bishop of Jerusalem; Basil, bishop of Caesarea; Chrysostom, bishop of Constantinople; Athanasius, bishop of Alexandria; Gregory of Nazianzus, bishop of Constantinople; Hippolytus, bishop of Portus; Tertullian, and Jerome (see Joseph Fielding Smith, *The Restoration of All Things,* Appendix).

Scripture strictly associates the ordinance of baptism with the washing away of impurities or sins. John the Baptist affirmed this link by preaching "the baptism of repentance for the remission of sins" (Mark 1: 4; Luke 3:3). Some Christians have tried to indicate that John's baptism was somehow different from later Christian baptisms, but this is contradicted by the scriptures and later authoritative statements. Peter instructed new converts on the day of Pentecost to "Repent, and be baptized, every one . . . in the name of Jesus Christ for the remission of sins" (Acts 2:38). Paul was like-wise commanded of Ananias to "be baptized, and wash away [his] sins" (Acts 22:16).

Tertullian, in the first century after the death of Christ, stated that "There is no difference whether one is washed in a sea or a pool, in a river or in a fountain, in a lake or in a channel: nor is there any difference between those whom John dipped in the Jordan, and those whom Peter dipped in the Tiber . . . We are immersed in the water" (see *Millennial Star,* vol. XXI, pp. 769-70 or James E. Talmage, *The Great Apostasy,* p. 125). Modern scriptures also confirm the role of baptism in the remission of sins (Alma 6:2; D&C 13; 55:1-2; 68:27; 84:64, 74; 138:33; JS—H 1:69), though the actual cleansing is accomplished through Christ's atonement (Mosiah 3:11, 18; Alma 7:14; D&C 20:37; 76:41, 69; Moses 6:59; see also p. 128 and following) and reception of the Holy Ghost.

Justin Martyr (ca. 150 AD) said the following regarding baptism:

> Those who are persuaded and believe, and promise that they can live accordingly, are instructed to pray and beseech God with fasting for the remission of their sins, while we pray and fast along with them. Then they are brought by us where there is water, and are reborn by the same manner of rebirth by which we ourselves were reborn; for then they are washed in the water in the name of God the Father and Master of all, and of our Saviour Jesus Christ, and of the Holy Spirit. For Christ said, "unless you are born again you will not enter the kingdom of heaven" (John 3:3-4) (*First Apology of Justin,* 61).

Origen, in about 220 AD, taught baptismal candidates, "Go and repent, catechumens, if you want to receive baptism for the remission of your sins. . . . No one who is in a state of sin when he comes for baptism can obtain the remission of his sins" (Jean Danielou, *Origin,* p. 54, Comm. John, 2, 37; De Princ. 4, 3, 12; Horn. Ez.1, 1).

The scriptures clearly state that baptism is a commandment. Luke reports that "the Pharisees and lawyers rejected the counsel of God against themselves, being not baptized of [John]" (Luke 7:30). Peter also "commanded" the Gentiles "to be baptized in the name of the Lord" (Acts 10:48). And finally, the importance of this ordinance was emphasized by Christ in his last admonition to the eleven apostles to "Go . . . and teach all nations, baptizing them in the name of the Father, and of the Son, and of the Holy Ghost" (Matt. 28:19). If baptism was not essential, why then the command to baptize all nations?

If baptism is for the remission of our sins and is a commandment, it must also be essential to salvation. The scriptures clearly affirms this: "The like figure whereunto even baptism doth also now save us" (1 Peter 3:21). Paul affirms that Christ "saved us, by the washing of regeneration, and the renewing of the Holy Ghost" (Titus 3:5) while adding that baptism is the appointed way to "put on Christ" (Gal. 3:27).

The Savior also clearly taught the link between baptism and salvation. Mark concludes his gospel with the Savior's teaching that "He that believeth and is baptized shall be saved; but he that believeth not shall be damned" (Mark 16:16). John likewise quotes Jesus Christ as saying that "Except a man be born again, he cannot see the kingdom of God" (John 3:3). When Nicodemus asked the meaning of this statement, Christ responded, "Except a man be born of water and of the Spirit, he cannot enter into the kingdom of God" (John 3:5).

Those who contend that baptism by water is not necessary have asserted that "born of water" implies only the necessity of physical birth from the water within the womb. Justin Martyr made it clear that this was not the true meaning of this verse in the second century AD. In describing his practice of the baptismal ceremony, he explains, "After [repentance] they are led by us to where there is water, and are born again in that kind of new birth by which we ourselves were born again. For upon the name of God, the Father and Lord of all, and of Jesus Christ, our Saviour, and of the Holy Spirit, the immersion in water is performed, because the Christ hath also said, 'Except a man be born again, he cannot enter into the kingdom of heaven' (*Dialogue with Trypho,* xiv, 1; see also *The Great Apostasy,* p. 125). Thus, the early Christian Fathers understood that the "new birth" referred to the baptism of water and not to one's physical birth.

Paul emphasized both the importance of water baptism and the authority to baptize in Acts 19:26. Upon finding some disciples who were apparently baptized by an unauthorized individual, Paul rebaptizes them and lays his hands upon them to give them the gift of the Holy Ghost. If baptism were either optional or acceptable under any authority, rebaptism would not have been necessary in this circumstance. The disciples could have proceeded directly to confirmation (i.e. the laying on of hands for the gift of the Holy Ghost) if this were the case, but instead they were first rebaptized.

Michael T. Griffith has also discussed the importance of authority and the baptismal ordinance in the early church. He cites Ignatius and other church leaders who declared that baptism was valid only under the proper authority:

> It is not right either to baptize or to celebrate the agape apart from the bishop; but whatever he approves is also pleasing to God, so that everything you do may be secure and valid (*The Apostolic Fathers*, p. 113).
>
> Cyprian, bishop of Carthage in the middle part of the third century, stated that no one outside of the church could administer a valid baptism (Jeffrey Burton Russell, *Satan: The Early Christian Tradition*, p. 106).
>
> On the necessity of the ordinance of baptism, Tertullian, known as the first great Latin theologian of ancient Christianity, taught the "sole necessary way" of obtaining Christ's protection against evil was through baptism (*Ibid.*, pp. 100-01). In fact it was universally believed in the Early Church that "we obtain the benefits of Christ's sacrifice by baptism" (*Ibid.*, p. 103) (*Signs of the True Church of Christ*, pp. 94-95).

An early Christian document known as the *Didache* (The Teaching) states that baptism was the accepted rite of admission to the church and "only those who have been baptized in the Lord's name" may partake of the sacrament (*Didache*, 9:5; see also J. N. D. Kelly, *Early Christian Doctrines*, pp. 193-211).

Justin Martyr, in about 150 AD, confirmed that "no one was allowed to partake [of the sacrament] except one who believes . . . and has received the washing for forgiveness of sins and for rebirth" (*First Apology of Justin*, p. 66).

Tertullian held that baptism was necessary for salvation (*De bapt.* 1:12-15; see also J. N. D. Kelly, *Early Christian Doctrines*, p. 209). He also suggested that children not be "baptized until they reached years of discretion" (*De bapt.* 1:18; J. N. D. Kelly, *Early Christian Doctrines*, p. 209).

J. N. D. Kelly also notes that Clement of Alexandria, Origen, and Hippolytus believed that baptism was very important. "Clement of Alexandria speaks of baptism as imparting regeneration, enlightenment, divine sonship, immortality, [and] remission of sins [where] sonship . . . is the result of regeneration worked by the Spirit" (J. N. D. Kelly, *Early Christian Doctrines*, p. 207; Paed. 1, 6, 26). Origen insisted on penitence, sincere faith and humility "as prerequisites to baptism as well as gradual transformation of the soul" (*Ibid.*, p. 208; Horn. in Lev. 6, 2; Luke 21; Ex. 10; 4). Hippolytus associated the remission of sins and reception of the Spirit with baptism (*Ibid.* p. 208; *trad. apost.* 22, 1).

It is clear that baptism is a doctrine of the true church (Heb. 6:2) and therefore was not subject to change by men (1 Cor. 11:2). Those who reject this ordinance "shall receive to themselves damnation" (Rom. 13:2) in that they "cannot enter into the kingdom of God" but will inherit a lesser kingdom (John 3:5; D&C 76:51-52, 62; see also *Teachings,* pp. 262, 360 and 361).

60. Do Latter-day Saints believe Christ's sacrifice was essential to salvation?

Despite anti-Mormon efforts to assert otherwise, the central doctrine of the LDS Church is the belief that "through the Atonement of Christ, all mankind may be saved, by obedience to the laws and ordinances of the Gospel" (Third Article of Faith). Bruce R. McConkie taught that "The very heart and core and center of revealed religion is the atoning sacrifice of Christ. All things rest upon it, all things are operative because of it, and without it there would be nothing. Without it the purpose of creation would be void, they would vanish away, there would be neither immortality nor eternal life . . . We believe and proclaim that salvation is in Christ, in his gospel, in his atoning sacrifice (2 Nephi 31:21; Mosiah 4:8; Acts 4:12). We are bold to say it comes by the goodness and grace of the Father and the Son" (*Doctrines of the Restoration,* pp. 57, 78).

The Book of Mormon teaches the necessity of the atoning sacrifice like no other book of scripture. Consider the following scriptures and the clear and convincing witness that they bear of this eternal truth:

• Wherefore, all mankind were in a lost and in a fallen state, and ever would be save they should rely on this Redeemer (1 Nephi 10:6).

• Wherefore, redemption cometh in and through the Holy Messiah; for he is full of grace and truth. Behold he offereth himself a sacrifice for sin, to answer the ends of the law, unto all those who have a broken heart and a contrite spirit; and unto none else can the ends of the law be answered. Wherefore, how great the importance to make these things known unto the inhabitants of the earth, that they may know that there is no flesh that can dwell in the presence of God, save it be through the merits, and mercy, and grace of the Holy Messiah, who layeth down his life according to the flesh, and taketh it again by the power of the Spirit, that he may bring to pass the resurrection of the dead, being the first that should rise. Wherefore, he is the firstfruits unto God, inasmuch as he shall make intercession for all the children of men; and they that believe in him shall be saved (2 Nephi 2:6-9).

• . . . there is none other name given under heaven save it be this Jesus Christ, of which I have spoken, whereby man can be saved. For we labor diligently to write, to persuade our children and also our brethren, to believe in Christ, and to be reconciled to God; for we know that it is by grace that we are saved, after all we can do. And we talk of Christ, we rejoice in Christ, we preach of Christ, we prophesy of Christ, and we write according to our prophecies, that our children may know to what source they may look for a remission of their sins (2 Nephi 25: 20, 23, 26).

• And now, my beloved brethren, after ye have gotten into this strait and narrow path, I would ask if all is done? Behold, I say unto you, Nay; for ye have not come thus far save it were by the word of Christ with unshaken faith in him, relying wholly upon the merits of him who is mighty to save. Wherefore, ye must press forward with a steadfastness in Christ, having a perfect brightness of hope, and a love of God and of all.men. Wherefore, if ye shall press forward, feasting upon the word of Christ, and endure to the end, behold, thus saith the Father: Ye shall have eternal life. And now, behold, my beloved brethren, this is the way; and there is none other way nor name given under heaven whereby man can be saved in the kingdom of God (2 Nephi 31:19-21).

• For behold, and also his blood atoneth for the sins of those who have fallen by the transgression of Adam, who have died not knowing the will of God concerning them, or who have ignorantly sinned. But wo, wo unto him who knoweth that he rebelleth against God! For salvation cometh to none such except it be through repentance and faith on the Lord Jesus Christ. And moreover, I say unto you, that there shall be no other name given nor any other way nor means whereby salvation can come unto the children of men, only in and through the name of Christ . . . and through the atoning blood of Christ, the Lord Omnipotent (Mosiah 3:11-12, 17-18).

• . . . And they all cried aloud with one voice, saying: O have mercy, and apply the atoning blood of Christ that we may receive forgiveness of our sins, and our hearts may be purified; for we believe in Jesus Christ, the Son of God, who created heaven and earth, and all things; who shall come down among the children of men. I say, that this is the man who receiveth salvation, through the atonement which was prepared from the foundation of the world for all mankind . . . even unto the end of the world. And this is the means whereby salvation cometh. And there is none other salvation save this which hath been spoken of; neither are there any conditions whereby man can be saved except the conditions which I have told you (Mosiah 4:2, 7-8).

• . . . were it not for the atonement, which God himself shall make for the sins and iniquities of his people, that they must unavoidably perish, notwithstanding the law of Moses (Mosiah 13:28).

• And now, ought ye not to tremble and repent of your sins, and remember that only in and through Christ ye can be saved? Therefore, if ye teach the law of Moses, also teach that it is a shadow of those things which are to come—Teach them that redemption cometh through Christ the Lord (Mosiah 16:13-15).

• And he shall come into the world to redeem his people; and he shall take upon him the transgressions of those who believe on his name; and these are they that shall have eternal life, and salvation cometh to none else (Alma 11:40).

• Now Aaron began to open the scriptures unto them concerning the coming of Christ, and also concerning the resurrection of the dead, and that there could be no redemption for mankind save it were through the death and sufferings of Christ, and the atonement of his blood (Alma 21:9).

• And since man had fallen he could not merit anything of himself; but the sufferings and death of Christ atone for their sins, through faith and repentance, and so forth; and that he breaketh the bands of death, that the grave shall have no victory, and that the sting of death should be swallowed up in the hopes of glory (Alma 22:14).

• And now, behold, I will testify unto you of myself that these things are true. Behold, I say unto you, that I do know that Christ shall come among the children of men, to take upon him the transgressions of his people, and that he shall atone for the sins of the world; for the Lord God hath spoken it (Alma 34:8).

• . . . nothing can save this people save it be repentance and faith on the Lord Jesus Christ, who surely shall come into the world, and shall suffer many things and shall be slain for his people (Helaman 13:6).

• And as many as have received me, to them have I given to become the sons of God; and even so will I to as many as shall believe on my name, for behold, by me redemption cometh, and in me is the law of Moses fulfilled (3 Nephi 9:17).

• And my Father sent me that I might be lifted up upon the cross; and after that I had been lifted up upon the cross, that I might draw all men unto me, that as I have been lifted up by men even so should men be lifted up by the Father, to stand before me, to be judged of their works, whether they be good or whether they be evil (3 Nephi 27:14)

• And because of the redemption of man, which came by Jesus Christ, they are brought back into the presence of the Lord; yea, this is wherein all men are redeemed, because the death of Christ bringeth to pass the resurrection, which bringeth to pass a redemption from an endless sleep, from which sleep all men shall be awakened by the power of God . . . being redeemed and loosed from this eternal band of death, which death is a temporal death (Mormon 9:13).

• Yea, come unto Christ, and be perfected in him, and deny yourselves of all ungodliness; and if ye shall deny yourselves of all ungodliness, and love God with all your might, mind and strength, then is his grace sufficient for you, that by his grace ye may be perfect in Christ . . . And again, if ye by the grace of God are perfect in Christ, and deny not his power, then are ye sanctified in Christ by the grace of God, through the shedding of the blood of Christ, which is in the covenant of the Father unto the remission of your sins, that ye become holy, without spot (Moroni 10:32-33).

It is clear that the Book of Mormon teaches the necessity of Christ's atonement to salvation as well as man's obligation to have faith in Christ and obey him. Members of The Church of Jesus Christ of Latter-day Saints witness to the world that Jesus Christ is the Savior and Redeemer of mankind and only those who trust in him shall enter into his kingdom (see also D&C 20:29; 38:4; 76:40-42, 69; 138:2).

61. Why don't Latter-day Saints still use wine in their sacrament? (Is it because they don't rely on Christ's atoning blood for salvation?)

Latter-day Saints emphatically affirm our reliance on the atoning blood of Jesus Christ for the remission of sins, as attested to in the Bible (Col. 1:14; 1 Peter 1:18-19; 1 John 1:7; Rev. 7:14) and modern scripture (1 Nephi 12:10; Mosiah 3:7, 11; 4:2; Alma 5:21, 27; 21:9; 24:13; 34:36; Helaman 5:9; Ether 13:10; Moroni 4:1; 5:2; 10:33; D&C 20:40; 27:2; 76:69; Moses 6:62).

Even the sacrament prayer for the administration of the water affirms the symbolism of the atoning blood. It states in part:" . . . bless and sanctify this water to the souls of all those who drink of it, that they do it in remembrance of the blood of thy Son, which was shed for them" (D&C 20:79).

As to our use of water in place of grape juice (new wine—see Isa. 65:8), it is important to note that initially grape juice was used in the sacrament both in the early church (Matt. 26:28-29) and in the latter-day Church (D&C 20:79; *History of the Church,* 1:78). As a precaution against enemies of the Church poisoning or adulterating the grape juice sold to the Saints, a change was authorized by the Lord (*History of the Church,* 1:106-08; *Church History and Modern Revelation,* 1:132; *Doctrine and Covenants Student Manual,* p. 55). The Lord revealed "that it mattereth not what ye shall eat or what ye shall drink when ye partake of the sacrament, if it so be that ye do it with an eye single to my glory— remembering unto the Father my body which was laid down for you, and my blood which was shed for the remission of your sins" (D&C 27:2).

It is interesting to note that the command throughout the scriptures was not to partake of the bread and wine but rather of the bread and the cup (Matt. 26:26-27; Mark 14:22-23; Luke 22:17, 1920; 1 Cor. 11:24-26). It therefore appears that it was not the wine that was being emphasized but the "bitter cup" (D&C 19:18) of which Christ would partake (Matt. 20:22-23; 26:39, 42; Mark 10:38; 14:36; Luke 22:20, 42; John 18:11; 1 Cor. 10:21). This is also in conformity with the Old Testament usage of the term "cup" to symbolize suffering (Ps. 11:6; 75:8; Isa. 51:17, 22; Jer. 25:15, 17; 49:12; see also *Jesus the Christ,* p. 620, note 8).

It is noteworthy that some early Christians used both water and wine in the sacrament. Justin Martyr (ca. 140 AD) recorded:

> On Sunday we hold a meeting in one place for all who live in the cities or the country nearby. The teachings of the Apostles or the writings of the prophets are read as long as time is available. When the reader has finished, the president gives a talk urging and inviting us to imitate all these good examples. We then all stand together and send up our prayers. As noted before, bread, wine and water is brought forth after our prayer. The president also sends up prayers and thanksgivings. The people unitedly give their consent by saying, "Amen" The administration takes place, and each one receives what has been blessed with gratefulness. The deacons also administer to those not present . . . We all choose Sunday for our communal gathering because it is the first day, on which God created the universe by transforming the darkness and the basic elements, and because Jesus Christ—our Redeeming Savior—rose from the dead on the same day (*First Apology,* pp. 65-67, as cited in Vestal and Wallace, *The Firm Foundation of Mormonism,* p. 231).

This practice was also mentioned by Pope Julius I (AD 337) in a decree which stated: "But if necessary let the cluster be pressed into the cup and water mingled with it" (Gratian, *De Consecratione,* Pars III, Dist. 2, c. 7, as cited by Leon C. Field, *Oinos: A Discussion of the Bible Wine Question,* New York, 1883, p. 91, and Samuele Bacchiocchi, *Wine in the Bible,* pp. 109-10). This practice of mixing wine and water may be related to the fact that both blood and water were shed on the cross. John recorded that "one of the soldiers with a spear pierced his side, and forth-with came there out blood and water" (John 19:34). John later recorded that "there are three that bear witness in earth, the Spirit, and the water, and the blood: and these three agree in one" (1 John 5:8). In like manner, baptism by water was also related by Paul to Christ's death (Rom. 6:3-5).

Samuele Bacchiocchi, a non-LDS scholar, has observed, "An investigation . . . of such Jewish Christian sects as the Ebionites, the Nazarenes, the Elkesaites, and the Encratites, might provide considerable support for abstinence from fermented wine in the Apostolic Church. The fact that some of these sects went to the extreme of rejecting altogether both fermented and unfermented wine using only water, even in the celebration of the Lord's Supper, suggests the existence of a prevailing concern for abstinence in the Apostolic Church" (*Wine in the Bible,* p. 181). It also suggests that early Christians understood that "it mattereth not what ye shall eat or what ye shall drink when [partaking] of the sacrament" (D&C 27:2).

Catholics, at a much later period, also substituted the eucharist for the bread and wine of the Lord's Supper, believing that it would literally be turned into the flesh and blood of the Lord (See *Mormon Doctrine,* p. 241 or James Cardinal Gibbons, *The Faith of our Fathers,* pp. 235-50).

Although the later practice was introduced during a period of apostasy, it nonetheless shows that some Christians felt it was permissible to modify the observance of the sacrament even without direction from the Lord. The LDS sacrament service, on the other hand, is always observed within the guidelines given by the Lord and as prescribed in the scriptures (See John 6:53-54; Acts 2:46; 20:7; 1 Cor. 11:23-30; Moroni 4 and 5; D&C 20:75-79; 27:1-4; for additional information on the LDS reliance on Christ's atonement see responses on pp. 122, 123, and 128 and Gilbert W. Scharffs, *The Truth About "The God Makers",* pp. 192-93).

62. In view of David's forgiveness in Psalms 16:9-11 and other scriptures, does Christ's sacrifice extend to murderers?

Although many Christians today believe that all sins may be forgiven, the Lord has declared that some sins will not be washed away by his atoning sacrifice. We are told, for example, that "blasphemy against the Holy Ghost shall not be forgiven unto men" (Matt. 12:31). We are likewise informed by Paul that "if we sin wilfully after that we have received the knowledge of the truth, there remaineth no more sacrifice for sins" (Heb. 10:26; see also D&C 29:17).

As to David's sin of murder (the shedding of Uriah's innocent blood), it would be premature to assume that David was fully forgiven this sin just because several Old Testament scriptures seem to imply that he was (see 2 Sam. 12:13; Ps. 16:9-11; 30:3; 86:13). We should first note that

Joseph Smith's inspired revision of 2 Samuel 12:13 indicates that the Lord had *not* put away David's sin (JST 2 Sam. 12:13). We should also note that although David was promised that his soul (spirit) would not be left in hell (Ps. 16:10; 30:3; 86:13), Peter remarked that David had still "not ascended into the heavens" at the time of Christ's resurrection (Acts 2:29-34) when the graves of the saints were opened and "many bodies of the saints which slept arose" (Matt. 27:52-53). David's sepulchre was apparently untouched at that time (Acts 2:29).

We should also note that although David's soul (spirit) would not be left in hell (prison—JST Acts 2:27), the intent was only to show that David would eventually be resurrected. The reference to the resurrection of Jesus Christ cited by Peter (Acts 2:27, 31) still remains in the Septuagint version of Psalms 16:10 but is absent in the Hebrew Masoretic text. Thus, the meaning of this particular scripture has been obscured to include spiritual salvation in modern Bibles when only physical salvation was originally intended.

We are also told by John that "no murderer hath eternal life abiding in him" (1 John 3:15; see also Gal. 5:19-21 and Rev. 22:15) and this truth has been confirmed by modern revelation (D&C 42:18-19; Alma 39:5-6). Although forgiveness of the sin of murder is available to some degree to those who do so ignorantly, as did Paul (1 Tim. 1:13), and to those who sin before receiving a knowledge of the truth (Luke 23:34; Rom. 4:15; 5:13), as did the Jews (Acts 2:36-38), it is not available to those who have received a full knowledge of the truth (Heb. 10:26). Modern revelation indicates that partial forgiveness may be achieved with great difficulty (Alma 39:5-6) and after suffering by the sinner himself (D&C 76:103-106; 132:26, 39).

The Prophet Joseph Smith indicated that "murderers . . . cannot have [complete] forgiveness. David sought repentance at the hand of God carefully with tears, for the murder of Uriah; but he could only get it through hell; he got a promise that his soul should not be left in hell" (*Teachings,* p. 339; see also pp. 188, 356-57).

Murderers may be forgiven their sins through their own suffering (D&C 19:17) but not forgiven to the point that they gain salvation in the celestial kingdom (D&C 42:18; 76:105-106; 112; 1 John 3:15; Rev. 22:15; see also *Mormon Doctrine,* pp. 92-93, 520, 737).

63. Do Latter-day Saints believe in salvation by grace through faith alone?

Great care must be taken in responding to this particular question because those who ask it usually have a different understanding of the terms salvation, grace, and even faith itself. Without agreeing on common definitions of these terms, most discussions in this area are futile.

For a detailed discussion of salvation the reader is referred back to pages 121-24 of this text. As was shown in these sections, the scriptures use the terms "save" and "salvation" with different meanings. Salvation may mean redemption from physical death, redemption from sin, redemption from sin and death, or in some instances eternal life with God. While most Protestants would generally define salvation as redemption from both death and sin, Latter-day Saints would add the reception of exaltation to this definition. Exaltation, by the LDS definition, means becoming like God through the atonement of Jesus Christ, as discussed at the beginning of this chapter. Salvation without exaltation is, by the LDS definition, only partial salvation.

The term "grace" is likewise defined differently by Protestants and Latter-day Saints. Protestants generally define grace as the unmerited favor of God. This definition, though brief, is incomplete and therefore misleading. This definition could, for example, exclude the need for any effort on the part of man. However, most Protestants would agree that faith on our part is also necessary, and most would add that repentance and a profession of faith in Jesus Christ are also required for salvation. Thus, some effort is required.

Latter-day Saints define grace as God's "love, mercy, and condescension towards his children" (*Mormon Doctrine,* p. 338). We agree that salvation is granted by God as a result of true faith but, as James pointed out, true faith is always coupled with works on our part (James 2:17-20). The *LDS Bible Dictionary* contains the following informative statement concerning the relationship of grace and works:

> It is through the grace of the Lord Jesus, made possible by his atoning sacrifice, that mankind will be raised in immortality, every person receiving his body from the grave in a condition of everlasting life. It is likewise through the grace of the Lord that individuals, through faith in the atonement of Jesus Christ and repentance of their sins, receive strength and assistance to do good works that they otherwise would not be able to maintain if left to their own means. This grace is an enabling power that allows men end women to lay hold on eternal life and exaltation after they have expended their own best efforts.
>
> Divine grace is needed by every soul in consequence of the fall of Adam and also because of man's weaknesses and shortcomings. However, grace cannot suffice without total effort on the part of the recipient. Hence the explanation, "It is by grace that we are saved, after all we can do" (2 Nephi 25:23). It is truly the grace of Jesus Christ that makes salvation possible (*LDS Bible Dictionary,* p. 697).

Beliefs concerning the concept of grace cover a spectrum between two doctrinal extremes. At these extremes there are two theological traps. The first extreme is belief in salvation by grace, alone which might lead to the conclusion that obedience and good works are irrelevant. The second extreme is a belief in salvation by works, which could cause men to trust wholly in their own labors and genius, erroneously supposing that they will be rewarded hereafter solely upon their own achievements (see Robert L. Millet, *By Grace Are We Saved,* p. 4). Both of these beliefs are dangerous and could potentially cause us to fall short of exaltation.

The concept of salvation by grace through faith alone is today taught by some who refer to themselves as orthodox Protestants. Their misunderstanding of this doctrine stems from a focus on certain Pauline epistles to the exclusion of other New Testament teachings. Many Protestant sermons today continue to emphasize faith without works, even though not one scripture specifically teaches that men are saved by faith alone. On the other hand, numerous scriptures conclusively link works with faith as an essential part of the plan of salvation (see pp. 145-49).

The Apostle Peter made a special effort to warn us that it is dangerous to rely solely on the epistles of Paul regarding salvation. He advises us that Paul's writings were difficult to understand and, if misunderstood, could lead to destruction (2 Peter 3:15-16). One would think this warning should prevent people from relying totally upon Paul's writings regarding salvation but this is precisely what many Protestants have done. They almost exclusively cite scriptures in Paul's epistles to the Romans, Galatians, and Ephesians in support of their doctrine of salvation. In so doing they "wrest [struggle with] . . . the other [Old and New Testament] scriptures [which speak of works], unto their own destruction" (2 Peter 3:16; see also 146-147 of this text for additional scriptural support regarding the importance of works).

In Paul's defense it should be pointed out that his emphasis on grace, like modern LDS emphasis on good works, was probably intended to correct the erroneous teachings of his day. In Paul's day, the Jewish converts often believed that compliance with the Law of Moses was essential to justification (redemption from sin) and salvation (see Acts 13:39; Rom. 2:17; 3:19-28; Gal. 2:16; 3:11-14, 24). Although Paul's statements about justification at first seem contradictory (see Rom. 2:13; 3:20; and Rom. 2:6; Gal. 2:16), it is clear to Latter-day Saints that the Law of Moses was only a "schoolmaster to bring us unto Christ" (Gal. 3:24) who is the "author of eternal salvation unto all them that obey him" (Heb. 5:9). Although the Law of Moses could not justify men without Christ's atonement (2 Nephi 2:5-6, Mosiah 13:28), "the doers of the law shall be justified" (Rom. 2:13; see also James 2:24) "through the redemption that is in Christ Jesus" (Rom. 3:24). Thus, according to Paul, we are expected to have faith coupled with righteousness in order to be justified before God and receive eternal life (Rom. 2:6-8; 14:17-18; 1 Tim. 6:18-19).

It is important to note that the word "grace," according to all four gospel writers, was never used by Jesus Christ. One would think that if grace alone were sufficient to salvation and exaltation, Christ would have taught this important truth himself. Yet we search in vain for this doctrine among Christ's own sayings. On the other hand, Christ repeatedly emphasized the importance of obedience to gospel teachings and the necessity of good works on our part (Matt. 5:16; 7:21-23; 11:21-23; 16:27; 25:46; Mark 10:17-21; 12:28-34; Luke 7:31-38; 10:25-28; 11:28; 13:3, 24-27; 14:12-14; John 5:29; 7:17; 8:31-34; 13:34-35; 14:15, 21; 15:10). Why should he do so if obedience and good works were unnecessary?

Because members and missionaries of the LDS Church often emphasize the importance of obedience and works, some mistakenly conclude that we reject the concept of grace. This is simply not the case, as references to our dependence on grace are found throughout LDS scriptures and writings. The Book of Mormon speaks of grace at least 35 times and the Doctrine and Covenants 28 times.

We find Lehi, the first Book of Mormon prophet, teaching "there is no flesh can dwell in the presence of God, save it be through the merits, and mercy, and grace of the Holy Messiah" (2 Nephi 2:8). Jacob likewise taught, "ye are free to act for yourselves—to choose the way of everlasting death or the way of eternal life. Wherefore, my beloved brethren, reconcile yourselves to the will of God . . . and remember, after ye are reconciled unto God, that it is only in and through the grace of God that ye are saved. Wherefore, may God raise you from death by the power of the resurrection, and also from everlasting death by the power of the atonement, that ye may be received into the eternal kingdom of God, that ye may praise him through grace divine" (2 Nephi 10:23-25).

Moroni, the last Book of Mormon prophet, after speaking of the requirements of baptism, gave instructions to the church to watch over new converts and nourish them "by the good word of God, to keep them in the right way, to keep them continually watchful unto prayer, relying alone upon the merits of Christ, who was the author and the finisher of their faith" (Moroni 6:4). Moroni's closing remarks exhort all men to "come unto Christ and be perfected in him, and deny yourselves of all ungodliness . . . and love God with all your might, mind and strength, then is his grace sufficient for you, that by his grace ye may be perfect in Christ; and . . . then are ye sanctified in Christ by the grace of God through the shedding of the blood of Christ" (Moroni 10:32-33).

These passages make it clear that works are necessary on our part, but our works in no way save us. Works are a sign of our faith, for "faith without works is dead" (James 2:26). Without the atoning sacrifice of Jesus Christ all men would be lost despite their good works (Eph. 2:8-10; Heb. 9:22); but without good works God will not justify any man (Rom. 2:13; 2 Cor. 5:10; 1 John 1:7; Alma 41:1315).

Steven E. Robinson has explained:

> Our best efforts to live the laws of God are required, but not because they earn the promised rewards—our efforts are infinitely disproportionate to the actual costs. Rather, our best efforts are a token of our good faith and of our acceptance of the offered covenant. Thus we participate in our own salvation . . . but we can never earn it ourselves or bring it to pass on our own merits, no matter how well we may think we are doing (*Are Mormons Christian?*, pp. 105-06).

When one understands the scriptural steps by which grace becomes operative, one finds that: (1) God's grace and love towards all men (John 3:16) were manifest in Christ's atoning sacrifice (Titus 2:11; 1 John 4:9-10); (2) when we keep God's commandments, we abide in that love (John 15:10; 1 John 4:7; 5:3); (3) and we are born of God (1 John 5:4, 18); (4) we are sanctified by the Spirit (2 Thes. 2:13); and (5) we receive eternal life through Jesus Christ (1 John 5:11). Although we are saved by the grace of God and Christ, we will also appear before the judgement seat to receive a reward according to our works (Matt. 16:27; Rom. 14:10-12; 1 Cor. 3:8; 2 Cor. 5:10; Rev. 20:12-13; for additional information see Robert L. Millet, By Grace Are We Saved, p. 9; "What the Mormons Think of Christ" (Brochure); Bruce R. McConkie, *Mormon Doctrine*, pp. 343-46; 670-72; Steven E. Robinson, *Are Mormons Christian?*, pp. 104-08; Richard Lloyd Anderson, *Understanding Paul*, pp. 177-83, 272-76, 355-62).

64. Is salvation a free gift to all?

Both the Bible (Rom. 5:14-18; 6:23) and the Book of Mormon teach that salvation is a free gift to all. Lehi taught, "Wherefore, I know that thou art redeemed, because of the righteousness of thy Redeemer; for thou hast beheld that in the fulness of time he cometh to bring salvation unto men. And thou hast beheld in thy youth his glory; wherefore, thou art blessed even as they unto whom he shall minister in the flesh; for the Spirit is the same, yesterday, today, and forever. And the way is prepared from the fall of man, and salvation is free" (2 Nephi 2:3-4).

Nephi asks, "Hath he commanded any that they should not partake of his salvation? Behold, I say unto you, Nay; but he hath given it free for all men; and he hath commanded his people that they should persuade all men to repentance. Behold, hath the Lord commanded any that they should not partake of his goodness? Behold, I say unto you, Nay; but all men are privileged the one like unto the other, and none are forbidden" (2 Nephi 26:27-28).

Bruce R. McConkie has affirmed:

> "Salvation is free" (2 Nephi 2:4). Justification is free. Neither of them can be purchased; neither can be earned; neither comes by the law of Moses, or by good works, or by any power or ability that man has. . . .
>
> When the prophets who were before Christ preached that salvation is free, they were announcing the same doctrine that would thereafter fall from apostolic lips in the pronouncement that we are saved by grace. The questions then are: What salvation is free? What salvation comes by the grace of God? With all the emphasis of the rolling thunders of Sinai, we answer: All salvation is free; all comes by the merits and mercy and grace of the Holy Messiah; there is no salvation of any kind, nature, or degree that is not bound to Christ and his atonement. Specifically, our Lord's atoning sacrifice brings all men forth in the resurrection with immortal bodies, thus freeing them from death, hell, the devil, and endless torment; and our Lord's atoning grace raises those who believe and obey, not only in immortality, but unto eternal life; it raises them to sit down with Abraham, Isaac, and Jacob in God's everlasting kingdom forever (*The Promised Messiah,* pp. 346-47).

Perhaps the confusion about this gift would be cleared up by considering a few of the many other scriptural gifts from God including numerous gifts of the Spirit (1 Cor. 12), the gift of the Holy Ghost (Acts 2:38), the gift of grace (Rom. 5:15; James 4:6), the gift of righteousness (Rom. 5:17), the gift of faith (Eph. 2:8; 1 Cor. 12:9), the gift of repentance (Acts 11:18), the gift of prophecy (1 Cor. 13:2), and the gift of wisdom (James 1:5). Each of these gifts is free in the sense that we cannot earn them, but that does not mean that they may be had without effort. Paul taught that we should "covet [i.e. seek or strive after; see D&C 46:8] earnestly the best gifts" (1 Cor. 12:31) and "desire spiritual gifts" (1 Cor. 14:1, 12). Throughout his epistles, Paul affirms that we must strive on our part to be worthy of all gifts and blessings of God (Rom. 2:7, 13; Gal. 6:7-9; Eph. 5:3-10; Phil. 2:12; 1 Tim. 6:18-19; Heb. 6:10-15).

The most important of all gifts of God is the gift of salvation and eternal life (Rom. 6:23). Modern revelation confirms that this gift is the greatest of all gifts (D&C 6:13; 14:7). The mission of Jesus Christ had two main purposes and resulted in two gifts: resurrection and eternal life. Each, as Brother McConkie has stated, is free, but the first is given to all men (1 Cor. 15:22) while the second is given only to those who obey the gospel of Jesus Christ (Heb. 5:9). The first overcomes physical death caused by Adam's transgression (Rom. 5:14-15, 18; Alma 11:40-45), and the second overcomes spiritual death caused by our own sins (Rom. 6:22-23; Rev. 2:11; 20:6, 14-15; Alma 12:16, 32-35). Because we suffer the first by no fault of our own, we are not held responsible; but because we suffer the second as a result of individual sin, we must seek forgiveness through the process of repentance (2 Cor. 7:10). Nothing we have done or can do will earn forgiveness, but our refusal to have faith in Christ and to follow him constitutes a refusal to accept his sacrifice for us (John 8:12, 24; Alma 34:15-16). If we reject him, we reject also his gift to us. In this sense we consider the gift of salvation in God's kingdom to be free, but conditional upon our obedience to the gospel of Jesus Christ (see Rom. 2:16; 10:16; 1 Cor. 15:1-2; and questions which follow).

King Benjamin stated it clearly in the Book of Mormon:

> I say unto you, if ye have come to a knowledge of the goodness of God, and his matchless power, and his wisdom, and his patience, and his long-suffering towards the children of men; and also, the atonement which has been prepared from the foundation of the world, that thereby salvation might come to him that should put his trust in the Lord, and should be diligent in keeping his commandments, and continue in the faith even unto the end of his life, I mean the life of the mortal body—I say, that this is the man who receiveth salvation, through the atonement (Mosiah 4:6-7).

Elder David B. Haight taught: "Immortality comes to us all as a free gift by the grace of God alone without works of righteousness. Eternal life, however, is the reward for obedience to the laws and ordinances of His Gospel" (October 1989 Conference Talk, *Ensign*, Nov. 89, p. 61). Thus, salvation in its fullest sense is a free gift given not because we earn it by our works, but because the Lord has chosen to reward those who have true faith coupled with obedience and good works. Without obedience our faith is dead (James 2:20-21) and without true faith (faith coupled with works) our hope for salvation is dead. (See also *Teachings,* pp. 68, 253, and 357).

65. Do Latter-day Saints believe in assured salvation?

A few scriptures in the Bible seem to imply that once one or two steps are taken, salvation will be assured (John 3:36; 6:27, 37-39; 10:28-29; Rom. 8:38-39; 10:9-13; Phil. 1:6; 1 John 5:13). However, a host of other scriptures list additional required steps for salvation (see pp. 123-24 of this text) and make it clear that man may fall from grace (Ezek. 18:24; 1 Cor. 9:27; 10:12; 2 Cor. 6:1; Gal. 5:1-6; 6:9; Phil. 2:12; 1 Tim. 1:18-19; 4:1; 5:12; Heb. 3:12-14; 4:10-11; 6:4-6; 10:26-29, 39; 12:15; 2 Peter 2:1-2, 20-21; 3:17; 1 John 5:16; 2 John 8-9; Rev. 2:5; 3:5). Modern revelation also confirms that "man may fall from grace and depart from the living God [and that members of] the church [must] take heed and pray always, lest they fall into temptation" (D&C 20:32-33; see also Gal. 5:4; Heb. 3:12; 12:15; and *Teachings,* pp. 338-39).

Though the scriptures do speak of being sealed up unto salvation (John 6:27; 2 Cor. 1:22; Eph. 1:13; 4:30; Mosiah 5:15; D&C 76:53; 88:3-4; 131:5; 132:19, 49) and making our "calling and election sure" (2 Peter 1:10) or receiving the "promise" of eternal life (Rom. 4:16; Eph. 1:13; 4:30; 2 Tim. 1:1; Heb. 9:15; 1 John 2:25), this promise is a covenant relationship, a sacred agreement between man and God (Gal. 3:16-17; Heb. 8:6; 12:24; 13:20; D&C 84:33-44).

If we accept Jesus Christ as our Savior and obey his gospel to the end of our lives, God promises to give us eternal life (See Mark 10:30; 2 Peter 1:3-11; Mosiah 18:9, 13; D&C 66:2). However, only when our faith has been sufficiently tried (1 Peter 1:7-10; Ether 12:6; Abr. 3:25-26), will we receive the promised blessing *in person* from Jesus Christ and God the Father (John 14:16-18, 21, 23; Heb. 9:15; 1 John 2:24-25; D&C 88:3-5) and have our salvation sealed to us by the Holy Spirit of Promise, the Holy Ghost (Eph. 4:30; D&C 76:53; 132:7). Since few Christians would claim to have had these blessings sealed in person by the Father and the Son, it is doubtful that their salvation is at this point assured.

We should also note that even Paul spoke of this promise given to the saints as a "hope of eternal life" (Titus 1:2) and not an *assurance* of such (Rom. 5:2; 8:24-25; 1 Cor. 15:19; Gal. 5:5; Phil. 1:20; Col. 1:5; 1 Thes. 5:8; Titus 3:7; Heb. 6:11; see also 1 Peter 1:13; 1 John 2:25). Furthermore, the Apostle Peter made it clear that even those who have "escaped the pollutions of the world through the knowledge of the Lord and Saviour Jesus Christ, [if] they are again entangled therein, and overcome, the latter end is worse with them than the beginning. For it had been better for them not to have known the way of righteousness, than, after they have known it, to turn from the holy commandment delivered unto them" (2 Peter 2:20-21). We thus learn that salvation is assured if we endure in righteousness to the end of our lives (Matt. 10:22; 24:13; Mark 13:13; Heb. 6:15). Until then, we are only given the promise that we shall obtain if we remain steadfast in our faith (Col. 2:5; 2 Tim. 4:7-8; Heb. 3:14; Mosiah 4:11-12; 5:15).

Many people quote 1 John 5:10-13 to show that we "may know that [we] have eternal life." Although there is a sense in which we may have an assurance that we will receive eternal life, this is not the same thing as assured (guaranteed) salvation. This was also not the original intent of the above scripture. The New International Version (NIV) translates these verses as follows: "Anyone who believes in the Son of God has this testimony in his heart . . . And this is the testimony: God has given us eternal life, and this life is in his Son. He who has the Son has life; he who does not have the Son does not have life" (see also 1 John 1:2). The intent here is therefore not to teach assured salvation but to show that we must have faith in Christ.

The NIV shortens verse 13 to make it less repetitious, but the King James Version follows the Greek Received Text which reads, "I wrote these things to you, the ones believing in the name of the Son of God, that you may know that you have eternal life, and that you may believe in the name of the Son of God" This redundancy indicates a probable transcription error in the original Greek text; it also clearly shows that the faith of those whom John was writing to was not sufficiently proven since he wrote to them so that they, at some future point, might have true faith in the Son of God unto eternal life (see 1 Peter 1:7-10; 1 John 5:1-4). Like the early Christian saints, we must endure in faith and righteousness to the end. If we fail to do so, our salvation may be lost.

Bruce R. McConkie had this to say about the assurance of salvation:

> As members of the Church, if we chart a course leading to eternal life; if we begin the process of spiritual rebirth, and are going in the right direction; if we chart a course of sanctifying our souls, and degree by degree are going in that direction; and if we chart a course of becoming perfect, and, step by step and phase by phase, are perfecting our souls by overcoming the world, then it is absolutely guaranteed—there is no question whatever about it—we shall gain eternal life. Even though we have spiritual rebirth ahead of us, perfection ahead of us, the full degree of sanctification ahead of us, if we chart a course and follow it to the best of our ability in this life, then when we go out of this life we'll continue in exactly the same course. We'll no longer be subject to the passions and appetites of the flesh. We will have passed successfully the tests of this mortal probation and in due course we'll get the fulness of our Father's kingdom—and that means eternal life in his everlasting presence (*Doctrines of the Restoration*, p. 54).

66. Is salvation instant?

Those who promote the concept of instant salvation often cite the story of the thief on the cross (Luke 23:39-43). What is interesting is that the thief requested only that Jesus remember him when he came to his kingdom. It is ironic that those who cite this passage as an example of instant salvation are generally the same people who teach that a person only has to "confess" that Jesus is his Lord and Savior to be saved (Rom. 10:9-10). While it is true that the thief did display faith and was at this point repentant, we find him expressing more a hope for the resurrection than a true faith in Christ's atoning sacrifice for his own sins. Clearly this scripture does not support the idea of instant salvation, for the thief did not fulfill the "requirements" listed by orthodox Protestants.

Some Protestants have tried to infer more from the Lord's reply to the thief than was originally intended. When the Lord said: "To day shalt thou be with me in paradise" (Luke 23:43), he was not saying that the thief was instantly saved and would go immediately with Jesus to his Father's kingdom (although the use of "paradise" in 2 Corinthians 12:2-4 and Revelation 2:7 might seem to support this belief). In reality, this statement could only have meant: Today you will be with me in the paradise of spirits (i.e. that portion of the spirit world reserved for the righteous dead). This can easily be demonstrated by examining the scriptural facts surrounding Christ's activities between his death and his resurrection three days later.

Regarding this period, Peter informs us that Christ was "put to death in the flesh, [but] quickened by the Spirit: By which also he went and preached unto the spirits in prison" (1 Peter 3:18-19; see also Eph. 4:8-9). Peter then adds: "For this cause was the gospel preached also unto them that are dead, that they might be judged according to men in the flesh, but live according to God in the spirit" (1 Peter 4:6). Christ, therefore, visited the spirit world to set the prisoners free by preaching the gospel as Isaiah had prophesied (Isa. 24:22; 42:5-7; 49:9; 61:1; Luke 4:18). This was accomplished while Christ's body lay in the tomb awaiting the resurrection. Jesus showed that he had not gone to his Father's kingdom during this period when he told Mary Magdalene, following his resurrection, "Touch me not; for I am not yet ascended to my Father: but go to my brethren and say unto them, I ascend unto my Father and your Father; and to my God and your God" (John 20:17). Thus, the paradise entered into by the Savior and the thief upon death was not the same place as the Father's Kingdom.

The Savior hinted at the divided nature of the spirit world in the parable of Lazarus and the rich man (Luke 16:19-31). In this parable he referred to the righteous portion of the spirit world as "Abraham's bosom" (Luke 16:22) and to the unrighteous portion as hell or Hades (see *LDS Bible Dictionary*—Hell). The preaching of the gospel in both portions of the spirit world was inaugurated incident to Christ's visit and is described in greater detail in Joseph F. Smith's vision (D&C 138; see also Ephesians 4:8-9; Alma 40:11-14, 21; *Mormon Doctrine,* Spirit World, pp. 761-62 and *LDS Bible Dictionary*—Paradise).

When we understand that paradise was a place of rest for righteous spirits awaiting the resurrection, it becomes clear that the assurance given by Christ to the penitent thief on the cross was not a promise of instant salvation and acceptance into heaven, but rather a promise that he would go that day to the spirit world where he could hear the gospel preached and be given the opportunity to accept or reject Christ's atonement for him. Salvation, in this case, was therefore not immediate but still pending an acceptance of and obedience to the gospel in the spirit world (see James E. Talmage, *Jesus the Christ,* p. 677).

The Savior, when asked by a lawyer what was required to inherit eternal life (Luke 10:25), responded: "What is written in the law? how readest thou?" The lawyer said unto him, "Thou shalt love the Lord thy God with all thy heart, and with all thy soul, and with all thy strength, and with all thy mind; and thy neighbor as thyself." The Savior's response was, "Thou halt answered right: this do, and thou shalt live" (Luke 10:28). Christ also taught, "blessed are they that hear the word of God, and keep it" (Luke 11: 28).

Some cite the story of the sinful woman who washed Jesus' feet with her tears (Luke 7:37-50) as proof of instant salvation. As with the previous example, there was no verbal confession nor any word spoken by this repentant woman. Jesus is reported to have said: "Thy sins are forgiven. . . . Thy faith hath saved thee; go in peace"(Luke 7:48, 50). It seems clear that, in this case, salvation from past sins was granted by the Lord (see 121-122 of this text). However, eternal salvation in the kingdom of God could be granted subsequently by the Savior only if the repentant woman endured in righteousness to the end of her life (see Bruce R. McConkie, *Doctrinal New Testament Commentary,* 1:265; Matt. 10:22; 24:13; Mark 13:13; Heb. 6:15; 1 Nephi 13:37; 22:31; 2 Nephi 31:15-16, 20; 33:4; Alma 32:13; 3 Nephi 27:6; D&C 18:22; 53:7; 76:50-53).

Paul is often cited in support of the premise of instant salvation (Rom. 6:23; 10:9-10, 13; Heb. 10:10, 14), but this assertion contradicts Paul's later teachings which emphasize the importance of remaining steadfast in faith and showing forth good works that we "may lay hold on eternal life" (1 Tim. 6:11-12, 18-19; 2 Tim. 4:7-8). Paul himself admitted that he still had imperfections and was striving to improve (2 Cor. 12:5, 9-10; Phil. 3:12-14) and that if they (Paul and the saints) did not "weary in well doing: [they would] in due season . . . reap" (Gal. 6:9) "life everlasting" (Gal. 6:8).

Peter likewise exhorted us to give "all diligence" to "add to [our] faith virtue; and to virtue knowledge; and to knowledge temperance; and to temperance patience; and to patience godliness; and to godliness brotherly kindness; and to brotherly kindness charity." If we are diligent to "do these things" we will not fall but "an entrance shall be ministered unto [us] abundantly into the everlasting kingdom of our Lord and Saviour Jesus Christ" (2 Peter 1: 5-7, 10-11). Thus, Peter is speaking of attaining salvation as a continuing process to which we must give "all diligence."

Peter similarly speaks of grace not as a one-time gift of God but of our need to "grow in grace and in the knowledge of our Lord and Saviour

Jesus Christ" (2 Peter 3:18). God does not grant the most precious of all gifts when we show the first signs of a broken heart and a contrite spirit, but he does "give to each person according to what he has done. To those who by persistence in doing good seek glory, honour and immortality, he will give eternal life" (NIV Rom. 2:6-7).

Salvation is not received solely as a result of a confession of faith, but follows a life of faith accompanied by works (Luke 10:25-28; 11:27-28; Acts 2:47; Rom. 11:26; 13:11; 1 Cor. 3:13-15; 1 Tim. 6:11-12, 18-19; Titus 1:16; Rev.2: 26; 3:5, 21; 12:10-11; 20:6, 12-15; 21:7; 22:12). Instant salvation is a false teaching conceived by Satan to rob those who accept it of true salvation, the salvation which is given to those who endure in faith and righteousness. See also Mosiah 2:41; Alma 32:15; D&C 50:5; 63:20; 66:12; James E. Talmage's *Articles of Faith,* pp. 85 and 87; and *A Sure Foundation,* pp. 226-28.

67. Do Latter-day Saints believe a man can save himself by his own works?

Anti-Mormon literature often claims that members of our Church believe in salvation by works, but this is not accurate. LDS beliefs are in accord with the teachings of both Paul and James. We believe in salvation by grace through faith in Jesus Christ (Rom. 5:2; Eph. 2:8; see also pp. 135 and following), but we also believe that faith without works is dead (James 2:17, 20). To understand LDS teachings in this area one must first understand the meaning and significance of faith in LDS theology.

Latter-day Saints firmly believe that the first principle of the gospel is faith in the Lord Jesus Christ—faith that he is our Savior and Redeemer and that he died for us. Our fourth Article of Faith begins, "We believe that the first principles and ordinances of the Gospel are: *first,* Faith in the Lord Jesus Christ." Thus, we believe that faith in Christ is the first step in obtaining salvation (see Alma 32 and pages 12-13 of this text).

We also believe, as taught by James, that sincere faith is always accompanied by good works (James 2:17, 20, 24, 26). Not one scripture tells us that men are saved through faith alone, but many scriptures tie faith and works inseparably together, as will be shown shortly. Our third Article of Faith states, "We believe that through the Atonement of Christ, all mankind may be saved, by obedience to the laws and ordinances of the Gospel." Those laws and ordinances include faith in Jesus Christ, repentance, baptism by water and the Spirit, and enduring to the end of our lives in obedience to the commandments. The Savior taught these basic principles of the gospel during his ministry (Matt. 4:17; 10:22; 19:17; 28:19-20; John 3:5, 17-18; see also pages 12-13 of this text). Converts to the Church of Christ were likewise taught these principles by the apostles (Acts 2:36-38; 10:35-36, 43, 47-48; 19:2-6).

These same principles, along with a belief in the resurrection and the judgement, were considered by Paul to be the milk of the gospel (Heb. 5:12-14; 6:1-2; see also 1 Cor. 3:2; 1 Peter 2:2; D&C 19:22; 50:40). Unfortunately, some Christians have never been weaned away from gospel milk but are still arguing about and striving to understand these basic teachings. The meat of the gospel, according to Paul, "belongeth to them that are of full age, even to those who by reason of use have their sense exercised to discern both good and evil" (Heb. 5:4). Paul is saying that the mature Christian lives as dictated by the Spirit of the Holy Ghost, making the right choices and producing good works. As Elder Glenn Pace has pointed out, ". . . we will not be saved by works if those works are not born of a disposition to do good, as opposed to an obligation to do good." He explains that this process "comes about through grace and by the Spirit of God, although it does not come about until we have truly repented and proven ourselves worthy" (*Spiritual Plateaus,* p. 63). A mature Christian is converted to the truth and is obedient to the gospel because he has undergone a spiritual transformation referred to in scripture as being "born again" (John 3:3-7, 1 John 2:29; 3:9; Mosiah 27:24-26; *LDS Topical Guide,* p. 306).

Members of The Church of Jesus Christ of Latter-day Saints have accepted the gospel of Jesus Christ and have thus accepted him as Savior by taking his name upon them in baptism (Mosiah 5:715). Latter-day Saints have also accepted the gospel basics which include true faith (belief followed by works) and the covenant of baptism which includes obedience to the commandments (Mosiah 5:5, 8, 15). Latter-day Saints understand the principle of enduring to the end (1 Nephi 22:31; 2 Nephi 31:16, 19-21) and it only remains for them to learn how to endure in righteousness and live by the Spirit. We believe, as Paul taught, that the emphasis after conversion should shift from milk (faith, repentance, etc.) to the meat (enduring in righteousness and living by the Spirit).

Emphasis on works is not unique to the LDS Church—it is also found in every major book of the New Testament. Consider the following scriptures: Matthew 5:19; 7:21-23; 16:27; 25:46; Mark 7:6-8; 12:30-31; Luke 11:28; 13:3, 27; 14:12-14; John 5:29; 13:15; Acts 3:23, 26; 10:35; Romans 2:5-8, 10, 13; 14:12, 17-18; 1 Corinthians 3:8, 14; 6:9; 10:10-12; 2 Corinthians 5:10; Galatians 6:4, 7-9; Ephesians 4:17-19, 25-32; 6:8; Philippians 2:12; 4:8; Colossians 1:10; 3:24-25; 1 Thessalonians 4:13; 5:22; 2 Thessalonians 2:12; 3:13; 1 Timothy 4:16; 5:8-10; 6:18-19; 2 Timothy 2:20-21; 3:17; Titus 1:16; 2:14; Hebrews 4:11-12; 5:9; 6:4-6; 10:24, 26; James 2:24, 26; 1 Peter

1:17; 2:12-15; 2 Peter 2:20-21; 3:17; 1 John 1:6-9; 2:3-4; 3:10; 2 John 9; 3 John 11; Jude 1:15; Revelation 2:23, 26; 14:12-13; 20:12-13; 22:14-15. If good works spontaneously spring from faith, why would every New Testament writer in nearly every New Testament book (all but Philemon) feel it necessary to exhort us to keep God's commandments?

We also find the fathers of the Early Church emphasizing obedience. According to Clement, Barnabas taught, ". . . the Son of God is in the Judean country, promising eternal life to all who will hear him, provided they will do certain things conformant to the will of Him who sent him, namely God the Father" (*Clementine Recognitions,* 1: 1-5 in Patrol., Graec, 1:1207-9 as quoted in Hugh Nibley, *The World and the Prophets,* p. 32).

Latter-day Saints do not rely on good works for salvation. Yet those outside our Church who believe we do often quote Ephesians 2:8-9 ("by grace are ye saved . . . not of works") as if we had rejected this doctrine. However, those who quote these verses rarely quote the next verse, which reads: "For we are his workmanship, created in Christ Jesus unto good works, which God hath before ordained that we should walk in them." When this passage is read as a whole, it is clear that good works are expected of those who are "born again" through grace. Thus, the gift of salvation, (eternal life) is promised to those who are spiritually transformed. It is bestowed by the Lord at the end of life's journey following the resurrection and judgement (see 2 Nephi 31: 19-20 and previous question).

Some have raised the question of "dead works" (Heb. 6:1), citing Romans 4:4-5 and Isaiah 64:6 to show that unless we are first saved, our righteousness is worthless. As has already been shown (p. 142), salvation is not instantly realized by confessing that Jesus is our Lord and Savior, but will be achieved by living in faith to the end of our mortal existence. The phrase "dead works" in Paul's epistle to the Hebrews referred to unrighteous behavior which was to be repented of and abandoned completely—not to righteous behavior. The New International Version makes this clear by translating the last portion of Hebrews 6:1 as, "not laying again the foundation of repentance from acts that lead to death" or in other words, sinful works of the flesh (see also Hebrews 9:14).

As was mentioned in an earlier response (p. 136), Paul's emphasis on grace was partially a reaction to the false Jewish belief that Mosaic "deeds of the law" would justify them. This is especially apparent in the verses preceding Romans 4:4-5. We read at the end of Romans 3 that Paul is teaching justification "by faith without the deeds of the law" of

Moses (Rom. 3:28). The deed he is specifically addressing is circumcision (verse 30). He explains that circumcision, though a righteous deed of the law, is of no value to the Jew unless he has faith in Christ. Paul then cites Abraham as an example of a man who, though uncircumcised (Rom. 4:12), was made "heir of the world [exalted] through the righteousness of faith" (Rom 4:13). Thus, the point he is making throughout this section is that true faith will produce righteousness and good works, but that works alone have no power unto salvation.

Isaiah 64:6, which speaks of our righteousness as "filthy rags," can also be translated as "soiled garments." An allusion to soiled garments is more in keeping with the rest of the scriptures (see Isa. 1:16-19) and fits perfectly with Alma's declaration that "there can no man be saved except his garments are washed white . . . through the blood of [Christ]" (Alma 5:21; see also Gen. 49:11; Rev. 7:14; Alma 13:11; 3 Nephi 27:19; Ether 13:10). Therefore, our works, like unclean garments, are of no value without Christ's cleansing atonement. Unlike dirty rags, soiled garments are valuable when cleaned and are therefore worth keeping. Good works likewise are of value when coupled with faith and with the atonement of Jesus Christ.

Our works are also of value in that they are a token of our obedience to the gospel of Jesus Christ (Luke 11:28; 2 Thes. 1:8; 1 Peter 4:17; D&C 138:4). When we obey God's commandments we also demonstrate our love for him (John 14:15, 21; 1 John 2:5; 5:3) and may thereby be born again (1 John 2:29) unto eternal life (John 3:3; 1 John 5:3-4, 11). Our works are a product of faith and the regenerating influence of the Holy Ghost (Rev. 14:12-13). Our works in no way earn any blessings from God, but true spiritual rebirth will produce righteous works. Therefore, without Christ's atonement no man can receive salvation; any good works produced without faith in him are of no saving value.

In the Book of Mormon, King Benjamin's discourse to his people illustrates the futility of trying to earn salvation. He declared:

> . . . if you should render all the thanks and praise which your whole soul has power to possess, to that God who has created you, and has kept and preserved you, and has caused that ye should rejoice, and has granted that ye should live in peace one with another
>
> I say unto you that if ye should serve him who has created you from the beginning, and is preserving you from day to day, by lending you breath, that ye may live and move and do according to your own will, and even supporting you from one moment to another—I say, if ye should serve him with all your whole souls yet ye would be unprofitable servants.
>
> And behold, all that he requires of you is to keep his commandments; and he has promised you that if ye would keep his commandments ye should prosper in

the land and he never doth vary from that which he hath said; therefore, if ye do keep his commandments he doth bless you and prosper you.

And now, in the first place, he hath created you, and granted unto you your lives, for which ye are indebted unto him.

And secondly, he doth require that ye should do as he hath commanded you; for if ye do, he doth immediately bless you; and therefore he hath paid you. And ye are still indebted unto him, and are, and will be, forever and ever; therefore, of what have ye to boast? (Mosiah 2:20-24)

In summary, to charge that Latter-day Saints believe in salvation by works is to grossly misrepresent LDS doctrine. As has been shown (pp. 128, 134), the teachings of the Church and the Book of Mormon affirm that Christ's sacrifice and God's grace are essential to our salvation. Our works are only important in the sense that they are tokens of faith and obedience (Heb. 5:9; James 2:26), but without Christ's atoning sacrifice no man may be saved (1 Nephi 10:6; 2 Nephi 2:5-7; Jacob 7:12; Mosiah 3:17; 16:10-13; Alma 21:9; 22:14). Those who rely solely on the grace of Christ, but who lack the good works which accompany true faith, may fulfill Christ's prophecy in Matthew 7:21-23. Even though they may claim faith and miracles in Christ's name, to them he will say, "depart from me, ye that work iniquity." If these are rejected, surely those who only profess Christ's name while failing to obey his gospel in deed will be rejected at the day of judgement. See also Mormon Doctrine—Good works, pages 328-31.

68. Do works precede salvation or are they a product of salvation?

In an effort to clarify the relationship of faith, works, and salvation, some have tried to address the issue using word formulas. The following formulas have been proposed by Protestants to resolve this question:

Faith + Works (does not equal) Eternal Life
Faith = Eternal Life + Works

These word formulas, however, do not hold up against the teachings of Jesus Christ. The Savior, when asked "Good Master, what good thing shall I do, that I may have eternal life?" responded: "if thou wilt enter into life, keep the commandments" (Matt. 19:16-17). This certainly indicates that keeping the commandments is a requirement for eternal life. As was addressed earlier (pp. 140 and following), eternal life (salvation in God's kingdom) is not a product of a confession of faith only (Rom. 13:10-12). Ultimate salvation is received following a life of obedience and good works (Matt. 19:17). Put in their proper perspective, the above formulas should read:

Christ's Atonement + True Faith = Eternal Life
(see John 3:16-21; Eph. 2:8; Alma 11:40)
where:
True Faith = Belief + Obedience + Works
(see Heb. 5:9; James 2:17-26; I John 2:3)

As the above illustrates, the atonement of Jesus Christ does become effective in our lives based on our faith, but that faith must be genuine. Genuine faith is always accompanied by obedience and good works. If we remain faithful to the end, enduring in righteousness, we will receive eternal life as a gift from God (Rom. 6:23). Our righteousness will not earn it, but our best efforts to live Christ-like lives will lead, little-by-little, to spiritual rebirth (1 John 2:29; 3:24; 5:4), justification (Rom. 2:13; James 2:24), and sanctification (2 Thes. 2:13; 1 John 3:7, 10).

John taught: "if we walk in the light, as he [God] is in the light . . . the blood of Jesus Christ his son cleanseth us from all sin" (1 John 1: 7), and "everyone that doeth righteousness is born of him" (1 John 2:29; 3:24). John also taught "he that doeth righteousness is righteous, even as he [God] is righteous" (1 John 3:7). We become righteous not because our works make us so, but because God sanctifies us through his Spirit based on our faith and efforts to obey him. It is for this reason that the apostles exhorted the saints to remain faithful and show forth the "righteousness of faith" (Rom. 4:13). Faith produces righteousness which is manifest in good works. Our faith with our works justifies us (Rom. 2:13; James 2:24) and enables us to please God (Heb. 11:6; 1 John 3:22) and be blessed.

The scriptures bear record that our ultimate reward (exaltation and eternal life) will be granted by the Lord according to our works, which are the visible token of our faith (Ex. 20:6; Ps. 62:12; Eccl. 12:14; Matt. 16:27; Rom. 2:6-8; 2 Cor. 5:10; Rev. 2:23; 20:12; 22:12; Alma 41:3). Those who believe that Christians will somehow escape the judgement are in error. The scriptures are clear that everyone, whether righteous or wicked, whether quick (alive) or dead will appear before the judgement seat of Christ (Ps. 50:4; Eccl. 3:17; Matt. 16:27; Acts 17:31; Rom. 14:10 2 Cor. 5: 10; Rev. 2:23; 20: 12-13; 22: 12; see also Acts 10:42, 2 Tim. 4:1, 1 Peter 4:5; Moroni 10:34). All will give an accounting. 1 Peter 4:17-18 states that judgement will begin with the "house of God" (i.e. the church); Peter then adds, "if it first begins at us, what shall the end be of them that obey not the gospel of God?" Those who have produced no fruit and have not obeyed God will be rejected, while those who brought forth fruit by doing the will of God will, through sanctification and rebirth, receive eternal life (Matt. 7:17-23).

If good works came automatically by acceptance of Christ, why did Christ, Paul, and the other apostles exhort us first to good works (Matt. 5:6; 7:21-27; 19:16-17; John 7:17; 8:31-32; Acts 10:35; 1 Tim. 6:18-19; 1 John 1:7; 2:17)? Why didn't they just preach faith and confession of Jesus Christ? Yet we read of the necessity of overcoming, enduring, and working out our salvation (Matt. 10:22; 24:13; Mark 13:13; Phil. 2:12; 1 Tim. 4:16; Rev. 2:7, 11; 3:5, 12, 21). Why the contradiction? Obviously, works are important and must precede salvation. The goal is therefore reached at the end of the road—not at the beginning (see also Acts 2:47; 11:13-14; 15:11; Rom. 5:9-10).

69. Is perfection attainable by man?

When speaking of salvation, Protestants typically emphasize man's sinful nature: "There is none righteous, no, not one . . . For all have sinned; and come short of the glory of God" (Rom. 3:10, 23). Though man is admittedly imperfect, we must not ignore the fact that Jesus called us to a better life and commanded us, "Be ye therefore perfect, even as your Father which is in heaven is perfect" (Matt. 5:48). Unless we believe that Jesus gave us an impossible commandment, we must admit that some degree of perfection is attainable by man.

The scriptures leave no doubt that we are expected to strive for perfection. In fact, the Bible refers to both Noah and Job as perfect men (Gen. 6:9; Job 1:1; 2:3) and alludes to other perfect men in Christ's day (1 Cor. 2:5-6; Heb. 12:23). Abram and the people of Israel were commanded to be perfect (Gen. 17:1; Deut. 18:13) and the New Testament church was specifically established to help men become perfect like Christ (John 17:22-24; Eph. 4:11-14). Paul exhorted the saints to be perfect in his day (2 Cor. 13:9-11; Heb. 11:40) and was striving for perfection himself (Phil. 3:12, 15). These and other scriptures make it clear that perfection should be our goal. Though man may only become "perfect in Christ Jesus" (Col 1:28; 1 Peter 1:18-19, 22; 5:10; 2 Nephi 2:8; D&C 76:69), or in other words, by way of his atonement, scriptural perfection, like true faith, seems to be associated with good works on our part (2 Tim. 3:17; Heb. 13:20-21).

Moroni provides what is perhaps the best scriptural explanation of the perfecting process. He invites us to "come unto Christ, and be perfected in him, and deny yourselves of all ungodliness . . . and love God with all your might, mind, and strength, then is his grace sufficient for you . . . and if by the grace of God ye are perfect in Christ, ye can in nowise deny the power of God. And again, if ye by the grace of God are perfect in Christ, and deny not his power, then are ye sanctified in Christ by the grace of God, through the shedding of the blood of Christ, which is in the covenant of the Father unto the remission of your sins, that ye become holy without spot" (Moroni 10:32-33).

Joseph Fielding Smith taught the following on the subject of perfection:

> Salvation does not come all at once; we are commanded to be perfect even as our Father in heaven is perfect. It will take us ages to accomplish this end, for there will be greater progress beyond the grave, and it will be there that the faithful will overcome all things and receive all things, even the fulness of the Father's glory . . . That will not come all at once, but line upon line, and precept upon precept, example upon example, and even then not as long as we live in this mortal life, for we will have to go even beyond the grave before we reach that perfection and shall be like God. But here we lay the foundation (*Doctrines of Salvation,* 2:18; see also *A Sure Foundation,* pp. 205-10).

70. How can Latter-day Saints believe in eternal marriage in view of Matthew 22:29-30 and other similar scriptures?

Before it can be fully understood, Matthew 22:29-30 must be viewed in the larger context that begins with verse 23. Similar versions of this same story are found in the gospels of Mark and Luke (Mark 12:18-25; Luke 20:27-36). To understand these verses, we need to understand both the context of this story and the total scriptural context of eternal marriage.

The context in which this question was posed makes it clear that the Sadducees were trying to entrap the Lord. Since the Sadducees did not believe in the resurrection (vs. 23), asking a question based on that belief (vs. 28) was an obvious ruse. We should also note that the Pharisees had made a similar attempt that same day which had failed to "entangle him" (Matt. 22:15-23).

The question posed by the Sadducees was based on a dilemma contrived from the law of Moses (Deut. 25:5-10). Under the Mosaic law, if a man died, his widow was to marry his brother so that the brother could raise up seed in the name of him who died. Because the law of Moses constituted a lower law, the law of marriage it contained was for this life only (Rom. 7:1-3). By contrast, the Lord was teaching the higher law of the gospel, which brought with it a higher law of marriage for eternity. This conclusion is reinforced by the Lord's response to a similar question posed by the Pharisees: "Have ye not read, that he which made them at the beginning made them male and female, And said, For this cause shall a man leave father and mother, and shall cleave to his wife: and they twain shall be one flesh? Wherefore they are no more twain, but one flesh. What therefore God hath joined together, let no man put asunder"

(Matt. 19:4-6). It is also important to note that the Sadducees' question confirms that the Lord and his disciples were teaching the eternal nature of marriage. How could the Sadducees hope to entrap the Savior with a doctrine he had never taught?

The answer Christ gave the Sadducees effectively dismissed their question about marriage so that he could get to the fundamental problem—the Sadducees disbelief in the resurrection. He told them, "Ye do err ["greatly err" in Mark's account], not knowing the scriptures nor the power of God" (Matt. 22:29). The scriptures, as the Lord was about to demonstrate, testified of the resurrection and of the power of God to raise men from the dead (see Luke 20:37-38) and to bind on earth and in heaven (Matt. 16:19). The scriptures also testify of eternal marriage, as will be shown shortly. The Savior's response in Luke (see Luke 20:34-36) is more specific and probably more accurate than the accounts of Matthew and Mark. Because it also helps explain these shorter versions, we will examine this account in detail. Joseph Fielding Smith, in *Doctrines of Salvation,* gave the following commentary on these verses:

> The Savior, answering them according to their folly, said: "The children of this world [i.e. the world to which the Sadducees belonged] marry, and are given in marriage." I call your attention to the fact that the Lord said that he and his disciples did not belong to this world (John 17:9-16); the Sadducees did.
>
> Then he added: "But they [those of "this world" who do not keep the whole law] which shall be accounted worthy to obtain that world [i.e. even those who obtain the celestial kingdom but being unmarried do not obtain an exaltation in that kingdom], and the resurrection from the dead, neither marry, nor are given in marriage: Neither can they die any more: for they are equal unto the angels; and are the children of God, being the children of the resurrection" (Luke 20:27-37; see also Matt. 22:23-32).
>
> . . . This is the only answer the Lord could have given to these unbelievers. It is in full accord with the revelation given to the Prophet Joseph Smith, wherein the Lord says that, "when they [those of "this world" who do not keep the whole law] are out of the world they neither marry nor are given in marriage; but are appointed angels in heaven, which angels are ministering servants, to minister for those who are worthy of a far more, and an exceeding, and an eternal weight of glory. For these angels did not abide the law; therefore they cannot be enlarged, but remain separately and singly, without exaltation, in their saved condition, to all eternity; and from hence-forth are not gods, but are angels of God forever and ever" (D&C 132:16-17).
>
> The answers are exactly the same and apply to those who may be worthy of some salvation, notwithstanding their rejection of the eternal marriage covenant. There will be no marrying, neither giving in marriage among those who reject the truth of the everlasting gospel. That privilege is confined to those who keep the commandments of the Lord in their fulness and who are obedient to the laws of God (*Doctrines of Salvation,* 2:72-73).

We should also note that though none would marry "in the resurrection" (i.e. after this life), this in no way excludes eternal marriages made binding by the power of God in mortality. Illustrating this is the marriage of Adam and Eve (Gen. 2:22-24). This marriage was performed by God before death entered the world and as such was for eternity. We are told that "whatsoever God doeth, it shall be for ever" (Eccl. 3:14).

The New Testament also confirms the doctrine of eternal marriage. Paul taught, "Nevertheless neither is the man without the woman, neither the woman without the man, in the Lord" (1 Cor. 11:11). Peter affirmed that man and woman can be "heirs together of the grace of life" (1 Peter 3:7). The New Testament likewise teaches that our earthly families are merely reflections of a heavenly family in which we are sons and daughters of God (John 20:17; Acts 17:28-29; Eph. 3:15; Heb. 12:9). Those who become "like him" (Matt. 5:48; 1 John 3:2) will thus have the opportunity to become fathers and mothers of other eternal families (2 Peter 1:3-4; D&C 132:19, 30-31; see also Legrand Richards, *A Marvelous Work and a Wonder,* pp. 188-200 and James E. Talmage, *Jesus the Christ,* p. 548).

The first fathers likewise emphasized the importance of marriage. Eugene Seaich observed that Irenaeus declared, "whosoever is not in the world and has not loved a woman so as to unite with her, is not of the truth" (*Against Heresies,* I, 6:4). He likewise points out that:

> Clement of Alexandria unequivocally taught that all should marry as the apostles did (*Who is the Real Man that Shall Be Saved?*, pp. 14, 22, 27). Eusebius (*History of the Church,* III: 30) lists Peter, Philip, and Paul among "the apostles that lived in marriage." Clement also understood Paul's words in 1 Corinthians 9:5 to mean that the apostles travelled about with wives; Acts 1:12-14 records that all were present with their wives and children in the Upper Room after the Resurrection. The Epistles generally indicate that marriage was expected of bishops, elders, deacons and the like (1 Tim. 3:2, 5; 5:14; Titus 1:6; Rom. 16:3; 1 Cor. 7:2; etc.). In fact, about forty of the early Popes were married (John A. O'Brian, *Why Priests Marry,* The Christian Century, 87:417; see also William Fops, *Was Jesus Married?,* p. 99). (Eugene Seaich, *Mormonism, the Dead Sea Scrolls, and the Nag Hammadi Texts,* pp. 35, 39)

Although the doctrine of eternal marriage is not clearly explained in Bible scripture, it should be apparent that the Lord's response to the Sadducee unbelievers differed significantly from teachings directed to believers (Matt. 19:4-6; Mark 10:6-9; 1 Cor. 11:11; 1 Peter 3:7) by the Lord and his apostles. LDS beliefs are easily reconciled with these later teachings.

71. Don't the spirits of the dead go directly to heaven or hell after death?

Protestants often cite Paul's epistles to the Corinthians (2 Cor. 5:8) and Philippians (Phil. 1:23) to show that "to be absent from the body" is "to be present with the Lord" It is clear that those who have endured, believing in Christ and keeping his commandments, dwell "in him" and "he in [them]" (1 John 3:23-24; 4:15-16; 5:3; see also John 6:56). In this sense, we will be in the Lord's presence after death, but we should not interpret this to mean that we return immediately to heaven. As was pointed out earlier (p. 142 of this text), righteous spirits awaiting the resurrection will rest in paradise while the wicked will be consigned to hell or a spirit prison (Luke 16:19-31; 23:39-43; John 20:17; Alma 40:9-14, D&C 138:11-16, 50). These places are unitedly referred to as the spirit world. The gospel will be presented to those who are in prison (John 5:25; 1 Peter 3:18-19), that all might have an opportunity to hear and understand the truth in its fulness, be judged as those who heard it in the flesh, and live while yet spirits as God lives—in righteousness (1 Peter 4:6).

Both Irenaeus and Tertullian taught that men's spirits go to a place of waiting to await the resurrection. Irenaeus criticized the Gnostic idea that the soul passes to heaven after death (*Haer.* 5, 31, 1). Tertullian felt that the soul remained in the underworld (*De anim.* 55-8; Marc 4, 34) while Irenaeus concluded that "the souls (of Christians) go to an invisible place designated for them by God, and sojourn there until the resurrection. . . . Afterward receiving bodies and rising again perfectly" (*Haer.* 4, 33, 9 as quoted in J.N.D. Kelly, *Early Christian Doctrines,* p. 468).

President Ezra Taft Benson, in the August 1991 First Presidency Message, stated the following on this subject:

> The spirit world is not far away. Sometimes the veil between this life and the life beyond becomes very thin. Our loved ones who have passed on are not far from us.
>
> The prophet Brigham Young asked, "Where is the spirit world?" and then answered his own question:
>
> "It is right here. . . . Do [spirits] go beyond the boundaries of this organized earth? No, they do not. They are brought forth upon this earth, for the express purpose of inhabiting it to all eternity" (*Journal of Discourses,* 3:369).
>
> "When the spirits leave their bodies they are in the presence of our Father and God, they are prepared then to see, hear and understand spiritual things. . . . If the Lord would permit it, and it was his will that it should be done, you could see the spirits that have departed from this world, as plainly as you now see bodies with your natural eyes" (*Journal of Discourses,* 3:368) (*Ensign,* Aug. 91, pp. 2-4; see also *Mormon Doctrine*—Spirit Prison, pp. 754-55 and *Spirit World,* pp. 761-62).

We know that at the time of the Second Coming, all the inhabitants of the spirit world must "appear before the judgement seat of Christ" (Rom. 14:10; 2 Cor. 5:10; see also Matt. 25:31) where, incident to the resurrection, "every knee shall bow" and "every tongue confess" the Lord's name (Rom. 14:11; Phil. 2:9-11). This event will mark the beginning of the millennium and will be followed by Christ's one-thousand-year reign on earth (Rev. 5:10; 20:4, 6). At the conclusion of the millennium, the earth will be renewed and glorified and will become a heaven (the Celestial Kingdom) to those who inhabit it (Rev. 21; D&C 88:17-20; 130:9). Thus, until that time, the permanent celestial world will not exist, and those who die must await the resurrection in the spirit world.

72. Do Bible scriptures justify a belief in salvation for the dead?

Before examining what the Bible has to say about salvation for the dead, it is important to understand that this aspect of the Lord's work was primarily reserved for the last days. Consequently, most Bible references in this regard emphasize either Christ's role in redeeming the dead or the yet future redemption of the spirit dead. Modern revelation, on the other hand, speaks of the immediate importance of this work and our duty in this respect (see *LDS Topical Guide*—Salvation for the Dead, Baptism for the Dead, and Genealogy and Temple Work).

The Bible contains many references to the ministry among the dead. Isaiah anciently referred to Christ's ministry to the prisoners of the spirit world in four separate passages of scripture (Isa. 24:21-22; 42:5-7; 49:9-10; 61:1). From these passages we learn that those who are to be punished will be shut up by the Lord in a pit or prison and after many days shall be visited (24:22). Those called by the Lord will open the eyes of the blind (42:7) by teaching them the Lord's way, bringing them out of the darkness of the prison house, and enabling them to make their abode in the high places (49:9). The "opening of the prison" (Isa. 61:1) was initiated by the Savior, as we shall see shortly.

Zechariah also makes reference to the "pit wherein is no water" (Zech. 9:11). Though this may be an allusion to the unacceptability of the baptismal ordinance in this place, it could also refer to the torment of the spirits who thirst for the living water of the gospel (see also Luke 16:24). Job likewise speaks of the pit to which the sinner's soul may go (Job 33:27-30) but from which a man's soul may be brought back "to be enlightened with the light of the living." Obadiah prophesied that "saviours shall come up on mount Zion to judge the mount of Esau; and the kingdom shall be the Lord's" (Obad. 1:21; see also *Teachings*, pp. 191, 223, 330). Though none of these Old Testament scriptures is clear by itself, the New Testament provides some keys to understanding these important passages.

Luke informs us that the Lord quoted Isaiah in order to confirm to the Jews in Nazareth that he had been "anointed" to "preach the gospel to the poor . . . heal the brokenhearted . . . preach deliverance to the captives, and recovering of sight to the blind, to set at liberty them that are bruised" (Luke 4:18). Peter, as was mentioned earlier, affirmed that Christ's ministry to the spirits of the dead in prison (1 Peter 3:18-19; 4:6) was to make it possible for them to live like "God in the spirit." In this context, Christ's statement that "the hour is coming, and now is, when the dead shall hear the voice of the Son of God: and they that hear shall live" (John 5:25) takes on new meaning. In like manner, Paul's declaration that Jesus is "Lord of the dead and living" (Rom. 14:9) makes more sense if we realize that "he led captivity captive" when he "descended first [prior to ascending up on high] into the lower parts of the earth [i.e. into the pit or spirit prison]" (Eph. 4:8-9).

In about AD 150, Justin Martyr debated with Trypho using a text which he said was still in some copies of Jeremiah. The text stated that, "The Lord God remembered his dead people of Israel who lay in the graves; and he descended to preach to them his own salvation" (*Dialogue with Trypho,* 72 in *Ante-Nicene Fathers,* 1:235).

In an early Christian text entitled *The Shepherd of Hermas* we are told that in addition to the Lord's personal visit to the spirit world, "These apostles and teachers who preached the name of the Son of God, having fallen asleep . . . preached also to those who had fallen asleep before them" (*The Shepherd of Hermas,* Similitude's 9.16.5, *The Apostolic Fathers,* 2:263). Many other early Christian scholars and historians perpetuated this teaching because they had clear evidence that it was taught by those living alongside the apostles. Among these were Hippolytus, Tertullian, Clement of Alexandria, and Origen (Richard Lloyd Anderson, *Ensign,* Oct. 91, p. 9).

Irenaeus, the last living associate of the first apostles, wrote in about 180 AD of Jesus' visit to the spirit world. He said, "The Lord descended into the regions beneath the earth, preaching his advent there also, and (proclaiming) the remission of sins received by those who believe in him. Now all those believed in him who had hope towards him, that is, those who proclaimed his advent, and submitted to his dispensation, the righteous men, the prophets, and patriarchs to whom he remitted sins in the same way as he did to us . . ." (Irenaeus, *Against Heresies,* IV, 27, ii; see also *Ensign,* Oct. 91, p. 9).

The work of salvation for the dead, though initiated by Christ, will be carried on by others. Malachi alludes to this work in the last verses of the Old Testament. We are informed that the Lord will send "Elijah the prophet before the great and dreadful day of the Lord" to initiate a new work. Since this was a latter-day event prophesied to occur prior to the Second Coming, we should not expect to see it completely explained in the New Testament. It is, however, mentioned. Paul refers to the righteous dead who "having obtained a good report through faith, received not the promise [of eternal life]: God having provided some better thing for us, that they without us should not be made perfect" (Heb. 11:39-40). Though these passages are admittedly unclear without modern revelation (see D&C 76:73-74; 88:99; 124:39; 128:15-18), it is clear that the dead will in some way rely on the Saints in the last days for their own salvation.

Paul, in his first epistle to the Corinthians, tells us, "If in this life only we have hope in Christ, we are of all men most miserable" (1 Cor. 15:19). He goes on to speak of some who "are baptized for the dead" (1 Cor. 15:29). Though some today interpret this concept to refer to a pagan ordinance, their interpretation seems an unlikely rationalization in the context of the scripture. It would be strange for an apostle of the Lord to interject an incorrect practice into the middle of a Christ-centered discussion, then cite this false practice as a proof of the resurrection. This verse also helps explain how the dead, with our help, could "be made perfect" (Heb. 11:40). These verses also make clear how we could be likened to "saviors" (Obad. 1:21) because we make possible their salvation through vicarious baptism. If this ordinance were accomplished by the children of those who lived without the gospel, it would also explain how the hearts of the children would turn to their fathers and vice versa (Mal. 4:6).

When we consider questions such as "What about my ancestors who never heard of Jesus Christ?" and "What about those in countries where Christ and his gospel are never taught?", we are faced with a dilemma. While some claim that everyone who is looking for Christ will find him, this explanation does not ring true. It seems an obvious attempt to justify an injustice wherein some races are almost totally excluded from salvation due to their circumstances. We are told that all men will be judged "according to their works" (Rev. 20:12-15) and unless all are given an equal chance, God would be unjust. 1 Peter 4:6 and 1 Corinthians 15:29 provide us with the key to understanding this dilemma: all will have the opportunity to hear the gospel in its fulness, have the saving ordinances performed by proxy, and live like God eternally. This is the LDS belief—that those who have not yet heard the gospel in mortality may yet hear it on the other side. It is not, as detractors say, a second chance to gain salvation after rejecting it (D&C 137:7-9).

As was explained in the beginning, this doctrine apparently was not crucial to the early saints and was therefore not explained in detail to them. We do find it explained in latter-day revelation when the time had fully come for Elijah to bring forth this great work. The hints of this doctrine in the New Testament are clear when read by the Spirit but will be misunderstood without it (see also Richard Lloyd Anderson, *Understanding Paul,* pp. 126-27; Appendix C, Baptism for the Dead).

73. Where does the Bible indicate that the temple was part of the New Testament church?

Jacob, the Old Testament prophet, equated the "house of God" to "the gate of heaven" (Gen. 28:17). Modern revelation affirms that in a very real sense, the highest kingdom of heaven can only be obtained through the ordinances of the temple (D&C 131:1-2). Although most Christians today recognize the importance of the temple to ancient Israel, they seem to ignore references to temple worship in the New Testament church. They reason that temples were only for blood sacrifices, and that when Christ became the final sacrificial "Lamb of God," blood sacrifices and the need for temples were "done away" (see 2 Cor. 3:14; Heb. 9:1-28; 10:1-20).

Those who hold that temples are no longer required ignore the biblical teachings that the Lord will return suddenly at the last day "to his temple" (Mal. 3:1-2) and that the anti-Christ will reveal himself "in the temple of God" (2 Thes. 2:4). We are also told by John the Revelator that those who "wash their robes and make them white in the blood of the Lamb" will serve God "day and night in his temple" (Rev. 7:14-15). We might ask then who will build this temple and why will it be used "day and night" if it is no longer needed?

We should also note that Christ and his disciples often taught and worshiped in the temple. Christ, according to all four gospels, "taught daily in the temple" (Matt. 26:55; Mark 14:49; Luke 2:46; 19:47; 21:37-38; John 7:28; 8:20; 18:20) and would not allow men to defile it (Matt. 21:12-15; Mark 11:15-18; Luke 19:45-46; John 2:14-17). There he taught his gospel (Luke 20:1) and healed the blind and the lame (Matt. 21:14). After the resurrection, we find the disciples "continuing daily . . . in the temple" (Acts 2:46) "praising and blessing God" (Luke 24:53). We also find the apostles teaching and healing at the temple as Christ had done (Acts 3:1-26). Significantly, Paul was praying in the temple and was there visited by the Lord in his glory (Acts 22:17-18). Later, in his first epistle to the Corinthians, Paul asks, "Do ye not know that they which minister about holy things live of the things of the temple?" (1 Cor. 9:13). How can we live of the things of the temple if there is no temple? Apparently then, the temple remained the center of Christian worship even after Christ's death (for additional information on early Christian temple rites see Eugene Seaich, *Ancient Texts and Mormonism,* pp. 56-68 and Darrick Evenson, *The Gainsayers,* pp. 79-92).

The importance of temples and temple work will increase as we enter the millennial period of the earth's history. Bruce R. McConkie has stated: "Salvation cannot be gained except through baptism of water and of the Spirit, nor can exaltation be achieved except through temple endowments and the sealing of families together for eternity. These saving and exalting ordinances are performed vicariously in the temples for the worthy dead who did not have the opportunity to receive them in this life. We are commanded to go to with our might, collect all the accurate genealogical data we can, and perform these saving and exalting ordinances for our worthy ancestors. Obviously, due to the frailties, incapacities, and errors of mortal men, and because the records of the past ages are often scanty and inaccurate, this great work cannot be completed for every worthy soul without assistance from on high. The millennial era is the time, primarily, when this assistance will be given by resurrected beings. Genealogical records unknown to us will then become available. Errors committed by us in sealings or other ordinances will be rectified, and all things will be arranged in proper order. Temple work will be the great work of the millennium" (*Mormon Doctrine,* pp. 500-01; see also *Doctrines of Salvation,* 2:251-52).

After the millennium there will come a day when temples will no longer be required (Rev. 21:22), but that day will not come until the end of the earth (Rev. 21:1) when God will dwell with his people (Rev. 21:3). Until that day, the Lord's people have been commanded to build houses to his holy name (D&C 124:39) that we, therein, might receive his ordinances and the revelation pertaining to this dispensation (D&C 124:40-41).

74. Do Latter-day Saints believe in an eternal hell as described in the Bible?

The confusion of many Christians today regarding the real nature of hell is, for the most part, the result of mistranslations of the words sheol, hades, and gehenna. The Hebrew word "sheol" and the Greek equivalent "hades" were general terms for the afterlife, and not a place of eternal punishment. King James scholars translated Sheol half the time as "grave" and the rest of the time as "hell" or "the pit." The *Cambridge Bible Dictionary* tells us that the Hebrew Sheol corresponds to the Greek hades and "signifies the abode of departed spirits . . . or the underworld. It often has been held, both in Jewish and Christian churches, that Hades consists of two parts, Paradise and Gehenna, one the abode of the blessed and the other of the lost. 'Gehenna' or 'Gehenna of fire,' is the Greek equivalent of the 'valley of Hinnom,' a deep glen south of

Jerusalem, where the idolatrous Jews offered their children to Moloch (2 Chron. 28:3; 33:6; Jer. 7:31; 19:2-6). It was afterwards used as a place for burning the refuse of the city (2 Kings 23:10) and in that way became symbolic of the place of torment (Matt. 5:22, 29, 30; 10:28; 18:9; 23:15, 33; Mark 9:43, 45, 47; Luke 12:5; James 3:6). All language about hell-fire is probably due to the impression produced on men's minds by the sight of this ceaseless burning" (*Cambridge Bible Dictionary,* Hell, p.50: see also *Teachings,* p. 310; *History of the Church,* 5:425).

Modern LDS authorities differentiate between the spirit world hell and the "lake of fire" hell (*Mormon Doctrine,* pp. 349-51). That there is a difference is made clear in Revelation 20:13-14 where death and the spirit world hell are delivered up to be judged. Those from this temporary hell who are condemned are then "cast into the lake of fire" (Rev. 20:14), a place where the devil and his servants reside in eternity (Rev. 20:10). 2 Nephi 9:16 informs us that the torment of this hell is "as" a lake of fire and brimstone and has no end.

Some Christians teach that Matthew 25:41, 46; Mark 9:43; Revelation 14:10-11, and 20:10, 15 prove that hell is a place of everlasting punishment and torment in which all the wicked will suffer throughout eternity. Although Latter-day Saints believe in a place of everlasting punishment where some will reign with the devil and his angels in eternity (D&C 76:43-44), they also believe that this place is reserved for exceedingly few "who deny the Son after the Father has revealed him" (D&C 76:43). These are commonly referred to by Latter-day Saints as "sons of perdition" (Matt. 12:31-32; Heb. 6:4-8; D&C 76:31-39; *Mormon Doctrine*—Sons of Perdition; see also page 244 of this text).

J. N. D. Kelly indicates that Origen was satisfied that hell was not eternal but must one day come to an end (*Early Christian Doctrines,* p. 473 citing C. Cels. 3, 79; 6, 26; in *Irem. hom.* 19, 4). Scriptures such as Job 33:27-30; Psalms 16:10; 86:13; and Acts 2:31 provide proof that the torment of hades or Sheol is not eternal since the prisoners there may be redeemed from this punishment to receive a lesser kingdom of glory (D&C 76:81-89). Bruce R. McConkie summarizes the LDS view of hell: "Thus, for those who are heirs of some salvation, which includes all but the sons of perdition (D&C 76:44), hell has an end, but for those who have wholly given themselves over to satanic purposes there is no redemption from the consuming fires and torment of conscience. They go on forever in the hell that is prepared for them" (*Mormon Doctrine*—Hell, p. 351; see the remainder of this article for further information; see also *Answers to Gospel Questions,* 2:208-10)

75. Does the Bible speak of more than one kingdom in heaven (degrees of glory)?

Paul, while speaking of visions and revelation, tells of a man who was "caught up to the third heaven" (2 Cor. 12:2) or "paradise" and "heard unspeakable words, which it is not lawful for a man to utter" (2 Cor. 12:4).

Both Latter-day Saints and Orthodox Protestants are fond of quoting this scripture. Latter-day Saints use it to show that there are at least three heavens, and Protestants use it in an attempt to show that the thief on the cross was given instant salvation since, they say, the paradise he was promised is, according to this scripture, heaven (see pages 142-143 of this text).

On the subject of paradise, the *Cambridge Bible Dictionary* informs us that the New Testament word translated as paradise is actually "a Persian word meaning a park. It is not found in the Old Testament. In the New Testament, Luke 23:43 and 2 Corinthians 12:4, it denotes that region of Hades (Sheol) in which the spirits of the blest await the general resurrection, the name being borrowed from the story of our first parents in the 'Garden of Eden', Gen. 2:8. We also find the word used in Rev. 2:7 to denote the place where they who 'overcome' will eat of the 'tree of life'" (*Cambridge Bible Dictionary*—Paradise, p. 77). Thus, paradise is a general term and does not always refer to the same place.

Protestants object to the LDS view that Paul was implying that there is more than one heaven (see D&C 76 and 88). They generally believe that the "third heaven" spoken of by Paul was the one and only heaven where God the Father dwells. The other two unmentioned heavens, by their reasoning, are the atmospheric heaven (Deut. 28:12; Ps. 147:8) and the heaven of the sun, moon and stars (Gen. 1:16-17). Before proceeding further, we should note that Latter-day Saints also believe that there is only one heaven wherein God the Father dwells. Other heavens or kingdoms are presided over by Jesus Christ and the Holy Ghost (D&C 76:77, 86). The Celestial Kingdom is God the Father's abode (D&C 76:62).

Bruce R. McConkie informs us in *Mormon Doctrine* (under the subject of Heaven, pp. 347-48) that the term "heaven" has been applied in scripture in at least seven ways:

1. Atmospheric heaven—Isa. 65:17; D&C 87:6; 89:14; 117:6
2. Sidereal heavens—Gen. 22:17; Ps. 19:1
3. God's dwelling place—Matt. 6:9; Luke 10:18; John 6:38; D&C 29:36
4. The dwelling place of translated beings—2 Kings 2:11; D&C 110:13

5. Paradise—Luke 16:19-31; Alma 40:11-14

6. All kingdoms of glory—D&C 76, section heading

7. The celestial kingdom of God—D&C 131:1

Thus, the biblical word heaven, like paradise and hell, is a general term which may be applied to many places. This conclusion is further illustrated by the original Hebrew and Greek words which were translated as heaven in the King James Version of the Bible. The original Hebrew words meaning heaven were also used to refer to the sky, clouds, dust, expanse (even of land), and the horizon (*Strong's Concise Dictionary of Hebrew*). *Strong's Exhaustive Concordance of the Bible* indicates that three Greek words were translated as heaven: (1) ouranos (also meaning air or sky), (2) mesouranema (translated as midst of heaven and possibly meaning mid-sky), and (3) epouranios (meaning above the sky or celestial). Though this alone would seem to affirm the Protestant view of three heavens, careful study of the usage of these words in scripture does not. For all practical purposes, the word "ouranos" is the only word used to denote God's heaven, as in Matthew 6:9, Luke 11:2, 2 Corinthians 12:2, Revelation 3:12; the sidereal heavens as in Revelation 6:13, 9:1, 12:4; and the atmospheric heavens as in Matthew 24:30, 26:64, Acts 14:17, James 5:18. The word ouranos was the only word translated as heaven in the gospels and Acts (if the word "heavenly" is excluded). The word mesouranema was translated as "heaven" or "midst of heaven" only in Revelation 8:13, 14:6, and 19:17. The word epouranios was most often translated as "heavenly," but with the added meaning of being high or exalted (Eph. 1:3, 20; 2:6; Heb. 3:1; 9:23; 12:22) and was nearly always employed by Paul; epouranios was translated as heaven only in Philippians 2:10. Therefore, Hebrew and Greek usage confirms that most biblical references to heaven were general in nature and must be considered to be subject to interpretation based on context. Thus, the Hebrew or Greek provide no definitive easy answers.

Members of the LDS Church often cite 1 Corinthians 15:40-42 to illustrate that men will be resurrected into various glories all differing in degree. They compare the glories of the sun, moon and stars to the celestial, terrestrial, and telestial kingdoms mentioned in modern revelation (D&C 76). Protestants counter that the main idea of these verses is the difference between our natural (terrestrial or earthly) body and the glorious spiritual or celestial body we shall receive in the resurrection (see verse 44). Although this argument has merit, it ignores verse 41, which differentiates between three or more glories. Why didn't Paul just mention the glory of the sun as compared to that of the stars if this was his purpose? Even though he is discussing bodies and not kingdoms, it is clear that we shall be glorified on many levels as determined at the judgement and shall receive rewards according to our works (Matt. 16:27; Rom. 14:10-12; 1 Cor. 3:8; Rev. 20:12-13).

The Prophet Joseph Smith stated that, "it was apparent that many important points touching the salvation of men, had been taken from the Bible or lost before it was compiled. It appeared from what truths were left, that God rewarded every one according to the deeds done in the body [and] the term Heaven as intended for the Saints eternal home must include more kingdoms than one" (*Teachings,* pp. 10- 11).

It is interesting that the vision found in D&C 76 was received after the above statements were made, while the prophet was making an inspired revision of the gospel of John (*Ibid.*). Although direct reference is made to John 5:29 (D&C 76:15), it would also seem probable that the statement by Jesus that "In my Father's house are many mansions" (John 14:2) also led Joseph Smith to ponder whether there might be more kingdoms than one. Joseph referred several times to this verse of scripture (*Ibid.,* pp. 311, 331, 359, 366), often saying it could have been translated more clearly. The concept of many kingdoms in heaven, according to him, was the original intent, though this meaning has been nearly lost (*Ibid.,* p. 366).

Other Bible passages also hint that there is more than one kingdom in heaven (1 Kings 8:27; Matt. 25:21, 23, 34; 2 Peter 3:13; Rev. 5:10), but the parable of the sower deserves further comment. Very few today have noted that among the seeds that "fell into good ground, and brought forth fruit, some [multiplied] and hundredfold, some sixtyfold, [and] some thirtyfold" (Matt. 13:8). The fact that these numbers are significant is accentuated by the next verse, "Who hath ears to hear, let him hear" (Matt. 13:9).

Eugene Seaich cites several of the first fathers on the subject of kingdoms, but two of the most convincing relate to the parable of the sower. He observed that:

> The very early Church Father, Papias [AD 160], who (according to the first-hand account of Polycarp; *Against Heresies,* V, 33, 4) had it personally from John (Jean Danielou, *The Theology of Jewish Christianity,* p. 46), writes that "as the Elders say, Those who are deemed worthy of an abode in heaven shall go there, others shall enjoy the delights of Paradise, and others shall possess the splendor of the city [Rev. 22:14]; for everywhere the Savior will be seen, according as they shall be worthy who see him [Rev. 22:4]. But that there is this distinction between the habitation of those who produce an hundredfold, and that of those who produce sixtyfold, and that of those who produce thirtyfold; for the fruit will be taken up into heaven; the second class will dwell in Paradise, and the last will inhabit the city; and that on this account the Lord said, 'In my house are many mansions'; for all things belong to God, who supplies all with a suitable dwelling place, even as

his word says, that a share is given to all by the Father, according as each is or shall be worthy" (*Relics of the Elders*, 5). . . .

Other early Church writers also taught that there were "three degrees of glory," for example, Irenaeus [AD 178], who says in *Against Heresies:* "The Elders, the disciples of the Apostles, affirm that (the thirtyfold, the sixtyfold, and the hundred-fold) are the gradation and arrangement of those who are saved, and that they advance through steps of this nature" (V, 36, 2)" (*Ancient Texts and Mormonism*, pp. 43-44).

On this same subject, Hugh Nibley notes that Peter explained to Clement that the Lord "has commanded us to go forth to preach, and to invite you to the supper of the heavenly king . . . and to give you your wedding garments, that is to say, the privilege of being baptized . . . you are to regard this as the first step of three, which step brings forth thirty commandments, as the second step does sixty, and the third one hundred, as we shall explain to you more fully at another time" (*Clementine Recognitions*, III, 34) . . . The very early Testament of Our Lord Jesus Christ opens with the admonition that the document is to come into the hands "only of proven saints who dwell in the third order (or level) next to the mansion of my Father who sent me" (*Test. Dom. n. J. Christi*, Rahmani, ed., 1:xviii, p. 22) (Hugh Nibley, *Since Cumorah*, pp. 110-11).

From the above comments by the first fathers, it is apparent that the doctrine of "degrees of glory" was taught and recorded by the apostles, though the surviving statements in the Bible do not clearly convey this today. Though the Bible does not contain a clear description of the mansions within God's house (John 14:2), reason should convince even the skeptic that a just God could not divide all mankind into two general categories, one destined for heaven and the other destined for hell. Clearly, the LDS view is a more just solution befitting a loving Heavenly Father.

Joseph Smith once stated "Could you gaze into heaven five minutes, you would know more than you would by reading all that was written on the subject" (*Teachings*, p. 324). He truly knew more than any Bible scholars on the subject. That Joseph Smith was instrumental in restoring these truths without any knowledge of the above statements, testifies of his divine calling as a prophet of God (see also Richard Lloyd Anderson, *Understanding Paul*, pp. 127-28, 142-45).

76. Will there be a rapture, and when will it occur?

To this point we have examined mostly LDS beliefs which were somewhat unique when compared to Christianity in general. This question deals with a unique Protestant belief which is being disputed by various factions today. Because the concept of a "rapture" is not universally accepted among Christians and is not understood by many, it is appropriate to start by first defining the term.

The word rapture is said to come from a Latin translation of the Greek word harpazo which is found in 1 Thessalonians 4:17. Harpazo is translated in English as "caught up." The term rapture, as it is used by orthodox Protestants, is based on a belief that, when Christ comes, he will instantly catch up all living believers to meet him in the air and translate them into immortal bodies without experiencing physical death. It is further believed that those who are caught up will be miraculously taken away from tribulations to be with the Lord in heaven. LDS scripture presents a different picture, especially on this last point. Protestant belief in the rapture is based on Matthew 24:31, 39-42; Luke 17:30-37; 1 Corinthians 15:51-54; and 1 Thessalonians 4:13-18; 5:9-10. Although other scriptures might also be applied to this event, their relationship is often questioned even among Protestants. There is also disagreement among Protestants regarding the rapture's timing in relation to the tribulation period spoken of in Matthew 24:21, 29; Mark 13:24; Luke 21:9-26, and Revelation 7:14. According to orthodox Protestant eschatology, the tribulation period will last seven years (two periods of 3 1/2 years; see Dan. 7:25; 12:7, 11; Matt. 24:21-22; Rev. 11:2-3; 12:6, 14; 13:5). Daniel 9:27 is usually cited in support of this conclusion, but Revelation 2:10 provides another figure (10 days or years).

Three or four theories have been suggested concerning the timing of the rapture. Those who hold that believers will be caught up before the tribulation period, to be with Christ in heaven and to return with him at the end of this period, are called "pre-tribulationists" Those who believe that Christians will go through the tribulation and be caught up at the end of this period are called "post-tribulationists." Those who believe that the church will go through half of the tribulation period (three and one-half years) before being caught up are referred to as "mid-tribulationists" If this were not enough, there is also a fourth interpretation commonly called the "partial rapture view" which holds that only some believers will be taken up at one or more points during the tribulation period.

All of these theories are of recent origin, having been developed in the last two hundred years. Modern revelation received through the Prophet Joseph Smith contains answers to these and other similar questions, and would settle these arguments if accepted. Unfortunately, many are "ever learning, and [yet] never able to come to the knowledge of the truth" (2 Tim. 3:7).

Although the Bible has clearly not provided sufficient information to settle this problem, it does provide a great deal of information on this subject. The gospels alone provide more information than can be considered in a brief discussion on this subject. To keep this answer short, we will only consider the timing of Christ's coming and the gathering of believers in relation to the tribulation period. Matthew tells us that, "Immediately after the tribulation of those days shall the sun be darkened . . . And then shall appear the sign of the Son of man in heaven: and then shall all the tribes of the earth mourn, and they shall see the Son of man coming in the clouds of heaven with power and great glory. And he shall send his angels with a great sound of a trumpet, and they shall gather together his elect . . ." (Matt. 24:29-31). Mark likewise tells us, "after that tribulation, the sun shall be darkened . . . And then shall they see the Son of man coming in the clouds with great power and glory. And then shall he send his angels, and shall gather together his elect from the four winds, from the uttermost part of the earth" (Mark 13:24, 26-27). Although Luke does not use the word tribulation, he describes these events in the same order (see Luke 21: 25-27). In each case, the Second Coming follows the tribulation and the gathering of the elect follows his coming. Not only is there no mention of Christ's appearance before or during this tribulation period, but believers are warned by all three writers that false Christs will appear to deceive many (Matt. 24:5, 23-24; Mark 13:6, 21-22; Luke 21:8). None of these accounts hints at multiple returns of the Savior.

The remainder of the New Testament reinforces the concept that the saints will not be spared tribulations. Paul told the Thessalonian saints, ". . . when we were with you, we told you before that we should suffer tribulation" (1 Thes. 3:4). In a second epistle he stated, "we ourselves glory in . . . your patience and faith in all your persecutions and tribulations that ye endure" (2 Thes. 1:4). He taught other saints that, "we glory in tribulations also: knowing that tribulation worketh patience" (Rom. 5:3) and "we must through much tribulation enter into the kingdom of God" (Acts 14:22). Matthew quotes Christ as saying that except the "great tribulation" were "shortened, there should no flesh be saved: but for the elect's sake those days shall be shortened" (Matt. 24:21-22). This is also the theme of the parable of the wheat and the tares (Matt. 13:24-30, 3643).

John the Revelator also makes it clear that the saints will pass through the tribulation period prior to Christ's coming. In Revelation 7:13-14, an elder asked John, "What are these which are arrayed in white robes? and whence came they? And [John] said unto him, Sir, thou knowest. And he said to me, these are they which came out of great tribulation, and have washed their robes, and made them white in the blood of the Lamb." John goes on to speak in chapter 13 of the period in which the beast would reign (42 months or 3 1/2 years—Rev. 13:5). During this period we are told that "it was given unto him to make war with the saints, and to overcome them" (Rev. 13:7). Directly following this, Christ comes with his elect to Mount Zion (Rev. 14:1) and in the clouds to execute judgement (Rev. 14:15-16). Note that in chapters 14 through 19 the Lord executes judgement.

Chapter 15 speaks of the exaltation of the just who "had gotten the victory over the beast, and over his image, and over his mark, and over the number of his name" (Rev. 15:2; compare Rev. 13:7, 15-17). Chapters 16 through 19 detail the "wrath of God" poured out upon the wicked (Rev 16:1) and at the end of chapter 19 the beast is defeated by Christ (Rev. 19:20-21). Remember the beast's reign was previously identified as 42 months or three and one-half years (Rev. 13:5), which seems to be the last half of the tribulation period. Therefore, this is further confirmation that these chapters describe events at the end of the tribulation (compare also Dan. 7:25; 12:7; Zech. 13:8-9; Mal. 3:2-3, 5-6; 4:1-3; Rev. 20:1-7 with 1 Thes. 4:16; and Rev. 12:14 with 12:17 and 13:5).

Joseph Smith's inspired revision of Matthew 24 informs us that the great tribulation will be "on the Jews and the inhabitants of Jerusalem" (JS—M 1:18) and "after the tribulation of those days . . . they shall see the Son of Man coming in the clouds of heaven . . . and he shall send his angels before him with the great sound of a trumpet, and they shall gather together the remainder of his elect" (JS—M 1:36-37; see also JST Luke 17:36-39). Doctrine and Covenants 29:8 tells us that the "tribulation and desolation" shall be "upon the wicked," but Joseph Smith added that, "it is a false idea that the Saints will escape all judgement whilst the wicked suffer; for all flesh is subject to suffer, and the righteous shall hardly escape [D&C 63:34], still many of the Saints will escape" (Teachings, p. 162).

Doctrine and Covenants section 63 provides us with additional insight regarding these events and also explains the LDS belief concerning the translation of believers at the coming of Christ. It states that "the saints also shall hardly escape; nevertheless, I, the Lord, am with them, and will come down in heaven from the presence of the Father and consume the wicked with unquenchable fire . . . he that liveth when the Lord shall come, and hath kept the faith, blessed is he; nevertheless, it is appointed to him to die at the age of a man [100 years? —see Isa. 65:20]. Wherefore, children shall grow up until they become old; old men shall die; but they shall not sleep in the dust, but they shall be changed in the twinkling of an eye" (D&C 63:34, 50-51). It also states that "in the day of the coming of the Son of Man . . . cometh an entire separation of the righteous and the wicked" (D&C 63:53-54)—not before!

Again in D&C section 88 the Lord warns, "prepare the saints for the hour of judgement which is to come; That their souls may escape the wrath of God, the desolation of abomination which awaits the wicked, both in this world and in the world to come" (D&C 88:84-85). "And the saints that are upon the earth, who are alive, shall be quickened and be caught up to meet him. And they who have slept in their graves shall come forth, for their graves shall be opened; and they also shall be caught up to meet him in the midst of the pillar of heaven—They are Christ's, the first fruits [of the resurrection], they who shall descend with him first, and they who are on the earth and in their graves, who are first caught up to meet him" (D&C 88:96-98). Thus begins the resurrection of the just and the millennial reign of Christ on the earth (see D&C 88:99-101; Rev. 20:4-6). Those who are caught up are not taken into heaven but reign "with Christ a thousand years" on the earth (Rev. 5:10; 20:4-6; *Teachings,* p. 318). Thereafter, "they shall reign for ever and ever" with him (Rev. 22:4-5).

Modern revelation makes it clear that the saints will remain on the earth through the tribulation period until Christ's coming. Those who are old or in the grave shall be changed to a resurrected state at that time. Younger saints will grow old and be changed in an instant at one hundred years of age (Isa. 65:20; D&C 101:30-31) to inherit a glorious resurrection with God and Christ.

7
Scripture

77. Why don't Latter-day Saints accept the Bible to be inerrant and infallible as most Protestants do?

Latter-day Saints love the Bible and rejoice in the truths that it teaches. We study and ponder its sayings and seek to live by the divine standards it proclaims (*Discourses of Brigham Young,* pp. 124-25). The Bible, as no other book, bears testimony of the life and ministry of our Lord Jesus Christ and testifies of his atoning sacrifice and resurrection. It contains the prophecies of patriarchs and seers that the Messiah-Christ would come, and also the testimonies of apostles and other witnesses that he did come. As first recorded, it was truly "the word of God" revealed to inspired men. By the providence of the Lord, it has been handed down from age to age and preserved as a witness to all mankind that God loves us and has provided a way for us to return to him.

Latter-day Saints affirm the importance of scripture in teaching gospel truths (2 Tim. 3:16; Alma 22:13-14; 31:5; D&C 42:12), but reliance on the Bible alone does not assure comprehension of those truths. The multiplicity of beliefs among the numerous Christian churches existing today attests to this fact. Many today emphasize a relatively limited number of Bible verses to support their own chosen beliefs while ignoring the more balanced gospel truths found elsewhere.

We must not put faith in aberrant doctrines that are supported by only one or two scriptures, especially those not supported by modern revelation. Use of isolated scriptures to prove a false belief may cause those that do so to reject other truths when they are presented. Some, for example, hold tenaciously to the belief that God the Father is a spirit being, citing John 4:24, then reject man's potential to become like him because man is fleshly and God, in their view, is spirit. This pitfall can be avoided if we remember to teach only those doctrines that are supported by "two or three witnesses" whether they be the witnesses of living prophets or of scripture. We should also remember that all scripture, to be properly understood, must be read by the Spirit (1 Cor. 2:7, 10-14).

Latter-day Saints are sometimes criticized for using modern scripture in preference to the Bible. The reason for this is found in the Book of Mormon. It testifies that "when [the Bible] proceeded forth from the mouth of a Jew it contained the fulness of the gospel of the Lord" but later, as it was handed down, evil men took "away from the gospel of the Lamb many parts which [were] plain and most precious" (1 Nephi 13:24, 26). The Prophet Jeremiah also spoke of unscrupulous men who were altering the word of the Lord saying, "'We are wise, we have the law of the Lord,' when scribes with their lying pens have falsified it" (*New English Bible,* Jeremiah 8:8; see also *Revised Standard Version, Jerusalem Bible,* and *New International Version*). Joseph Smith said, "I believe the Bible as it read when it came from the pen of the original writers. Ignorant translators, careless transcribers, or designing and corrupt priests have committed many errors" (*History of the Church,* 1:132, 245; 6:51; *Teachings,* pp. 9-10, 327; Eighth Article of Faith). That this was actually the case is well known to reputable scholars of all faiths, but will be shown in more detail in the responses to questions which follow.

Some Bible cultists today believe that the Bible is inerrant and infallible. They assert that the Bible is "completely authoritative and trustworthy in all that it asserts as factual, whether in matters of theology, history, or science" (Gleason L. Archer, *Encyclopedia of Bible Difficulties,* p. 19). They also assert that the Bible canon is closed for all time and is therefore complete and sufficient to answer all-important questions. Those that hold these views believe a myth. As will be shown shortly, the Bible itself professes no such doctrine.

It is difficult to understand how anyone could assert that the Bible is inerrant and infallible. With the endless succession of Bible translations (150 translations in the first 75 years of this century alone) and with the numerous textual and translational problems found throughout all the available manuscripts, no one can be sure that any modern text is completely accurate. The above-cited problems have forced many to conclude that while errors exist in our modern Bible, the original manuscripts, as written by inspired men, must have been perfect. Whether they were or not, no originals exist today and the end result is the same. To know that the original version was correct is of little value to scholars when no original manuscript exists, nor can one be fully reconstructed. Daniel-Rops quoted Origen (185-243 AD) as saying: "Today the fact is evident, that there are many differences in the manuscripts, either through the negligence of certain copyists, or the perverse audacity of some in correcting the text" (*L'Eglise des Apotres et des Martyrs,* p. 313 as quoted in James L. Barker, *Apostasy from the Divine Church,* p. 14).

Most authorities agree that soon after the apostles disappeared, a multiplicity of texts rapidly developed. By the fourth century, "they had to deal with a great welter of various readings and of mixed texts" (Frederic G. Kenyon, *The Text of the Greek Bible,* p. 248). Dr. Kenyon concedes, "Hardly any manuscript is free from influences from authorities of a different complexion from itself" (*Ibid.,* p. 213). This intermixing has made it impossible to reconstruct one original. The best that textual scholars have been able to do is to trace our modern New Testament back to five main types of texts at the end of the second century (Fredrick Grant, *An Introduction to the Revised Standard Version of the New Testament,* pp. 38-39). Unfortunately, no one can agree which of these groups more closely resembles the theoretical original Greek manuscripts (see Hugh Nibley, *Since Cumorah,* pp. 27-28). Without further knowledge, men are at a loss to identify what was originally written by our New Testament authors (see also Michael Griffith, *Refuting the Critics,* pp. 117-18).

Several Bible passages are cited in support of Bible inerrancy. One of the scriptures cited most often is found in Paul's second epistle to Timothy. It states: "All scripture is given by inspiration of God, and is profitable for doctrine, for reproof, for correction, for instruction in righteousness" (2 Tim. 3:16). In order to understand Paul's statement to Timothy we must first understand several facts:

1. Scripture in Paul's day was understood to mean the Old Testament (Bruce R. McConkie, *Doctrinal New Testament Commentary,* 3:113). Most scholars agree that the earliest gospel, that of Luke, was written shortly after Paul wrote this epistle. Although many epistles or letters had been written by this date, they were not yet considered scripture. At this point, the epistles were separate scrolls meant to be read by the individuals or groups to which they were addressed; none of these texts as yet had been compiled for general use (see article by Leland H. Gentry in *The New Testament and the Latter-day Saints,* pp. 85-86).

2. If Paul intended the word "scripture" to include both present and future writings of inspired men, then we can also include the Book of Mormon, the Doctrine and Covenants, and the Pearl of Great Price. These were also inspired of God.

3. The Joseph Smith Translation of this passage reads, "All scripture given by inspiration of God, is profitable for doctrine." It is interesting to note that the Greek texts we have today do not contain the word "is" The Greek reads: "All scripture given by God and [or also] profitable for teaching, for reproof, for correction, for instruction—in righteousness." The problem of placement of the verb in this passage is apparent in the New International Translation which inserts the word "is" in two places: "All scripture is God-breathed and is useful for teaching, rebuking, correcting, and training in righteousness." In any case, nowhere does Paul say that the scriptures will remain infallible through time.

4. The remainder of this passage is rarely quoted by our Protestant critics. It summarizes the reason Timothy is being exhorted to study the scriptures: "that the man of God may be perfect, thoroughly furnished unto all good works" (2 Tim. 3:17). The emphasis is not that scripture is perfect, but that we may become perfect by showing forth good works as exemplified and commanded in scripture. The last portion of this passage is often overlooked by critics possibly because it teaches the importance of good works, a doctrine with which they disagree.

Peter's statement in 2 Peter 1:20-21 is also quoted to support biblical inerrancy: "Knowing this first, that no prophecy of the scripture is of any private interpretation. For the prophecy came not in old time by the will of man: but holy men spake as they were moved by the Holy Ghost." This passage proves only that these holy men wrote as they were inspired by the Spirit, and not that what they wrote was infallible. Even in the days when Paul's original writings were available to the saints, they were misunderstood (2 Peter 3:16) and being handled deceitfully (2 Cor. 4:2). What is worse, erroneous interpretations were leading some into "error" and "destruction" (2 Peter 3:16-17). Can scripture, which even in its pure state causes many to falter, be termed inerrant or infallible?

In D&C 68:4 the Lord informs us that whatsoever is spoken "when moved upon by the Holy Ghost shall be considered scripture;" but even perfect scripture, if it exists, cannot be understood properly unless read by the Spirit (1 Cor. 2:7, 10-14; D&C 50:17-20). The Lord provides an example of this principle in the gift of tongues. Paul taught that this gift was not meant solely as a sign to believers but was also meant to edify the saints. He taught that where "any man speak in an unknown tongue . . . let one interpret. But if there be no interpreter, let him keep silence in the church; and let him speak to himself, and to God" (1 Cor. 14:27-28). Thus, where one spoke by the Holy Ghost it was also necessary that another translate by the same Spirit. Without the translation, it was not edifying (1 Cor. 14:26). The same is true of scripture. When read without the Spirit as our personal translator, scripture may be misunderstood.

Some today try to prove with scripture that the Bible has been preserved by the Lord without error. A statement by Peter in 1 Peter 1:23-25 is cited in support of this assertion. In these verses Peter is quoting Isaiah 40:8 (note that there are differences between Isaiah's words and those quoted by Peter). Peter says, "Being born again . . . by the word of God, which liveth and abideth for ever . . . And this is the word which by the gospel is preached unto you." It is generally suggested that the gospel, as contained in the Bible, is the word. But clearly in this passage, the gospel contains information about the "word" which "endureth for ever." Although, the "word" spoken of here may properly apply to Christ or the Spirit, since both of them are eternal (see Gen. 21:33; Deut. 33:27; Ps. 90:2; Isa. 9:6; Heb. 9:14; Rev. 4:9-10; 5:14; 10:6; 15:7), it is more likely that Peter is speaking of eternal gospel truths. The truths of the gospel, and not the words men write, abide forever (see discussion of missing scriptures, p. 178).

Proponents of Bible inerrancy often make extravagant claims about the accuracy and consistency of Bible manuscripts in existence today. Although it is true that we have more than 5000 Greek manuscripts containing all or part of the New Testament, it is also true that no two of those manuscripts are identical. Scholars continue to debate the authenticity of various Bible passages and the reliability of different texts.

Those defending the Bible's accuracy often insist that differences do not affect doctrinal issues and are therefore minor. However, it is interesting to note that when Mark 16:16 is cited as proof that baptism is essential to salvation, the same people who claim biblical inerrancy will point out that "most reliable early manuscripts" do not contain the last 12 verses of Mark. Thus, more than half of the last chapter of Mark is considered by many Protestant scholars to be of questionable authority. The fact that one of these verses states: "He that believeth and is baptized shall be saved" (Mark 16:16) blatantly defies their doctrinal irrelevancy assertion.

To this example, we could add many other similar passages. Four of the more obvious examples include John 7:53-8:11; Acts 8:37; 9:5-6; and 1 John 5:7-8. Each of these passages has been omitted from one or more New Testament Bible translations because early Greek manuscripts do not contain these verses. We should also note that some scholars even question the authenticity of the final phrase of the Lord's Prayer: "For thine is the kingdom, and the power, and the glory, for ever. Amen" (Matt. 6:13; see also Luke 11:2-4 and *Answers to Gospel Questions,* 3:133-35). These discrepancies are more often the rule than the exception. The author has noted more than 100 New Testament verses where all or part of the verse is missing in some manuscripts, and more than 100 other passages where significant wording variations occurred between the Nestle Greek text and the King James Received text.

Discrepancies between texts are not just found in the New Testament. The Old Testament contains similar examples of textual variances. Scholars note that the Septuagint translation, which was used by early Christians, omits 1 Samuel 17:12-31, 41, 50, and 55-58. While this might seem to be a mistake, the story of David and Goliath becomes less contradictory and reads more smoothly when these verses are left out. It is quite possible these verses were added later (*Rediscovering the Book of Mormon,* ed. John L. Sorenson and Melvin J. Thorne, p. 17).

Matthew 5:18, 24:35, Mark 13:31, and Luke 21:33 are also cited as proof that the Bible will be preserved by the Lord. There is no doubt that the Lord preserved the scriptures and especially Christ's words, but these verses do not support the assertion that all of his words or even all scriptures have been preserved. The scriptures are, according to John, incomplete in the details of Christ's life (John 21:25) and the manuscripts we have today differ in many of the details they contain.

Although Christ did state that not "one jot or one tittle shall . . . pass from the law, till all be fulfilled" (Matt. 5:18), this in no way refers to preservation of scripture. The law spoken of is the law of Moses and "all" seems to refer to the prophetic symbolism represented in the law of Moses. Therefore, the law of Moses would be observed until Christ fulfilled "all things" pertaining to his life and mission represented in the law, as well as in the prophets and the psalms (Luke 24:44). After the law had been fulfilled (Gal. 5:14), it was changed (Heb. 7:12; 8:8-13). As Paul states, "Wherefore the law was our schoolmaster to bring us unto Christ that we might be justified by faith. But after that faith is come, we are no longer under a schoolmaster" (Gal. 3:24-25). Thus, it was only the law of Moses which was preserved, and then it was only until Christ came. This passage in no way justifies a claim that the Bible or any scripture will be preserved without error. The above explanation also applies to Psalm 19:7.

Modern Christians who refuse to admit that God can reveal scripture today as he did anciently have devised a God who is not the same yesterday and today. By refusing to live by every word which proceeds forth from God, they are falling into the same trap as the Jews of Christ's day. The Jews in that day used their scriptures to show that Christ's teachings went far beyond the revelations of the prophets. Thus, they refused the gospel blessings available to those who accept Christ and his teachings. Many modern Christians are using the Bible as their sole standard while rejecting the Book of Mormon and other modem revelation. In so doing they are refusing not only the additional understanding these scriptures bring but most importantly, the blessings of exaltation available only through the restored priesthood and Church of God. (See *LDS Bible Dictionary,* Bible, pp. 622-25, and Writing, p.790 for additional information concerning the preservation of the Old and New Testament texts.)

78. What are some of the errors in our Bible?

For centuries Bible scholars have written volumes documenting the errors, omissions, and contradictions found in the Bible after the "plain and precious" parts were removed (1 Nephi 13:26-40); yet today some are still unaware that errors have crept into modem biblical texts. These errors may have been introduced inadvertently because of imperfect sight, inattentiveness of copyists, human frailties, or they may have been introduced intentionally where contradictions, variations, inconsistencies, or alleged errors were detected during copying, translation, or revision. Despite overwhelming evidence to the contrary, there are still many "fundamentalists" today that insist that "the Bible" (presumably some unspecified Protestant version) is inerrant and infallible.

Some textual errors have been mentioned previously in other chapters of this text. These included:

1. Jeremiah's false prophecy concerning Zedekiah—Jer. 34:4-5; 52:10-11; see also p. 42 of this text
2. The three varying accounts of Paul's vision—Acts 9:3-8; 22:6-11; 26:13-18; see also p. 45
3. Other contradictions regarding marriage, women's role, and drinking wine—see p. 67
4. God's need to repent—see p. 73

Hebrew and Greek manuscripts in our possession today contain these same errors and offer little help in explaining the above contradictions. Other errors and contradictions may be added to the above list. The following sampling of some of the more obvious problem scriptures gives an idea of the abundance of errors found in our modem King James Bibles:

1. Number of Israelites killed by a plague—Num. 25:1, 9; 1 Cor. 10:8
2. Sisera's death—Judges 4:21-22; 5:25-27
3. Jepthah's burnt offering—Judges 11:30-40; see Ex. 20:13
4. Evil spirits from the Lord—1 Sam. 16:14-16, 23; 19:9
5. Saul's death, a suicide or murder?—1 Sam. 31:4-5; 2 Sam. 1:10; 21:12
6. Number slain of David—2 Sam. 10:18; 1 Chron. 19:18
7. God or Satan provoked David—2 Sam. 24:1; 1 Chron. 21:1
8. Dead arose—2 Kings 19:35; Isa. 37:36
9. God creates evil—Isa. 45:7
10. Lord makes us err and hardens our hearts—Isa. 63:16-17
11. Differences in the genealogies of Christ—Matt. 1:6-16; Luke 3:23-38; see *Jesus the Christ,* pp. 85-90
12. The Lord leads us into temptation—Matt. 6:13; James 1:13
13. Man or men with an unclean spirit—Matt. 8:28-34; Mark 5:1-18; Luke 8:26-39
14. The sign of Jonas (2 or 3 nights)—Matt. 12:40; 28:1; Mark 15:42; 16:1-2

15. Christ baptized followers—John 3:22; 4:2
16. Blind man or men healed at Jericho—Matt. 20:29-34; Mark 10:46-52; Luke 18:35-43
17. Mother or apostles request—Matt. 20:20-28; Mark 10:35-45
18. Death of Judas—Matt. 27:5; Acts 1:18
19. Misattribution—Matt. 27:9-10; Zech 11:13
20. Crucifixion inscriptions—Matt. 27:37; Mark 15:26; Luke 23:38; John 19:19
21. Christ's last words—Luke 23:46; John 19:30
22. Angels at the tomb—Matt. 28:2; Mark 16:5; Luke 24:4; John 20:12
23. Mistranslations of Hebrew words:
    a. Book (Gen. 5:1; Ex. 17:14; etc.)—scroll or tablet
    b. Brass (Gen. 4:22; Ex. 25:3; etc.)—possibly copper
    c. Oak (Isa. 1:29; Ezek. 27:6; etc.)—possibly elm
    d. Whale (Gen. 1:21; Job 7:12; etc.)—large fish
24. Mistranslations of Greek words:
    a. Virtue (Mark 5:30; Luke 6:19; 8:46)—see p. 20 this text
    b. Parable (John 10:6)—should be allegory
    c. Easter (Acts 12:4)—should be Passover
    d. Charity (1 Cor. 13:1-4, 8; etc.)—should be love
    e. Hell (Matt. 10:28; 11:23; etc.)—see p. 160

To these can be added errors of grammar, punctuation, and numerous misquotations of scripture, but these flaws are admittedly more trivial. What is important is that we realize that our modern Bible translations do contain some errors and therefore cannot be read without discernment. The fact that we find most of the above contradictions and errors in all available manuscripts leads us to one of two conclusions: either the originals, as written by inspired writers, contained the same errors, or copying errors were made in the very earliest manuscripts and continued to be propagated in subsequent copies of copies. Neither of these conclusions is acceptable to those who hold the Bible to be inerrant and infallible. When confronted with these problems, some avoid the issue, stating that these differences are compelling evidence for the historicity of the events and the lack of collusion on the part of the writers. Although this statement is certainly true, it nevertheless fails to explain the contradictions in these various accounts and demonstrates that either the writers, scribes, or translators have introduced errors at some point.

The inconsistencies and errors listed above do not shake the faith of Latter-day Saints for several reasons: first, modern scriptures and Joseph Smith's inspired revision of the Bible restore many plain and precious portions of the gospel that were lost (see 1 Nephi 13:24-26; and p. 170 of this text); second, we have the additional witness of modern prophets and apostles to help us; third, we have an assurance that the Holy Ghost will guide us in understanding not only the scriptures but "all truth" (John 14:26; 16:13; Moroni 10:4-5; D&C 121:26). Many other Christians today have no such assurance because they rely solely on their interpretations of the Bible for all truth. They have also chosen to ignore all of God's word revealed in these latter days and have denied the need for a restoration of God's priesthood power through which the gift of the Holy Ghost is given (4th and 5th Articles of Faith). As Paul taught, no man knoweth the things of God except the Holy Ghost reveal it unto him (1 Cor. 2:10-13). Though members of the various Catholic and Protestant denominations may gain an understanding of many gospel truths by the inspiration of the Spirit, they will not be guided to "all truth" without receipt of the gift of the Holy Ghost by the laying on of hands from those authorized to bestow it (see chapter 9).

79. Are portions of scripture missing?

Many scriptures mentioned in modern Bibles either no longer exist or have been altered to the point that they are no longer accepted as authoritative. These include:

1. The book of the covenant—Ex. 24:4, 7*
2. The book of the wars of the Lord—Num. 21:14
3. The manner of the kingdom recorded by Samuel—1 Sam. 10:25*
4. The book of Jasher—Josh. 10:13; 2 Sam. 1:18
5. A book of statutes—1 Sam. 10:25
6. The book of the acts of Solomon—1 Kings 11:41
7. The book of Samuel the seer—1 Chron. 29:29
8. The book of Nathan the prophet—1 Chron. 29:29; 2 Chron. 9:29
9. The book of Gad the seer—1 Chron. 29:29
10. The prophecy of Ahijah—2 Chron. 9:29
11. The visions of Iddo the seer—2 Chron. 9:29; 12:15; 13:22
12. The book of Shemaiah the prophet—2 Chron. 12:15
13. The book of Jehu—2 Chron. 20:34
14. The acts of Uzziah recorded by Isaiah—2 Chron. 26:22*
15. The sayings of the seers—2 Chron. 33:19
16. An epistle of Paul to the Corinthians—1 Cor. 5:9
17. An epistle of Paul to the Ephesians—Eph. 3:3
18. An epistle of Paul to the Laodiceans— Col. 4:16
19. An additional epistle of Jude—Jude 1:3
20. The prophecies of Enoch—Jude 1:14
* Possibly included in current Bible books

Some have objected to the above list, saying that those writings not included in our Bible must not have been truly inspired. We might then ask, why would we exclude the books of Samuel and Gad the seers, the prophecies of Ahijah and Enoch, the visions of Iddo the Seer, the book of Shemaiah the Prophet, the three missing epistles of Paul, and a missing epistle of Jude? It is hard to believe that the writings of prophets, seers, and apostles would be considered uninspired, especially when they are mentioned in the scriptures as worthy of further study.

To the above list we can add missing prophecies which include: Matthew's reference to a prophecy that Christ would be a Nazarene (Matt. 2:23; see *LDS Bible Dictionary*, p. 726), a prophecy that Elias "shall first come, and restore all things" (Matt. 17:10-13), and a prophecy by Jeremiah concerning the 30 pieces of silver (Matt. 27:9). None of these prophecies is found in our modern Old Testaments. We might also add to the above prophecies references that do not match Old Testament scripture, such as Matthew's quote from Jesus referring to Zecharias, son of Barachias, being slain between the temple and the altar (Matt. 23:35; see also *Jesus the Christ*, p. 567, note 9), John's reference to a scripture about "living water" (John 7:38), Paul's mention of Jannes and Jambres the Egyptian magicians (2 Tim. 3:8), James' reference to a scripture about envy (James 4:5), and John's reference to wicked deeds of Balaam not specifically mentioned in the Old Testament (Rev. 2:14).

Stephen E. Robinson makes an interesting point regarding the Bible "canon" which deserves mention:

> The real Achilles heal of canonical exclusion . . . lies in the idea that there is one single Christian canon or one single Christian Bible, for historically there has not been one Christian canon or one Christian Bible, but many. For example, just before AD 200 someone in the Christian church at Rome wrote a list of books that were accepted as canonical by the Roman church at that time. A copy of this canon list was discovered in 1740 by Lodovico Muratori in the Ambrosian Library in Milan, and for this reason it is called the Muratorian Canon. According to it, the Roman church at the end of the second century did not consider Hebrews, James, 1 Peter, or 2 Peter to be scripture, and they accepted only two of the letters of John, although we cannot be sure which two. They did accept as canonical, however, two works now considered to be outside the New Testament, the Apocalypse of Peter and the Wisdom of Solomon. Clearly their canon of scripture was different from that of modern Christians, but does that mean that the second- and third-century Roman church was not Christian? Remember that they were the same people who were dying in the arenas for the sake of Christ. Can anyone seriously argue that they weren't Christians just because their canon was different?
>
> The famous church historian Eusebius of Caesarea, writing about AD 300, proposed another canon (Eusebius, *History of the Church*, 3.25.1-7). He listed only twenty-one books as "recognized," and listed Hebrews, James, 2 Peter, 2 and 3 John Jude, and Revelation as questionable or spurious . . . Metzger summarizes, "The Eastern Church as reported by Eusebius about AD 325, was in considerable

doubt concerning the authority of most of the Catholic Epistles as well as the Apocalypse" (*The Canon of the New Testament,* p. 209).

Saint Gregory of Nazianzus rejected the book of Revelation in his fourth-century cannon list, which was ratified three centuries later in 692 by the Trullan Synod, . . .

Before the fifth century the Syrian Christian canon included 3 Corinthians and Tatian's Diatessaron, but excluded the four Gospels, Philemon, the seven general Epistles, and the book of Revelation. Syrian Christians from the fifth century on accepted the Syriac Peshitta version of the Bible which included the four Gospels in place of the Diatessaron and excluded 3 Corinthians, but recognized only twenty-two books in all as canonical: the four Gospels, the book of Acts, the fourteen letters of Paul, James, 1 Peter, and 1 John. To this day both the Syrian Orthodox church and the Chaldean Syrian church recognize only these twenty-two books, rejecting 2 Peter, 2 and 3 John, Jude, and the book of Revelation. It is also interesting to note that the Greek Orthodox Church has never included the book of Revelation in its official lectionary. . . .

The Abyssinian Orthodox church has in its canon the twenty-seven books of the modern New Testament, but adds the Synodos and Qalementos (both attributed to Clement of Rome), the Book of the Covenant (which includes a post-resurrection discourse of the Savior), and the Ethiopic Didascalia. To the Old Testament the Abyssinian canon adds the book of Enoch (cited as prophetic by the canonical book of Jude) and the Ascension of Isaiah. . . .

Among Protestants, Martin Luther suggested that the New Testament books were of varying worth and divided them up into three separate ranks. In the prefaces of his early editions of the New Testament, Luther denied that the lowest rank (Hebrews, James, Jude, and Revelation) belonged among "the true and noblest books of the New Testament," and went so far as to call the Epistle of James "a letter of straw." He complained that Hebrews contradicted Paul by teaching that there was no repentance after baptism; that James contradicted Paul in teaching justification by works; and that Jude merely copied from second Peter and from apocryphal books; and that Revelation dealt with material inappropriate for an Apostle, it didn't teach enough about Christ, and its author had too high an opinion of himself (W. G. Kummel, *Concordia Theological Monthly,* #37 (1966), "The Continuing Significance of Luther's Prefaces to the New Testament," pp. 573-78). As a direct result of Luther's judgement, some subsequent Lutheran editions of the Bible separated Hebrews, James, Jude, and Revelation from the rest of the New Testament, and even went so far as to label them "apocryphal" and "noncanonical." As Bruce Metzger points out: "Thus we have a threefold division of the New Testament: 'Gospels and Acts,' 'Epistles and Holy Apostles,' and 'Apocryphal New Testament'—an arrangement that persisted for nearly a century in half a dozen printings" . . .

Finally, it should be understood that there is still no single Christian canon or Bible, for Protestants and Catholics disagree on whether the "Deuterocanonical books" (what Protestants call the Apocrypha) are scripture. At the Council of Trent in 1546, Roman Catholics officially adopted a canon of scripture that included the Apocrypha as fully inspired and fully the word of God. Consequently these twelve books are found in modern Catholic editions of the Bible. The collection of books includes Tobit, Judith, the Wisdom of Solomon, Ecclesiasticus or Ben Sirach, Baruch, the Letter of Jeremiah, 1 Maccabees, 2 Maccabees, additions to Esther, and additions to Daniel (comprised of the Prayer of Azariah and the Song of the Three Young Men, Susanna and the Elders, and Bel and the Dragon).

These books were part of the Greek translation of the Old Testament known as the Septuagint, which was in use in Egypt as early as the second century BC. The Septuagint was also the version of the Old Testament used by the early Christian church, and so had passed into the Latin Vulgate of the Roman church, and is still the version used by the Greek Orthodox. The conciliar decree De Canonicis Scripturis, issued on 8 April 1546, declared that all who did not accept these deuterocanonical books (the Apocrypha) as Christian scripture were anathema (accursed). . . .

On the other hand, most Protestants broke with the centuries-old tradition of accepting the Septuagint and all its contents, and preferred the version of the Old Testament which had been preserved in Hebrew by the Jews. These medieval copies of the Hebrew Old Testament did not have the Apocrypha in them as the Greek Septuagint translation did, and consequently the books of the Apocrypha are not generally accepted as scripture by Protestants. . . . in the interests of Christian unity Protestants and Catholics have "agreed to disagree" among themselves on the issue of canon (Stephen E. Robinson, *Are Mormons Christian?*, pp. 51-55; see also Hugh Nibley; *Since Cumorah*, pp. 32-51).

Many scholars have observed that several other books not included in the King James Bible were routinely quoted by early Christians. These include:

1. The Testament of Levi (3:1-4) quoted by the Savior in the Sermon on the Mount (Eugene Seaich, *Mormonism, the Dead Sea Scrolls, and the Nag Hammadi Texts,* p. 48)
2. The Testament of the 12 Patriarchs (*Ibid.,* p. 2)
a. Joseph 28:2-Matt 5:44
b. Levi 13:5-Matt 6:19
3. The Shepherd of Hermas—widely quoted in the church from the second to fourth century AD (*Mormonism, the Dead Sea Scrolls, and the Nag Hammadi Texts,* p. 2)
4. 2 Baruch—considered as legitimate Christian scripture by the early church (*Ibid.,* p. 3)
5. 4 Ezra—considered as scripture by the early church (*Ibid.,* p. 3)
6. Odes of Solomon—considered as scripture by early Christians (*Ibid.,* p. 3)
7. The Assumption of Moses—quoted in Jude 1:9 (Joseph Fielding McConkie, *Prophets and Prophecy,* p. 149)
8. Wisdom—quoted in 1 Clement (ca. 95 AD) and Barnabas (70-132 AD) and by Irenaeus (ca. 190 AD) (J. N. D. Kelly, *Early Christian Doctrines,* pp. 52-60)
9. Ecclesiasticus—quoted in Barnabas (*Ibid.,* p. 54)
10. Tobit—quoted by Polycarp (ca. 136 AD) (*Ibid.,* p. 54)
11. Didache—quoted by Polycarp (*Ibid.,* p. 54) 52-60)
12. History of Susannah—quoted by Irenaeus (*Ibid.,* pp.
13. Bel and the Dragon—quoted by Irenaeus (*Ibid.,* pp. 52-60)

Justin Martyr gave two examples of writings in the second century AD that had been removed from Jeremiah (Dialogue with Trypho as quoted in *Ante-Nicene Fathers,* 1:234-35). Dionysius, Bishop of Corinth (168-177 AD), complained of falsification of the gospels and his own letters (Joseph Fielding McConkie, *Sons and Daughters of God,* pp. 60-65).

To these we could add other Apocryphal books (such as the Maccabees, Judith, etc.) quoted or listed as inspired by Tertullian (ca. 200 AD), Hippolytus (ca. 200 AD), Clement of Alexandria (ca. 200 AD), Origen (ca. 240 AD), and Cyprian (246 AD) (*Ibid.,* pp. 52-60; Jean Danielou, *Origen,* p. 137).

Modern scriptures also attest to the fact that large portions of scripture have been lost (1 Nephi 19:10-16; 2 Nephi 3; Jacob 5; 6:1; Words of Mormon 1:1-11; Alma 33:3-17; 34:7; Helaman 8:19-20; 15:11; 3 Nephi 10:16; Ether 1:1-5; 4:1-7; D&C 84:7-13; 107:56-57; Moses 6:5; and others; see also *History of the Church,* 1:363; Bruce R. McConkie, *Mormon Doctrine,* Lost Scriptures, pp. 453-55, Joseph Fielding McConkie, *Prophets and Prophecy,* pp. 149-50). All of the foregoing omissions attest to the fact that our present Bible does not contain all the words that the Lord revealed to his people in former times. We can only conclude that our modern Bible is incomplete since so many important prophecies, sacred books, and epistles now appear to be missing from our modern Bible text (see Michael T. Griffith, *Signs of the True Church of Christ,* pp. 86-87 and Peterson and Ricks, *Offenders for a Word,* pp. 117-28 for additional references on this subject).

80. Don't newly discovered manuscripts prove the Bible is inerrant?

Proponents of biblical inerrancy often imply that the Dead Sea Scrolls prove that our Bible text has changed very little, even after centuries of recopying. They usually point to the relatively infrequent differences which exist between the Isaiah text and Modern Hebrew versions of Isaiah. We are also led to believe that the Dead Sea Scrolls prove the accuracy of the entire Old Testament—but this is not the case. Those who try to persuade us to believe these claims ignore some significant details about the Dead Sea Scrolls and other important discoveries made this century. We will first clarify what the Dead Sea scrolls actually reveal.

Although fragments of all Old Testament books except Esther have been found in 11 Dead Sea caves, most of the 200 biblical manuscripts which have been identified were not scrolls but fragments of scrolls. Over 80,000 fragments representing seven to eight hundred different manuscripts were found in one cave alone. The work of assembling these fragments has gone on for more than 40 years and will probably continue for another 40 years.

At the time of the initial discovery, seven major scrolls were made available to scholars. Within ten years of their discovery a translation of these scrolls was also made available. This included a translation of a complete Isaiah scroll originally recorded on leather—the only complete Bible book found. A second partial Isaiah scroll was also among these seven scrolls. The other five scrolls contained the *Habakkuk Commentary,* the *Manual of Discipline,* the *Thanksgiving Hymns,* the *War Scroll* (also known as the *War of the Sons of Light against the Sons of Darkness*), and the *Genesis Apocryphon* (See Vernon W. Mattson Jr., *The Dead Sea Scrolls and Other Important Discoveries,* pp. 13-14). Two other more or less complete Bible scrolls have since been added to the Isaiah scrolls: a Psalm scroll and an Aramaic Job scroll.

The remainder of the Old Testament is represented only by fragments and will never be totally complete. No New Testament books, of course, were found in any of the Dead Sea caves. Although translations of the more complete scrolls were quickly made available to all, the fragmented manuscripts have only recently been published and made available. What has been published indicates that the Qumran library contained a canon which is not identical to traditional Judaism but which instead preserved "a variety of textual traditions" (Geza Vermes, *Dead Sea Scrolls—Qumran in Perspective,* pp. 204-06).

The two Isaiah scrolls are typical of the variety found in the rest of the manuscripts. One scroll corresponds to the Modern Hebrew Bible while the other corresponds more closely to the Masoretic or traditional Hebrew text relied upon heavily by King James scholars. Detailed examination of the Dead Sea Scroll Isaiah texts leads us to conclude that although these two Isaiah manuscripts were undoubtedly preserved by God for the last 2000 years, they were not as well preserved by man from 700 BC to 200 BC (the time the Qumran texts were produced). Otherwise, there would not have been two very different versions after the first 500 years.

Proponents of biblical inerrancy seldom mention that scholars have found evidence of an effort by ancient scribes to eliminate discrepancies by consulting different texts. Small inconsistencies were eliminated by comparing three model texts and "choosing as official and binding the reading attested by at least two of the model scrolls. Thereafter, every text which departed from the canonized scripture was held to be an unauthorized version" (*Ibid.,* pp. 208-09). This might explain how so many later texts were said to have matched, even though they consistently contained obvious contradictions and errors.

We should further note that among the writings discovered at Qumran, there were about five times more non-biblical texts as there were biblical texts, and yet many of the non-biblical texts appear to have been valued as highly as modern scriptures. Today many of these valued texts are classified as apocryphal or pseudepigraphal writings. While works such as *Jubilees,* the *Testament of Levi,* the *Book of Enoch* and others found at Qumran have proven their antiquity and their value to understanding the inter-Testamental period, they remain largely ignored by modern Christianity.

The discoveries of Jewish writings at Qumran were quickly followed by the discovery of previously unknown Jewish and Christian writings at other Middle East locations. These included the discovery of the Nag Hammadi library in Egypt, fifteen thousand clay tablets at Ebla, gold and silver tablets at Persepolis, manuscripts at Masada, and others. Hugh Nibley noted twenty important manuscript finds between 1844 and 1947 in his book *Since Cumorah,* pages 52 and 53. Through these finds, the world has been provided with an unblemished and unaltered record of early Christian beliefs along with their scriptural library. Though all of these writings were discovered prior to 1975 and much of it prior to 1950, most of Christianity remains ignorant of what these discoveries have to teach us.

81. Why don't Latter-day Saints accept Bible scripture as complete and sufficient for salvation?

Protestant "Orthodoxy" has decreed that the Bible is perfect and sufficient for them, and that no additional scripture is expected or needed. Those who hold this belief have built a wall around their scriptures which will include no more and no less. They have dammed their growth and progress by refusing to accept the possibility that all of God's word was not included in their modern Bible. They also refuse to admit that God may yet reveal more knowledge than is now contained in their Bible, either through discoveries or through modern prophets.

Isaiah and Ezekiel both prophesied the coming forth of additional knowledge. Isaiah prophesied that a fallen people would speak to us "out of the dust" (Isa. 29:4). Ezekiel foretold a time when the record of Judah (the Bible) would be joined to the record of Joseph (Ezek. 37:16-17). Although these prophecies best describe the Book of Mormon, they also may apply to the discoveries mentioned previously, since these records were also brought forth out of the ground (see also Ps. 85:11; Isa. 29:4; Mormon 8:4; Moroni 10:27; D&C 101:32-35). If these discoveries are part of the "marvelous work and a wonder" that the Lord promised he would perform, they should cause the wisdom of wise men to perish and the understanding of the prudent to be hid (Isa. 29:14). Isaiah adds that "in that day shall the deaf hear the words of the book" and the "blind shall see out of obscurity, and . . . darkness" (Isa. 29:18). Those who will not "hear" or "see" these restored words of God by refusing to read them will certainly not be among the wise and prudent spoken of, but will instead be among the foolish who remain in darkness (verse 18).

Ezekiel identifies the time of fulfillment of his prophecy with the gathering of the children of Israel "into their own land" (Ezek. 37:21). It is interesting to note that both the Dead Sea Scrolls and the Nag Hammadi manuscripts were found within a year of the date that Israel was reestablished as a nation (1947).

Members of The Church of Jesus Christ of Latter-day Saints seem to be unique among Christians today in that they believe God "will yet reveal many great and important things pertaining to the kingdom of God" (9th Article of Faith). LDS scholars are studying these new finds with great interest and are not afraid to compare them to our own beliefs. These writings include doctrines such as the premortal existence of man's spirit; the necessity of the fall of Adam, righteous works and baptism, a belief in a latter-day restoration of truth, and other beliefs foreign to some but familiar to Latter-day Saints. Critics of the LDS Church often challenge the reliability of these works by pointing out that they contain what they regard as errant gnostic doctrines. What they fail to realize is that many of these same writings were also read and quoted by the Lord and his disciples (see p. 181). In view of this fact, it is odd that many still reject these writings as "uninspired."

Revelation 22:18-19 is often cited in an effort to show that the scriptural canon is complete. As was shown previously (p. 51), this passage cannot reasonably be interpreted to mean that no further scripture will be revealed by God. In this regard, the Book of Mormon contains an interesting prophecy concerning the day when that book (the Book of Mormon) would come forth: "Wo be unto him that shall say: We have received the word of God, and we need no more of the word of God, for we have enough! For behold, thus saith the Lord God: I will give unto the children of men line upon line, precept upon precept, here a little and there a little; and blessed are those who hearken unto my precepts, and lend an ear to my counsel, for they shall learn wisdom; for unto him that receiveth I will give more; and from them that say, We have enough, from them shall be taken even that which they have" (2 Nephi 28:29-30). The Lord adds, "Wherefore, because that ye have a Bible ye need not suppose that it contains all my words; neither need ye suppose that I have not caused more to be written" (2 Nephi 29:10). As soon as the Book of Mormon had been published many began to say, "A Bible! A Bible! We have got a Bible, and there cannot be any more Bible" (2 Nephi 29:3). They had no idea that in so doing they were fulfilling one of the prophecies this new book of scripture contained.

Concerning the power of scripture to bring us salvation, Brigham Young has declared:

> We have learned much from the Bible. We have also learned much from the Book of Mormon and the book of Doctrine and Covenants; but all the salvation you can obtain by means of those books alone is comparatively of little value. They contain a history of what other men have done, show the path they have walked in, and the way in which they obtained the words of eternal life for themselves; but all the scriptures from the days of Adam until now cannot, alone, save one individual. Were they all committed to memory so perfectly that they could be recited with the greatest ease, that alone would not save one of the smallest of God's creatures, nor bring any person nearer the gate of the celestial kingdom (*Discourses of Brigham Young*, pp. 127, 330; *Journal of Discourses*, 7:332; see also 5:327).

On this same subject, Joseph Fielding McConkie has pointed out an interesting parallel between the Jews of Christ's day and Christians today. He states that:

> Though their nation professed to be the true believers, both pious and devout, there were but few of the people in Jesus' day who listened to and believed his words. It was the religious leaders, the Sadducees and Pharisees, who bitterly opposed Christ and his teachings. The Sadducees professed a belief in the Torah (the first five books of Moses), declaring them to be absolute, immutable, and not open to new interpretations. The Pharisees also accepted the Torah, but added to it their beliefs in the traditions of the fathers. Both effectively rejected the principles of living prophets and continuous revelation. For them the heavens were sealed, revelation had ceased, and they warred with vigor against any who opposed their views. They put Christ to death and sought the lives of his followers. Stephen was stoned to death on the pretense that he rejected Moses—even though his dying testimony was that he accepted Christ because Moses had prophesied of him (Acts 6:9-15; 7:1-53).
>
> So it is in our day. The names of the religious sects have changed, but the "war of words and tumult of opinions" remains the same. While the so-called Christian world piously professes allegiance to the Bible, few have actually listened to and believe the book for which they have professed such reverence. The Bible makes no profession to being a comprehensive, exhaustive, or even systematic apology of the gospel—for such it is not! As Paul testified, "Our gospel came not unto you in word only, but also in power, and in the Holy Ghost, and in much assurance" (1 Thessalonians 1:5). All the Bible professes to be is an account of some of God's dealings with some of his children in some of the ages past. The essence of its message is that whenever God has had a people that he acknowledged as his own, he communicated his will to them by revelation, both on a personal basis and through his prophets. Well might those who, like the Sadducees of old, hold to the Bible as absolute and immutable, remind themselves that the experiences that the apostles shared with Christ during the three years of his mortal ministry, and of which we

have preserved for us only a fragmentary account, were not sufficient to fully convert them. Their conversion came in large measure from those teachings and sacred experiences they shared with Christ after his resurrection, teachings they felt to be too sacred to preserve for us. How, then, are we to be converted by a partial account of those experiences which did not convert the apostles? (*Seeking the Spirit,* pp. 52-53; see also *Teachings,* pp. 61, 327; and *Mormon Doctrine,* pp. 82-83, 421-23)

The church established by Jesus Christ was not governed according to the Bible, for the New Testament as we know it today did not exist until hundreds of years later. The Bible did not then and does not now contain the power and authority to baptize or give the gift of the Holy Ghost. It likewise cannot heal the sick or bestow the gifts of the Spirit. It is only a record of those who had this power conferred upon them. The early church was governed by revelation received by apostles and prophets. Inspired leaders recorded the word of God revealed to them so that all members of the church would benefit thereby. The same Spirit that influenced these leaders also witnessed to the truthfulness of their teachings to the members in that day. We must in like manner seek that same Spirit as a witness of truth today.

82. Is the Bible always accurate in scientific matters?

Latter-day Saints accept the fact that errors have been introduced into the Bible through copying and translation whether it be in scientific, historical, or doctrinal matters. Whenever men are involved in receiving, recording, or interpreting the word of God, there are occasions for errors to be introduced into that which God has revealed. This was discussed earlier in this text (pp. 37, 42) in relation to prophets and error. Eight misconceptions about the earth, as recorded in the Bible, were specifically cited in this regard (see p. 47). We could also note that men have often cited the Bible in support of other erroneous theories about the earth. The geocentric or earth-centered solar system and the flat-earth theory were held to be Bible-based religious truths for many centuries. To these we could add apparent errors in other scientific fields. Without a doubt those who hold the Bible to be inerrant will say that many of these are not actually errors but only figurative language. It will be left to the reader to decide.

1. Jacob's misconception of genetics—Gen. 30:37-43
2. Both the hare and the badger (coney) described as chewing the cud—Lev. 11: 5-6; Deut. 14:7; *Cambridge Bible Dict.,* Coney, p. 28
3. Fowl that creep on all four—Lev. 11: 20
4. Mythical beasts which were considered real
   a. Unicorn—Num. 23:22; 24:8; Deut. 33:17; Job 39:9-10; Ps. 22:21; 29:6; 92:10; Isa. 34:7

b. Dragon—Job 30:29; Ps. 74:13; 91:13; Isa. 13:22; 27:1; 51:9; Jer. 14:6; 49:33; 51:34; Micah 1:8; Mal. 1:3

c. Behemoth—Job 40:15-17 (erroneously identified as a hip popotamus or elephant, see verse 17)

d. Leviathan—Job 41:1-34; Ps. 74:14; 104:26; Isa. 27:1

5. Brass (alloy of copper and zinc) dug from the ground—Deut. 8:9; Job 28:2

6. Eagles bearing young on wings—Deut. 32:11

Of this last scripture Brother Joseph Fielding McConkie has written: ". . . within the scriptures we even find the verities of heaven taught with incorrect illustrations. Moses wrote of eagles bearing their young upon their wings (Deut. 32:11), something that eagles simply cannot do, though until the nineteenth century it was thought that they did" (*Prophets and Prophecy,* p. 124).

We also find instances in the scriptures where bats are classified as birds or fowl (Lev. 11:13, 19; Deut. 14:11, 18) and whales seem to be classified as fish (Jonah 1:17 cross-reference Matt. 12:40) though this seems to be only a semantics problem. The above scriptures admittedly involve only minor scientific errors and in some cases can be explained, but they nonetheless illustrate the fact that a faith in total scientific inerrancy depends a lot on one's perspective. Those who take a more literal view of the interpretation of scripture will either have to rationalize the scriptures cited above or admit that some scientific errors do exist.

83. Why don't Latter-day Saints study Greek and Hebrew texts to discern the true meaning of the scriptures?

Many Latter-day Saints do study Greek, Hebrew, and other ancient languages in order to shed additional light on the scriptures. The prophet Joseph Smith often referred to the Hebrew (*Teachings,* pp. 290, 300, 348, 371-72) and Greek texts (*Ibid.,* pp. 262, 300, 349, 372) and made use of a lexicon in his studies (*Ibid.* p. 310; *History of the Church,* 5:425). Today, the LDS Bible includes hundreds of footnotes where Hebrew and Greek alternative translations are offered as an aid to our Bible study. Additionally, many LDS scholars also refer to the available Greek and Hebrew texts to better understand certain passages of Bible scripture. Indeed, this author has also frequently consulted Hebrew and Greek inter-linear translations to better discern the original intent of the ancient writers.

Bruce R. McConkie listed a knowledge of Hebrew and Greek as one of a number of keys to understanding the Bible, but warned that it can be used improperly when not guided by the Spirit (*Doctrines of the Restoration,* pp. 284-85). Those that rely on reason alone to interpret scripture are relying on the "arm of flesh" (2 Chron. 32:8; Jer. 17:5) or "man's wisdom" (1 Cor. 2:13) to know the things of God. Paul tells us clearly that spiritual things of God are known only by the Holy Ghost (1 Cor. 2:10-13; see also John 16:13; Moroni 10:4-5).

Joseph Fielding McConkie observed:

> We ought not to lose sight of the fact that the original language of every revelation is the language of the Spirit, the language of the Holy Ghost, which is our only sure source of light in understanding the intent of our ancient mentors the prophets. . . . The professing Christian who refuses to admit the necessity of the spirit of revelation in understanding the New Testament will see no more of the true meaning of that book than the professing Jew can see of the true meaning and intent of the Old Testament writers. Jews who could quote and expound scripture endlessly failed to recognize the Christ when he came, because they rejected the spirit of prophecy and the responsibility to live worthy of it. Similarly, there is no shortage of Bible believers in our day who also quote and expound that book endlessly but will fail to recognize either Christ or his gospel because they too have rejected the spirit of prophecy and the necessity of living worthy of it (*Prophets and Prophecy,* pp. 114-15).

Those who assume that a knowledge of ancient scriptural languages alone is sufficient to discover the true meaning of the scriptures are deluding themselves. Scholars in various religious denominations still disagree on doctrinal beliefs despite the added insight provided by a knowledge of ancient languages. It is essential that the scriptures be read with the inspiration of the Spirit, for without this help we will only "lean" to our "own understanding" (Prov. 3:5) and become more entrenched in error.

84. Does Isaiah 29 refer to the Book of Mormon, or is it just pronouncing various woes on Ephraim and Jerusalem for trusting in foreign alliances?

Anti-Mormon critics seek in vain a way to explain the prophecy found in Isaiah chapter 29. The explanation that Isaiah chapters 28 through 31 describe the "woes of Ephraim and Jerusalem for trusting in foreign alliances against God's will" ignores several facts. It ignores, first of all, that Isaiah often interjected prophetic events into his commentary about his day. Chapters 5, 7, 9, 11, 13, 14, 24, 26, 40, 43, 45, 53, 63, and 65 provide many examples of prophetic visions of past and future events interwoven with the prophet's preaching to his own generation.

Critics also ignore the fact that the descendants of Joseph (through Ephraim and Manasseh) would be spread like "a fruitful bough by a well; whose branches run over the wall . . . unto the utmost bound of the everlasting hills" (Gen. 49:22, 26). The Western Hemisphere has the longest mountain range in the world. The Rocky Mountains extend from the northern tip of North America to the southern tip of South America. It is significant that the people who wrote the Book of Mormon left Jerusalem shortly after Isaiah's day (600 BC) and were themselves descendants of Joseph. Thus, it appears that when Isaiah spoke of Ephraim, he naturally connected the fate of all of Joseph's posterity in all parts of the earth (Isa. 28:22). Isaiah 29:1 speaks of "Ariel, the city where David dwelt," (i.e. Jerusalem) and then changes the subject, focusing on another place, saying "*it* shall be unto me *as* Ariel" (verse 2). He then speaks of the "heaviness and sorrow" of the descendants of Joseph and goes on to describe the fate of a people who would suffer the wrath of the Lord and would "speak out of the ground . . . as of one that hath a familiar spirit" (Isa. 29:4). The Book of Mormon was written in a style which is similar to Isaiah's own writing and was translated from records buried in the ground. The book is an account of the descendants of Joseph who passed away "at an instant suddenly" (Isa. 29:5; see also Mormon 6).

The Book of Mormon is the only "book" which has fulfilled the prophecies found in Isaiah 29 verses 11 through 14. The book of Revelation does not. The Dead Sea Scrolls do not. Other books discovered in the twentieth century do not. Only the Book of Mormon fulfills these prophecies in every point (see JS—H 1:51-52, 63-65; 2 Nephi 26:14-19; 27:1-26). This book alone has caused "the wisdom of . . . wise men" to "perish" and "the eyes of the blind" to "see out of obscurity, and out of darkness" (Isa. 29:14, 18). The coming forth of the Book of Mormon was in a day when the eyes of prophets, rulers, and seers were "covered" (Isa. 29:10; 30:10) and just prior to the time when the Jews began to turn back from their error and "come to understanding" (Isa. 29:23-24). The day when "Truth shall spring out of the earth; and righteousness shall look down from heaven" (Ps. 85:11) has come.

The coming forth of the Book of Mormon was also predicted by Ezekiel in the day when Israel would be restored as a nation (Ezek. 36:24-37:14). In that day, the record of Joseph the branch of Ephraim was to be joined to the record of Judah and the children of Israel were to be gathered "from among the heathen" and brought "into their own land" (Ezek. 37:15-21). This gathering was not the temporary gathering after their exile in Assyria but was the permanent gathering when they would dwell in the land of Jacob "for ever" (Ezek. 37:25-26) and the Lord would sanctify his people Israel (Ezek. 37:27-28).

If Isaiah chapter 29 is not a prophecy of the coming forth of the Book of Mormon, then our critics have utterly failed in their attempt to produce a satisfactory answer as to what it does describe. They have failed to identify the sealed book described in verse 11 or the "marvelous work and a wonder" which will confound the wise and prudent (verse 14). Truly the fulfillment of this prophecy correlates in too many details with the coming forth of the Book of Mormon to ascribe it to coincidence. The Book of Mormon is causing the wisdom of the wise and prudent to perish. Those who choose to ignore it will remain in obscurity and darkness, blind to the truth (Isa. 29:18, 24).

85. Is it true that the Book of Mormon contains no new doctrine and few unique teachings?

The assertion that the Book of Mormon contains no new doctrine has been made by those who are critical of LDS beliefs. Possibly they hope to deter other Christians from reading it and learning the truth about its contents. Although the teachings it contains are quite similar to the Bible, it does contain many doctrines not found in Bible scripture. The Book of Mormon denounces, for example, the belief that God is restricted to a single volume of scripture (2 Nephi 29:7-10).

Gilbert W. Scharffs and other authors have compiled extensive lists of unique LDS doctrines not found in the Bible yet are found in the Book of Mormon (*The Truth About "The God Makers,"* pp. 49-51). A sample of a few of those unique doctrines follows:

1. "Adam fell that men might be; and men are, that they might have joy" (2 Nephi 2:25).
2. In hell "torment is as a lake of fire and brimstone" (2 Nephi 9:16).
3. "His blood atoneth for the sins of those who . . . have died not knowing the will of God concerning them, or who have ignorantly sinned" (Mosiah 3:11).
4. "The atonement . . . has been prepared from the foundation of the world" (Mosiah 4:6).
5. God can't save unrepentant sinners because of the law of justice (Mosiah 15:27).
6. It is not wrong to use available remedies, in addition to faith, to cure sickness (Alma 46:40).
7. Christ's church must bear his name (3 Nephi 27:8).
8. "Wo unto him . . . that shall say the Lord no longer worketh by revelation" (3 Nephi 29:6).
9. The premortal Jesus had a spirit body that looked like his mortal body (Ether 3:6-16).
10. Exact sacramental prayers are given (Moroni 4:3 and 5:2).
11. "For behold, the Spirit of Christ is given to every man, that he may know good from evil" (Moroni 7:16).
12. "Little children need no repentance, neither baptism . . . but little children are alive in Christ" (Moroni 8:11-12).

13. The truthfulness of the Book of Mormon may be determined by sincere study, pondering and prayer (Moroni 10:3-5).

14. "Despair cometh because of iniquity" (Moroni 10:22).

To this list Brother Scharff adds many Bible doctrines which are clarified or expanded in the Book of Mormon (*The Truth About "The God Makers"*, pp. 52-56).

The Book of Mormon also adds much to our understanding of many fundamental Bible doctrines which have been misinterpreted in our day. It clarifies concepts such as the apostasy (1 Nephi 13; 22; 2 Nephi 26-28); opposition in all things (2 Nephi 2:11); freedom of choice (2 Nephi 2:27-28; 10:23, Helaman 14:30-31); the nature of the Godhead (2 Nephi 2:28; 3 Nephi 11:10-11, 14; Ether 3:16); Christ's identity and mission (2 Nephi 9; 25:18-19; Mosiah 3-4; 3 Nephi 15:4-5); the need for an infinite atonement (2 Nephi 9:7; Alma 34:10); the importance of baptism (2 Nephi 31:5-13; Alma 7:14-15; 3 Nephi 11:21-27, 33-34); the necessity of enduring in righteousness (2 Nephi 31:16; Alma 38:1-2; 3 Nephi 27:16, 19-20); plural marriage (Jacob 2:24-30); being born again (Mosiah 5; 27:24-26; Alma 5:12-19); authority (Mosiah 23:17; 3 Nephi 11:25; 12:1; Moroni 2:1-2; 3:1-4); the resurrection (Alma 11:40-45); forgiveness of serious sins (Alma 39:5-6); why the righteous suffer (Alma 60:13); why miracles may be withheld (Mormon 9:20); and the sacrament (3 Nephi 18:1-12; Moroni 4 & 5).

Those who believe that the Book of Mormon does not teach unique doctrines have misunderstood the purpose of the book. It was not given to reveal new latter-day doctrines but rather to serve as another witness that Jesus is the Christ and to lead men to him (Book of Mormon title page). In this regard, Joseph Fielding McConkie has stated, "The Book of Mormon has no peer in teaching the doctrines of the fall, the atonement, and the need for a redeemer. The clarity with which it testifies that Jesus is the Christ is unmatched in any other scriptural record" (*Seeking the Spirit*, p. 73; see also Vestal and Wallace, *The Firm Foundation of Mormonism*, pp. 259-65). One author noted that "the Book of Mormon has 476 references to the Lord Jesus Christ by name. With 531 pages in the text of the 1981 LDS edition, that averages nearly one reference per page. Of all the other Christian scriptures, only the Gospels . . . have more references to him by name" (Charles D. Tate, *Ensign,* April 92, p. 63). When all references to Deity are considered in the Book of Mormon and the New Testament, we find that the Book of Mormon has more references to the Lord, despite the fact that it has 1,349 fewer verses. Tate found that only 30 of 531 pages in the Book of Mormon contain no specific name reference to Deity and that the book of Moroni alone contains

215 references to Christ (*Ibid.*). Truly the Book of Mormon is another witness of Christ.

The Book of Mormon also excels in leading men to Christ in that it provides us with the clearest definition of any scripture of the basics of the Gospel and the plan of salvation (2 Nephi 31; 3 Nephi 27; Moroni 8:24-26; see also Ensign, Sept. 92, pp. 7-13). As such it contains the fulness of the Gospel (D&C 20:9; 27:5; 42:12). Many Christians today, though accepting Christ as Savior, still stumble over the basic principles of the gospel because many plain and precious portions of that gospel were kept back (1 Nephi 13:26, 29, 32). The Book of Mormon restores those plain gospel truths (1 Nephi 13:35-36, 40).

86. Why does the Book of Mormon borrow extensively from the Bible, and why are so many quotes from Isaiah identical to the King James Version?

Some Christians today question the need for so many similar verses in both the Book of Mormon and the Bible. They sometimes assert that many Book of Mormon verses were copied from the King James Bible, which in their opinion makes the Book of Mormon a fraud. While this might appear to be true to the casual Book of Mormon reader, a closer look at these duplicate texts actually provides an additional witness of the Book of Mormon's authenticity.

The 21 chapters of Isaiah which are quoted in the Book of Mormon (Chapters 2-14, 29, and 48-54) either partially or completely represent about one-third of the book of Isaiah, but less than two and one-half percent of the total Book of Mormon. We also find that more than half of all verses quoted from Isaiah (234 of 433) differ from the King James Version available to Joseph Smith (see Book of Mormon note to 2 Nephi 12:2). The Book of Mormon apparently follows the King James (Masoretic) text only when it conveys the original meaning.

We often find differences in Book of Mormon Isaiah texts where modern texts disagree (see also Vestal and Wallace, *Firm Foundation of Mormonism,* pp. 70-72). One Book of Mormon verse (2 Nephi 12:16), is not only different but adds a completely new phrase: "And upon all the ships of the sea" This non-King James addition agrees with the Greek (Septuagint) version of the Bible, which had not been translated into English in Joseph Smith's day (*Book of Mormon,* 1981 edition, p. 82, footnote 16a; Gilbert Scharff, *The Truth About "The God Makers",* p. 172; see also Hunter & Ferguson, *Ancient America and the Book of Mormon,* pp. 100-02; Hugh Nibley, *Since Cumorah,* pp. 129-43; Franklin S. Harris, Jr., *The Book of Mormon Message and Evidences,* p. 50).

Another interesting quote—2 Nephi 20:29-changes Isaiah's spelling of "Ramah" (Isa. 10:29) to "Ramath" Ramath is the early Hebrew spelling which was later changed to Ramah (*Preliminary Report of the Isaiah Variants in the Book of Mormon,* p. 102). It is also significant that the chapters of Isaiah actually quoted in the Book of Mormon (chapters 2-14 and 48-54) are those which modem scholars widely agree correspond closely to the original Isaiah collection and therefore would have been the most likely to have existed in Lehi's day (Hugh Nibley, *Since Cumorah,* pp. 142-43). How could Joseph Smith have known these things? If Joseph or anyone else actually tried to plagiarize the Bible, and if he "wrote" rather that "translated" the Book of Mormon, critics have failed to show the source of the remaining 93% (when all similar texts are removed). A 100% non-biblical book of scripture wouldn't have been much more difficult to produce.

It is also interesting to note that one Bible scholar has found that the four gospels attest to the fact that Jesus Christ and the apostles consistently quoted scripture. He calculated that over "ten percent of the daily conversation of Jesus consisted of Old Testament words quoted literally" and nearly 50% of the Lord's words as quoted by John were quotations from the Old Testament (Jay P. Green Sr., *The Interlinear Bible, Hebrew-Greek-English,* p. 975).

When we consider the fact that Isaiah is the most quoted of all prophets, being more frequently quoted by Jesus, Paul, Peter, and John (in his Revelation) than any other Old Testament prophet, it should not surprise us that both the Book of Mormon and Doctrine and Covenants also quote Isaiah more than any other prophet (*LDS Bible Dictionary,* p. 707). The Lord told the Nephites that "great are the words of Isaiah" (3 Nephi 23: 1). The prophet Nephi confessed, "My soul delighteth in his words . . . for he verily saw my Redeemer, even as I have seen him" (2 Nephi 11: 2).

It is clear that the writings of Isaiah held special significance for Jesus Christ and Nephi (see 2 Nephi 11:8; 25:5; 3 Nephi 20:11; 23:1-3). Isaiah's prophecies might also have been quoted frequently because they were largely concerned with latter-day events. Isaiah wrote about the restoration of the gospel through Joseph Smith (see Isa. 49), the gathering of Israel in the last days (Isa. 18), the coming forth of the Book of Mormon (Isa. 29), wickedness in the last days (Isa. 33), the Savior's Second Coming, and the millennium (Isa. 13, 26, 27, 63). While he also wrote about the Savior's first coming (Isa. 32: 1-4; 53) and events in his own time (Isa. 20, 23), most of what he wrote about is yet to be fulfilled

(Bruce R. McConkie, "Ten Keys to Understanding Isaiah," *Ensign,* Oct. 73, pp. 78-83, see also *Melchizedek Priesthood Personal Study Guide,* vol. 3, p. 26).

When one considers that New Testament writers literally quoted hundreds of Old Testament scriptures, including 76 verses from Isaiah (*LDS Bible Dictionary,* pp. 756-59) it should not surprise us that Book of Mormon writers did likewise. After all, these writings were part of the Old World scriptures brought by Lehi's descendants to the New World (1 Nephi 19:22-23). If the prophets of the Book of Mormon had not quoted Isaiah, we might have questioned the authenticity of their words. That they did quote him extensively shows that they understood his writings as did Jesus and other apostles and prophets.

If critics are making an accusation of plagiarism, then they are by the same logic indicting their own Bible. Close examination of the Old Testament reveals many passages which are copied nearly word for word, including grammatical errors. Micah, who lived hundreds of years after Isaiah, prophesied word for word in Micah 4:1-3 what Isaiah prophesied in Isaiah 2:2-4, without once giving him credit (see A. Melvin McDonald, *Day of Defense,* p. 49). We also find the genealogy from Genesis 5,10-11, 36 repeated in 1 Chronicles, and much of the history in Samuel and Kings is repeated in Chronicles. Isaiah 36:2 through 38:6 is the same as 2 Kings 18:17 through 20:6. Although Old Testament scripture was often quoted by Old and New Testament writers without giving credit, the Book of Mormon most often makes it clear from whom passages were quoted. There was obviously no intent to plagiarize in either book. But to find fault with the Book of Mormon, critics must equally fault the Bible; otherwise, they are using a dual standard to judge.

Paul has been cited as the most original of all New Testament writers, but investigations of his epistles show that Paul often quoted from classical writers, orators, dramas, law courts, sports commentaries, and ancient religious rites. Even the well-known Pauline formula of "faith, hope, and charity," which also appears in the Book of Mormon, has been found in Babylonian writings (Hugh Nibley, *Since Cumorah,* p. 128).

Some have also questioned the use of the name JEHOVAH in 2 Nephi 22:2 and the use of some italicized King James Version words in the Book of Mormon. It seems clear that Joseph Smith was led to translate many passages as they appear in the King James Bible and made changes specifically by exception. Use of the proper name Jehovah, which is an anglicized form of the Hebrew Yahweh, was common in the Bible (Ex. 6:3; Ps. 83:18; Isa. 12:2; 26:4) and was also in common use in Joseph Smith's day (D&C 109:34, 42, 56, 68; 110:1-3;

128:9; *Teachings,* pp.220, 221, 250-51). Although the name Jehovah is of more recent origin than the original Book of Mormon plates, it does not mean this name could not properly be used in translating a more ancient Hebrew title denoting the eternal I AM. Why should Joseph Smith be criticized for using the same name that King James translators used?

Some have questioned why the Book of Mormon Isaiah passages often contain the exact wording of the King James Bible, including italicized words. The italicized King James words found in Isaiah passages were inserted by scholars for clarification of the meaning in the English translation but were not in the original Hebrew text. As was stated earlier, Joseph Smith apparently made changes to Isaiah and other passages with biblical parallels only by exception (i.e. where clarification was needed), though witnesses and internal evidence indicate that Joseph Smith did not have a Bible with him as he translated (*Review of Books on the Book of Mormon,* vol. 5, p. 51; vol. 6, pp. 100-01, 127-30). It only stands to reason that Joseph Smith would not remove or change the King James words which clarify the meaning unless they were misleading or in error. Examples of this are found in 2 Nephi 12:2 (compare Isa. 2:2); 2 Nephi 12:6 (Isa. 2:6); 2 Nephi 12:12-14 (Isa. 2:12-14); and 2 Nephi 12:20 (Isa. 2:20).

We should note that in the first chapter where Book of Mormon passages parallel Isaiah's record (Isa. 2), eight verses contained italicized words and Joseph modified six of them. The two verses left unchanged would have been confusing without the italicized words they included. Although these passages may not be representative of all Isaiah passages, the types of changes cited above are. Indeed, Book of Mormon chapter summaries encourage the reader to compare the related Isaiah passages. When this is done without bias, the changes found in the Nephite record testify to the authenticity of this work and the inspiration involved in its production. The reader is encouraged to make this comparison, noting especially the italicized words, and then challenge critics to do likewise (see also p. 201 of this text concerning chiasmus; John A. Tvedtnes, *Preliminary Report of the Isaiah Variants in the Book of Mormon,* FARMS, p. 136).

87. Are there any scientific or historic proofs of the authenticity of the Book of Mormon?

Some critics claim that the Book of Mormon fails many scientific and historic tests which should validate its trustworthiness. A number of anachronisms in the Book of Mormon are often cited in support of their assertion that the book is a fraud. We cannot ignore the belief many share that just as Christianity in general stands or falls on the reality of the resurrection, Mormonism stands or falls on the authenticity of the Book of Mormon (*Ensign,* Nov. 86, p. 6). Either Joseph Smith has perpetrated a great religious hoax or he was a prophet of God and the Book of Mormon is truly the word of God. There are no other alternatives. If it is a hoax it should be easy to tell. If it is "of God," that should be verifiable also (see Orson Pratt, *The Restoration of All Things,* p. 86).

What our Christian friends fail to realize is that scientific and historic scholarship can never provide definitive answers about the "things of God" As the scriptures tell us, "the things of God knoweth no man, but [by] the Spirit of God" (1 Cor. 2:11). Intellectual proofs may reassure us but it is the Spirit of the Holy Ghost which convinces us beyond any doubt. Just to set the record straight, let's consider some of the scientific and historic tests which are cited or patently ignored by our critics.

The Book of Mormon was sometimes ridiculed in Joseph Smith's day by scientists and scholars for what they considered to be obvious blunders. The mention of white-skinned races, horses, wheels, steel, glass, cement, silk, barley, and metal plates in pre-Columbian America was ridiculed as the product of an unschooled farmboy's imagination. At that time the existence of these items among the early inhabitants of the Americas was widely held to be scientifically insupportable. Since that day, criticisms concerning all these items have been quieted among knowledgeable scholars, although occasional criticisms still persist among the uninformed. Although archaeology has verified the early existence of the above-mentioned anachronisms, further research is still needed. Archaeologists have excavated fewer than one percent of all *known* ancient sites of the Book of Mormon period (Vestal and Wallace, *The Firm Foundation of Mormonism,* p. 103). There is much yet to be learned by scientific efforts in this area.

As a detailed discussion of all pertinent scientific and historic discoveries is not possible in this text, only a summary of references and findings will be given in this response. Those who require more information are encouraged to read the pertinent references cited.

Anachronisms

1. *Iron and Steel* (2 Nephi 5:15, Ether 7:9)—Book of Mormon references to the working of metals such as iron and steel were often touted as mistakes in the early days of the Church, but recent discoveries indicate that such metals were indeed in use in Book of Mormon times in both the New and Old World. Although the "steel" in use in that day may not have been forged in the same manner as today's steel, early historians nonetheless reported the use of a type of "steel" in antiqui-

ty in both the New and Old World. (See *An Ancient American Setting for the Book of Mormon*, pp. 278-87; see also *Since Cumorah*, p. 254; *Lehi in the Desert and the World of the Jaredites*, pp. 210-13; *A Challenge to the Critics*, p. 28; "An Evaluation of the Smithsonian Institute's statement regarding the Book of Mormon," FARMS Reprint, *Ancient America and the Book of Mormon*, pp. 263-64, 276-77; *Refuting the Critics*, p. 45).

2. *Silk* (Alma 1:29, Ether 9:17)—Although Chinese silk was probably not used in ancient America, other silky fabrics made with western materials were woven in the New World (*A Challenge to the Critics*, p. 28; see also *Lehi in the Desert and the World of the Jaredites*, p. 216; *Reexploring the Book of Mormon*, pp. 162-64).

3. *Glass* (Ether 3:1)—Glass was known in the ancient world prior to 3000 BC. Note that the Book of Mormon mentions glass in about 2200 BC, but only in the Old World (*Lehi in the Desert and the World of the Jaredites*, pp. 213-16; see also *A Challenge to the Critics*, p. 28).

4. *Horses* (1 Nephi 18:25, etc.) and *Elephants* (Ether 9:19)—The existence of pre-Columbian animals such as the horse and elephant, while still being debated by experts, seems more and more probable. The remains of horses and mammoths dating from Book of Mormon times have been found in Florida, Mexico, and the Yucatan Peninsula (*An Ancient American Setting for the Book of Mormon*, pp. 288-99; see also *Since Cumorah*, pp. 256-57; *Lehi in the Desert and the World of the Jaredites*, pp. 216-21; *Trial of the Stick of Joseph*, pp. 94-95; *A Challenge to the Critics*, pp. 50-56; *A Companion to Your Study of the Book of Mormon*, p. 117 as quoted in *Book of Mormon Student Manual*, p. 46; *Ancient America and the Book of Mormon*, pp. 312-14; *Reexploring the Book of Mormon*, pp. 98-100).

5. *Bees* (Ether 2:3)—Some critics assert that the Book of Mormon places bees in America at about 2000 BC, but all references to bees or honey in the Book of Mormon belong to the Old World. The Jaredites carried hives of bees from Babel into the wilderness, but they were apparently not taken on their ships (Ether 6:4). The existence of the honeybee at this early period in the old world is attested to by the Bible (Ex. 3:8; Deut. 1:44; Judges 14:8). Since there is no mention in the Book of Mormon of bees in the New World this is really a non-issue, but findings do indicate that bees were in America at a very early date (*Lehi in the Desert and the World of the Jaredites*, pp. 184-89; see also *The Truth About "The God Makers*," p. 174; *A Challenge to the Critics*, pp. 56-57).

6. *Cement* (Helaman 3:7-11)—The mention of the use of cement in the Book of Mormon was initially thought to be a gross error on Joseph

Smith's part, but more recent findings reveal that ancient Americans did use cement, concrete, and gypsum in their roads and buildings (*Since Cumorah*, p. 254; West, *The Trial of the Stick of Joseph*, pp. 86-88; *Book of Mormon Student Manual*, pp. 354-55; *Reexploring the Book of Mormon*, pp. 212-14; *Ancient America and the Book of Mormon*, pp. 261-63, 269).

7. *Wheels* (Jarom 1:8; 3 Nephi 3:22)—It is clear that ancient Americans knew the wheel. Sixty examples of wheeled objects have been found. One of these, a child's toy with four little stone wheels, was unearthed in a Mexico City excavation, and large, nine-foot-diameter stone wheels have been found in Bolivia (*The Trial of the Stick of Joseph*, pp. 92-94; Small and large stone wheels are pictured in the *Book of Mormon Student Manual*, p. 56, 187; see also *A Challenge to the Critics*, pp. 58-64; *Ancient America and the Book of Mormon*, pp. 259-61; *Refuting the Critics*, pp. 56-57).

8. *Money* (Alma 11:1-20)—Some have mistakenly assumed that Alma 11 describes a coinage system, when in fact the word coin does not appear in the Book of Mormon text (the word "coinage" in the chapter heading was added by a nineteenth century editor). The system described is based on fractional measurements of grain (Alma 11:7) and proportionate weights of metal. Both the grain standard and the exact proportions cited in the Book of Mormon (1, 2, 4, 7) correspond very closely with an ancient but extremely practical Egyptian monetary system (*The Firm Foundation of Mormonism*, pp. 93-98; *Since Cumorah*, pp. 255-56; *An Ancient American Setting for the Book of Mormon*, pp. 232-33; *A Challenge to the Critics*, pp. 46-48; *Refuting the Critics*, p. 60).

9. *Barley* (Alma 11:7, 15)—Many experts have claimed that barley did not exist in ancient America. However, barley has been found at a Phoenix, Arizona Hohokam site dating from 300 BC. Barley was found in abundance at that site and was found to have been grown domestically (*A Challenge to the Critics*, p. 27; December 1984 FARMS Update, Barley in Ancient America; *Reexploring the Book of Mormon*, pp. 130-32; *Ancient America and the Book of Mormon*, pp. 303-08; *Ancient American Setting for the Book of Mormon*, p. 184).

10. *Israelites inhabited pre-Columbian America* (1 Nephi 5:14; 6:2)—Though anthropologists are still arguing the presence of Israelites in ancient America, there is abundant proof of the existence of white-skinned races among the ancestors of Indian tribes of Central and South America. To this day many paintings in the temples at Bonampak and Chichen Itza, terracotta pottery and sculptures depict white skinned, bearded Caucasian and Semitic-appearing people.

Bearded figures were depicted frequently in bas reliefs, sculptures, and terra cotta portraits until 385 AD, even though Indians today do not grow beards. The sudden disappearance of this characteristic matches exactly the Book of Mormon history's dating of the Nephite decline. Could this be coincidence? (*A Challenge to the Critics*, pp. 24-36, 115-32; see also *Since Cumorah*, p. 246; *The Trial of the Stick of Joseph*, p. 108; *An Ancient American Setting for the Book of Mormon*, pp. 81-91; *Archaeology and the Book of Mormon*, pp. 25-33, 46-57, 182-282; *Ancient America and the Book of Mormon*, pp. 240-56; *Refuting the Critics*, pp. 50-51).

11. *Metal plates*—Joseph Smith was ridiculed by many because he claimed to have translated the Book of Mormon from gold plates. In addition, Book of Mormon prophets described other Old World writings on metal plates (1 Nephi 3:3; 19:1; Mosiah 8:9). Since that day more than 60 plates of gold, silver, brass, and other metals have been found dating to as early as 3000 BC and as late as the eighth century AD (see *Those Gold Plates!*, pp. 4-5, 10-32; *The Firm Foundation of Mormonism*, p. 106; *A Challenge to the Critics*, pp. 37-45; *Refuting the Critics*, p. 46).

12. *Stone boxes*—Stone boxes like the one which Joseph Smith described (JS—H 1:51-52) though virtually unknown in that day, have since been found in both the New and Old World. To date, over 50 stone boxes have been found in Mesoamerica. One box found near a temple in Kulkulcan, Mexico had a lid which was very similar to the one described by Joseph Smith (see JS—H 1:51; *A Challenge to the Critics*, pp. 43-45; *Those Gold Plates!*, pp. 26-27).

Other Evidences

1. *Tree of Life*—The tree of life symbol found in the Book of Mormon (1 Nephi 8, 11; 2 Nephi 2:15; Alma 5:34, 62; etc.) has been depicted in bas-reliefs throughout the New World. One of these (Izapa Stella #5) has been found to agree in over one hundred details with Lehi's vision of the tree of life. Surprisingly, many of the hundreds of tree of life symbols combine the form of the cross with the tree (*The Firm Foundation of Mormonism*, pp. 120-22; *A Challenge to the Critics*, pp. 69-75; *The Messiah in Ancient America*, pp. 71-111; *Ancient America and the Book of Mormon*, pp. 213-14).

2. *Language*—Evidence of both Hebrew and Egyptian cultures is found throughout the Book of Mormon (1 Nephi 1:2; Mosiah 1:4; Mormon 9:32-34). Hebrew idioms, grammar, and names are found throughout the text but, at the same time, distinctly Egyptian names and cultural traits may also be found there. This Egyptian influence is further sub-

stantiated by Mesoamerican pyramids and inscriptions discovered after Joseph Smith's day (*Rediscovering the Book of Mormon*, pp. 77-91; *The Firm Foundation of Mormonism*, pp. 173-79, *A Challenge to the Critics*, pp. 76-89; *The Trial of the Stick of Joseph*, pp. 83-86; *Lehi in the Desert and the World of the Jaredites*, pp. 13-17; *Book of Mormon Student Manual*, p. 42; *Reexploring the Book of Mormon*, pp. 183-85; *Ancient America and the Book of Mormon*, pp. 264-68; *Refuting the Critics*, pp. 40-42, 73-74).

3. *Ancient writing patterns*—Several different characteristics of ancient writings have recently been identified for the first time. These include the *colophon*, which was often used in Egyptian compositions, and *chiasmus* which is a distinctly Hebraic literary form. Both are found in the Book of Mormon despite the fact that these characteristics were unknown to scholars in Joseph Smith's day.

The *colophon* is essentially a writer's preface which follows a fixed pattern. It most often includes the writer's name, background, qualifications for writing, and a summary of the text. At times, the text is also concluded with a similar pattern. Colophons are found throughout the Book of Mormon (*Rediscovering the Book of Mormon*, pp. 32-37; *Lehi in the Desert and the World of the Jaredites*, pp. 17-20; *The Firm Foundation of Mormonism*, p. 147; *Reexploring the Book of Mormon*, pp. 13-16).

Chiasmus is an ancient literary form which resembles poetry. Instead of repeating sounds or following a rhyming pattern, chiasmus repeats ideas or words in a systematic pattern which reverses at its center point. Many examples of chiasmus have been identified in the Hebrew Bible, but the Book of Mormon contains some of the most complex examples of chiasmus known today. Alma's chiasm in Alma 36 is made up of 17 elements with all but the center element repeated twice ("Chiasmus in the Book of Mormon" *The New Era*, Feb. 72, p. 9; *Rediscovering the Book of Mormon*, pp. 114-31; *The Firm Foundation of Mormonism*, pp. 155-70; *Book of Mormon Authorship*, pp. 33-52; *A Challenge to the Critics*, pp. 94-99; *Reexploring the Book of Mormon*, pp. 230-35). H. Clay Gorton has found that four of the ten chiasma that are common to the Isaiah chapters in both the Book of Mormon and the King James Bible contain seriously degraded chiasmic structures in the Bible. A fifth chiasm was entirely eliminated in the King James Version (KJV). He observes that "the fact that five of the ten common chiasma appear in the KJV in a degraded form clearly demonstrates that the KJV is an altered form of the [earlier] Brass Plates Isaiah that had been copied by Nephi and then translated by Joseph Smith" (*The Legacy of the Brass Plates of Laban*, p. 65).

4. *Writing styles*—A number of scientific tests have been devised to examine the authenticity of the Book of Mormon. Two tests which deal with writing styles have produced some exciting (yet largely ignored) results which anti-Mormon critics cannot explain. A new computer-assisted analysis technique referred to as "stylometry" or more commonly "wordprint analysis" was developed to identify an author's writing style, much like a fingerprint or voiceprint is used to identify an individual. Wordprint analyses identify both the usage rate of non-contextual words and total new word usage rates. Both have produced significant results and will be addressed.

The non-contextual words used in wordprint analysis are the filler words, such as prepositions and conjunctions, which are repeated subconsciously through patterns developed early in life. Although the conscious features of a given author's style might be imitated, the subconscious features cannot. Analysis indicates that an author's wordprint style remains consistent despite the passage of time, change of subject matter, or literary form. Most importantly, the accuracy of a wordprint analysis is retained even after an author's work has gone through a strictly literal translation into another language. (*Reexploring the Book of Mormon,* pp. 221-26).

Wordprint studies have been used to determine authorship in the examination of letters, biblical books, and ancient Greek works. More recently, the technique was applied to the Book of Mormon. In a 1979 report, Wayne Larsen and Alvin Rencher showed that the Book of Mormon text contained more than 20 distinct wordprint styles which were internally consistent with the authors identified in the text. Even more surprising to anti-Mormon critics was the fact that none of the Book of Mormon wordprint styles matched Joseph Smith's own style or that of any other suggested nineteenth-century author (See *Book of Mormon Authorship,* pp. 157-88). Despite the fact that Joseph Smith's own wordprint style is not found in the Book of Mormon, a consistently limited working vocabulary similar to Joseph Smith's is found throughout the book (See FARMS paper entitled *Book of Mormon "Wordprint" Measurement using "Wraparound" Block Counting*).

The rate at which new words are introduced throughout the Book of Mormon is consistently low, while individual wordprint styles vary consistently throughout the book according to the textually identified author. The only reasonably acceptable explanation for these two statistically observable results is that "the Book of Mormon is a continuous literal translation of non-English writings by different original authors, expressed by a literal translator using a restricted English vocabulary" (*Ibid.*).

The conclusion that Joseph Smith or any contemporary could have written the Book of Mormon is scientifically indefensible in light of the findings mentioned above. When coupled with the internal writing patterns and Egyptian and Hebrew characteristics mentioned earlier, the only rational conclusion that can be reached is that the Book of Mormon was not the product of any nineteenth-century author's imagination. It can only be what Joseph Smith claimed it to be: a translation of an ancient record written by men familiar with both Hebrew and Egyptian language characteristics. (Additional information on wordprint may be found in *The Signature of God; They Lie in Wait to Deceive,* vol. 2, chap. 9; *Sunstone Magazine,* vol. 6, num. 2, pp. 15-26; and *BYU Studies,* Spring 1980, pp. 225-51).

5. *Migration Routes*—Some people both in and out of the LDS Church have erroneously assumed that the Book of Mormon is the history of all pre-Columbian civilizations in the Western Hemisphere. In reality, it is a religious account of three groups that came to the Americas prior to 589 BC. Undoubtedly, there were other groups which came to the New World at other times and by other routes, but these are not mentioned in the Book of Mormon narrative. The primary group described in the Book of Mormon is that of Lehi the prophet. Dr. Eugene England has made a detailed comparison of this group's Arabian journey with modern geographical features. His study revealed numerous correspondences and no contradictions. In fact, more than twenty significant geographical details described in the Book of Mormon, but unknown in Joseph Smith's day, serve as evidence that it is indeed an ancient document, written from firsthand information (*Book of Mormon Authorship,* p. 143; see also *The Truth About "The God Makers,"* pp. 130-32; *Refuting the Critics,* pp. 44-45).

The theory that the American Indian is basically Mongoloid and came to the Americas via the Bering Strait is widely accepted today. However, Diane Wirth has observed that "blood types of the American Indians do not correspond to those of East Asian peoples. . . . In fact, a more plausible theory is that their ancestors came by sea, from non-Mongoloid parts of the Old World. Blood types are genetically inherited and passed from father to son, from one generation to the next. Among Asians, blood types A and B are common; among American Indians blood type O predominates. Except for the Eskimos, and some Athapascan groups such as the Apache and the Navajo, blood group B is virtually nonexistent among American Indians throughout North, Middle, and South America. In essence what we have is a chain of interrelated populations which cannot be regarded as typical Mongoloids. Artifacts found in the Bering Strait suggest the influence of a rather small number of Asians—far below any number that would have been needed to produce the large populace which existed" (*A Challenge to the Critics,* p. 25; see also *Since Cumorah,* p. 246; *Refuting the Critics,* pp. 48-49).

Jack West cites several legends recorded by great historians which further substantiate the Book of Mormon account. These legends describe migrations soon after the dispersion of the human family in which several different groups came "through the sea" (*The Trial of the Stick of Joseph,* pp. 69-75; see also *The Firm Foundation of Mormonism,* pp. 110-15).

6. *Early writing and legends*—Though much of the written record of early native Americans was lost or destroyed, surviving codices such as the Popol Vuh, the works of Ixtlilxochitl, the Title of the Lords of Totonicapan, the Annals of the Cakchequels, and the Nuttall Codex affirm many teachings and events found in the Book of Mormon. These records affirm that various groups came to the Americas by ship, a great destruction near the period of Christ's death, the visit of a fair white God, and other significant Book of Mormon events. They also refer to biblical topics such as the creation, Adam and Eve, the great flood, the closed ark, the tower of Babel, the confusion of languages, and belief in fasting and baptism; topics also found in the Book of Mormon and the Brass Plates (1 Nephi 5:10-12; 3 Nephi 27:1, 16; Ether 1:3, 33; 6:7; see also *Ancient America and the Book of Mormon,* pp. 18-35, 89-93, 203, 219; *The Messiah in Ancient America,* pp. 20-21, 31-35, 53-56, 114-31, 232, 286). One of the virtually universal beliefs found among Indian tribes of both North and South America concerns a white, bearded God who visited their ancestors. They record that at the end of his visit, he left a promise that he would return one day. These legends are well documented in a book entitled *He Walked the Americas* by L. Taylor Hansen.

One North American legend describes the childhood of this "white God." It says, "He told them that he was born across the ocean, in a land where all men were bearded. In this land he was born of a virgin on a night when a bright star came out of the heavens and stood over his city. Here, too, the heavens opened and down came winged beings singing chants of exquisite beauty" (*He Walked the Americas,* p. 48).

Other legends speak of the priesthood he established with his 12 disciples, the changes he made in their temple worship, the prayers he spoke, the miracles he did, and even the marks in his hands received in the land of his birth when he was nailed to a cross (*Ibid.,* pp. 150-53; see also *Those Gold Plates!,* pp. 78-88; *The Messiah in Ancient America,* pp. 1-28; *A Challenge to the Critics,* pp. 133-47; *The Trial of the Stick of Joseph,* pp. 81-83; *Archaeology and the Book of Mormon,* pp. 29-33, 39-45, 89-92; *Ancient America and the Book of Mormon,* pp. 195-222).

7. *Modern Witnesses*—In addition to the ancient historical accounts found among Indian tribes of North and South America, we have testimonies of many modern witnesses of the authenticity of the Book of Mormon. Besides Joseph Smith, there were eleven other men who saw and handled the plates from which the Book of Mormon was translated. Three of these men saw the angel who brought the plates and heard a voice from heaven declaring that the translation had been done by the gift and power of God and was true. Eight of the witnesses viewed the plates and the unusual characters engraven upon them and were allowed to "heft" the plates. All eleven men signed sworn legal affidavits attesting to these events as firsthand witnesses. Despite persecution, attempts to discredit their testimonies, and even the excommunication of some, none of these witnesses ever denied his testimony of these events. Anti-Mormon critics have often attempted to prove otherwise, but available records lend no support to their assertions. The dying words of the three witnesses leave no doubt that Joseph Smith's account of the origin of the Book of Mormon was true (*Investigating the Book of Mormon Witnesses*). To these accounts, we could also add the testimonies of friends and relatives who took part in these events (see *Ensign* articles, Feb. 89, p. 36 and July 92, pp. 53-55).

The Bible affirms that "In the mouth of two or three witnesses shall every word be established" (2 Cor. 13:1). No other revelation from God is attested to by so many modern witnesses or has been reaffirmed personally by the Father and Son (D&C 1:29-30; 17:6; Testimony of the Three Witnesses in the Book of Mormon). We should not ignore this veritable "cloud of witnesses" (Heb. 12:1), but should heed the words of the prophets and look unto Christ and his word as contained in the Bible (Heb. 12:2) and the Book of Mormon (2 Nephi 2:28; 25:24-26).

Although the above historical and scientific details may affirm our testimony of the truthfulness of the Book of Mormon, they cannot by themselves produce a complete testimony. The only way to gain a lasting testimony is through the confirmation of the Spirit as directed in Moroni 10:4-5. See chapter 10 of this text for further details. For further information on the apparent lack of archaeological remains confirming the Book of Mormon see *An Approach to the Book of Mormon*, Appendix A.

88. Could the Book of Mormon have been taken from either the Spaulding Manuscript or Ethan Smith's View of the Hebrews?

Non-Mormons have suggested two theories to explain the origin of the Book of Mormon. The most popular theory, especially among anti-Mormon critics, is that a manuscript written by Presbyterian minister Solomon Spaulding (also spelled Spalding), was the source for the Book of Mormon. In spite of the lack of evidence, this theory continues to find adherents from time to time. Recently the theory was resurrected once more when handwriting analysts revealed what they regarded as similarities between the Spaulding manuscript and a portion of the Book of Mormon manuscript. The alleged similarities have since been dismissed by experts, but the search for a flaw in Joseph Smith's account of the Book of Mormon's origin probably will continue among enemies of the Church. A more recent anti-Mormon theory suggests that a work by Ethan Smith (no relation to Joseph Smith) entitled "View of the Hebrews" was the source of the Book of Mormon. This theory, like the Spaulding theory, lacks any substantial evidence that indicates that Joseph Smith either saw this work or borrowed from it. Although a detailed study of these theories is not possible in this text, a summary of points raised by various authors will be set forth with references for those who desire a more in-depth analysis.

The Solomon Spaulding Manuscript. This manuscript was written sometime between 1809 and 1816 and thereafter misplaced; it was rediscovered in 1884. When the manuscript was found to have only superficial similarities with the Book of Mormon, speculation about a second manuscript began. To date no other manuscript has been found. In 1977, an attempt was made to show that Solomon Spaulding's handwriting matched twelve pages of the Book of Mormon manuscript. The intended implication was that the Book of Mormon was a fraud and that a portion of the speculated missing manuscript was used in the Book of Mormon manuscript. This theory was quickly disproven when Church historians produced the original transcription of D&C 56 in the same handwriting. Since that revelation, dated June 1831, could never have been written by Solomon Spaulding who had died 15 years earlier, it had to have been written by an as-yet unidentified scribe. Additional support for the existence of this unknown scribe was also found in the numerous differences between Spaulding's handwriting and the handwriting on the disputed pages, as well as the content and continuity of this portion of the Book of Mormon manuscript. In addition, wordprint analysis (see p. 202) has revealed no similarities between Spaulding's writing style and any of the more than 20 identifiable writing styles found within the Book of Mormon. This scientific evidence clearly refutes the theory that any written text was taken from an existing or speculated work by Solomon Spaulding (see Lester E. Bush, Jr., *The Spaulding Theory Then and Now,* Mormon Miscellaneous Reprint Series #1; Robert and Rosemary

Brown, *They Lie in Wait to Deceive,* vol. 2; *A Sure Foundation,* pp. 54-60; Bruce R. McConkie, *Mormon Doctrine,* p. 749; Welch, *Reexploring the Book of Mormon,* p. 223; *Ensign,* Sept. 76, pp. 84-87; Michael T. Griffith, *Refuting the Critics,* chapter 4).

Ethan Smith's *View of the Hebrews.* This work was first published in 1823 during the period when Joseph Smith was being visited annually by the Angel Moroni. Although it was technically possible that this book was available to Joseph Smith, the many dissimilarities in content and style clearly indicate that the books are completely separate works and that no plagiarism occurred. Although it is true that B. H. Roberts identified some 50 parallels between the two works, the similarities are not convincing and are no more than might be considered coincidental. Later comments by B. H. Roberts make it clear that his own testimony of the Book of Mormon remained firm despite the existence of these identified parallels. Indeed, the Book of Mormon contradicted Ethan Smith's work on many key points; for example:

1. *View of the Hebrews* argues that the American Indians were descendants of the lost tribes; the Book of Mormon does not.

2. *View of the Hebrews* begins at the destruction of Jerusalem by the Romans whereas the Book of Mormon starts prior to the destruction of Jerusalem by the Babylonians (about 700 years earlier) and includes the migration of a much earlier group from the tower of Babel at least 2000 years earlier.

3. *View of the Hebrews* asserts that the ten tribes came to America via the Bering Strait as most authorities then believed, while the Book of Mormon states that three different groups came to America separately by ship (see p. 203 of this text).

4. *View of the Hebrews* describes the Israelite spread from north to east then south whereas the Book of Mormon describes a general movement from south to north.

5. *View of the Hebrews* describes a general war about AD 1400 while the Book of Mormon maintains that the destruction of the Nephites occurred just after AD 400.

6. *View of the Hebrews* argues that Quetzalcoatl was Moses, while the Book of Mormon emphasizes Christ's visit to the Americas but makes no mention of Quetzalcoatl. Christ's visit is never mentioned in *View of the Hebrews.*

Such differences in content are significant, and many more could be added, but differences in writing style may be even more significant. As with Solomon Spaulding's work, one would expect that any borrowed names, words, or phrases or other plagiarisms would easily be substantiated, but no such plagiarisms have been identified. Also, word-print analysis revealed no similarities between Ethan Smith's writing style and the 20-plus writing styles found in the Book of Mormon.

Ironically, those who taut the Ethan Smith theory ignore the purpose of *View of the Hebrews:* to explain the remnants of Hebrew culture among the American Indians. The Book of Mormon verifies what Ethan Smith and others have recognized—that there is a distinct thread of ancient Judaism woven throughout ancient American cultures. How odd that critics have twisted *View of the Hebrews* to be seen as evidence *against* the Book of Mormon when it helps verify a major premise of the Book of Mormon.

Those who try to show that one of the above sources were used by Joseph Smith have selectively ignored facts to the contrary. As has been shown, the writings of Joseph Smith, Sidney Rigdon, Solomon Spaulding, and Ethan Smith were unlike any of those contained in the Book of Mormon. Hebrew idioms, chiasmus, Hebrew and Egyptian features, writing styles, and computer textual analysis all indicate that no nineteenth-century author produced this work. The Book of Mormon was, as claimed, written by ancient prophets as they were inspired by God (see also pp 201-03; *A Sure Foundation,* pp. 63, 69-71; *The Truth About "The God Makers,"* pp. 167-70; *View of the Hebrews: An Unparallel,* FARMS Update, 1983; *Studies of the Book of Mormon—B. H. Roberts (A Parallel),* ed. Brigham D. Madsen, pp. 323-44; *Ensign,* Sept. 76, pp. 84-87).

89. Why were nearly 4000 changes made in the Book of Mormon between the 1830 edition and present-day editions?

Critics of the Book of Mormon commonly assume that because God does not change, nothing that comes from God should change (see previous discussion on p. 71 of this text). They often cite Joseph Smith's declaration "that the Book of Mormon was the most correct of any book on earth" (Nov. 28, 1841, *Teachings,* p. 194). They also cite D&C 17:6 where the Lord declares the translation to be "true." What they fail to understand is that the Book of Mormon never was labeled as perfect or infallible.

Book of Mormon authors themselves admitted their susceptibility to error (1 Nephi 19:6; 2 Nephi 33:11; 3 Nephi 23:12-13; Mormon 8:12, 16-17; 9:31; Ether 12:23-25). Even the Book of Mormon title page admits, "if there are faults they are the mistakes of men; wherefore, condemn not the things of God" Although Latter-day Saints accept the Book of Mormon as the word of God, they do not believe it to be perfect or infallible. Men, some of them uninspired, took part in the recording, copying, and publishing of the first and successive editions of the Book of Mormon. Hugh Nibley has observed that "once the possibility of human error is conceded, why should the idea of a corrected Book of Mormon be offensive? Revised and improved editions of the Bible are constantly coming from the press, and the Mormons have never believed in an infallible book or an infallible anything in which men have had a hand. God allows fallible humans to be co-workers with him on the road to a far-distant perfection, but he expects them to make lots of mistakes along the way" (*Since Cumorah,* p. 4).

Robert J. Matthews notes that during the Prophet Joseph Smith's life-time, "three editions of the Book of Mormon were printed. Each time he amended the text in a few places to more correctly convey the intended meaning of his translation. Other changes in these and successive edi-tions were made to correct typographical errors, improper spelling, and inaccurate or missing punctuation and to improve grammar and sentence structure or eliminate ambiguity. None of these changes, individually or collectively, alters the message of the Book of Mormon" (*A Sure Foun-dation,* p. 34).

Sidney B. Sperry affirmed that, "The sense of the first edition has not been disturbed in later editions, and the thousands of changes are rela-tively minor in nature, in matters of punctuation, spelling, diction, cor-rection of errors and the like. The thing that counts still remains, the message and sense of the original translation" (*Problems of the Book of Mormon,* p. 209, as quoted in Stan Larson's *Changes in Early Texts of the Book of Mormon,* FARMS Reprint).

Gilbert W. Scharffs observed that, "Ninety-nine percent of the orig-inal edition of the Book of Mormon has not been changed. Indeed, 4000 changes seems amazingly few. . . . Dozens of articles and books have been written on the subject of Book of Mormon changes and these changes have logical explanations and almost every change is trivial. It seems inconsistent for the authors to criticize the Book of Mormon that has but a small fraction of the number of changes that have been made in the Bible" (*The Truth About "The God Makers",* p. 160; see also *Scrapbook of Mormon Polemics,* num. 1, pp. 2-3, Mor-mon Miscellaneous).

When one considers that the Book of Mormon "manuscript was one solid paragraph, without punctuation mark, from beginning to end" (Nib-ley, *Since Cumorah,* p. 4) and that the printer was given free hand with punctuation and spelling, it should not surprise us that corrections were necessary in later editions. In fact, of the nearly 4000 changes noted by our critics, approximately 2000 were grammatical errors (Joseph Field-ing McConkie, *Seeking the Spirit,* p. 38). Lack of standardization of spelling and grammar in those days and the use of multiple scribes in the translation process surely made later changes necessary to improve readability. Even when these are discounted, we still have a small number of textual changes which remain.

Critics most often cite those changes that might be construed as doctrinal changes. Typical of these is the Godhead issue. Our critics contend that after publishing the Book of Mormon, Joseph Smith changed his concept of God from a trinitarian view to the present LDS view. This assertion is based on changes to four verses in the 1830 edition where "Son of" was added in the 1837 edition (1 Nephi 11:18, 21, 32; 13:40). Van Hale has pointed out that "both editions teach that Jesus is the Son of God, and the Son of the Father, and both editions teach that Jesus is God, and that he is the Father." He further notes that both editions clearly teach that Jesus and his Father are separate and distinct persons (*Scrapbook of Mormon Polemics,* num. 2, p. 35, Mormon Miscellaneous). He cites the following references found in all editions of the Book of Mormon to establish this point:

1. *Jesus is the Son of God*—1 Nephi 10:17; 11:6-7, 24; 2 Nephi 25:16, 19; 31:11-21; Jacob 4:5-11; Helaman 3:28; 3 Nephi 9:15.
2. *Jesus is the Son of the Father*—Alma 5:48; 3 Nephi 11:7; 12:19; 14:21; 18:27; 28:8, 10; Moroni 4:3; 5:2; etc.
3. *Jesus is God*—Title page; 2 Nephi 10:3-7; 11:7; Mosiah 27:31; Mormon 3:21; Ether 3:18; etc.
4. *Jesus is the Father*—The Eternal Father: Mosiah 15:4; 16:15; Alma 11:38, 39. Father of all things, Father of heaven and earth: 2 Nephi 25:12; Mosiah 3:8; 7:27; 15:4; Alma 11:39; Ether 4:7; Helaman 14:12; 16:18. Father of the redeemed: Mosiah 5:7; Ether 3:14.
5. *Jesus is both the Father and the Son*—Mosiah 15:2-3; 3 Nephi 1:14; Mormon 9:12; Ether 3:14; 4:12.
6. *Jesus has a Father and God who is a separate and distinct person*—Jacob 4:5; 3 Nephi 11:7, 32; 17:16; 19:18-31; 20:46; 26:2, 15; 27:28-30; Moroni 7:27; 9:26.

An attempt has been made in subsequent editions of the Book of Mormon to eliminate errors by referring back to the original or printer's emended manuscripts. Unfortunately, much of the original manuscript was destroyed while stored in the cornerstone of the Nauvoo House, but 144 pages still remain and the printer's manuscript is still in good condition. After consulting these manuscripts, many corrections were made in the 1981 edition, bringing it more into conformity with the originals and further improving the correctness of the text.

In 1977, Stan Larson calculated that the Book of Mormon text as then published was 99.9% correct (*Textual Variants of the Book of Mormon Manuscripts*, p. 1). Of the 50 textual variances he cited in his study, about 70% were corrected in the 1981 edition. Those that were not corrected do not change the sense of the text itself. Although some minute errors possibly remain in present-day editions, it is still without doubt "the most correct of any book on earth"—a comment which undoubtedly was made by Joseph Smith in reference to its profound doctrinal truths rather to its editorial correctness (*Teachings*, p. 194; see also Joseph Fielding Smith, *Answers to Gospel Questions*, 2:199-201; Paul R. Cheesman, *The Keystone of Mormonism—Early Visions of the Prophet Joseph Smith*, pp. 93-96; Welch, *Reexploring the Book of Mormon*, pp. 9-12, 21-23; Stan Larson, *Changes in Early Texts of the Book of Mormon, and Textual Variants in the Book of Mormon Manuscripts*, FARMS reprints).

90. How do Latter-day Saints explain the fact that the papyri from which the Book of Abraham was translated have been shown to be an Egyptian Book of the Dead?

A little historical background is needed to properly answer this question. On November 27, 1967, the New York Metropolitan Museum of Art presented to the Church eleven recently rediscovered fragments of papyri originally purchased by the Saints of Kirtland in July, 1835 (*History of the Church*, 2:235-236). A twelfth fragment had been in the Church's possession for many years, but the reappearance of those eleven additional papyrus fragments has sparked a controversy which may linger for years to come. The controversy centers around the authenticity of the Book of Abraham and Joseph Smith's ability to translate Egyptian hieroglyphics. There is as yet no definitive answer to the above question, but two possible explanations have been proposed by LDS researchers.

There is no doubt that the fragments now in our possession do not contain the text of the Book of Abraham. An *Improvement Era* article published in January, 1968 identified the recovered papyri as funerary texts from the Book of the Dead (also called the Book of Breathings). Scholars, both LDS and otherwise, have since confirmed this evaluation. Recovered documents also appear to be of more recent origin than the time of Abraham (Abraham lived before 2000 BC while the scrolls are dated to around 100 BC). What is not certain is whether the papyri originally purchased by the Church in 1835 actually contained the Book of Abraham or just contained ceremonial symbols derived from the original Book of Abraham.

Soon after the purchase of the original papyri, Joseph Smith stated that he "commenced the translation of some of the characters or hiero-glyphics, and . . . found that one of the rolls contained the writings of Abraham, another the writings of Joseph of Egypt" (*History of the Church*, 2:236). In December of that year, he said that "The Record of Abraham and Joseph, found with the mummies, is beautifully written on papyrus, with black, and a small part red, ink or paint, in perfect preser-vation" (*History of the Church*, 2:348). Hugh Nibley points out that the Book of Breathing text is "entirely different" from the record of Abra-ham described by Joseph Smith. The Book of Breathing papyri were neither beautifully written nor well preserved and were devoid of rubrics (passages in red). Thus, on each of these three points, the Book of Breathing manuscript conspicuously fails to qualify as the manuscript Joseph described (Nibley, *Judging and Prejudging the Book of Abra-ham*, p. 6 and *The Message of the Joseph Smith Papyri*, pp. 2-3).

Hugh Nibley further observed that one of the three or more original scrolls was described as long enough that when "unrolled on the floor, [it] extended through two rooms of the Mansion House" (*Dialogue*, vol. 3, no. 2, 1968, p. 101). He also noted that in 1906, Joseph F. Smith remembered "his 'Uncle Joseph' down on his knees on the floor with Egyptian manuscripts spread out all around him . . . When one consid-ers that the eleven fragments now in our possession can easily be spread out on the top of a small desk . . . it would seem that what is missing is much more than what we have" (*Judging and Prejudging the Book of Abraham*, as reprinted in *They Lie in Wait to Deceive*, p. 243). We should also add that only one of the three Abraham facsimiles were among the rediscovered fragments. This fact alone demonstrates that significant portions of the original scrolls are still lost. The traditional opinion held by LDS scholars has been that the Book of Abraham papyri are among those fragments which are still lost.

An alternate view, which is either expressly stated or hinted at by sev-eral LDS writers, is that the text of the Book of Abraham was not actu-ally contained in the papyri purchased by the Saints. This opinion revolves around the meaning of the word "translation" as it was used by Joseph Smith. Kirk Vestal, Arthur Wallace, Eugene Seaich, and James Harris speculate that Joseph did not actually "translate" as we define the term today, but instead produced the text through divine inspiration (*History of The Church*, 4:136-137). The Joseph Smith Translation of the Bible (D&C 76:15; 93:53; 94:10; 124:89; *History of the Church*, 1:211, 215, 219, etc.) illustrates this broader usage of the term "trans-late" Joseph restored over 120 verses concerning Enoch to Genesis chapter 5 where only 5 verses exist in our modem Bibles (compare

Moses chapter 6). He did not claim to translate this missing text from other ancient sources, but restored it by revelation.

These scholars believe that the Egyptian papyri purchased by the Church did not actually contain the text restored by Joseph Smith, but instead contained symbolic references to a more ancient primary document dating from 2500 BC (Vestal and Wallace, *The Firm Foundation of Mormonism,* pp. 183-86). Because the three Book of Abraham facsimiles also contained many ancient symbols and allusions to this primary document, Joseph Smith used them to illustrate his Abraham text. All of the authors cited above seem to agree that the facsimiles were not part of the original Abraham text but were more likely included because of the deeper symbolism they contained (Seaich, *Ancient Texts and Mormonism,* p. 106; Nibley, *Judging and Prejudging the Book of Abraham,* p. 7; *A Study of the Joseph Smith Egyptian Papyri,* p. 16; Vestal and Wallace, *The Firm Foundation of Mormonism,* pp. 183-86).

What is important is not that the facsimiles and text are only remotely related (because this is apparent from the Book of Abraham text) but that Joseph Smith's explanations attached to the facsimiles are accurate. Vestal and Wallace note that 25 of Joseph Smith's 30 facsimile explanations corresponded closely to the interpretation of Egyptologists, while the remaining 5 did not conflict (*Ibid.,* p. 188; see also p. 234 of this text).

That Joseph's translation is so similar to those of Egyptologists is even more remarkable when one considers that neither Joseph Smith nor his associates had any prior knowledge of either Egyptology or Egyptian hieroglyphics.

It appears that after the Book of Abraham was completed, Joseph Smith, W. W. Phelps, and others tried to work out an Egyptian grammar and alphabet. In so doing, they attempted to match up the "translated" text of the Book of Abraham with the Egyptian characters on the papyri. The idea was apparently to use the Book of Abraham as a type of Rosetta Stone or sure translation (Nibley, *Judging and Prejudging the Book of Abraham,* p. 6; *The Meaning of the Kirtland Egyptian Papers*). The experiment was doomed to failure, but it nonetheless indicated that: (1) they had very little knowledge of ancient Egyptian hieroglyphics, (2) they believed the text to be a true translation of papyri scrolls in their possession, and (3) there was no attempt to deceive others by claiming a knowledge of Egyptian hieroglyphics (see Hugh Nibley, *Judging and Prejudging the Book of Abraham,* p. 5 or Robert and Rose Mary Brown, *They Lie in Wait to Deceive,* pp. 238-40).

Though the above has been used in an attempt to discredit Joseph Smith and the Church, it is clear to those that read the Book of Abraham and study Joseph Smith's explanation of the three facsimiles that this work was inspired. An in-depth examination of the validity of the Book of Abraham cannot be provided in this text due to the complexity of the subject, but it has been accomplished by knowledgeable authors. For further information the reader should consult the references cited above and p. 61 of this text. Additional historical background is available in Jay M. Todd, *The Saga of the Book of Abraham.*

91. Why don't Latter-day Saints use the Joseph Smith Translation of the Bible?

Some critics of the Church accuse us of ignoring the Joseph Smith Translation (also referred to as the inspired version) of the Bible because it is, in their opinion, untrustworthy. Such is not the case. Most of the significant changes made by Joseph Smith in his inspired revision of the Bible are either found in the Pearl of Great Price (Moses and Joseph Smith—Matthew) or in the footnotes or appendix of the LDS Bible. The Church does use these inspired changes in its teaching but does not consider the Joseph Smith Translation to be complete. Although important changes were made to over 2000 Bible verses, it is apparent that "there are yet thousands of passages to be revised, clarified, and perfected. After his work of revision, the Prophet frequently quoted parts of the King James Version, announced that they contained errors, and gave clarified translations—none of which he had incorporated into his prior revisions of the Bible" (Bruce R. McConkie, Mormon Doctrine, p. 385; see also Merrill Y. Van Wagoner, *The Inspired Revision of the Bible,* pp. 21, 41-59).

Some question the reason for starting this inspired revision if it was never finished. The Lord's intent was apparently not to produce a perfect Bible but to involve Joseph Smith in a systematic study in which many important revelations could be given. Joseph Fielding McConkie has noted that sections 44, 74, 76, 77, 84, 86, 88, 91, 93, 107, 113, and 132 of the Doctrine and Covenants were all revealed in response to Joseph Smith's appeal for understanding as he struggled with his revision of Bible texts (*Seeking the Spirit,* pp. 41-42).

Although Joseph Smith's inspired revision is incomplete for now, perhaps there will come a day when all necessary changes will be made and the Joseph Smith Translation will be used by Latter-day Saints instead of the King James Version (McConkie, *Mormon Doctrine,* p. 385 and Joseph Fielding Smith, *Answers to Gospel Questions,* 2:206-07). Until that day, the Church will use both the King James Version for its accuracy and acceptance among Christians, and the Joseph Smith Translation for the insights it provides (see also *LDS Bible Dictionary,* p. 717, Joseph Smith Translation).

92. Why was additional scripture given?

Although the general purpose for modern revelation was discussed in detail in chapter four of this text, the specific reason for additional scripture was not. For additional information on the need for modern revelation, the reader is referred to p. 51 and following.

Many Christians today believe that the Bible is sufficient for our modern needs. They ignore the fact that God has called prophets in every dispensation. The Prophet Amos declared, "Surely the Lord God will do nothing, but he revealeth his secrets unto his servants the prophets" (Amos 3:7). This declaration leads us to conclude that either God has ceased to communicate with man and is therefore doing nothing today, or God is the same yesterday, today and forever and continues to reveal his secrets to those he has called as prophets. One or the other must be true. If, as Latter-day Saints believe, God is communicating with men today, then those truths being given by inspiration of God are scripture (2 Tim. 3:16; D&C 68:4).

As has been shown previously in this chapter, the Bible is neither complete nor sufficient for salvation (pp. 170-87) and it does not claim that it is. Latter-day Saints do not dispute its value, for it is the word of God and the only source of many inspired teachings, including most of the teachings of Jesus Christ during his mortal ministry. However, the record is incomplete because some portions have been lost or because the Lord chose to keep them hidden until the dispensation of the fullness of times when all things will be restored (Acts 3:21; Eph. 1:10; 2 Nephi 27:22). The Lord has promised the righteous of this dispensation that he will reveal "all the hidden mysteries of [his] kingdom from days of old, and for ages to come" (D&C 76:7) and "in that day when [he] shall come, he shall reveal all things" (D&C 101:32-34).

The hidden mysteries apparently include truths revealed in our day to Joseph Smith and subsequent prophets. These revelations have been assembled into three volumes which Latter-day Saints consider to be scripture like the Bible. The purpose of this additional scripture is clear when they are read and understood. The *Book of Mormon* contains the writings of ancient prophets on the American Continent and is meant to witness to the "Jew and Gentile that Jesus is the Christ, the Eternal God, manifesting himself unto all nations" (title page, Book of Mormon). The *Doctrine and Covenants* includes revelations given in our day as part of the restoration of all things. It contains specific commandments, advice, and warnings for those who live in this time of the earth's history. The *Pearl of Great Price* contains truths revealed to Moses and Abraham and restored in this dispensation. It also includes an inspired revision of

Matthew chapter 24 and Joseph Smith's own account of the early events of the restoration. All of these scriptures reveal doctrines and principles of great worth to God's children as they prepare for the Second Coming of Jesus Christ.

But the restoration of all things is not complete. It will continue until Christ returns and beyond. Indeed, "many great and important things pertaining to the Kingdom of God" will yet be revealed (Article of Faith #9). These include the sealed portion of the Book of Mormon (Ether 3:27; D&C 10:45-46); the records of the lost tribes (2 Nephi 29:12-13); the fulness of the record of John (1 Nephi 14:18-28; Ether 4:13-16; D&C 93:6, 18); the fulness of the record of the Brother of Jared (Ether 4:6-7): the record of Enoch (D&C 107:57); and perhaps other writings of prophets and inspired men in the days of Adam (Moses 6:5). See also A New Witness for the *Articles of Faith,* pp. 481-86; *Doctrines of Salvation,* 3:201-2.

As Brother McConkie has written, "Fools say 'Revelation has ceased and the canon of scripture is full.' The Saints of God testify, Revelation has scarcely begun; and if we are true and faithful, we shall receive revelation upon revelation until we know all things and therefore become like Him from whom revelation comes" (*A New Witness for the Articles of Faith,* p. 486).

8
Specific Modern
Scriptural Difficulties

93. Isn't the name Sam, used in the Book of Mormon, an American and not a Jewish name (1 Nephi 2:5)?

The possibility that Sam could be a Jewish or Hebrew name seems quite plausible when other similar Bible names are examined. We find Dan and Daniel, Micha and Michael, Nathan and Nathaniel, Uz and Uzziah, Shema and Shemaiah, El and Eloheim, Eli, Elijah and Elias, and many more. Apparently, the shortening or adding of syllables to Hebrew names was the rule rather than the exception. Is Sam, then, a shortened form of Samuel? Possibly, but we also find that Sam is both an Egyptian and Arab name (Vestal and Wallace, *The Firm Foundation of Mormonism,* p. 175). Could Joseph Smith have guessed that Sam would have Jewish, Egyptian and Arabic roots? (see also Michael T. Griffith, *Refuting the Critics,* p. 74).

94. Why does the Book of Mormon describe a river which emptied into the Red Sea when none exists today (1 Nephi 2:8)?

Hugh Nibley, in *Lehi in the Desert and the World of the Jaredites,* pages 91-95, shows that many authorities are "convinced that the peninsula has supported some quite respectable rivers even in historic times" He has also noted that Lehi made his discovery in the spring of the year (the commencement of the first year of the reign of Zedekiah, where the first month always refers to the first spring month). He observed that rushing torrents can be found even in desert mountains at that time of the year. He also noted that the expression "river of water" (verse 6) is a biblical term (Joel 1:20; 3:18; Song 5:12) referring to a country where rivers do not run all the time. Nibley also cites several instances of broad streams in this area. The Bible in like manner describes similar rivers now unknown to us (Gen. 2:13-14; Jud. 5:21; 2 Kings 5:12).

95. Why does it seem that many Book of Mormon passages are identical to passages in the King James New and Old Testament?

Many instances are cited where Book of Mormon verses are similar to modem Bible scriptures. Although this may seem strange at first, it must be remembered that Joseph Smith translated the Book of Mormon in 1829 and was familiar with the King James Bible. Modem translators in like manner consult similar verses in our modem Bible when translating the Dead Sea Scrolls (see also *Book of Mormon Student Manual,* p. 90). Although some verses in the Book of Mormon are similar to the King James Version, modem wordprint analysis techniques have confirmed that Joseph Smith literally translated Mormon's abridgement of ancient records (see pp. 202-03 of this text).

The following passages in the Book of Mormon are sometimes cited as examples of plagiarism:

1 Nephi 4:13 and John 11:50—Most critics use ellipses to make these verses sound more alike. This should alert the impartial reader to the detractor's real intent. The contents of these verses are completely different and the meaning being conveyed is also different. The resemblance seems to be coincidental.

I Nephi 10:8 and John 1:27—When one considers that this Book of Mormon scripture is a prophecy of John the Baptist's ministry, we are left with the conclusion that this was a correct prophecy of the words which John would speak. We should note, though, that John recorded only half of this message. The rest is found in other Gospels. Isaiah also made a similar prophecy (Isa. 40:3) of John's words which was fulfilled in Matthew 3:3; Mark 1:3; Luke 3:4; and John 1:23. We should also note that large revelatory passages of Isaiah, Jeremiah, Ezekiel, Nahum, Obadiah, and Zephaniah are similar as to be interchangeable ("Response to Mormonism—Shadow or Reality," Mormon Misc. Response Series #6, p. 21).

I Nephi 10:9 and John 1:28—This is again a prophecy. Only four words (in Bethabara beyond Jordan) are actually the same. We should note that "Beth-barah" and "Jordan" are also linked in Judges 7:24. It is also very probable that Joseph Smith might have used similar prophetic words due to his familiarity with the Gospel of John. If we conclude that use of similar words or phrases is proof of fraud, then fairness requires that all scripture must also bear no resemblance to any previously recorded scripture. Similarities between Isaiah 2:2-4; Micah 4:1-3; 2 Kings 19:1-37; and Isaiah 37:1-38 prove that this is not true in the Bible. John the apostle quoted extensively from the Old Testament. Scholars have found that about 278 verses of the 404 total verses of John contain references from the Old Testament, yet in no case does he specifically mention a book of Jewish scripture, and seldom does he quote it verbatim (*The Interpreters Bible,* 12:358).

1 Nephi 11:22 and Romans 5:5—This may be another case where Joseph Smith's familiarity with the Bible may have led him to use a somewhat familiar biblical expression (the love of God is shed abroad in our hearts) when translating. Note that this verse is not word-for-word the same. It would be a challenge for anyone familiar with the Bible to translate similar passages of scriptures without using any Bible phrases, but it seems that this is what some of our critics expect.

1 Nephi 11:27 and Luke 3:22—Note first that Matthew, Mark, Luke, and John used the words "descending" and "like a dove" to describe this event. 1 Nephi refers to the Holy Ghost and not "the Spirit" as Matthew, Mark, and John and uses the expression "in the form of a dove" which is not found in the Bible. Again, this is a prophecy of this event. If it bore little or no resemblance, it wouldn't be much of a prophecy.

1 Nephi 14:11 and Revelation 17:1, 15—To make these verses similar we have to bridge fourteen verses of John's book of Revelation. Note that Nephi saw the same vision as John but was commanded not to write it (1 Nephi 14:25-27). That he used similar words should not be surprising. Many Old Testament writers did likewise when they saw similar visions. Note the similarities between the following Old Testament prophecies and similar prophecies in the book of Revelation:

1. Isa. 48:12 and Rev. 1:17; 2:8-First and last
2. Gen. 2:9 and Rev. 2:7; 22:2-Tree of Life
3. Ps. 62:12 and Rev. 2:23; 20:13-To every man according to works
4. Zech. 6:1-3 and Rev. 6:4-8-Red, white, black, and pale horses
5. Joel 2:31 and Rev. 6:12-Sun darkened and moon turned to blood
6. Hos. 10:8 and Rev. 6:16-Mountains, fall on us
7. Zech. 4:2-3 and Rev. 11:4-Two olive trees and candlestick(s)
8. Dan. 7:4-7 and Rev. 13:2-Leopard, bear, lion, and dragon
9. Dan. 7:21 and Rev. 13:7-A beast makes war with the saints and prevails
10. Dan. 7:7 and Rev. 17:12-A beast with ten horns
11. Isa. 21:9 and Rev. 18:2-Babylon is fallen
12. Isa. 52:11 and Rev. 18:1   Come out of her
13. Isa. 65:17 and Rev. 21:1-New heaven and new earth
14. Isa. 60:14-20 and Rev. 21:23-A holy city lit by the Lord's glory
15. Deut. 4:2 and Rev. 22:18-Add not unto these words

1 Nephi 20 and 21 and other similar quotes from Isaiah have sometimes been cited as examples of plagiarism. Plagiarism is defined as "copying or imitating another author and passing off the same as one's own work." Since Nephi makes it clear that he is quoting Isaiah each time he does so (1 Nephi 19:23-24; 2 Nephi 11:8; 25:1-5) and since the summary at the beginning of each chapter instructs the reader to compare the appropriate chapter in Isaiah, it is hard to see how this can be considered plagiarism on anyone's part. As was mentioned earlier, John never gave the source of his gospel quotes. Are his quotes also plagiarism? See also pp. 193-96 of this text and *A Companion to Your Study of the Book of Mormon*, pp. 141-42.

1 Nephi 22:15 and Malachi 4:1—Although these verses resemble each other, they also differ in several points: Satan's loss of power over the hearts of the children of men, the proud and wicked will be "as" stubble, and it is not "the day" that will burn them up but the wrath of God (verse 16) that will burn them at that day. Also note that other prophets spoke of these events in similar terms (Ps. 83:13-14; 89:46; Isa. 33:14; Joel 2:1-5). It is not unlikely that both Malachi and Nephi quoted a now unknown prophet. It is clear that the brass plates contained the prophecies of Ezias, Zenock, Neum, Zenos, and Joseph the son of Jacob (1 Nephi 19:10; 2 Nephi 4:1-2; 3 Nephi 10:16-17). None of these is found in our present Old Testament (*Book of Mormon Student Manual*, p. 19; *A Companion to Your Study of the Book of Mormon*, p. 244; see also 2 Chronicles 9:29; Jude 1:14; and other references on p. 178 of this text).

2 Nephi 4:17 and Romans 7:24—It is true that a portion of Nephi's words in the above cited verse are the same. The phrase "O wretched man that I am!" does contain the same King James wording as Paul's declaration recorded nearly 600 years after Nephi's time, but the above phrase is very short. Six words in a verse containing forty words can hardly be considered plagiarism. In a book as long as the Book of Mormon (more than 500 pages), a few similarities of this type should be expected.

2 Nephi 26:9 and Malachi 4:2—"Sun of Righteousness" as used in Malachi, is a confusing term. Nephi used words which Joseph Smith translated as "Son of Righteousness." Other than the similar sounding titles and a reference to healing, these verses are completely different. Third Nephi 25:2 quotes Malachi making the same change (Sun to Son) and making other changes at the same time. If this is an error, at least Joseph Smith was consistent. Son of Righteousness was also used in Ether 9:22 which antedates 2 Nephi by thousands of years. Both Book of Mormon scriptures refer to the Son of Righteousness as a source of peace, which Malachi does not.

Alma 10:2 and Daniel 5:5—This reference is very brief and contains no details. Historical similarities of this type are also very common in the Bible. Note the similarity between Elijah's restoration of life to the widow's son (1 Kings 17:17-24) and the following New Testament stories: Acts 9:36-42; 20:6-12 (compare also Matt. 14:17-21; 15:36-38; 21:12-18; John 2:14-16).

Helaman 12:25-26 and John 5:29—This passage, which was written in 6 BC, has been criticized as a quote from John 5:29 which was composed nine decades later. Though it is unlikely that the Book of Mormon quoted Daniel, we find that both scriptures are very similar to Daniel 12:2 which was written about 550 BC. If all three scriptures are compared, the quote found in Helaman appears closer in several points to the one found in Daniel.

3 Nephi 28:21-22 and Daniel 3:6—Similarities between Book of Mormon scriptures and Old Testament scriptures written after Lehi's departure are often questioned by critics. A typical example is found in 3 Nephi 28:21-22, but similarities between this passage and the misadventures of Shadrach, Meshach, and Abednego (Dan. 3:6) and Daniel (Dan. 6:16) don't hold a candle to similarities between Peter's and Paul's ministries found in Acts:

1. Acts 3:1-11; 14:8-18-Healed a man lame from birth
2. Acts 5:15-16; 19:11-12-Healings without direct contact
3. Acts 5:17; 13:45-Jewish jealousy
4. Acts 8:9-24; 13:6-11-Dealings with a sorcerer
5. Acts 8:17; 19:6-Laying on of hands
6. Acts 9:36-41; 20:9-12-Raised another to life
7. Acts 10:10; 22:17-Received revelation in a trance
8. Acts 10:10-48; 22:17-21-Shown in a vision the need to take the Gospel to the Gentiles
9. Acts 10:25; 14:11-12-Worshiped by men
10. Acts 12:5-12; 16:25-34-Imprisoned, set loose

There are many events in history which seem to repeat. The above similarities are just a few examples. Apparently, as Ecclesiastes says, ". . . there is no new thing under the sun" (Eccl. 1:9).

Moroni 7:1 and 1 Corinthians 13:13—The use of the phrase "faith, hope, and charity" is found throughout the Book of Mormon, not just in Moroni. We also find it in Alma 7:24 and Ether 12:28. The Book of Mormon also speaks of faith, hope and love (Alma 13:29) informing us that charity is love (2 Nephi 26:30), the "pure love of Christ" (Ether 12:34; Moroni 7:47). As was mentioned earlier (p. 195 of this text), Paul often quoted from other sources. This well-known formula of faith, hope, and charity was no exception. It has also been found in ancient Babylonian writings (Hugh Nibley, *Since Cumorah,* p. 128; see also Vestal and Wallace, *The Firm Foundation of Mormonism,* p. 38 and Daniel Ludlow, *A Companion to Your Study of the Book of Mormon,* p. 336).

Moroni 10:9-17 and 1 Corinthians 12:8-11—Daniel Ludlow has stated that "several plausible explanations of this similarity could be given; however, the following possibility seems to be most reasonable: The Savior could have given a great sermon on the manifestations or gifts of the Spirit on both the Eastern and Western continents. Thus both Paul and Moroni would have been acquainted with the teachings of this sermon, just as they were both acquainted with the teaching of the Sermon on the Mount. Neither the New Testament nor the Book of Mormon claims to contain all the teachings of Jesus Christ. In fact, the Book of Mormon specifically states the "more part" of the teachings of the resurrected Christ were not included on the plates of Mormon (3 Nephi 26:6-11). John indicated that not all of the teachings of the Savior were contained in the New Testament (John 21:25). Two other possible explanations of this similarity are as follows: (1) These teachings on the gifts of the Spirit could have been recorded by a prophet in Old Testament times, and thus could have been available to Moroni through the brass plates of Laban and to Paul through one of the manuscripts that has not been included in our Old Testament; (2) the truths of the gospel are revealed to man through the power of the Holy Ghost, and the teachings concerning the gifts of the Spirit could have been revealed to both Moroni and Paul in essentially the same order" (A Companion to Your Study of the Book of Mormon, pp. 340-41).

96. How could a devout Jew not know which tribe he was from (1 Nephi 5:14)?

Since Lehi was a descendant of Joseph, he was not technically a Jew (of the tribe of Judah) but was instead an Israelite (of the tribe of Joseph). According to the Bible, both Ephraim and Manasseh were gathered by Asa to Jerusalem in 941 BC (2 Chron. 15:9). When many members of these tribes were carried away to Babylon in 721 BC it surely must have divided families and caused some confusion of lineage. Other Israelites of this time also did not know their tribe as is noted in the Bible. A description of those who sought their lineage and lived in the same century as Lehi is found in Ezra 2:62 and Nehemiah 7:64. Also, Paul warned Timothy of false genealogies which were common among the Jews (1 Tim. 1:4).

97. Why does Lehi use the Elizabethan
poetic word "methought" in 1 Nephi 8:4?

Joseph Smith translated the entire Book of Mormon into King James English using words such as "yea," "thee," "thy," "wo," "behold," "smite," etc. throughout the book. We can only guess why this was done but it appears that Joseph felt free to use any words which best conveyed the meaning and spirit of the original text. Clearly this language does not detract from the message of the Book of Mormon when read by the Spirit.

98. Aren't titles such as "Son of God"
and "Lamb of God" New Testament terms?

Use of such phrases as "Son of God" as found in 1 Nephi 10:17 and "Lamb of God" as found in 1 Nephi 10:10 and 11:21 has been questioned by critics. Although "Son of God" was only used once (Dan. 3:25) and "Lamb of God" was never used in the Old Testament, many scriptures do speak of God's Son and the symbolism of the sacrificial lamb:

Son of God—Prov. 30:4; Isa. 7:14; 9:6; Dan. 7:13; Hos. 1:10; 11:1

Lamb of God—Gen. 22:8; Isa. 53:7 likens Christ to a lamb (Mosiah 14:7); Jer. 11:19; see also Ex. 12:5, 21; 29:39; Lev. 14:10-12; 23:12; Num. 28:4

We should also note that John the Baptist spoke to the Pharisees about Jesus saying: "Behold the Lamb of God" (John 1:29, 36). Why would he use this title if it were not already in existence and if it would not be understood by them? Surely the Old Testament prophecies cited above suggest these titles, even if they were not actually translated in these exact words.

99. Why was faith given to the ball
in 1 Nephi 16:28-29 and not to God?

The ball mentioned in these passages was an instrument used by God (verse 26) to guide the righteous followers of the prophet Lehi. Similar symbolism is found in the Old Testament stories of the pillar of fire and a cloud (Ex. 13:21) and the brass serpent (Num. 21:9). In these stories the Israelites looked to these physical manifestations for guidance and physical salvation, each symbolized God's mercy and ability to save those who follow him. We may have faith in many things, but it is only faith in the Lord Jesus Christ that leads to true salvation. Many passages in the Book of Mormon make it abundantly clear that we are only saved through faith in the Lord Jesus Christ (see 1 Nephi 7:12; 10:6; 15:11; 2 Nephi 9:23; 33:7, 10; etc.).

100. Wasn't the Jewish "land of promise" the land called Canaan (2 Nephi 1:3)?

Critics often confuse the descendants of Joseph (1 Nephi 5:14, 6:2) with those of Judah. The "land of promise" for Judah was the land of Canaan as Genesis 13:14-18 states, but the blessing given to Joseph in Genesis 49:22-26 indicates that Joseph's posterity would "run over the wall . . . unto the utmost bound of the everlasting hills." The longest continuous chain of mountains in the world is found running through North and South America. It is also interesting to note that Ezekiel recorded a commandment of the Lord for both Judah and Joseph to "write" separate histories for each of their tribes (Ezek. 37:15-20). The Jews have written the Bible, but where is the record of the tribe of Joseph? Both the location of Lehi's descendants and the fact that the descendants of Joseph (the Nephites) would write their histories fulfills Bible prophecy, but these points are ignored by Book of Mormon critics.

101. Did Joseph Smith borrow 2 Nephi 1:14 from Shakespeare?

2 Nephi 1:14 refers to death as "the cold and silent grave, from whence no traveler can return" while Shakespeare speaks of death as "The undiscovered country from whose bourn no traveller returns" (Hamlet 3.1.78-79). Similar expressions have been used in many ancient documents. We find similar passages, for example, in Job 10:21 and 16:22. Job says, "Before I go hence I shall not return, even to the land of darkness and the shadow of death" and "When a few years are come, then I shall go the way whence I shall not return." The possibility that Lehi's words might have been inspired by these passages is strengthened by the fact that the word translated as "way" in Job 16:22 is "orach," which also means "traveler." It is possible that these passages or similar ancient near eastern poetry may have been available to Lehi on the brass plates, but it is equally likely that the similarity might have been coincidental. Hugh Nibley, for example, cites a poem by the first century BC Roman poet Catullus, which is nearer to Lehi's language than to Shakespeare's, though it would be unreasonable to assume any connection (*Since Cumorah*, pp. 184-85; *An Approach to the Book of Mormon*, pp. 228-29). *The Book of Mormon Student Manual* observes that critics who "use such a flimsy basis for criticizing this record . . . need to pay less attention to the choice of words in verse 14 and more attention to the counsel in verse 13!" (pp. 61-62).

102. How could the love of God cause flesh to be consumed (2 Nephi 4:21)?

The consuming of fleshly sins and desires, as symbolized by a refiner's fire (Isa. 48:10; Mal. 3:3), seems to be the intended meaning of this passage. Similar metaphors are used throughout Bible scripture. Deuteronomy 4:24 and Hebrews 12:29 speak of God as a consuming fire and similar symbolism is used in Psalms 21:9; 50:3; Isaiah 10:16-18; 24:6; 33:14; Malachi 3:2-3; 4:1; Matthew 13:40-42; 2 Thessalonians 1:8; and 2 Peter 3:10-12.

103. How could Lehi's family grow into two nations so quickly, and how could they build a temple within thirty years (2 Nephi 5)?

Note that the word "nation" was never used in 2 Nephi chapter 5. Nephi spoke of families (verse 6) and people (verses 8-9, 14, 15, 17, 22, 24, 26, 29, 32-33) but never nations. Actually, twenty or more people were in the Lehi party which crossed the sea (1 Nephi 4:35; 7:6; 16:7; 18:7; 2 Nephi 5:6). The nine or more families which departed in 592 BC (Lehi, Ishmael, Laman, Lemuel, Nephi, Zoram, Sam, Ishmael's 1st son, Ishmael's 2nd son) and multiplied (2 Nephi 5:13) could have been seventy or more twenty-two years later (2 Nephi 5:28). It is not unreasonable to think that thirty-five of these might have helped build a temple (2 Nephi 5:6).

John L. Sorenson discussed population growth in the Book of Mormon in a September 1992 Ensign article. He noted that "growth rates derived from modern population studies are useless if they refer to conditions unlike those prevailing in Book of Mormon times. . . . Although the Book of Mormon is silent on population growth and decline as such, it does provide glimpses of how the numbers were growing. For example, the data on armies and battle casualties indicate quite consistent growth" (Ensign, Sept. 92, pp. 27-28).

2 Nephi 5:16 says that the "manner of the construction [of their temple] was like unto the temple of Solomon" but the materials according to the context were different (not so precious). Solomon's temple was not much larger than many of our meetinghouses, measuring 90 feet in length by 30 feet in width and height (Book of Mormon Student Manual, p. 64). The time it took to build the temple is not actually specified, but a similar temple was finished in less than three years when the LDS Church was about five years old (the Kirtland temple was started in June 1833 and finished in March 1836). The Nauvoo temple was constructed

in five years (1841-1846) during a period of intense persecution of the Church. That a smaller group could have constructed a temple in less than 30 years (2 Nephi 5:28) seems quite practical.

104. Doesn't 2 Nephi 5:21-23 indicate racial bias?

2 Nephi 26:33 makes it clear that skin color makes no difference to God. At times, however, he does try to separate the faithful from the unbelievers. In this case, the Lord accomplished this separation by giving the unbelieving Lamanites a darker skin, "that they might not be enticing" to the Nephites. New Testament saints were similarly commanded to not be "unequally yoked together with unbelievers" (2 Cor. 6:14) and similar prohibitions are found throughout the Old Testament (Gen. 24:3; Deut. 7:3; Josh. 23:11-13; Ezra 10:10; Neh. 10:30; 13:25).

The curse upon the Lamanites was separation from God; their dark skin was simply the mark of that curse. When a large portion of the Lamanites were converted to the Lord, "the curse of God did no more follow them" (Alma 23:18), yet they retained their darker skin. Decades later, the mark was also removed from all the descendants of Laman, Lemuel and the Sons of Ishmael who believed (3 Nephi 2:12-16).

At times, the righteousness of the dark-skinned Lamanites exceeded that of the fair-skinned Nephites, and the Lord blessed them (Jacob 3:3, 7; Helaman 6:1-9). In fact, many of the most important prophecies in the Book of Mormon were revealed to Samuel the Lamanite during just such a period (Helaman 13:1-7; 14:1-6, 20-28). This Lamanite prophet revealed the signs of Christ's birth and death to the Nephites, also telling them that wickedness would result in their "utter destruction" within four hundred years (Helaman 13:9-10). The Lamanites were not destroyed but were preserved to fulfill the many great promises made to this dark-skinned branch of the house of Israel (Enos 1:13-18; Jarom 1:2; Alma 9:16-17; Helaman 15:16).

105. Isn't 2 Nephi 10:7 a false prophecy since the Jews are back in their own land but in unbelief?

The Jews are turning to Christ and have been doing so since the days of Joseph Smith. We should also note that Isaiah likewise prophesied that "the ransomed of the LORD shall return, and come to Zion with songs" (Isa. 35:10) and "the redeemed of the Lord shall return, and come with singing unto Zion" (Isa. 51:11). The Bible clearly teaches that only the believer can be redeemed by Christ (Gal. 3:13). Are Isaiah's prophecies also false? It appears that the final gathering and restoration of the Jews is yet to come (see p. 55 of this text for further details).

106. The name "Jesus" was not known in Old Testament times and "Christ" was not a name but a title. Why does 2 Nephi 25:19 refer to the name "Jesus Christ" more than 500 years before his birth?

Some have criticized 2 Nephi 25:19 for referring to Jesus Christ as a name prior to the New Testament era. Several points must be understood when considering this.

First, according to John 1:41, the titles "Messiah" and "Christ" are equivalent Hebrew and Greek titles. It is apparent that Book of Mormon authors recognized this since they repeatedly referred to the Lord as "Jesus the Christ" (2 Nephi 26:12; Mormon 5:14; Moroni 7:44) or as "the Messiah" (1 Nephi 15:13; 2 Nephi 1:10; 2:6; 2:26).

Second, the inspired writers of the New Testament repeatedly refer to the "name of Jesus Christ" as in Acts 2:38; 3:6; 4:10; 8:12; 1 Corinthians 1:2, 10; 2 Thessalonians 3:6. Also note that the name "Jesus" used in the New Testament was actually the Greek form of the name "Joshua" or "Yeshua" meaning "Jehovah is salvation" (*Strong's Exhaustive Concordance of the Bible,* Universal Subject Guide—Jeshua; *LDS Bible Dictionary,* p. 713).

Third, Arthur E. Glass, a Jewish-Christian scholar, has observed that Isaiah 62:11 and several other Old Testament phrases translated as "my salvation" or "thy salvation" should properly be translated as the proper name Yeshua or Jesus (Yeshua in the Tenach—Brochure; see also Gen. 49:18; Ex. 15:2; 1 Sam. 2:1; Ps. 9:14; 91:16; Isa. 12:2, 49:6, Luke 2:29-32; etc.). This would lead to the conclusion that Nephi and other prophets could have known Jesus Christ's name before his birth. In Hebrew, "Jesus the Messiah" would have been "Yeshua Mashiyach." Joseph Smith simply translated the Nephite name for him as Jesus Christ, the Anglicized Greek equivalent we use today (see also *Ensign,* Sept. 84, pp. 24-25).

107. Doesn't 2 Nephi 28:8-9 contradict the Latter-day Saint doctrine of repentance after death?

Some criticize the Book of Mormon's condemnation of deathbed repentance (2 Nephi 28:8-9) as contradictory to the doctrine of repentance after death, but this assessment is not well thought out. Deathbed repentance is motivated by fear and may not be sincere. Repentance after death, as implied in 1 Peter 3:18-19 and 4:6 is available to those "who have died without a knowledge of [the] gospel, who would have received it if they had been permitted to tarry" (D&C 137:7). This obviously does not include those who would repent upon their deathbed, since these have received the gospel already and have chosen not to live it.

108. Why was the French word "adieu" used in 544 BC (Jacob 7:27)?

There should be no problem with the word "adieu" since it was in common usage at the time Joseph Smith translated this passage (his mother and others also used it). It is also found in most English dictionaries today. It means "I commend you to God," a quite appropriate scriptural phrase. We should also remember that "adieu" was a translation of a reformed Egyptian (Mormon 9:32) equivalent to a Hebrew word used in 544 BC. The Hebrew word Lehitra'ot has essentially the same meaning as the word "adieu" (Daniel H. Ludlow, *A Companion to Your Study of the Book of Mormon,* p. 163). Those who criticize Joseph Smith for using a French word must, in fairness, also criticize King James translators for using French words such as tache (Ex. 26:6, 11), laver (Ex. 30:18, 28), and bruit (Jer 10:22; Nah. 3:19) which were derived from French words meaning mark, wash, and noise. Should we delete them because they are no longer in current use in the English language today? See also *A Sure Foundation,* pp. 16-18.

109. How could Nephites offer sacrifices when Exodus 28:41 and Hebrews 7:5-14 say that only Levites could perform this ordinance?

The authority by which Nephites and Lamanites made sacrifices was the Melchizedek and not the Levitical priesthood (Alma 4:16-20; 13:1-14; see also Joseph Fielding Smith, *Answers to Gospel Questions,* 1:124-26; Bruce R. McConkie, *The Promised Messiah,* pp. 410-12). That there are two priesthoods is clear in Hebrews 5:1-10 and 7:5-28. Both the Levitical (or Aaronic) priesthood and the higher Melchizedek priesthood were exercised in Old Testament times, and the higher priesthood was used to offer sacrifice (Heb. 7:26-27). Five Old Testament prophets who were not Levites are mentioned in connection with the offering of sacrifices:

1. Joshua (Ephraimite)—Josh. 8:30-31; 24:30
2. Samuel (Ephraimite)—1 Sam. 1:1-2, 20; 2:18; 7:9-10; 11:14-15
3. Elijah (Gad or Manasseh)—1 Kings 17:1; 18:31-38
4. David (Judah)—1 Chron. 16:2; Matt. 1:2-6
5. Solomon (Judah)—1 Kings 3:2-3; Matt. 1:2-6

The *Cambridge Bible Dictionary* affirms that although Samuel was "not a priest he performed priestly functions and constantly offered sacrifice at various places" (*Cambridge Bible Dictionary—*

Samuel, p. 90; see also *LDS Bible Dictionary*, pp. 599-600, 768). Latter-day Saints believe that all prophets from Adam to Moses held the higher or Melchizedek priesthood (Teachings, pp. 180-81). Until Moses, no other priesthood existed. All sacrifices offered prior to that time were done by the authority of the Melchizedek priesthood (Gen. 4:4; 8:20-21; 31:54; 46:1; Ex. 5:3, 8, 17; D&C 107:41-53). Since the Nephites held this priesthood, they also were empowered to offer sacrifices, just as Old Testament prophets had (see also *A Companion to Your Study of the Book of Mormon*, pp. 132-34; *Ensign*, March 94, p. 54).

110. "Alma" in Hebrew means "betrothed virgin." Why was this name given to a man?

Although the Hebrew word "almah" is most often translated as damsel, maid, or virgin, we cannot be sure the name Alma was derived from this word. Other Hebrew words like "alman," meaning bereaved or forsaken, or "almown," meaning hidden or secret, might also have been the source. We might also note that the equivalent Greek word translated as virgin by King James scholars was used to refer to men in Revelation 14:4.

Speaking of the Dead Sea Scrolls, Hugh Nibley stated; "In 1966, Professor Yadin found deeply buried in the floor of the Cave of Manuscripts the deed to a farm. Today the visitor entering the Shrine of the Book in Jerusalem will find the very first display on his left hand to be this deed, a strip of papyrus mounted on glass with the light shining through; and there written in a neat and legible hand is the name 'Alma, son of Judah'—one of the owners of the farm" (*Nibley on the Timely and Timeless*, p. 172; see also Yigael Yadin, *Bar-Kokhba Rediscovery of the Legendary Hero of the Second Jewish Revolt against Rome*, p. 176).

It is also possible that an Egyptian word or name might have inspired the name (see Hugh Nibley, *Since Cumorah*, pp. 192-94). Other Book of Mormon names such as Lehi, Laban, Zoram, and Sariah were obviously derived from Hebrew names (Lehi—Jud. 15:9, 14, 19; Laban—Gen. 24:29; Zoram—Jud. 13:2; Sariah—Gen. 17:15; see also *Since Cumorah*, pp. 194-96).

However, the name Alma was first used in the Book of Mormon in 148 BC, some 450 years after Lehi left Jerusalem. If the meaning of the word "gay" in English could change in less than 10 years, it is logical that the Hebrew used by the Nephites could have been substantially altered within 450 years. Linguistic changes were freely admitted by one Book of Mormon writer (Mormon 9:33) and would explain the use of non-Hebrew names at a later date in the Book of Mormon. For these reasons, the existence of one Book of Mormon name which doesn't have an obvious Hebrew connection cannot be considered proof of error or fraud.

111. Why does the Book of Mormon say that Jesus was born in Jerusalem (Alma 7:10)?

This apparent error in the birthplace of Jesus is in reality a proof of the Book of Mormon's authenticity. An Old Testament prophet in 2 Kings 14:20 uses the identical words "at Jerusalem" to refer to the "city of David" or Bethlehem (Luke 2:4). It is apparent that the word "at" was meant to convey the meaning of the area around a city. It is important to understand that Bethlehem is only five miles south of Jerusalem. Also, it is clear that Nephites designated cities and the lands surrounding them by the same name (Alma 47:20). Even today many of our counties have the same name as the major city they surround. Since Nephite prophets were familiar with the city of Jerusalem and not Bethlehem, it is only reasonable that they would use these words in describing the location of the Savior's birth (see also *Answers to Gospel Questions*, 1:172-75; *Reexploring the Book of Mormon*, pp. 170-71; Michael T. Griffith, *Refuting the Critics*, chapter 1).

112. Why do Latter-day Saints say Ezekiel 37:15-20 is a prophecy of the Book of Mormon when Lehi was a descendant of Manasseh, not Ephraim (Alma 10:3)?

Ishmael, who was as much a father of the Nephite and Lamanite civilizations as Lehi, was a descendant of Ephraim (*Journal of Discourses*, 23:184-85; *The Improvement Era*, vol. 8, p. 781; see also *Book of Mormon Student Manual*, pp. 19, 64; *A Companion to Your Study of the Book of Mormon*, pp. 100, 199). Thus, the Nephites and Lamanites were actually descendants of both tribes. It is interesting that Ezekiel specified in verse 19 that the Lord would accomplish this work through the "stick of Joseph [Ephraim and Manasseh], which is in the hand of Ephraim." Joseph Smith and many members of the LDS Church are descendants of Ephraim. Thus, the record of Joseph was in the hand of Ephraim when it was brought forth and united with the stick of Judah (The Bible). Also, as Ezekiel 37:16 states, the stick of Ephraim was written for Joseph and "all the house of Israel his companions." It is clear from this that more than one tribe was to be represented in the Book of Mormon account, and this is exactly what we find (see also Joseph Fielding Smith, Answers to Gospel Questions, 1:142-43, 3:197-98).

113. Why does the Book of Mormon say there were Christians in the New World (Alma 46:15)?

Mormons do not dispute that the Greek word which was translated as "Christian" was first applied to disciples in the Old World in about AD 43 (Acts 11:26). But Luke surely had no knowledge of the New World and could not have known that believers in the Americas used a similar expression which could be translated as "Christian." Mesoamerican believers in the coming of the Messiah had to be called by some name. Just as Christ and Messiah are equivalent titles in Greek and Hebrew (John 1:41), there was apparently an equivalent Nephite word to denote believers in Christ. That word was translated into the closest modern English term by Joseph Smith: "Christian" Joseph Smith also used the closest available word for terms like baptism (1 Nephi 10:9), Holy Ghost (1 Nephi 10:11); and Bible (2 Nephi 29).

114. Doesn't Samuel the Lamanite contradict the Bible's account of Christ's death (Helaman 14:20, 29)?

Although Samuel did say "that darkness should cover the face of the whole earth for the space of three days" (Helaman 14:27), the verses immediately prior to this statement make the meaning clear. Helaman 14:20 states that "there shall be no light on the face of *this land . . .* for the space of three days" Therefore the thick darkness described in the New World had nothing to do with the darkness described by Matthew and Mark (Matt. 27:45 and Mark 15:33; see also 1 Nephi 19:10-13; 2 Nephi 10:20). The thick darkness described in 3 Nephi 8 was called a vapor which obscured the sun (verses 20-23). Moses noted that a similar darkness was once over the land of Egypt (Ex. 10:21; 20:21).

Similar localized events have been recorded as a result of large forest fires and volcanic activity which obscured the sun. Fires set by "lightnings," or volcanic dust from eruptions which were described as "quakings," very easily might have obscured the sun as described in verse 22 (Nibley, *Since Cumorah,* p. 266-67). This also would not have affected the events surrounding the resurrection, as some authors contend.

The timing of this event is a further witness to the authenticity of this account: 3 Nephi 10:9 tells us that the crucifixion occurred "in the morning," while the Bible places the event in the afternoon between the 6th (noon) and 9th hours (3 PM). Critics should note that 3 PM in Jerusalem would be about 6 AM on the American continent.

115. Why wasn't 3 Nephi 13:12 changed
as it was in the Joseph Smith Translation?

Joseph Smith changed the clause "Lead us not into temptation" to "And suffer us not to be led into temptation" in his inspired revision of the Bible. Some have asked why this phrase was not also changed in the Book of Mormon. It seems clear from other similar passages in the Book of Mormon that Joseph Smith tried to retain the biblical phraseology whenever possible. It appears that his wording for similar passages followed the wording of the King James Bible except when a change was absolutely necessary. In this case, the Bible text may have seemed sufficiently clear to Joseph at the time the Book of Mormon was being translated, but appeared somewhat misleading when the prophet undertook his inspired revision of the Bible years later. As was explained in chapter four (p. 68), Latter-day Saints accept God's right to expand on previously revealed scripture "line upon line" and "precept upon precept," "here a little, and there a little" (Isa. 28:10-13). It seems clear that this was the case in this passage (see also Daniel Ludlow, *A Companion to Your Study of the Book of Mormon*, pp. 267-68).

116. Why did one of the Lord's disciples
have the Greek name Timothy (3 Nephi 19:4)?

Stephen D. Ricks addressed this question in detail in an October 1992 *Ensign* article. He says that "Although we do not know for certain, there are several plausible explanations for the appearance of this name in the Book of Mormon. It may be that the name Timothy, as well as other manifestations of Greek influence, was brought to the New World by the Mulekites." The Mulekites may have come to the New World on a Phoenician ship which had regular contact with the Greeks. He notes that "Lachoneus and Timothy, the only two names in the Book of Mormon that seem to be of Greek origin, appear . . . only after the Mulekite contact with the Nephites. Another possibility . . . is that we have a Greek doublet—a name in one language that has the same or nearly the same meaning as a name in another language. For example, in the New Testament, the Greek name Petros (Peter) is a doublet of the Aramaic Cephas, both of which mean a "rock" Likewise, the Greek Didymus is a doublet of the Aramaic Thomas, meaning "twin"

The name Timothy means "God-fearer" and might be a doublet for a similar-meaning Nephite name. Alternatively, Timothy may simply be a rendering of a like-sounding Nephite name that is otherwise completely unrelated to the Greek" Brother Ricks also indicates that the name Timothy may have originated from Israelite contacts with Greeks prior to

Lehi's time. Professor Cyrus H. Gordon found that trade and other cultural contacts existed between the Greeks and the ancient Near East from the middle of the second millennium BC (*Ensign,* Oct. 1992 pp. 53-54).

117. Why did 4 Nephi 6 require 57 words to say that 59 years had passed?

Anyone who records a journal in ink will find that when updating a history at intervals where little has taken place, the narrative may become wordy. Considering that an eraser was not available to those engraving the plates, it is surprising that there are not more passages like this. We should also note that phrases like "it came to pass" were most likely one word in the Nephite language. In both Hebrew and Greek one word is used. It is hayah (pronounced haw-yaw) in Hebrew and ginomai (pronounced ghinom-ahee) in Greek (see *Strong's Exhaustive Concordance*—Hebrew and Greek Dictionaries).

118. If the Jaredites were to become a great nation, where are they today?

The promise in Ether 1:43 concerning the descendants of Jared becoming a great nation unto the Lord is not fully explained in the short book of Ether, but it is apparent that they numbered in the millions (Ether 15:2) and endured for nearly two thousand years upon the American continent. Certainly they would have been one of the great nations of that era, a fulfillment of that prophecy. It is also possible that one or more righteous groups left the wicked Jaredite nation at some point and are yet upon the earth.

119. How could the brother of Jared be so bold as to instruct the Lord (Ether 2)?

The conclusion that the brother of Jared gave instructions to God in Ether 2 is erroneous. Ether 2:5, 16, 20, and 22 make it clear that the Lord gave instructions throughout the chapter. It was only when it came to the problem of providing light within closed seagoing vessels that the Lord gave the brother of Jared the opportunity to devise an appropriate solution (Ether 2:23-25). To imply that a prophet instructed the Lord is drawing an unwarranted conclusion and is not factual.

120. How could the brother of Jared be redeemed without Christ's sacrifice (Ether 3:9-13, 19)?

Some critics contend that these verses imply that the brother of Jared was "redeemed from the fall because he saw the finger of the Lord." Verse 9 makes it clear that it was because of "such exceeding great faith" in God (also referred to as knowledge, verse 19) that he was redeemed.

Biblical scriptures in John 3:36; 20:31; Acts 10:43; and Romans 5:2 confirm this principle. The Book of Mormon clearly teaches the necessity of Christ's atoning sacrifice in regard to salvation (see p. 128 of this text). It also teaches that the atonement of Christ provided salvation to those who died before his coming, as well as for those who came after.

121. How could the canopic jars in the Book of Abraham facsimiles 1 and 2 look alike, yet have different meanings?

The answer to this question is also a witness to Joseph Smith's divine calling as a prophet. Joseph Smith identifies the jars in Facsimile #1 as four idolatrous gods while in Facsimile #2 he identifies them as representing "the earth in its four quarters." James R. Harris observes that these jars do, in fact, represent the Sons of Horns, who are the gods of "the four lands adjacent to Egypt: on the east, Elkenah (Canaan); on the west, Libnah (Libya); on the north, Mahmackrah (Anatolia); and on the south, Korash (Cush). The east, west, north, and south orientation of these lands is consistent with the tradition that these Sons of Horns were guardians of the pillars 'which formed the four cardinal points.' The four gods who held the pillars of heaven and earth in position, were thus gods of the four cardinal points who embrace the four Pure Lands . . ." or four quarters of the earth (*The Facsimiles of the Book of Abraham, A Study of the Joseph Smith Papyri,* p. 37). How could Joseph Smith, who knew nothing of Egyptology, have known this unless he was indeed a prophet and seer?

9
The Holy Ghost and Truth

122. How should scripture be interpreted?

According to Chauncey Riddle, scripture may be read in three different ways: (1) by private interpretation (using personal understanding), (2) by scholarly interpretation, or (3) by prophetic interpretation (*The New Testament and the Latter-day Saints,* pp. 264-71). Although Peter warned that "no prophecy of the scripture is of any private interpretation" (2 Peter 1:20-21), it seems clear that many Christians nevertheless interpret scripture in this way.

Many Protestants today believe that scholarly interpretation holds the key to a correct interpretation of scripture. While first-class scholarship can add significantly to our understanding of scripture, it cannot be relied upon to lead us to all truth. As has been stated elsewhere in this text, scriptural scholars exist in all major denominations today and yet they still disagree on many basic doctrinal issues. Though each may find support for his own personal beliefs in scripture, a consensus is difficult if not impossible to obtain on doctrines such as baptism, the requirements of salvation, the Godhead, and many other crucial tenets.

Men have been arguing about the true interpretation of scripture since revelation was first put into written form. Even when they were written in a language in current use, they were often misunderstood (2 Peter 3:16). Early Christians also had a hard time living the principles they contained (Rom. 1:18, 22, 25; Gal. 1:6-7; 2 Peter 2:2) even though Christ's divine example was still fresh in the minds of many. Can scholars today hope to understand scripture better than the first Christians?

Latter-day Saints and some Protestants believe that personal revelation is necessary to correctly interpret scripture. Paul, in 1 Corinthians 2:11, tells us that, "the things of God knoweth no man but [by] the Spirit of God." He adds that these things of God "also we speak, not in words which man's wisdom teacheth, but which the Holy Ghost teacheth; comparing spiritual things with spiritual" (verse 13). Jesus likewise taught that truth comes by revelation of God through the Holy Ghost. He declared that when "he, the Spirit of truth, is come, he will guide you into all truth . . . and he will show you things to come" (John 16:13).

Latter-day Saints also have modern scriptures which teach the necessity of the Spirit in understanding the truths of scripture. We are taught to read, ponder, and pray so that the Holy Ghost "will manifest the truth of it" unto us (1 Nephi 10:17-19; Moroni 10:4-5; D&C 11:12; 42:14; 45:57; 50:17-20; 84:43-47). Bruce R. McConkie has stated: "In the final analysis there is no way, absolutely none, to understand any scripture except to have the same spirit of prophecy that rested upon the one who uttered the truth in its original form. Scripture comes from God by the power of the Holy Ghost. It does not originate with man. It means only what the Holy Ghost thinks it means. To interpret it, we must be enlightened by the power of the Holy Spirit. It takes a prophet to understand a prophet, and every faithful member of the Church should have 'the testimony of Jesus' which 'is the spirit of revelation' (Rev. 19:10; Ensign, Oct. 73 p. 82; see also *Teachings,* pp. 11-12 and *Doctrines of the Restoration,* p. 229).

123. How may a knowledge of truth be obtained?

The Lord has established some basic rules for obtaining a knowledge of truth. Some of these rules were mentioned in the answer to the previous question. The following are also recommended in this regard:

1. Living the gospel to the best of our ability (John 3:20-21; 14:15-17)
2. Exercising faith in Christ through prayer (Matt. 7:7-11; James 1:5-6; Alma 22:16; Moroni 10:4; D&C 11:14; 42:14)
3. Searching the scriptures in humility and with an open mind (Prov. 1:2-5; 3:5-7; Acts 17:11-12; 2 Tim. 2:15; 3:15; D&C 11:12, 22; 136:31-32)
4. Listening for answers revealed through the Spirit (Luke 12:11-12; John 16:13: 2 Peter 1:21)
5. Testing answers through application, whenever possible, to observe if the fruit is good (Matt. 7:14-20; 1 Thes. 5:21; 1 John 4:1; Alma 32:29-33)

We should note that the above rules are not based on logic but on scripture. Since God's word is truth (John 17:17), these rules can be relied upon to lead us to "all truth"

We may ask why many do not receive the truths of the Restored Gospel. For some, it is apparently because they are not sufficiently humble, teachable, and receptive to the Spirit. Those who refuse to read the Book of Mormon, for example, are either not sincerely searching for truth or have allowed pride in their own false knowledge to harden their hearts to the possibility that the Book of Mormon is the word of God. They refuse to try Moroni's promise or lack the faith that God will reveal to them "the truth of all things" (Moroni 10:5) as he has promised.

Some Protestants today teach that the Bible is the absolute authority on truth and that any inspiration which contradicts the Bible, as they understand it, is in error. In contrast to this, Ignathius in his letter to the Philadelphians warned, "For the ancient records [archeiois] ought not to be preferred to the Spirit" (Alexander Roberts, *The Apostolic Fathers* in *The Ante-Nicene Fathers,* 10 vols., 1:84 as quoted in *Review of Books about the Book of Mormon,* vol. 5 p. 323). We differ from Protestants in that we use both ancient and modern scriptures as our standard. We consider revelation through the Lord's prophet to be scripture, and like all scripture, we seek to know the truth of it for ourselves by the confirmation of the Holy Ghost.

In many instances, people are not relying on the Spirit for answers and may even mock the trustworthiness of relying on the Spirit (see p. 241). Those who do so are putting their "trust in the arm of flesh" and not in the Lord (Prov. 3:5; Jer. 17:5; 2 Cor. 5:7; 2 Nephi 4:34; D&C 1:19).

124. What is the Holy Ghost?

Marion G. Romney stated: "The Holy Ghost is a person, a spirit, the third member of the Godhead. He is a messenger and a witness of the Father and the Son. He brings to men testimony, witness, and knowledge of God the Father, Jesus Christ His Son, and the truths of the gospel. He vitalizes truth in the hearts and souls of men" (*Ensign,* May 77, p. 43).

Although modern revelation teaches this concept clearly (2 Nephi 31:21; Alma 11:44; D&C 20:26-27; 130:22; Moses 1:24; 5:9; 7:11), there are many Christians today who believe that the Holy Ghost is only God's influence and not a separate personage. We should also note that all three of the writers of the synoptic gospels describe the Holy Ghost as a separate personage from both the Father and the Son (Matt. 3:16-17; Mark 1:10-11; Luke 3:22). Many other Bible scriptures also distinguish the Holy Ghost from the other members of the Godhead (Matt. 28:19; John 14:16, 26; 15:26; Acts 7:55-56; 10:38; 2 Cor 13:14; 1 John 5:7).

The terms "Spirit" and "Ghost" are used interchangeably in scripture. The term "Holy Ghost" is the King James Version's translation of the Greek "pneuma hagios" which is used 87 times in the New Testament from Matthew (1:18) to Jude (1:20). These words are often translated as Holy Spirit in other Bible translations, and were so translated by King James scholars in Luke 11:13.

The terms Spirit (Matt. 12:18), Spirit of God (Matt. 12:28), Spirit of the Lord (Luke 4:18), Spirit of your Father (Matt. 10:20), Spirit of Christ (Rom. 8:9), Spirit of Jesus Christ (Phil. 1:19), Spirit of truth (John 15:26), Spirit of holiness (Rom. 1:4), Spirit of life (Rom. 8:2), and Spirit of the living God (2 Cor. 3:3) are similarly used by New Testament writers, although not always to refer to the Holy Ghost (see *Strong's Exhaustive Concordance of the Bible*).

The Greek word "pneuma," which is common to all these terms, can also be translated as breath (2 Thes. 2:8), wind (John 3:8), life (Rev. 13:15) or, as it is most often translated, spirit. The word can be applied to either the divine Spirit (Luke 4:1), to an unclean spirit (Mark 1:23), or to the human spirit (Acts 7:59). John 20:22 indicates that Jesus gave the Holy Ghost to his apostles after the resurrection and that he "breathed on them" to accomplish this. We also find God breathing the breath of life (man's spirit) into Adam in Genesis 2:7. Although pneuma was often used in the New Testament to refer to "the spirit" with a small "s" (Mark 14:38; John 11:33; Rom. 7:6; 1 Cor. 2:12; etc.), many of these seem to allude to the influence of the Holy Ghost. The majority of the time when pneuma was used in the New Testament it was referring to the Holy Spirit. The King James Version capitalizes the first letter in these instances. When used uncapitalized, it is generally referring to a spiritual fervor which may or may not be the influence of this Holy Ghost (Acts 18:25).

The scriptures testify that the Holy Ghost is:

1. A guide (Luke 4:1; John 16:13; Acts 16:6-7; Alma 30:46; D&C 45:57)
2. A revelator and a teacher (Luke 12:12; John 14:26; 1 Cor. 2:10, 13; 2 Peter 1:21; Moroni 10:4-5)
3. A comforter (John 14:16, 26; Rom. 5:5; 15:13; D&C 42:17)
4. The Spirit of truth (John 14:17; 15:26; 16:13; D&C 6:15)
5. A witness (John 15:26; Acts 5:32; 20:23; Heb. 10:15; 1 John 5:6-7; 2 Nephi 31:18)
6. A reprover (John 16:7-8; D&C 121:43)
7. A glorifier (John 16:14)
8. A messenger (Acts 1:2)
9. A quickening power (Rom. 8:11)
10. An intercessor (Rom. 8:27)
11. A sanctifier (Rom. 15:16; 2 Thes. 2:13; Titus 3:5; 2 Nephi 31:17)
12. A source of testimony (1 Cor. 12:3; 2 Nephi 33:1; D&C 8:2)
13. A source of spiritual gifts (1 Cor. 12:3-11; D&C 46:13-25)
14. A sealer (D&C 76:53; 132:7)
15. A companion (D&C 121:46)

See also *Discourses on the Holy Ghost*.

125. Why is the gift of the Holy Ghost necessary, and why do Latter-day Saints believe it must be given by the laying on of hands?

As was pointed out in chapter 6 (p. 124), both reception of the Holy Ghost and sanctification by the Spirit are necessary for salvation. Christ taught that "Except a man be born of water and of the Spirit, he cannot enter into the kingdom of God" (John 3:5). Paul declared that the saints were chosen unto "salvation through sanctification of the Spirit and belief of the truth" (2 Thes. 2:13). Joseph Smith also made it clear that the baptism of water is ineffective without the baptism of the Spirit (*History of the Church, 6:316; Teachings,* p. 314).

Bruce R. McConkie has declared, "There is nothing as important as having the companionship of the Holy Ghost. Those who first receive this endowment and who then remain in tune with this member of the Eternal Godhead will receive a peace and a comfort that passeth all understanding; they will be guided and preserved in ways that are miraculous; they will be instructed until they receive all truth; they will sanctify their souls so as to dwell spotless before the Sinless One in his everlasting kingdom" (*A New Witness for the Articles of Faith,* p. 253).

New Testament scripture makes it clear that the gift of the Holy Ghost was conferred in the early church by the laying on of hands (Acts 8:14-20; 9:17; 19:6; 1 Tim. 4:14; 2 Tim. 1:6). It is interesting that few if any Christian churches today, other than the LDS Church, bestow the gift of the Holy Ghost in this manner. When asked how the LDS religion differed from other religions of that day, Joseph Smith replied that, "we differed in mode of baptism, and the gift of the Holy Ghost by the laying on of hands" (*History of the Church,* 4:42).

That these ordinances also had to be done by those having authority was demonstrated earlier in this text (p. 20 and following) and is implied by these same scriptures.

Modern revelation leaves no doubt that the baptism of fire and the Holy Ghost is promised as a gift to those who are baptized by water and are confirmed members of the Church by the laying on of hands of the priesthood (D&C 20:41; 33:11, 15; 39:23; 49:14; 76:52; Article of Faith #4). Although this gift is bestowed by the ordinance of the laying on of hands by an authorized servant of the Lord, the priesthood bearer cannot "give the Holy Ghost" but only bestows the right to "receive" that gift. Therefore, the Holy Ghost will only be manifest as one strives to be worthy (*see Gospel Doctrine,* pp. 60-61; *Journal of Discourses,* 13:157 as quoted in *The Gospel: God, Man, and Truth,* pp. 58-61; see also *Mormon Doctrine,* pp. 312-13, 438; Richard Lloyd Anderson, *Understand-*

ing Paul, pp. 61, 208; *LDS Bible Dictionary,* p. 723 — Laying on of hands; David Yarn, *The Gospel: God Man, and Truth,* p. 56).

It is clear that the laying on of hands was the method by which priesthood bearers in the ancient church blessed others (Gen. 48:14, 20; Matt. 19:13-15; Mark 10:13, 16); healed the sick (Matt. 9:18; Mark 5:23; 16:18; Luke 4:40; Acts 9:12, 17; 28:8); set men apart for service (Num. 8:10-11; 27:18, 23; Acts 13:2-3); and ordained men to the priesthood (Acts 6:6; Alma 6:1; Moroni 3:1-2; JS—H 1:68-69). It is also clear that Paul spoke of this ordinance as a doctrine (Heb. 6:2). This doctrine referred to as the second baptism (note baptism is plural in this verse) was also called the baptism of fire or the gift of the Holy Ghost (note verse 4 refers to the "heavenly gift" given "partakers of the Holy Ghost;" see Acts 2:38; 10:45).

Concerning the priesthood power, Bishop John of Bristol said, "the power of working miracles was not extended beyond the disciples upon whom the apostles conferred it by the imposition of hands. As the number of those disciples gradually diminished, the instances of the exercise of miraculous powers became continually less frequent, and ceased entirely at the death of the last individual on whom the hands of the apostles had been laid" (*Eccl. Hist of the 2nd and 3rd Cent.,* London, 1825, p. 48f).

Tertullian (ca. 200 AD), though somewhat uncertain when the Holy Ghost was received, concluded from Genesis 48:14 and Acts 19 that the bishop's hand, when imposed in blessing summoned and invoked the Holy Spirit (J. N. D. Kelly, *De bapt.* 8; 10 as quoted in *Early Christian Doctrine,* p. 209). Cyprian (Bishop of Carthage from 249 to 258 AD), while discussing baptism and the gift of the Holy Ghost, asked, "if they attribute the effects of baptism to the majesty of the name, so that they who are baptized anywhere and anyhow, in the name of Jesus Christ, are judged to be renewed and sanctified; wherefore in the name of the same Christ are not hands laid upon the baptized persons among them, for the reception of the Holy Spirit? Why does the same majesty of the same name avail in the imposition of hands, which they contend, availed in the sanctification of baptism?" (Cyprian, *Epistle LXXIII,* 9 as quoted in James L. Barker, *Apostasy from the Divine Church,* p. 169).

Early Christian writings indicate that until the third century the gift of the Holy Ghost was bestowed by the laying on of hands just after baptism. With time, this ordinance was no longer associated with the reception of the Holy Ghost but was thought to be a strengthening ordinance since, they supposed, the Holy Ghost was already given at baptism. As a result, the second ordinance came to be known as confirmation and was delayed until later in life (J. N. D. Kelly, *Early Christian Doctrines,* pp. 432-36).

126. Why do Latter-day Saints believe in a "burning in the bosom" when it doesn't seem to be a biblical principle?

Some critics of the LDS beliefs come very close to blasphemy when they belittle the spiritual witness which is described as a "burning in the bosom." They claim that feelings cannot be relied upon when our eternal destiny is at stake. They will often claim that the Bible is the only reliable standard of truth and must be relied upon as the final authority. They will also assert that Satan could cause us to have a "burning in the bosom" to deceive us.

Let us compare the teachings of scripture with those of our critics. Paul taught that "the kingdom of God is not in word, but in power" (1 Cor. 4:20). The power to save is not found in the preaching of men or even in the scriptures alone. We must also have the "priesthood, the gift of the Holy Ghost, revelation, visions, miracles, [and] manifestations of God's power. . . . Where God's power is manifest, there is the Church and kingdom of God on earth" (Bruce R. McConkie, *Doctrinal New Testament Commentary,* 2:333). It appears as though our critics believe, the kingdom of God is not in power but in the word alone.

Paul taught that "the things of God knoweth no man but [by] the Spirit of God" (1 Cor. 2:11). Joseph Smith agreed with this principle, and taught that "no man can know that Jesus is the Lord, but by the Holy Ghost" (*Teachings,* p. 223). Our critics, on the other hand, seem to be saying, Man must not trust in the Spirit of God to reveal things of God with certainty. They contend that the Bible is infallible and can be used to prove that Jesus is the Lord as well as any and all doctrinal truths.

John the Apostle recorded that Jesus taught, "the Comforter, which is the Holy Ghost, whom the Father will send in my name, he shall teach you all things, and bring all things to your remembrance, whatsoever I have said unto you" (John 14:26) and later "the Spirit of truth . . . will guide you into all truth" (John 16:13).

Some today criticize the description of a "burning in the bosom" found in D&C 9:8 as unbiblical and possibly of the devil. If it is not biblical, then the early disciples were also deceived. The two disciples who were taught by Christ on the road to Emmaus described the witness they received saying, "Did not our heart burn within us, while he talked with us by the way, and while he opened to us the scriptures?" (Luke 24:32).

The reference to a burning in the bosom can be misleading when not understood in its proper context. Even some within the LDS Church mistakenly believe that this is the only way the Spirit can manifest itself. We should remember that D&C 9 was a revelation given specifically to Oliver Cowdery while he was attempting to translate the Book of Mormon record. This manifestation of the Spirit surely does not apply to all persons and circumstances. Critics also focus on the words in verse eight which describe the physical manifestation Oliver would feel, while ignoring the important instructions which apply to those seeking spiritual confirmation: "you must study it out in your mind; then you must ask me if it be right, and if it is right . . . you shall feel that it is right. But if it be not right you shall have no such feelings" (D&C 9:8-9). We should remember that the inspiration of the Spirit may also come as a still small voice (1 Kings 19:12; D&C 85:6) or as enlightenment to the mind and joy to our hearts (Job 32:8; D&C 8:2-3; 11:13) which "leadeth to do good . . . to walk humbly, to judge righteously; and . . . [will] fill your soul with joy" (D&C 11:12-13; see also Joseph Fielding McConkie, *Seeking the Spirit,* pp. 74-75; *Melchizedek Priesthood Study Guide* #4, pp. 1-4).

Because LDS beliefs are different from those of mainstream Christianity, we are often accused of teaching another gospel (Gal. 1:6-8) even though the principles we teach are firmly based in New Testament scripture (see chapter 1 of this text for additional details on this subject). On the other hand, some Protestant leaders today teach that following the promptings of the Holy Ghost is a heretical doctrine. Because these individuals possibly have not known or listened to the witness of the Spirit, they deny that it exists. They teach men "with their lips" to trust in Christ for their salvation, but do not trust him in "their hearts" to reveal truth in the manner he promised (Isa. 29:13; John 14:16-17, 26). The following principles were taught by Jesus and his apostles in relation to truth:

1. The Holy Ghost teaches truth (John 14:26; 15:26; 16:13; 1 John 5:6)

2. Those who live according to God's word shall know the truth (Jer. 17:10; John 3:21; 8:31-32; 1 John 3:22)

3. Wisdom shall be given to those who ask God in faith through prayer (Matt. 7:7-8; James 1:5-6; 1 John 3:21-22)

4. Although we should study to show ourselves approved of God (2 Tim. 2:15), we must realize that the Spirit is essential to a proper and complete understanding of the word of God (1 Cor. 2:11)

5. Relying on man's wisdom will result in failure to recognize truth when it is given to us (Prov. 3:3-7; Jer. 17:5-7)

The Prophet Nephi declared: "the evil spirit teacheth not a man to pray, but teacheth him that he must not pray" (2 Nephi 32:8). Speaking of those who were trying to hinder the restoration of the truth, the Lord declared, "Satan has great hold upon their hearts; he stirreth them up to iniquity against that which is good; And their hearts are corrupt and full of wickedness and abominations; and they love darkness rather than light, because their deeds are evil; therefore they will not ask me" (D&C 10:20-21).

127. Why do Latter-day Saints say that the gift of the Holy Ghost follows baptism when Cornelius and others received it prior to baptism?

Joseph Smith taught that "There is a difference between the Holy Ghost and the gift of the Holy Ghost. Cornelius received the Holy Ghost before he was baptized, which was the convincing power of God unto him of the truth of the Gospel, but he could not receive the gift of the Holy Ghost until he was baptized. Had he not taken this sign or ordinance upon him, the Holy Ghost which convinced him of the truth of God, would have left him. Until he obeyed these ordinances and received the gift of the Holy Ghost, by the laying on of hands, according to the order of God, he could not have healed the sick or commanded an evil spirit to come out of a man, and it obey him; for the spirits might say unto him, as they did to the sons of Sceva: 'Paul we know and Jesus we know, but who are ye?'" (*Teachings,* p. 199; *History of the Church,* 4:555).

Joseph F. Smith taught that the "'gift' of the Holy Ghost simply confers upon a man the right to receive at any time, when he is worthy of it and desires it, the power and light of truth of the Holy Ghost, although he may often be left to his own spirit and judgement" (*Gospel Doctrine,* pp. 60-61).

Bruce R. McConkie observed, "In similar manner, in this day, many nonmembers of the Church, 'by the power of the Holy Ghost' (Moroni 10:4-5), learn that the Book of Mormon is true, or that Joseph Smith is a prophet of God, but unless they repent and are baptized, that flash of testimony leaves them. They never receive the continuing, renewed assurance that comes from the companionship of that Spirit Being whose mission it is to whisper truth to the spirits within men" (*Mormon Doctrine,* p. 313).

Some might ask, "What about Acts 10:45 where we are told that the gift of the Holy Ghost was poured out upon the Gentiles prior to baptism?" This is a case where a gift of the Spirit, namely the gift of tongues, is confused with the "gift of the Holy Ghost." The King James scholars who translated this passage apparently did not differentiate between these two types of gifts. For this reason, they translated the Greek word pneuma as ghost and not as spirit (see pp. 237-38 of this text). Verse 46 makes it clear that certain spiritual gifts, as listed in 1 Corinthians 12:1-11, were bestowed as a sign to God's church that they too were acceptable to God and should be accepted into the church. After receiving baptism, they would have received the gift of Holy Ghost as did other Christians before and after them (Mark 1:8; Acts 1:5; 2:38; 11:16; 19:5-6).

128. What is the unpardonable sin?

The doctrine of unpardonable sin has been misunderstood by much of Christianity despite the fact that three of the four gospels and the book of Hebrews speak of it. Protestant perplexity over this doctrine seems to be a result of a false conclusion that since Christ paid for all sin, there is no sin which cannot be forgiven. Let us examine what the Bible teaches concerning this subject:

Matthew quotes the Savior as saying, "All manner of sin and blasphemy shall be forgiven unto men . . . but whosoever speaketh against the Holy Ghost, it shall not be forgiven him, neither in this world, neither in the world to come" (Matt. 12:31-32). Mark's record states that Christ taught: "All sins shall be forgiven . . . but he that shall blasphemeth against the Holy Ghost hath never forgiveness but is in danger of eternal damnation" (Mark 3:28-29). Luke's account records that Jesus said, "And whosoever shall speak a word against the Son of man, it shall be forgiven him: but unto him that blasphemeth against the Holy Ghost it shall not be forgiven" (Luke 12:10).

Paul declared, "For if we sin wilfully after that we have received the knowledge of the truth, there remaineth no more sacrifice for sins" (Heb. 10:26). He also taught that "it is impossible for those who were once enlightened, and have tasted of the heavenly gift, and were made partakers of the Holy Ghost, And have tasted of the good word of God, and the powers of the world to come, If they shall fall away, to renew them again unto repentance; seeing they crucify to themselves the Son of God afresh, and put him to an open shame" (Heb. 6:4-6). These are also described as those "who draw back unto perdition" (Heb. 10:39).

Although other Bible scriptures allude to the unpardonable sin (John 17:12; 2 Peter 2:20-22; 1 John 5:16), the doctrine is best explained in modern revelation. Doctrine and Covenants 76:31-39 and 43-44 explains that those that come to know the Lord's power and partake thereof and yet deny the truth and defy his power will become sons of perdition. Those who deny the Holy Spirit after having fully received it also deny the Son and will receive no forgiveness, but instead will inherit everlasting punishment reserved for the devil and his angels (see also JST Matt. 12:37-38).

Bruce R. McConkie taught that to commit the unpardonable sin spoken of in Hebrews 6:4-8 and D&C 76:34-35, "a man must receive the gospel, gain from the Holy Ghost by revelation the absolute knowledge of the divinity of Christ [*Teachings,* p. 358], and then deny 'the new and everlasting covenant by which he was sanctified, calling it an unholy thing, and doing despite to the Spirit of grace' (*Ibid.,* p. 128). He thereby commits murder by assenting unto the Lord's death, that is, having a perfect knowledge of the truth he comes out in open rebellion and places himself in a position wherein he would have crucified Christ knowing perfectly the while that he was the Son of God" (*Mormon Doctrine,* pp. 816-17; 746; see also Jacob 7:17-20; Alma 39:5-6; D&C 64:7; 132:27; Joseph Fielding Smith, *Answers to Gospel Questions,* 1:62-64, 68-74; 3:30-31; and *Doctrines of Salvation,* 1:47-49, 2:218-25).

129. What does it mean to be born again?

The Bible contains an extensive amount of information about being born again, though only three verses refer to it using these exact words (John 3:3, 7; 1 Peter 1:23). It is referred to elsewhere as being born of the Spirit (John 3:6, 8; Gal. 4:29), being born of God (1 John 3:9; 4:7; 5:1, 4, 18), being baptized with fire (Matt. 3:11), being baptized of the Holy Ghost or of the Spirit (Matt. 3:11; Mark 1:8; Luke 3:16; John 1:33; Acts 1:5; 11:16; 1 Cor. 12:13), or even being filled with the Holy Ghost or with the Spirit (Acts 2:4; 4:31; 9:17; 13:9; etc.), although this last phrase was not just reserved for this specific event (see Acts 4:8; 6:3; 7:55; 11:24; etc.).

The Bible makes it clear that a spiritual birth is produced by the Holy Ghost (John 3:3, 5, 8; Titus 3:5) when the recipient demonstrates faith in Christ (1 John 5:1) and obedience to the truth (1 Peter 1:22-23). Paul taught that this spiritual rebirth caused a great change and a resulting newness of life (Rom. 6:4-11; 2 Cor. 5:17) and produced, in turn, the "fruit of the Spirit" which are "love, joy, peace, longsuffering, gentleness, goodness, faith, meekness, [and] temperance" (Gal. 5:22-23). John describes those who are "born of God" as righteous (1 John 2:29; 3:9-10) and loving children of God (1 John 3:10-11; 4:7; 5:1).

Modern scripture affirms that spiritual rebirth is accomplished when one "yields to the enticings of the Holy Spirit" (Mosiah 3:19; 27:24) through faith in Christ (Mosiah 5:7; Alma 7:14; 22:16; Helaman 3:35) and obedience to gospel truth. Modern scripture states that obedience to the gospel also entails humility before God (Alma 13:13; Helaman 3:35), fasting and prayer (Helaman 3:35), repentance from sin (Mosiah 27:24; Alma 5:49; 7:14; 22:16), baptism by water (Alma 7:14; D&C 5:16; Moses 6:59), the reception of the gift of the Holy Ghost by the laying on of hands (D&C 20:41), and faithfulness in our callings (D&C 84:33). Note that the principles which enable one to be born again are nearly identical to those which are essential to salvation, as cited earlier in this text (see p. 12, 13, 123-24). This reinforces the Lord's statement that in order to "enter into the kingdom of God" a man must "be born again . . . of water and of the Spirit" (John 3:3-5).

Modern scriptures expand our understanding of the "mighty change" (Mosiah 5:2) which is wrought in our hearts as a result of this new birth. In addition to filling the soul with joy (Alma 36:20, 24; Helaman 3:35), the redemption from sin and torment (Mosiah 27:29; Alma 36:19, 23) allows us to become children of Christ (Mosiah 5:7; 27:25). Through our faith in him, we are also made new creatures; changed from a fallen state to one of righteousness (Mosiah 27:25-26; Alma 13:12). This process causes a purification and sanctification of our hearts (Helaman 3:35), enables justification from sins (Moses 6:60) and allows us to be filled with the Holy Ghost (Alma 36:24). In putting off the "natural man," we become meek, humble, patient, full of love, and submissive to the Lord. We also become true saints through the atoning sacrifice (Mosiah 3:19) and eventually inherit the kingdom of God (Mosiah 27:26; Alma 13:13; *Teachings,* pp. 12, 360).

The process of justification and sanctification is succinctly explained in Moses 6:60, which states: "For by the water [baptism] ye keep the commandment, by the Spirit [or Holy Ghost] ye are justified, and by the blood [of Christ's atonement] ye are sanctified."

Marion G. Romney taught: "One is born again by actually receiving and experiencing the light and power inherent in the gift of the Holy Ghost" (*Ensign,* May 77, p. 44). Thus, membership in the Lord's church is not enough to assure salvation in God's kingdom. We must be born again unto eternal life through faithful obedience to the truths of the gospel while following the promptings of the Holy Ghost.

Although this new birth might at first seem to be a one-time event, sanctification and perfection occur over a period of time. Gaining salvation is a process. Paul affirmed to the saints at Rome that "now is our salvation nearer than when we believed" (Rom. 13:11), and to the Galatians he advised, "he that soweth to the Spirit shall of the Spirit reap life everlasting. And let us not be weary in well doing: for in due season we shall reap, if we faint not" (Gal. 6:8-9; see also pp. 142, 145 of this text).

Bruce R. McConkie explained that "a person may get converted in a moment, miraculously. That is what happened to Alma the Younger. He had been baptized in his youth, he had been promised the Holy Ghost, but he had never received it. He was too worldly-wise. . . . In his instance the conversion was miraculous in the snap of a finger, almost . . . But that is not the way it happens with most people. With most people conversion is a process" (Address to BYU First Stake Conference, 11 February 1968 as quoted by McConkie and Millet in *The Holy Ghost,* p. 102). On another occasion he added:

> We say that a man has to be born again, meaning that he has to die as pertaining to the unrighteous things in the world. . . . We are born again when we die as pertaining to unrighteousness and when we live as pertaining to the things of the Spirit. But that doesn't happen in an instant, suddenly. That . . . is a process. Being born again is a gradual thing except in a few isolated instances that are so miraculous that they are written up in the scriptures. As far as the generality of members of the Church are concerned, we are born again by degrees, and we are born again to added light and added knowledge and added desire for righteousness as we keep the commandments" (*Jesus Christ and Him Crucified,* 1976 Devotional Speeches of the Year, p. 399, as quoted in *The Holy Ghost,* p. 102).

Thus, if we, the disciples of Christ, await the righteous judgement of God by patient continuance in well doing, with the aid of the Spirit, we will eventually, receive eternal life (Rom. 2:5, 7; see also Joseph Fielding Smith, *The Way to Perfection,* pp. 192-93; Bruce R. McConkie, *Mormon Doctrine,* pp. 73-74, 100-01; McConkie and Millet, *The Holy Ghost,* pp. 89-103).

10
Testimony

130. What is a testimony?

Bruce R. McConkie has done an excellent job discussing the concept of testimony. He states:

> A testimony of the Gospel is the sure knowledge, received by revelation from the Holy Ghost, of the divinity of the great latter-day work. In former dispensations a testimony was the revealed knowledge of the divinity of the work in that day. A testimony in this day automatically includes the assurance of the truth of the same gospel in all former ages when it has been on the earth ...
>
> Three great truths must be included in every valid testimony: 1. That Jesus Christ is the Son of God and the Savior of the world (D&C 46:13); 2. That Joseph Smith is the prophet of God through whom the gospel was restored in this dispensation; and 3. That The Church of Jesus Christ of Latter-day Saints is "the only true and living church upon the face of the whole earth" (D&C 1:30).
>
> Embraced with these great revealed assurances are a host of others, as that the Book of Mormon is true, that holy messengers restored keys and priesthood to men in this day, and that the present leadership of the Church has the right and power to direct the Lord's work on earth. To bear one's testimony is to make a solemn attestation that personal revelation has been received certifying to the truth of those realities which comprise a testimony (*Mormon Doctrine*, pp. 785-86; see also *Melchizedek Priesthood Study Guide* # 2, pp. 16-17).

As Brother McConkie has stated, and as discussed in chapter 9 (page 238), the Holy Ghost is the source of a testimony. It is on this point that I would like to take a more personal approach and share my own testimony as I conclude this work. In the introduction to this book, I discussed the testimony or witness that we receive of spiritual truths. I pointed out that the scriptures teach us that we should "seek learning, even by study and also by faith" (D&C 88:118; 109:7), so that we might receive a witness in both our minds and our hearts (D&C 8:2).

There are those in the LDS Church and in other churches who have gained an intellectual testimony of many truths of the gospel through study, but have not sought a spiritual witness of these same truths. These individuals often do not fully live the commandments because they are not fully converted in their hearts. Disobedience to the commandments in turn prohibits the Spirit from dwelling in them and witnessing to their own spirits so that they might be guided in all truth and be unshaken in their testimonies. These individuals may also be subject to nagging doubts about certain teachings and doctrines and may never accept the fullness of the restored gospel. Teachings in areas such as polygamy, evolution, women's rights, abortion, and the like may make them uneasy because they rely on their own wisdom and not the wisdom and revelations of God. Because they base their testimonies primarily on the knowledge they have obtained through study, they may at times have those testimonies shaken when challenged on issues and questions for which they have no reasoned answers.

Brother McConkie in the same article cited above explained:

> If the sole source of one's knowledge or assurance of the truth of the Lord's work comes from reason, or logic, or persuasive argument that cannot be controverted, it is not a testimony of the gospel. In its nature a testimony consists of knowledge that comes by revelation, "for the testimony of Jesus is the spirit of prophecy" (Rev. 19:10), and anyone gaining that knowledge from the Holy Ghost could, if the Lord willed, receive knowledge of future events also and prophecy of them.
>
> Logic and reason lead truth seekers along the path to a testimony, and they are aids in strengthening the revealed assurances of which a testimony is composed. But the actual sure knowledge which constitutes "the testimony of Jesus" must come by "the spirit of prophecy" This is received when the Holy Spirit speaks to the spirit within men; it comes when the whisperings of the still small voice are heard by the inner man. Receipt of a testimony is accompanied by a feeling of calm, unwavering certainty. Those who have it can use logic and reasoning in defending their position and in bearing their testimonies, but it is the promptings of the Spirit rather than reason alone that is the true foundation upon which the testimony rests (*Mormon Doctrine*, pp. 785-86).

Though reliance on reason and logic alone is unwise, the same may be said for total reliance on the Spirit. Unfortunately, some members of the Church today rely almost exclusively on the spiritual witness they have received in their hearts and have neglected the continuous gospel study that is also essential to a firm testimony. When these members are challenged to give a reason for their faith (1 Peter 3:15), they may have trouble defending or even understanding their position. They may "know the Church is true" because they "prayed about it" and received a witness of its truthfulness, but be unable to use the scriptures to support and explain LDS doctrines and teachings (2 Tim. 3:16). If this kind of member is confronted by an intellectual outsider with scriptural or logical contradictions to LDS beliefs, that person will often have his or her testimony seriously shaken.

A few years ago, I had an experience with a close friend of the family who was a recent convert to the Church. She was a senior in high school, had a strong spiritual testimony, was actively involved in seminary, and attended Church meetings every Sunday. She needed to go to Utah and had arranged to ride with the family of one of her high school teachers. Her teacher's husband was staunchly anti-Mormon and made every effort during the six-hour trip to bring up every anti-Mormon criticism he could. By the time they reached Utah, our friend was extremely distressed and concerned that she had few, if any, answers to the criticisms she had heard. She asked my son some of the questions she had been challenged with earlier that day, and he tried to reassure her somewhat, but she still felt very confused.

Only after receiving satisfying answers to the questions which perplexed her did she again feel at peace with herself and her beliefs. Unfortunately, there are many missionaries and new members who have had similar experiences but have lacked the time and resources to find answers to these tough questions when they needed them most.

As a side note, I should add that it was for these family members and friends that I originally wrote this volume. Initially, I thought my two sons, who were going on missions, would have the greatest need for this information. To my surprise, my daughters have actually had more frequent need—with friends who were asking the questions which I have tried to answer here.

It seems clear that a balance between our spiritual and intellectual testimonies is important and can be developed only through study *and* the exercise of faith. We must pray constantly for guidance while searching the scriptures and intellectually striving for insight on the challenges we encounter each day. The leaders of the Church have recently reemphasized the importance of both prayer and scripture study. Experience has shown that members who do not neglect these two areas have strong testimonies and live the principles of the gospel more fully.

This link between spiritual and mental exertion also applies to personal revelation. Oliver Cowdery found that when he tried to translate the Book of Mormon, it was not enough to merely ask the Lord for help. He had to first study questions out in his mind (reason logically) then ask the Lord if the solution he had arrived at was "right." We learn from the Lord's instruction to Oliver that if we combine studying, pondering, and prayer, we will receive answers through his Spirit (D&C 9:7-9).

When we choose to ignore this revealed process, expecting answers before we have done as the Lord commanded, we are likely to be misled by the first thought that comes into our mind. It is only when we learn to distinguish between our own uninspired hopes and desires and the inspiration which comes from the Holy Ghost that we can be sure of the course we take. We must not only remember to pray for the inspiration of the Spirit, but we also must pay the intellectual price by using the intelligence the Lord has given us to study and ponder his words as contained in the scriptures. It has been said that we talk to God through prayer but God talks to us through the scriptures. To a large extent this is true.

I had an experience while on a military assignment in southern France which illustrates this point. As district clerk, I had become aware of a problem in one of the larger branches of that area. A young French returned missionary had been called to lead the branch. Many of the older members were upset that a young, single man had been called to that position. One Sunday, my duties required me to visit that branch and to attend their sacrament meeting. It turned out to be fast Sunday. I sat in the congregation pondering this problem as the sacrament was being passed. I knew that discord would continue in this branch until the hearts of the members were softened and they sustained their president; but some of the members might resist this council if it came from their own branch president. I wondered if I, an outsider, could—or should—try to help.

The thought came to me that I should search the scriptures for an answer. I opened my French triple combination to Doctrine and Covenants 121 and began reading. Almost immediately I read an unmarked verse (verse 16) which in English states: "Cursed are all those that shall lift up the heel against mine anointed, saith the Lord, and cry they have sinned when they have not sinned before me, saith the Lord, but have done that which was meet in mine eyes, and which I commanded them."

I was a little reluctant to use this scripture in bearing my testimony but I knew by the Spirit that the Lord wanted me to. I took my turn, bearing testimony that the calling of their branch president was inspired of the Lord; then I read the above scripture. I know it had a profound impact on some of the members of that branch because I could see tears in the eyes of many. As far as I know, no further problems of this nature came to the attention of the district presidency.

I am grateful that the Lord used me to bear testimony and read this scripture, allowing the Spirit to prick their hearts and accomplish this minor miracle. I have since searched in vain for a more appropriate scripture for this occasion and am convinced that the Holy Ghost inspired me to find that exact verse and read it at that time to that branch. Though the only prior effort I had made was to ponder the problem, and although I had been unaware that this scripture even existed, the Lord knew, and he knew that this branch had a profound need to hear it. The Lord communicated his answer to me through a scripture revealed more than 130 years earlier by the Spirit. Through that same Spirit, he witnessed to that branch their failings in this area.

Since that time, I have received many similar answers to questions through my study of the scriptures. As I endeavored to answer the questions in this text, I often found that inspiration came to me according to the effort I expended. Where I put forth much effort, I received much inspiration. Where I put forth little, I received little. I was truly amazed that so many answers to so many tough questions could be found as a result of a detailed study of the scriptures and other inspired literature. I believe this principle applies not only to our own search for answers, but to all things we do. Those readers, for example, who simply read this work will find little that will excite them in their quest for truth. On the other hand, those who study both the answers contained herein and the scriptural references cited will come away with a much greater appreciation for the scriptures and the Lord's wisdom in giving them to us.

I received a testimony that Jesus Christ was our Savior and Redeemer at a young age and have an unwavering conviction that he lived and died for us. My studies in the scriptures have reinforced that testimony to the point today that I can state that I *know* Jesus Christ is the Son of God and my Savior. He truly died for me and made possible my resurrection and exaltation. I have also gained a testimony of Joseph Smith's calling as God's prophet in these last days.

As a teenager, I remember the Joseph Smith story being recited by a returned missionary in Sunday School class, exactly as it is contained in our scriptures. At that time, the Holy Ghost witnessed to my spirit that the account that I was hearing was true. I have never received as strong a witness of the Book of Mormon or any other modern revelation, but I know they are also true as a result of this initial witness I received. If Joseph Smith was a prophet—and I knew he was—then these other revelations must also be true. To this day, I cannot read the Joseph Smith story without receiving a similar assurance that these events actually occurred as Joseph Smith recorded.

This account is the key to the restoration. Either Joseph Smith was a prophet of God and the restored gospel is true, or Joseph Smith was a fraud and The Church of Jesus Christ of Latter-day Saints is in error. Either he saw God and his Son, Jesus Christ, or he didn't. There is no gray area of truth. It is either all true or all a hoax. It is my testimony that it is true and that no man could have done what Joseph Smith did without the help and inspiration of God. I hope this fact was made clear in the many answers I have given in preceding chapters, but in case it was not, I am affirming it here. I know that Joseph Smith was a prophet and that he was called of God to begin the final preparations for the Second Coming of Jesus Christ. Through him, the gospel and the power of the priesthood were reestablished on the earth as part of the restoration of all things. Those who guide this Church today are likewise called of God and receive inspiration in leading his Church.

Some have argued that Joseph Smith might have been deceived by Satan or been misled by his imagination, but these arguments fail an objective analysis using the scriptures as our standard of truth. As was demonstrated in chapter 3 (pp. 35, 36)—the teachings of Joseph Smith, the Book of Mormon, and the Church all affirm that Jesus is the Christ and that he came in the flesh as prophesied and affirmed in scripture. To claim that Satan inspired these latter-day truths goes counter to Christ's teaching that a house divided against itself cannot stand (Matt. 12:25-26; see also Matt. 9:33-34; Mark 3:22-30; Luke 11:14-26; *Jesus the Christ,* pp. 265-66). To believe that an uneducated farm boy could have imagined these things and convinced so many others of their veracity is difficult to justify, especially in view of the testimonies of all those who were also intimately involved as eyewitnesses to many of these same events (see p. 205).

Indeed, to deny that these events took place, as so many witnesses have testified, takes more faith (blind faith perhaps) than to accept the accounts as factual. Joseph Fielding McConkie points out: "Many a pretender to the prophetic office has claimed to entertain angels or to have spoken with God, but who other than Joseph Smith introduced his angels to others? Joseph Smith introduced Moroni to Oliver Cowdery, David Whitmer, and Martin Harris. He was never alone when priesthood or keys were restored. . . . He and Sydney Rigdon received the revelation on the degrees of glory together. Together they saw legions of angels, along with the Father and the Son (see D&C 76:21-23). Oliver Cowdery was with Joseph Smith when John the Baptist came to restore the Aaronic Priesthood, and when Peter, James, and John came to restore the Melchizedek Priesthood. Oliver was also with Joseph Smith when Christ came to accept the dedication of the Kirtland Temple, and Moses, Elias, and Elijah restored their keys, powers, and authorities" (*Sons and Daughters of God,* pp. 194-95). The accounts of these and other eyewitnesses mentioned earlier (p. 205) stand as a testimony to the world that Joseph Smith was a true prophet of God and that the Church of Jesus Christ was in fact restored through divine messengers.

The LDS faith is an intelligent and reasonable faith. The evidence is clear to all who are intellectually honest in their investigation of the truth. When LDS teachings are given a fair hearing and when the witness of the Spirit (Heb. 10:15) is sought in sincerity, the truth will be revealed. Sound and accurate logic is not enough, though, to enable us to understand these truths. The assistance of the Holy Spirit is essential (1 Cor. 2:11).

It seems clear that orthodox Christianity has erred in this principle. Although they have come to Christ in faith, many deny the need to be obedient to all his commandments. They make no effort to perfect themselves, citing Isaiah and Paul in an attempt to prove that good works are as "filthy rags" (Isa. 64:6; Eph. 2:8-9; Titus 3:5). Obedience and good works are scorned, as is the need for the witness of the Spirit. The Prophet Nephi, in his closing words, spoke of the Holy Ghost and those who would not accept his promptings, saying "But behold, there are many that harden their hearts against the Holy Spirit, that it hath no place in them; wherefore, they cast many things away which are written and esteem them as things of naught" (2 Nephi 33:2).

The scriptures testify that the Spirit will not dwell in defiled or unholy temples (1 Cor. 3:16-17; Alma 34:35-36). They also teach that truth is revealed only to those doing the Lord's will. Jesus made this clear when he said, "If any man do his will, he shall know of the doctrine, whether it be of God" (John 7:17; see also John 8:31-32; 14:23; Alma 7:14-16; D&C 130:20-21).

Though we must have faith in Christ and in his saving grace, we must also be obedient to his teachings. As John taught, "He that saith, I know him, and keepeth not his commandments, is a liar, and the truth is not in him. But whoso keepeth his word, in him verily is the love of God perfected" (1 John 2:4-5). It is clear that a testimony of the truth and the sanctifying influence of the Spirit comes as a result of our obedience to gospel principles, and not the other way around as Protestant Orthodoxy teaches. Truth is revealed to those who keep his commandments and strive to walk even as Christ walked (1 John 2:4, 6).

It is my hope that this text will help those who read it to more fully understand the truths taught in the scriptures and through the Holy Ghost. It is also my prayer that they will put forth the effort required to receive the kind of spiritual witness and testimony which will quench the "fiery darts of the adversary" (Eph. 6:16; 1 Nephi 15:24; D&C 3:8; 27:17) and bring victory over the world and eternal life through Christ (1 John 5:4-5, 11).

May the Lord bless us all to this end, I ask in the name of Jesus Christ, our Savior. Amen.

Bibliography

Adams, L. Lamar. *The Living Message of Isaiah*. Salt Lake City: Deseret Book, 1981.

Anderson, Richard Lloyd. *Investigating the Book of Mormon Witnesses*. Salt Lake City: Deseret Book, 1981.

Anderson, Richard Lloyd. "Parallel Prophets: Paul and Joseph Smith." BYU Devotional Address, Aug. 9, 1983

Anderson, Richard Lloyd. *Understanding Paul*. Salt Lake City: Deseret Book, 1983.

Angus, S. *The Ante-Nicene Fathers*. Grand Rapids, Michigan: William B. Eerdmans Publishing Company, reprint 1985.

Archer, Gleason L. *Encyclopedia of Bible Difficulties*. Grand Rapids, Michigan: William B. Eerdmans Publishing Company, 1982.

Arrington, Leonard J. and Bitton, Davis. *The Mormon Experience: A History of the Latter-day Saints*. New York: Vintage Books, 1979.

Athanasius. *Against the Arians*.

Athanasius. *On the Incarnation of the Word*.

Augustine. *On the Psalms*.

Bacchiocchi, Samuele. *Wine in the Bible*. Berrien Springs, Michigan: Biblical Perspectives, 1989.

Backman, Milton V. Jr. *Joseph Smith's First Vision*. Salt Lake City: Bookcraft, 1971.

Barber, Ian. *What Mormonism Isn't: A Response to the Research of Jerald and Sandra Tanner*. Auckland, New Zealand: Pioneer Books, 1981.

Barker, James L. *Apostasy from the Divine Church*. Salt Lake City: Deseret News Press, 1960 (This text was expanded for the course of study for the Melchizedek Priesthood Quorums from 1952 to 1954).

Barlow, Philip. "Unorthodox Orthodoxy: The Idea of Deification." *Sunstone*. Salt Lake City: Oct. 1983, pp. 13-18.

Basil of Caesaria. *On the Holy Spirit*.

Benson, Ezra Taft. *Come unto Christ*. Salt Lake City: Deseret Book, 1983.

Bettenson, Henry. *The Early Christian Fathers*. New York: Oxford University Press, 1956.

Book of Common Prayer. New York: S. Buckley for the Church of England, 1903.

Book of Mormon. Salt Lake City: The Church of Jesus Christ of Latter-day Saints, 1981.

Book of Mormon Student Manual (Religion 121-122). Salt Lake City: The Church of Jesus Christ of Latter-day Saints, 1979.

Brown, Robert L. and Rosemary. *They Lie in Wait to Deceive: A Study of Anti-Mormon Deception*. 3 vols. Mesa, Arizona: Brownworth Publishing Company, 1985-1986.

Bryan, William Cullen (ed.). *Picturesque America*. New York: D. Appleton and Company, 1872.

Bush, Lester E., Jr. "The Spaulding Theory Then and Now" (reprint). Sandy, Utah: Mormon Miscellaneous, 1984.

Bushman, Richard L. *Joseph Smith and the Beginnings of Mormonism*. Chicago, Illinois: University of Illinois Press, 1984.

Cambridge Bible Dictionary. In *The Holy Bible* (specially bound for The Church of Jesus Christ of Latter-day Saints). Cambridge, Great Britain: Cambridge University Press, 1950.

Cheesman, Paul R. *The Keystone of Mormonism*. Salt Lake City: Deseret Book, 1973.

Clark, James R. (comp.). *Messages of the First Presidency*. 6 vols. Salt Lake City: Bookcraft, 1965.

Clement. *Clementine Recognitions*.

Clement. *Patrologia Graec.* In Nibley, Hugh. *The World of the Jaredites*. Salt Lake City: Bookcraft, 1952.

Coombs, Kenneth E. *The True Sabbath—Saturday or Sunday*. Salt Lake City: Paragon, 1948.

Crowther, Duane S. *Doctrinal Dimensions*. Bountiful, Utah: Horizon Publishers, 1986.

Crowther, Duane S. *The Prophecies of Joseph Smith*. Bountiful, Utah: Horizon Publishers, 1983.

Daniel-Rops. *L'Eglise des Apotres et des Martyrs*. In James L. Barker. *Apostasy from the Divine Church*. Salt Lake City: Deseret News Press, 1960.

Danielou, Jean. *Origen*. New York: Sheed and Ward, 1955.

Danielou, Jean. *The Theology of Jewish Christianity*. London, England: 1964. In Eugene Seaich. *Ancient Texts and Mormonism*. Murray, Utah: Sounds of Zion, 1983.

Didache, The. In Lightfoot, J. B. and Harmer, J. R. *Apostolic Fathers*. Grand Rapids, Michigan: Baker House, 1989.

Doctrine and Covenants. Salt Lake City: The Church of Jesus Christ of Latter-day Saints, 1981.

Doctrine and Covenants Student Manual (Religion 324-325). Salt Lake City: The Church of Jesus Christ of Latter-day Saints, 1981.

Eichrodt, Walter. *Theology of the Old Testament*. Philadelphia, Pennsylvania: Westminster Press, 1961.

Encyclopedia Americana. 30 vols. New York: Americana Corporation, 1972 edition.

Ensign (magazine). Salt Lake City: The Church of Jesus Christ of Latter-day Saints.

Eusebius. *The History of the Church* (also called *Ecclesiastical History*). Middlesex, England: Penguin Books, 1965.

Evenson, Darrick T. *The Gainsayers*. Bountiful, Utah: Horizon Publishers, 1989.

Field, Leon C. *A Discussion of the Bible Wine Question*. New York, 1883. In Bacchiocchi, Samuele. *Wine in the Bible*. Berrien Springs, Michigan: Biblical Perspectives, 1989.

Forrest, Bill. "Are Mormons Christian?" (brochure), *Mormon Miscellaneous Response Series*. Sandy, Utah: Mormon Miscellaneous, n.d.

Forrest, Bill and Hale, Van. *Scrapbook of Mormon Polemics,* Mormon Miscellaneous Scrapbook numbers 1 and 2 (booklets). Sandy, Utah: Mormon Miscellaneous, 1986.

Foxe, John. *John Foxe's Book of Martyrs*. Boston: Little, Brown and Company, 1965.

Gentry, Leland H. "Seducing Spirits and Doctrines of Devils." In *The New Testament and The Latter-day Saints*. Orem: Randall Book Company, 1987, 75-87.

Gibbons, James Cardinal. *The Faith of our Fathers*. Baltimore, New York: John Murphy Company, 1906.

Gorton, H. Clay. *The Language of the Lord*. Bountiful, Utah: Horizon Publishers, 1993.

Gorton, H. Clay. *The Legacy of the Brass Plates of Laban*. Bountiful, Utah: Horizon Publishers, 1993.

Gibson, Stephen W. *One-Minute Answers to Anti-Mormon Questions*. Bountiful, Utah: Horizon Publishers, 1995.

Glass, Arthur E. "Yeshua in the Tenach" (brochure). Orangeburg, New York: American Board of Missions to the Jews, n.d.

Grant, Fredrick. *An Introduction to the Revised Standard Version of the New Testament*. n.l.: International Council of Religious Education, 1946.

Greek-English Lexicon. Oxford, England: Clarendon Press, 1959.

Greek-English Lexicon of the New Testament and Other Early Christian Literature. Chicago: University of Chicago Press, 1957.

Green, Jay P., Sr. *The Interlinear Bible:* Hebrew-Greek-English. Peabody, Massachusetts: Hendrickson Publisher, 1976.

Gregory of Nazianzus. *Orations.*

Griffith, Michael T. *A Ready Reply,* Bountiful, Utah: Horizon Publishers, 1994.

Griffith, Michael T. *Signs of the True Church of Christ*. Bountiful, Utah: Horizon Publishers, 1989.

Griffith, Michael T. *Refuting the Critics*. Bountiful, Utah: Horizon Publishers, 1993.

Hale, Van. "Defining the Mormon Doctrine of Deity" (brochure). Reprint #6. Sandy: Mormon Miscellaneous, 1985.

Hale, Van. "What about the Adam-God Theory" (brochure). Response #3.Sandy: Mormon Miscellaneous, 1982.

Hamerton-Kelly, Robert. *Pre-Existence, Wisdom and the Son of Man; a Study of the Idea of Preexistence in the New Testament.* Cambridge: University Press, 1973.

Hamson, Robert L. The Signature of God. Solano Beach, California: Sandpiper Press, 1982.

Hansen, L. Taylor. He Walked The Americas. Amherst, Wisconsin: Amherst Press, 1963.

Harris, Franklin S., Jr. Book of Mormon Message and Evidences. Salt Lake City: Deseret News Press, 1953.

Harris, James R. The Facsimiles of the Book of Abraham, A Study of the Joseph Smith Papyri. Payson, Utah: Harris House Publisher, 1990.

Hastings, James. *Dictionary of the Bible.* 4 vols. Edinburgh: Clark, 1903. In Seaich, Eugene. *Ancient Texts and Mormonism.* Murray, Utah: Sounds of Zion, 1983.

Hastings, James. *Encyclopedia of Religion and Ethics.* In Seaich, Eugene. *Ancient Texts and Mormonism.* Murray, Utah: Sounds of Zion, 1983.

Hilton, John L. "Book of Mormon Wordprint Measurement using Wraparound Block Counting" (reprint). Provo, Utah: Foundation for Ancient Research and Book of Mormon Studies (FARMS), 1988.

Hippolytus. *Against the Heresy of Noetus.* In Barker, James L. Apostasy from the Divine Church. Salt Lake City: Deseret News Press, 1960.

Hippolytus. *Refutation of Heresies.*

Hopkins, Richard R. *Biblical Mormonism.* Bountiful, Utah: Horizon Publishers, 1994.

Horsley, A. Burt. *Peter and the Popes.* Salt Lake City: Bookcraft, 1989.

Hunter, Milton R. *Archaeology and the Book of Mormon.* Salt Lake City: Deseret Book, 1956.

Hunter, Milton R. and Ferguson, Thomas S. *Ancient America and the Book of Mormon.* Oakland, California: Kolob Book Company, 1950.

Improvement Era (magazine). Salt Lake City: The Church of Jesus Christ of Latter-day Saints.

Interpreter's Dictionary of the Bible. Nashville: 1962. In Seaich, Eugene. *Ancient Texts and Mormonism.* Murray, Utah: Sounds of Zion, 1963.

Irenaeus. *Against Heresies.*

Jerome. *The Homilies of St. Jerome.*

John Westley's Works, vol. 7, sermon 89. In Perrie, C. Johann. *What Every Christian Should Know.* Provo, Utah: Perry and Associates, 1990.

Journal of Discourses, 8th reprint. Liverpool: F.D. and S.W. Richards, 1854-1886.

Kaye, John. *Ecclesiastical History of the 2nd and 3rd Centuries.* London, England: Francis and John Rivington, 1845.

Kelly, 1. D. N. *Early Christian Doctrines.* San Francisco: Harper and Row, 1978.

Kenyon, Frederic G. *The Text of the Greek Bible; A Student Handbook.* London, England: Duckworth, 1937.

Kimball, Edward L. (ed.). *The Teachings of Spencer W. Kimball.* Salt Lake City: Bookcraft, 1982.

Larson, Stan. "Changes in the Early Texts of the Book of Mormon" (reprint). Provo, Utah: Foundation for Ancient Research and Book of Mormon Studies (FARMS), 1976.

Larson, Stan. "Textual Variants in Book of Mormon Manuscripts" (reprint). Provo, Utah: Foundation for Ancient Research and Book of Mormon Studies (FARMS), 1977.

Larson, Wayne A. and Rencher, Alvin. "Who wrote the Book of Mormon? An Analysis of Word Prints." In Noel B. Reynolds (ed.) *Book of Mormon Authorship.* Provo, Utah: Brigham Young University Religious Studies Center, 1982.

Larson, Wayne A., Arvin, Rencher, and Tim Layton. "Who wrote the Book of Mormon? An Analysis of Word Prints." In *BYU Studies,* vol. 20, num. 3. Spring 1980. Provo, Utah: Brigham Young University Press, 225-251.

Lash, Symeon. *Westminster Dictionary of Christian Theology.* Philadelphia: Westminster Press, 1983.

LDS Bible Dictionary. In *The Holy Bible.* Salt Lake City: The Church of Jesus Christ of Latter-day Saints, 1979.

LDS Missionary Bible Ready References. In *The Holy Bible* (specially bound for The Church of Jesus Christ of Latter-day Saints). Cambridge, Great Britain: Cambridge University Press, 1950.

LDS Topical Guide to the Scriptures. Salt Lake City: The Church of Jesus Christ of Latter-day Saints, 1977. Also in *The Holy Bible.* Salt Lake City: The Church of Jesus Christ of Latter-day Saints, 1979.

Lightfoot, J. B. and Harmer, J. R. *Apostolic Fathers.* Grand Rapids, Michigan: Baker House, 1989.

Lyon, T. Edgar. *Apostasy to Restoration.* 1960 Melchizedek Priesthood Study Guide. Salt Lake City: The Church of Jesus Christ of Latter-day Saints, 1960.

Ludlow, Daniel H. *A Companion to Your Study of the Book of Mormon.* Salt Lake City: Deseret Book, 1976.

Lundwall, N. B. (ed.). *Discourses on the Holy Ghost.* Salt Lake City: Bookcraft, 1959.

Lundwall, N. B. (comp.) *Lectures on Faith.* Salt Lake City: 1835.

Madsen, Brigham D. (ed.). *Studies of the Book of Mormon—B. H. Roberts* (A Parallel). Chicago, Illinois: University of Illinois Press, 1985.

Madsen, Truman (ed.). *Nibley on the Timely and Timeless.* Provo, Utah: Brigham Young University Religious Studies Center, 1978.

Madsen, Vernon W., Jr. *The Dead Sea Scrolls and Other Important Discoveries*. Salt Lake City: Buried Records Productions, 1978.

MaGill, Frank N. (ed.). *Masterpieces of Christian Literature*. New York: Harper and Row Publishers, 1963.

Martyr, Justin. *Dialogue with Trypho.*

McConkie, Bruce R. *A New Witness for the Articles of Faith*. Salt Lake City: Deseret Book, 1985.

McConkie, Bruce R. "Are the General Authorities Human?" University of Utah Address to the Institute of Religion, Oct. 28, 1966. In McConkie, Joseph Fielding and Millet, Robert L. *Sustaining and Defending the Faith*. Salt Lake City: Bookcraft, 1985.

McConkie, Bruce R. *Doctrinal New Testament Commentary*. 3 vols. Salt Lake City: Bookcraft, 1987.

McConkie, Bruce R. (comp.). *Doctrines of Salvation*. 3 vols. Salt Lake City: Bookcraft, 1956.

McConkie, Bruce R. *Doctrines of the Restoration*. Salt Lake City: Bookcraft, 1989.

McConkie, Bruce R. "Jesus Christ and Him Crucified." 1976 Devotional Speeches of the Year. In McConkie, Joseph Fielding and Millet, Robert L. *The Holy Ghost*. Salt Lake City: Bookcraft, 1989.

McConkie, Bruce R. *Mormon Doctrine*. 2nd Edit. Salt Lake City: Bookcraft, 1966.

McConkie, Bruce R. *The Mortal Messiah*. 4 vols. Salt Lake City: Deseret Book, 1981.

McConkie, Bruce R. *The Promised Messiah*. Salt Lake City: Deseret Book, 1981.

McConkie, Joseph Fielding. *Prophets and Prophecy*. Salt Lake City: Bookcraft, 1988.

McConkie, Joseph Fielding. *Seeking the Spirit*. Salt Lake City: Deseret Book, 1978.

McConkie, Joseph Fielding. *Sons and Daughters of God*. Salt Lake City: Bookcraft, 1994.

McConkie, Joseph Fielding and Perry, Donald W. *A Guide to Scriptural Symbols*. Salt Lake City: Bookcraft, 1990.

McConkie, Joseph Fielding and Millet, Robert L. *The Holy Ghost*. Salt Lake City: Bookcraft, 1989.

McConkie, Joseph Fielding and Millet, Robert L. *Sustaining and Defending the Faith*. Salt Lake City: Bookcraft, 1985.

McDonald, A. Melvin. *The Day of Defense* (booklet). Denton, Texas: 1963.

Melchizedek Priesthood Study Guide. 4 vols. Salt Lake City: The Church of Jesus Christ of Latter day Saints, 1988-1990.

Millennial Star. Nauvoo, Illinois: The Church of Jesus Christ of Latter-day Saints.

Millet, Robert L. *By Grace Are We Saved*. Salt Lake City: Bookcraft, 1989.

Millet, Robert L. *To Be Learned Is Good If.* Salt Lake City: Bookcraft, 1987.

Moulton, James Hope. *The Vocabulary of the Greek Testament.* Grand Rapids, Michigan: William B. Eerdmans, 1952.

Morgan, Willard. *From Critic to Convert.* Bountiful, Utah: Horizon Publishers, 1995.

Mourett. *Histoire General de L'Eglise.* In Barker, James L. *Apostasy from the Divine Church.* Salt Lake City: Deseret News Press, 1960.

New America Bible. New York City: Catholic Book Publishing Company, 1968.

Nibley, Hugh. *An Approach to the Book of Mormon.* Salt Lake City: Deseret Book, 1957.

Nibley, Hugh. "Judging and Prejudging the Book of Abraham" (reprint). Provo, Utah: Foundation for Ancient Research and Book of Mormon Studies (FARMS), 1979.

Nibley, Hugh. "The Meaning of the Kirtland Egyptian Papers" (reprint). Provo, Utah: Foundation for Ancient Research and Book of Mormon Studies (FARMS), 1971.

Nibley, Hugh. *Message of the Joseph Smith Papyri.* Salt Lake City: Deseret Book, 1975.

Nibley, Hugh. *Lehi in the Desert and the World of the Jaredites.* Salt Lake City: Bookcraft, 1952.

Nibley, Hugh. *Myth Makers.* Salt Lake City: Bookcraft, 1961.

Nibley, Hugh. *Since Cumorah.* Salt Lake City: Deseret Book, 1967.

Nibley, Hugh. *The World and the Prophets.* Salt Lake City: Deseret Book, 1954. Origen. Against Celcius.

Origen. *On the Gospel of John.*

Origen. *On First Principles.*

Pace, Glenn. *Spiritual Plateaus.* Salt Lake City: Deseret Book, 1991.

Pearl of Great Price. Salt Lake City: The Church of Jesus Christ of Latter-day Saints, 1981.

Perrie, C. Johann. *What Every Christian Should Know.* Provo, Utah: Perry and Associates, 1990.

Peterson, Daniel C. and Ricks, Stephen D. *Offenders for a Word.* Salt Lake City: Aspen Books, 1992.

Petersen, Mark E. *Those Gold Plates!* Salt Lake City: Bookcraft, 1979.

Peterson, Mark E. "Which Church is Right" (brochure). Salt Lake City: The Church of Jesus Christ of Latter-day Saints, 1982.

Priesthood. Salt Lake City: Deseret Book, 1981.

Random House American College Dictionary. New York: Random House, 1965.

"Response to Mormonism—Shadow or Reality?" (brochure), Mormon Miscellaneous Response Series #6. Sandy, Utah: Mormon Miscellaneous, 1983.

Reynolds, Noel B. (ed.). *Book of Mormon Authorship.* Provo, Utah: Brigham Young University Religious Studies Center, 1982.

Richards, LeGrand. *A Marvelous Work and a Wonder.* Salt Lake City: Deseret Book, 1978.

Richardson, Cyril C. *Early Christian Fathers.* New York: Macmillan Publishing Company, 1970.

Roberts, B. H. *Comprehensive History of the Church.* 6 vols. Provo, Utah: Brigham Young University Press, 1957.

Roberts, B. H. *Mormon Doctrine of Deity* (reprint). Bountiful, Utah.: Horizon Publishers, 1903

Robinson, Steven E. *Are Mormons Christian?* Salt Lake City: Bookcraft, 1991.

Russell, Jeffrey Burton. *Satan: The Early Christian Tradition.* Ithica, New York: Cornell University Press, 1981.

Scharffs, Gilbert W. *The Truth About "The God Makers."* Salt Lake City: Publishers Press, 1986.

Schweibert, E. G. *Luther and His Times: The Reformation from a New Perspective.* St. Louis: Concordia Publishing House, 1950.

Seaich, Eugene, *Ancient Texts and Mormonism.* Murray, Utah: Sounds of Zion, 1983.

Seaich, Eugene. *Mormonism, the Dead Sea Scrolls, and the Nag Hammadi Texts* (Booklet). Murray, Utah: Sounds of Zion, 1980.

Seastrand, James K. and Seastrand, Rosel. *Journey to Eternal Life and Distractions along the Way.* North Las Vegas, Nevada: Newmark Publishing, 1991.

Shepherd of Hermas. In Lightfoot, J. B. and Harmer, J. R. *Apostolic Fathers.* Grand Rapids, Michigan: Baker House, 1989.

Smith, Joseph, Jr. *History of the Church.* 6 vols. Salt Lake City: Desert Book, 1978.

Smith, Joseph F. *Gospel Doctrine.* Salt Lake City: Deseret Book, 1975.

Smith, Joseph F. *Ready References.* Cambridge, England: Cambridge Press, 1917.

Smith, Joseph Fielding. *Church History and Modern Revelation.* Salt Lake City: Council of the Twelve Apostles of The Church of Jesus Christ of Latter-day Saints, 1946.

Smith, Joseph Fielding. *Doctrines of Salvation.* 3 vols. Salt Lake City: Bookcraft, 1954-1956.

Smith, Joseph Fielding. *Man: His Origin and Destiny.* Salt Lake City: Deseret Book, 1954.

Smith, Joseph Fielding. *Religious Truths Defined.* Salt Lake City: Bookcraft, 1959.

Smith, Joseph Fielding. *The Restoration of All Things.* Salt Lake City: Deseret Book, 1973.

Smith, Joseph Fielding (comp.). *Teachings of the Prophet Joseph Smith.* Salt Lake City: Deseret Book, 1977.

Smith, Joseph Fielding. *The Way to Perfection.* Salt Lake City: Deseret Book, 1972.

Smith, Joseph Fielding, Jr. *Answers to Gospel Questions.* 6 vols. Salt Lake City: Deseret Book, 1960.

Sorenson, John L. *An Ancient American Setting for the Book of Mormon.* Salt Lake City: Deseret Book and Foundation for Ancient Research and Book of Mormon Studies (FARMS), 1985.

Sorenson, John L. 'An Evaluation of the Smithsonian Institute 'Statement Regarding the Book of Mormon'' (Reprint). Provo, Utah: Foundation for Ancient Research and Book of Mormon Studies (FARMS), 1982.

Sorenson, John L. and Thorne, Melvin J. *Rediscovering the Book of Mormon.* Provo, Utah: Deseret Book and Foundation for Ancient Research and Book of Mormon Studies (FARMS), 1991.

Sparks, Jack N. (ed.). *The Apostolic Fathers.* Nashville, Tennessee: Thomas Nelson Publishers, 1978.

Strong, James. *The New Strong's Exhaustive Concordance of the Bible.* Nashville, Tennessee: Thomas Nelson Publishers, 1984.

Strong's Greek Dictionary of the New Testament. In Strong, James. *The New Strong's Exhaustive Concordance of the Bible.* Nashville, Tennessee: Thomas Nelson Publishers, 1984.

Strong's Concise Dictionary of Hebrew. In Strong, James. *The New Strong's Exhaustive Concordance of the Bible.* Nashville, Tennessee: Thomas Nelson Publishers, 1984.

A Sure Foundation: Answers to Difficult Gospel Questions. Deseret Book. Salt Lake City, Utah, 1988.

Taylor, John. *Mediation and Atonement.* Salt Lake City: Deseret News Press, 1882.

Talmage, James E. *Articles of Faith.* Salt Lake City: Deseret Press, 1899.

Talmage, James E. *Jesus the Christ.* Salt Lake City: Deseret Press, 1915.

Talmage, James E. *The Great Apostasy.* Salt Lake City: Deseret Book, 1968.

"The Church as Organized by Jesus Christ" (brochure). Salt Lake City: The Church of Jesus Christ of Latter-day Saints, 1982.

"The Great Prologue: A Prophetic History and Destiny of America" (brochure). Salt Lake City: The Church of Jesus Christ of Latter-day Saints, 1976.

The Life and Teachings of Jesus and His Apostles, New Testament Institute Manual. Salt Lake City: The Church of Jesus Christ of Latter-day Saints, 1980.

Todd, John M. *Martin Luther, A Biographical Study.* Westminster, Maryland: Newman Press, 1964.

Tvedtnes, John A. "Preliminary Report of the Isaiah Variants in the Book of Mormon." Provo, Utah: Foundation for Ancient Research and Book of Mormon Studies (FARMS), 1981.

Uharriet, Thomas E. "Who is Jehovah?" (brochure). Marysville, Washington: Peace Publishers, 1988.

Underhill, Edward Bean. *Struggles and Triumphs of Religious Liberty.* New York: Colby, 1851. In Anderson, William F. *Apostasy or Succession, Which?* Independence, Missouri: Church of Christ, Temple Lot, n.d.

Van Wagoner, Merrill Y. *The Inspired Revision of the Bible* (booklet). Salt Lake City: Deseret News Press, 1963.

Vermes, Geza. *Dead Sea Scrolls—Qumran in Perspective.* Cleveland: Collins World, 1978.

Vestal, Kirk Holland and Wallace, Arthur. *The Firm Foundation of Mormonism.* Los Angeles: LL Company, 1981.

View of the Hebrews: An Unparallel. Provo, Utah: Foundation for Ancient Research and Book of Mormon Studies (FARMS), 1983.

Von Rad, Gerhard. *Theology of the Old Testament.* New York: Harper, 1962.

Warren, Bruce W. and Ferguson, Thomas Stuart. *The Messiah in Ancient America.* Provo, Utah: Book of Mormon Research Foundation, 1987.

Webster's Ninth New Collegiate Dictionary. Springfield, Mass.: Merriam Webster Inc., 1983.

Welch, John W. (ed.). *Reexploring the Book of Mormon.* Salt Lake City: Deseret Book, 1992.

Wells, Robert E. *We Are Christians Because . . .* Salt Lake City: Deseret Book, 1985.

West, Jack. *Trial of the Stick of Joseph.* Salt Lake City: Sounds of Zion, 1981.

"What the Mormons Think of Christ" (brochure). Salt Lake City: The Church of Jesus Christ of Latter-day Saints, 1982.

Widtsoe, John A. (comp.). *Discourse of Brigham Young.* Salt Lake City: Deseret Book, 1954.

Wirth, Diane E. *A Challenge to the Critics.* Bountiful, Utah: Horizon Publishers, 1985.

Yadin, Yigael. *Bar-Kokhba: Rediscovery of the Legendary Hero of the Second Jewish Revolt against Imperial Rome.* Jerusalem: Steimatzky's Agency, 1971.

Yarn, David. *The Gospel: God, Man, and Truth.* Salt Lake City: Deseret Book, 1979.

Zondervan Parallel New Testament in Greek and English. Grand Rapids, Michigan: Zondervan Bible Publishing, 1975.

Index